Leadership

Leadership

Marian Iszatt-White

and

Christopher Saunders

OXFORD

UNIVERSITY PRESS

OXFORD
UNIVERSITY PRESS

Great Clarendon Street, Oxford, OX2 6DP,
United Kingdom

Oxford University Press is a department of the University of Oxford.
It furthers the University's objective of excellence in research, scholarship,
and education by publishing worldwide. Oxford is a registered trade mark of
Oxford University Press in the UK and in certain other countries

Impression: 1

Published in the United States of America by Oxford University Press
198 Madison Avenue, New York, NY 10016, United States of America

British Library Cataloguing in Publication Data
Data available

Library of Congress Control Number: 2013956988

ISBN 978-0-19-964173-4

Printed in Great Britain by
Ashford Colour Press Ltd, Gosport, Hampshire

Links to third party websites are provided by Oxford in good faith and
for information only. Oxford disclaims any responsibility for the materials
contained in any third party website referenced in this work.

Acknowledgements

The authors would like to thank the following individuals and organisations for their permission to reproduce the case studies which appear in this text:

Simon Kitchener, Stuart Proffitt on behalf of Carillion plc, Langdale and Ambleside Mountain Rescue Team, Carrie Pemberton, Priya Kishore, Dr Pragnya Ram on behalf of Aditya Birla Group, Kevin Roberts, Oluwafunke Amobi, Maik Leonhardt, Shankar Muthamperumal, Andrew Ponnambalam, Jeff MacKenzie, and Pulaq Pathak.

The authors have made every attempt to secure permission to reproduce any copyright material which appears in the text, and grateful acknowledgement is made to all the authors and publishers concerned. In particular, the authors would like to acknowledge the following for granting permission to reproduce material from the sources below:

Avolio, B.J. (2010) Full Range Leadership Development (2nd Edition). Extract reproduced with permission of Sage Publications, Inc.

Northouse, Peter G. (2010) Leadership theory and practice (5th Edition). Extracts produced with permission of Sage.

Hofstede, G. (2003) Culture's consequences: International differences in work-related values (2nd Edition). Extract produced with permission of Sage Publishing.

Trompenaars, Fons and Hampden-Turner, Charles (2012) Riding the Waves of Culture: understanding diversity in global business (3rd Edition). Extract reproduced with permission of Nicholas Brealey Publishing.

Katzenbach, Jon R. and Smith, Douglas K. (1993) The wisdom of teams. Extract reproduced with permission of Harvard Business School Press.

Kotter, J.P. (2012) Leading Change, With a New Preface by the Author. Extract reproduced with permission of Harvard Business Review Press.

Dunphy, D.C. (1988) Transformational and Coercive Strategies for Planned Organizational Change: Beyond the O.D. Model. Organization Studies, 9 (3) 317–34. Extract reproduced with permission of Walter de Gruyter GmbH & Co. KG.

Balogun, J. and Hope Hailey, V. (2008) Exploring Strategic Change (3rd Edition). Extracts reproduced with permission of Financial Times/Prentice Hall.

Rohlin, Lennart, Skärvad, Per-Hugo and Nilsson, Sven Åke (1998) Strategic leadership in the Learning Society. Extract reproduced with permission of MiL Publishers AB.

Avery, G.C. and Bergsteiner, H. (2011) Sustainable Leadership: Honeybee and locust approaches. Extracts reproduced with permission of Taylor Francis (Routledge).

"Friends in High Places", Management Today, October 2012, 48–51 www.managementtoday.co.uk. Quoted with permission of Haymarket Media Group.

Yukl, G. (2010) Leadership in Organization (7th Edition). Upper Saddle River, NJ: Prentice Hall. Extract reproduced with permission of Elsevier.

Blake, Robert R. and McCanse, Anne Adams (1991) Leadership Dilemmas – Grid Solutions, Houston: Gulf., by Scientific Methods, Inc. Extracts reproduced with permission of Elsevier.

Likert, R. (1979) From production and employee centeredness to systems 1-4 Journal of Management, 5 (2), 147–56. Extracts reproduced with permission of Sage.

Wilkinson, J. (2011) Jonny: *My Autobiography.* Headline Publishing Group. Extracts reproduced with permission of Hodder & Stoughton.

Caza, A. and Jackson, B. (2011) Authentic leadership. In A. Bryman, D. Collinson K. Grint B. Jackson and M. Uhl-Bien (eds) The Sage Handbook of Leadership, pp. 352–64. SAGE. Extract reproduced with permission of Sage.

Day, D.V. (2011) Leadership Development. In A. Bryman, D. Collinson, K. Grint. B. Jackson and M. Uhl-Bien. (eds) The Sage Handbook of Leadership, pp. 37–50. SAGE. Extract reproduced with permission of Sage.

van Dierendonck, D. (2011) Servant Leadership: A review and synthesis. *Journal of Management*, 37(4), 1228–61. Extract reproduced with permission of Sage.

World Business Council for Sustainable Development & Tomorrow's Leaders. (2006) From Challenge to Opportunity: The role of business in tomorrow's society. WBCSD Earthprint Ltd.. Extract reproduced with permission from WBCSD.

Chouinard, Y. and Stanley, V. (2012) The Responsible Company: What we learned from Patagonia's first 40 years. Patagonia Books. Extract reproduced with permission from Patagonia.

Kolb, D., Osland, J., and Irwin, R. (1995) Organizational Behavior: An Experiential Approach. (6th Edition). Prentice Hall. Extract reproduced with permission of Pearson Education.

Finally, the authors would like to thank the following colleagues for their various contributions to the completion of this project:

Lorenz Herfurth and Dr Anne Parsons for their work on gaining copyright permissions, Dr Peter Lenney and Neil Ralph for their thinking and contributions in relation to mindfulness, Paul Ferguson for giving us the time and money to complete the book, and our students for constantly challenging our thinking about leadership.

Dedications

To Simon, my ever-patient husband, who spent a lot of weekends on his own while this book was being written. All my love, always. Marian

For my lovely wife Fiona, without whom very few of my mad ideas, including this book, would ever be realised! Love you! And for my Dad, Alan Saunders. Your influence and example generated my passion for developing managers and leaders. Had you still been with us I'm sure we would have had long discussions about leaders, leadership and leading.

Guide to the Online Resource Centre

There are a range of accompanying online resources available for students and registered lecturers.

Visit the Online Resource Centre at www.oxfordtextbooks.co.uk/orc/iszattwhite_saunders/ to access all of the supporting content.

For students:

Web links to related sites

Links to relevant and reliable online content will simplify your Internet research, and allow you to widen your reading from a selection of authoritative sources.

Links to feeds from topical journals

This resource points you towards to a number of relevant journals, and provides a good starting point to begin further research.

Online glossary

A searchable list of key terms from the book ensures you have a firm grasp of relevant leadership terminology. This resource is also a useful revision tool.

For registered lecturers

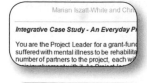

Integrative case studies

Access a number of additional and extended case studies linking to content covered in the book.

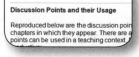

Suggestions for discussion points

This resource offers suggestions and guidance for using the discussion points featured in the text in tutorials, group work, and as essay questions.

Video clips

Support class discussion with a selection of video clips and accompanying teaching notes.

Contents

Contents

Why study leadership?

Learning outcomes

On reading this introductory chapter you will:

● Understand where we have positioned this book in relation to the extensive field of leadership literature, and why we decided to write it

● Have been introduced to some of the benefits of studying leadership from a theoretical perspective, and how this relates to the challenges of leadership as a practice

● Understand some of the ways in which leadership theory can support the development of improved leadership practice

● Be familiar with the format and features of the book, and how you can best use it to support both your critical understanding of leadership theory and the development of your own leadership practice

Why study leadership? Why study it theoretically?

There was a very silly joke one of the authors (MIW) remembers hearing in her childhood about a Martian landing on Earth and the first thing he saw was a petrol station. Mistaking the petrol pump for the resident life form of the planet, he went up to it and said 'take your finger out of your ear, and take me to your leader!' This childish play on the 'anatomical' features a human might have in common with a petrol pump nonetheless demonstrates the prominence which leadership as an idea has in our minds, even from an early age. Indeed, it is a measure of the ubiquity of leadership in our lives that even the average 5-year-old will have some concept of what it is: as children in school we have all had the experience of lining up for class, in the playground or on a school trip, and so recognize 'the leader' as 'the one in front'. And our concept of leadership develops along with our own development and experience of the world: we begin by following the guidance and strictures of our parents, taking the lead from them in many important aspects of our lives. As we move out into the world, we become subject to the attempts of others—politicians, social and religious leaders, and peers—to turn us into followers, or perhaps we become leaders ourselves. The media bombards us with images of leadership, from the public speech-making of our politicians, to the high profile activities of the CEOs of our favourite brand name companies. We are witness, too, to quieter leadership—leaders in schools working to deliver high quality education to our children, or community activists fighting for better health care, more public transport, or the rights of the disadvantaged. Thus the word 'leadership' can be seen as something of an empty signifier—a word which has no meaning per se, until we fill it with specific meanings of our own based on our own experience of it. To return to our Martian friend, their understanding of leadership—and who they would expect to be presented to when they ask to be taken to 'the leader'—may be very different from our own. They could be seeking an administrative official, a religious or spiritual guide, someone at the forefront of science or ideas, or just someone who can tell them where they are and what they should do next. For us too, a leader can be all of these things.

With so many examples of leadership—good and bad, effective and less so—surrounding us it is hardly surprising that considerable effort has been devoted over the centuries to trying to understand what leadership really is, how it works, and how we can do it better. Putting aside the debate as to whether leaders are born or made (which is discussed in Chapter 4), the widely held belief in the power of learning, and the notion that 'practice makes perfect', suggest a strong rationale for the study of leadership by would-be practitioners, whilst our natural thirst for knowledge for its own sake can, perhaps, explain more academic levels of interest. By observing the leadership of others, and the impact it has on potential follow-ers, we can hope to identify those behaviours and approaches most likely to be effective for ourselves as leaders and for leaders generally. By systematically exploring what works and what doesn't, what is effective in this situation but not that, what works for the many or has resonance for only the few, we can develop more consistent success in our leadership at-tempts compared with if we just randomly pursue what seems to be a likely course of action at the time, or repeatedly behave in a way which feels comfortable for us even if we don't al-ways achieve the results we are looking for. So from a practitioner perspective, there are clear benefits to the study of leadership practice and the systematic attempt to develop a portfolio of effective leadership practices of our own based on the observation of others.

This is particularly so at a time when much is expected of leaders and leadership, and the challenges of being an effective leader have never been greater. In our global economy, or-ganizations are more complex than ever before, and must be highly competitive if they are to survive. Technological advances bring benefits, but also the complexities of leading virtual teams and dealing with constant change. Leaders must be sensitive to the cultural differences entailed in doing business around the world and deal with the ethical dilemmas of sustain-ability. They must lead through redundancies and restructuring (a current issue for high street retailers as significant shopping activities move online), governance issues (making the head-lines in the banking sector) and serious accidents and health and safety issues (the oil industry and power generation are obvious candidates here but the issues exist in most organizations), balancing sound business decisions with issues of ethics and humanity. In this challenging environment, even experienced executives must reflect on past experience and constantly engage with their own learning and development if they are to keep pace with what is de-manded of them. And the leadership literature—along with wider expectations presented in the media—make what it is to be an effective leader a moving target. Largely gone are the old 'command and control' models based on authority—although the military and other simi-lar organizations would be an exception here. More recent models of transformational and charismatic leadership are under increasing scrutiny—as are leaders themselves—in the face of some striking examples of the downsides (and 'dark sides') to these previously lauded icons of the leadership art. Now leaders are told to be 'quiet'(Badaracco, 2002), to be servants to their followers (Greanleaf, 2002), to use their emotional intelligence (Antonakis, Ashkanasy, and Dasborough, 2009), at the same time as being held accountable for organizational out-comes often beyond their control. The 'audit society' (Power, 1997) sees governance issues being given increasing prominence, and leader performance being measured and assessed at every turn: this is particularly the case in the public sector, where managers are under increasing pressure to operate more like their business counterparts at the same time as being answerable to the communities they serve for delivering an ever-increasing level of service. And in the midst of grappling with all these issues, we are asking leaders to take time out to reflect: to speculate on what good leadership might really consist in and to consider how their own practice might measure up to this ideal. Are we just laying another burden at the would-be leader's door, or can academic sources of knowledge really support the development of working practitioners? We believe the latter, and that this text can make a meaningful contribution to structuring and informing such learning and reflection.

So why study leadership theoretically— or academically—if your aim is to become a better practitioner (which is, we would expect, the ultimate goal of most potential readers of this book)? What can theory offer us that first-hand observation can't? We would suggest that it can offer a number of benefits. First, it enables us to tap into a much wider and more rigorous range of observations: whereas we as individuals might have half a dozen leaders around us that we can observe and imitate, leadership studies can offer us insights into hundreds of different leaders in a much wider range of settings than we are likely to experience ourselves. Secondly, the process of debate and peer review which goes on routinely within the academic field ensures that the ideas which finally reach us have been robustly tested and are based on sound evidence. They are not—as we inevitably are in our own daily lives—subject to the many biases and heuristics which can often invalidate the kind of 'quick and dirty' conclusions we draw from our own limited experience. Thirdly, and perhaps most importantly, theoretical frameworks offer us a shared language for talking about leadership and a series of benchmarks against which to test our own ideas and measure our own experiences. In so doing they enable us to examine our own practice, and that of others, in a more reasoned and analytical manner, adding objectivity and alternative perspectives to our own thinking. In saying this, we are most definitely not saying that theory can somehow provide us with 'the answer' to effective leadership: as you will see throughout this text we are very clear that leadership theory constitutes a useful tool on the path to better leadership practice, but that it is only as good as the criticality with which we apply it. For this reason, you will also see that we will rigorously critique the theories we present, and encourage you to do the same.

So what qualifies us to write a book about leadership?

As you will no doubt have guessed, the authors of this textbook are academics. But we have also been leadership practitioners. Marian spent five years working in commercial banking before moving into corporate treasury. In this role, she worked in specialist engineering, the hotel industry, and the energy sector. In the last of these, she was Group Treasurer of Enterprise Oil plc, at the time the largest independent upstream oil and gas company in the UK and a Top-100 plc (it is now part of Shell). Reporting directly to the Board of Directors, her role entailed leading a high-profile team, and being responsible for all aspects of treasury strategy and implementation, including risk management (including a £600m investment portfolio and debt of £1bn), liquidity and funding, capital structure, and a departmental budget in excess of £2m. Major projects included development of a strategy and procedures for integrating the treasury function and personnel of a hostile take-over target into the Enterprise organization, and working at a senior level with Asset Teams to instigate changed working practices aimed at adding value to marginal projects. Marian studied for her PhD within the Centre for Excellence in Leadership in Lancaster University Management School, conducting ethnographic research into the everyday accomplishment of leadership work in the learning and skills sector, with a particular interest in strategy as a 'perennially unfinished project' and leadership as 'emotional labour'. Prior to that, she had gained an MSc in Organizational Behaviour at London's Birkbeck College, writing her thesis on valuing practices and 'what makes employees feel valued by their employer', an area of study which she has subsequently linked to her work on leadership as emotional labour.

Chris' 'real world' experience is very different but equally important in providing a rich resource for underpinning our 'take' on leadership and our interest in understanding it further. As General Manager of a small business—the Golden Hinde Educational Museum Ship—Chris was responsible for every aspect of running the business, including recruitment, training and management of staff, operations management of a busy visitor attraction, design and development of educational programmes run by the Museum, financial management, promotion and marketing, and business development. At the same time as keeping the ship afloat (literally as well as metaphorically!) Chris had a 'front of house' role to play within the vibrant, ever-changing environment of this most active of hands-on museums. He maintains a hands-on link with the business world as an Independent Board Member for Bolton at Home, a housing association responsible for 18,000 council-owned properties in Bolton. In this role Chris is the Board Champion for Organisational Development, and is Chair of the Audit Committee. Bolton at Home is a limited company with charitable status, and a Board member role requires a combination of solid business sense with sensitivity to the values and aims of the institution.

At Lancaster Chris has led the design and development of many leadership programmes for corporate clients, including Rexam Plc, My Travel Plc, the Riverside Group, and the Guinness Partnership. He is Director of Leadership for Housing programme, run in partnership with the National Housing Federation.

Chris has an MBA from Lancaster University, within which his dissertation investigated the successful implementation of the EFQM Business Excellence model and the role of leadership in using this quality improvement tool to raise organizational performance. In 2003 he gained an MPhil in Critical Management, with a thesis entitled 'Perspectives on self-interest and greed: A critical examination of the core assumptions in Western capitalism in the light of recent corporate failures'.

We hope you will agree that both Chris and Marian are likely to have some interesting tales to tell on the basis of this very varied experience, and that they will have had some experience of what it is like to practise leadership and how the academic theories measure up to this real world, lived experience. We are both Directors of MBA programmes (full time and Executive respectively) within Lancaster University Management School, and continue to learn through our students. As you go through this text, you will find our 'voice'—collective and individual—appearing in its pages. The intention here is to share some of our own experience in order to clothe the theory in practice and suggest directions for your own reflective learning. We will also be sharing some of our research interests, and the findings we have produced (although these will often be anonymized). In neither case are we suggesting that this somehow makes the related theory 'right' or our experience incontrovertible—if your own experience disagrees with ours, we hope you will use this as a basis for critical reflection as to why this might be the case and what learning you can derive from the combined total of our differing perspectives.

About this book

Whilst there are numerous books—many of them of a high quality—written on the subject of leadership, the vast majority are presented either as academic monographs or edited collections of stand-alone papers. Texts by Yukl (2009), Grint (2005a), Northouse (2010), and the like provide scholarly discussions of the leadership field as a whole, whilst other authors—for example Ciulla (2005), on ethical leadership—home in on specific themes or issues within the broader field. Some of these authors (most notably Northouse) have supplemented their original texts with case studies and other learning support materials, but they remain essentially scholarly texts, with all the advantages (such as rigour and criticality) and disadvantages (some of them make difficult or dense reading for the uninitiated, for example) which this format suggests.

Such books provide valuable insights into our understanding of leadership—and in some cases, the development of personal leadership practice—but they are not designed to support the systematic study of leadership by management and other students. Rather, they are the academic source material from which the curriculum for such students should be drawn, and the distillation of the debates and discussions which form the core topic areas for such a curriculum. This book thus draws upon these important works with the aim of offering their collected content in the format of a quality leadership *textbook*: that is, a book that is designed and formatted as a study text for would-be students of leadership, which draws on the insights and discussions of academic writers in order to pull together the different strands within this literature and present them in an accessible and interesting manner.

As such, *Leadership* aims to discuss the core themes and debates within the field of leadership and to provide case study and other materials designed to help readers make the transition from theory to practice. The book takes a thematic approach to its subject area—for example, the leadership versus management debate; are leaders born or made; leaders or leadership—and critically discusses the key theories and approaches relating to each topic. This format is intended to provide a structured approach to understanding the subject matter at the same time as engaging readers in the exercise of thinking critically about theory and supporting them in developing their own perspectives on the material presented. The use of learning outcomes and chapter summaries, discussion prompt boxes, full academic referencing, and suggestions for further reading, we believe, mark the book out as a study text, as does the natural progression of topics from underpinning debates, through historical developments in our understanding of leadership, to recent developments, and hot topics. Using case studies (real and fictional), film and media parallels, and 'blog boxes', the format of the book aims to bridge the gap between critical understanding of leadership theory and the development of personal leadership practice in a manner that is accessible to those with limited leadership experience at the same time as offering challenging real-world parallels to those who have progressed further into their careers.

Two of these pedagogical features are seen as particularly helpful in this regards. First, the case studies bridge the gap between theory and practice by presenting readers with the lived experiences of others, to supplement and provide comparison with their own experiences. In many instances, the case studies used are drawn from the authors' own research and hence draw on real organizations and real people—although some of these cases have been anonymized where the original remit of the research did not extend to their use in teaching materials or where the subject matter (for example, failed leadership) requires sensitive handling. In other cases, we draw on publicly available data to construct cases around well known organizations or public figures: these are often used to illustrate wider issues in the field of leadership, such as the role of charisma. Lastly, we have sometimes invented cases where this has seemed to us the best way of illustrating a particular point or drawing out a specific theme. Where this is the case, there will still be some element of our own experience underpinning what we have written, which we hope will enable readers to draw parallels with their own experience and shed light on the complex issues which form part of the 'situated curriculum' (Kempster and Stewart, 2010) of leadership learning.

Secondly, the 'blog boxes' encourage readers to engage with their own experience in a more critical and reflective way, using the theories presented to structure this activity. These boxes are presented in two ways: first as prompts to readers to review past experience from a new perspective through consideration of the questions posed, and secondly by presenting snippets of the authors' own leadership 'apprenticeships' (Kempster, 2006) which are expected to have resonance with readers' similar experiences and which illustrate the application of theory. At all stages throughout the text, the activities and features are designed to engage readers in an active learning process involving critical evaluation, personal reflection, the making of linkages, and the drawing out of insights. We've done the writing work in putting the book together: now you need to do the learning work as you read it!

As noted above, the book provides a solid grounding in all the core topics one would expect to see in a taught leadership programme. It is aimed primarily at postgraduate students, those with personal experience of organizations and the working world, and anyone who seeks to engage critically with the current state of knowledge and understanding in relation to this most ubiquitous of topics. For teachers of leadership, it offers a purpose written text, with accompanying materials for both students and teachers, which can be expected to provide a thorough grounding in the subject area for postgraduate and similarly experienced students. Given that wider reading is a key element of the expected mode of study for most postgraduate programmes, the book also supports this need with comprehensive referencing of the theories and models discussed, and suggestions for further reading.

Using this text to support leadership practice development

As a text to accompany the teaching of a core leadership module for postgraduate and similarly experienced students, the thematic progression of the text matches that likely to occur in the module itself, with key themes covered first and current hot topics bringing readers into the forefront of current debates in the field. The inclusion of discussion prompts, blog boxes— aimed at prompting an ongoing discipline of structured personal reflection—case studies, and film and media parallels encourage the reader to engage with the material at a critical and personal level and suggest ways in which learning can be extended beyond the main body of the text. The inclusion of learning outcomes and chapter summaries, full academic referencing, and suggestions for further reading are intended to support the learning process and increase accessibility. The adoption of a clear and direct style should enable complex ideas and debates to be presented in a manner that readers can engage with, and which supports the application of learning to individual practice. By including examples from our own experience as practising leaders, we hope to add another layer of authenticity to the links between theory and practice. We have also tried to be culturally diverse in the language and case studies/examples we present, recognizing that there is a need to counter the current over-emphasis on Western (and in particular UK, US, and Australian) perspectives within the leadership literature if we are to truly engage with the experiences of our readership. As mentioned above, both authors are Directors of MBA programmes with strongly international student bodies—it is with our own students in mind that we have designed and written this book.

Specifically, the book includes a number of pedagogical features which will help you to develop a critical understanding of leadership theory, and to apply this in developing your own leadership practice. These features are briefly outlined below and will be prominent throughout the text.

Learning outcomes

Each chapter starts with a brief list of the learning outcomes it is intended to deliver. This provides the reader with an accessible overview of what the chapter covers, together with an indication of how it is anticipated they will need to engage with the material presented.

Mainstream and critical perspectives

Within each chapter we cover the mainstream views surrounding the topic as the basis for understanding the most commonly held beliefs in this area—in many instances this constitutes what may be viewed as the core undergraduate curriculum, the starting point for study in the field. We then offer a range of critical perspectives around the same topic, which constitute the more challenging material we anticipate postgraduate and similarly experienced readers will be interested in. These perspectives are also the basis upon which we expect readers to challenge their own beliefs and expectations, and to critically engage with the core themes of the book.

Case studies

Each chapter includes a number of illustrative mini-case studies to allow readers to see how the theory might apply in practice. They also include a larger, integrative case study, including what are hopefully thought provoking questions, to enable readers to review and internalize their learning from the chapter. These longer case studies also suggest how the complexity and messiness of everyday life might still be amenable to the theories under consideration. In many instances, these case studies are drawn from our own research but, as noted above, they may be anonymized if the original remit of the research did not extend to their use for teaching materials or if the issues being discussed require sensitive handling. Where this is the case, it will be noted in the text accompanying the case. We also include film and media examples to illustrate themes within the book and as possible discussion activities for learning groups.

'Research in focus'.

Each chapter will include one or two 'feature' pieces of research, which summarize interesting research papers in more detail in order to develop the readers' understanding of key strands within the topic. These will sometimes be the work of central authors within the field, but may also draw attention to lesser-known writers who nonetheless make significant contributions to our understanding or who provide balance by presenting a strong critique of mainstream views.

Blog boxes

When working with our own students, we ask them to write regular blogs on specific aspects of the programme they are studying, and to use this as a means of developing a habit or discipline of structured reflection. We prompt them by posing questions in relation to programme content, or by drawing on discussions that take place in class which seem worthy of further development. The blog boxes dotted about this text aim to fulfil the same function—to prompt readers to get into a regular habit of reflecting on their own practice and using whatever tools—theory, the experience of others, observations, ideas heard in conversation—come to hand as a way of structuring this activity and broadening their perspectives. Two types of boxes are included—those which pose specific questions relating to the adjacent text, and those which offer snippets of the authors' experience or opinions, again, relating to the adjacent text. Whether you literally create a blog, write notes in a learning journal, or find some other way to record your thinking, we hope you will use these prompts to engage more fully with the material presented. The act of writing down our thoughts can be a powerful tool in causing us to question our assumptions and see the flaws in our own arguments. We would also encourage you to discuss your ideas with others—either face-to-face or virtually—as another means of challenging your own assumptions and opening yourself up to alternative perspectives.

Culturally diverse examples

The authors are well aware of the current over-emphasis on Western sources in the majority of leadership writing available to students today. We are also aware, from our own teaching, that leadership students come from all over the world and want to see examples and names that they recognize and that have resonance with their own cultural heritage and experience. In an attempt to counter the current Western bias we have worked hard to draw our case study examples from a range of countries and cultures, and to recognize when the theories we are presenting do not do justice to this richness of experience. We appreciate that there is still a long way to go in this effort: in token of which, we would be delighted to hear from readers wishing to suggest case study sources from their own cultures, or which otherwise counter the current narrowness of vision often found in leadership writing.

Clear signposting

The text utilizes a clear heading and sub-heading structure to signpost key topics and different elements of format. This is intended to allow readers to find specific topics efficiently and to navigate their way through the book easily. We also aim to flag up how different theories interlink or where a topic touched on in one chapter is expanded elsewhere. Such is the way with textbooks that we recognize that readers will often dip in and out of topics as they become relevant to their studies, rather than reading from cover to cover: the clear signposting utilized here should make that as painless a process as possible! There is also a full topic and author index at the end of the book.

Quality tables and figures

On the basis that 'a picture paints a thousand words', we have incorporated quality tables and figures where we feel these will add value in illustrating theories and models, comparing different approaches, and summarizing typologies.

Discussion points

Each chapter includes a number of discussion questions or reflective activities which can be used to prompt personal or critical reflection, review learning, or as a basis for in-class discussion. These are intended to encourage criticality in relation to the material presented, to offer a challenge to preconceived ideas and assumptions, and to prompt readers to apply their learning to their own practical context.

Chapter summaries

In keeping with the learning outcomes at the start of each chapter, there is also a summary of key points at the end. These act as a brief reminder of the key theories and debates which have been addressed in the preceding pages.

Further reading

Each chapter concludes with suggestions of books and journal articles, in addition to specifically referenced material, through which readers can extend their knowledge of the topic area. There is also a full list of references at the end of the book.

Supplementary material

In addition to the pedagogical features within the book itself, there are supporting materials available on the accompanying Online Resource Centre. The ORC site contains additional resources for both students and lecturers. www.oxfordtextbooks.co.uk/orc/iszattwhite/

How to use this book

We have written and organized this book with the intention that it provides readers with a logical progression through the core topics they need to address in order to gain a thorough understanding of leadership as it exists today. Obviously, that being the case, we would suggest that readers start at the beginning and work their way through to the end! We recognize, however, that readers may have (a) limited time or (b) particular areas of interest. We hope that the structure, format, and signposting within the text will allow these readers to dip in and out as interest or necessity dictates. Whatever the pattern of study, we would encourage readers to really engage with the subject by utilizing the discussion points and case studies, delving into the suggested further reading and original references to which the book refers, and—most importantly—by testing what they read against their own knowledge, beliefs, and experience. It is through this interaction with the text—this bringing together of theory and practice—that we believe the most is to be gained. From our own personal experience of learning about leadership, we would also suggest this will promote the most enjoyable experience.

An overview of the book

This introductory chapter concludes with a guide to the sections and chapters within the remainder of the book, offering readers an overview of the issues and debates they will encounter as they read on. The first part of the book, entitled 'Key themes in leadership' addresses the core topics which have shaped leadership thinking, both for academics and practitioners, over the past 50 or more years. These are topics for which one would expect any mainstream text on leadership to provide a thorough grounding. The second part of the book, which we have headed 'Hot topics in leadership' reflects some of the current debates that are still raging within the field, and some newer issues which a changing world are bringing to the attention of all those concerned with understanding or practising leadership. Some of our views here may be more speculative or more radical, but the aim is still the same—to provide readers with a solid grounding in these issues that will enable them to form their own views and shape their own practice going forward. A brief summary of the chapters in each section is given below.

Part 1: Key themes in leadership

Chapter 2: Leadership, power, and influence: Defining the leadership construct

This chapter introduces some foundational ideas about the nature of leadership that will be explored in greater depth in subsequent chapters. The core of this chapter focuses on how these ideas of leadership align with ideas of power and influence. We explore the sources of power and the possible use of these sources by leaders, and investigate the concept of influence and how this links to power and leadership. On a practical note, there are ideas on how a leader can develop and use influencing tactics to achieve organizational results. The chapter concludes with a critical look at the theories of power and influence with regards to leadership.

Chapter 3: The leadership/management debate: Is there a difference and does it matter?

This chapter sets out one of the key underpinning debates in the field, and one which shapes all subsequent discussions of what leadership is and how we might go about it. Drawing on key writers in the field, it explores the notion that 'management is about coping with complexity whilst leadership is about coping with change' (Kotter, 1990), together with varia-tions on this theme—all of which suggest leadership is somehow more exciting, and more ex-ceptional, than management. In contrast, it presents Mintzberg's (1975) more tempered view that leadership is just one among many skills that the competent manager needs to acquire. A more radical enquiry will also be made as to whether there is, in fact, a difference between leadership and management—whether these are meaningful categories into which to deposit different behaviours—and if there is, whether it is a useful distinction for us to make. Case studies from the authors' own research will be used to underpin this more radical position.

Chapter 4: Are leaders born or made: Early approaches to understanding leadership

This chapter considers the claims of two competing views of leadership, and the theories/models they have generated. In so doing, it combines a historical review of the origins of lead-ership theory with what is still a current debate within the field. Trait theory—the view that the ability to lead is determined by the possession of a collection of key traits, which are innate and thus cannot be learned—represents the earliest attempt by academics and industrialists to understand the phenomenon of leadership. This search for a 'one best way' to lead is ex-amined, as are the trait profiles which resulted. These are contrasted with the behavioural ap-proaches which succeeded them, and which are premised on a belief that one can learn the behaviours needed to be a successful or effective leader. Key models under the behavioural approach—for example, Hersey and Blanchard's (1969) Situational Leadership matrix, also known as the 'Skill/Will' model—are explored, as is the partial resurgence of trait approaches in the form of modern competency frameworks.

Chapter 5: Transformational and charismatic leadership: Vision and values at the top?

This chapter discusses transformational and charismatic views of leadership, which emerged in the wake of the restructuring and redundancies of the 1970s as a universal panacea. With a climate of economic downturn and employment uncertainty, the need for leaders to in-spire renewed commitment through the presentation of a powerful vision came to the fore. Whilst transformational leadership had its roots in a desire to 'convert leaders into moral agents' (James MacGregor Burns, 1978) who would produce a similar effect on those they led, charismatic leadership is less clear about the need for particular underpinning values. The role of a number of corporate scandals (most notably Enron) in bringing the notion of highly visible, character-driven leadership into disrepute is explored. The difficulty of 'routinizing' charisma—that is, sustaining its effect in the absence of its originator—is also discussed as an alternative explanation for this approach to leadership falling out of fashion.

Chapter 6: In the eye of the beholder: Leadership as a social construction

Whilst most mainstream writing discusses leadership from the perspective of the leader—their traits, their behaviours, their vision—the socially constructed view of leadership explored in this chapter acknowledges the key role of followers and followership. Drawing on the semi-nal work of Uhl-Bien (2006), it contrasts a view of followers as passive recipients of leadership influence with that of active constructors of leaders and leadership. On this view, what counts is how the actions of would-be leaders are perceived rather than what their intentions were in performing them. The implications of this thesis for our understanding of leadership, and some of the specific theories to emerge, are outlined and critiqued. As a corollary to the notion that leadership is 'in the eye of the beholder' the chapter also critiques its current status via Meindl, Ehrlich, and Dukerich's (1985) thesis of 'romantisization'—the idea that both in practice and in the media the whole notion of leadership is 'hyped up' to produce undeliverable expectations and beliefs.

Chapter 7: Leaders and leading: Everyone is a leader now!

As the previous chapter challenged the focus on leaders to the exclusion of followers, so this chapter challenges the focus on 'leaders' in preference to 'leadership'. Drawing on the work of Gronn (2003) and the domain of educational leadership where his perspective has its roots, it presents the thesis that the complexity and pace of change in modern organizations invalidates models of leadership which rely on a small number of senior—and often distal—leaders. Instead, he suggests a more proximal and distributed framework of leadership in which a range of leadership skills are exercised by a wide spread of organizational members independent of their position in the hierarchy. The chapter also critiques the somewhat disingenuous premise for this thesis, which rests on what are presented as the 'conceptual inadequacies' of the leadership construct.

Chapter 8: Leading teams: Delivering team performance

This chapter taps into the links between organizational behaviour and leadership to explore the leader's role in delivering team performance. In so doing, it sets out why team leadership constitutes a separate topic area from leadership per se and examines mainstream approaches to understanding leadership within teams. In this context, it explores models of team formation and performance as a prelude to understanding what a leader contributes to effective team processes before discussing two widely known models of team leadership deriving from Susan Kogler Hill (2002) and Richard Hackman (2002). As a counter to the historical association of leadership with team performance—dating back to the emergence of an interest in teams as part of the human relations movement—the idea of self-managing teams is explored. Finally, the challenge presented to team leadership by virtual teams is also considered.

Part 2: Hot topics in leadership

Chapter 9: Leading change: Leadership's natural habitat?

If we accept the distinctions discussed in Chapter 3 in relation to leadership versus management, then change presents itself as the leader's natural habitat: it is in changing situations that leadership is most needed to show direction, provide inspiration, and solve problems. This chapter considers the change process in organizations, from both micro and macro perspectives, and the role of leadership in successful change implementation. At a macro level, it considers the relative merits of n-step change models—such as Kotter's (1996) 'eight stages' model—versus more contextualized approaches—such as Balogun and Hope-Hailey's (2008) change kaleidoscope. At the micro level, individual responses to change, and in particular issues of resistance, are explored and frameworks such as the transition curve are presented as potential aids to understanding and addressing these issues. Also, the alignment between leadership as change agency and some existing theories of change—in particular transformational and charismatic—is explored and critiqued.

Chapter 10: Critical approaches to leadership

This chapter presents the student with an overview of some of the main critiques of leadership, from the thesis that it is fundamentally problematic because it bolsters the dominant belief in patriarchal social structures that serve to oppress under the guise of empowerment (Sievers, 1994), to the more issue-driven critiques based on feminist or other standpoints. Gemmill and Oakley's (1992) classic description of leadership as an 'alienating social myth' is explored, as is Puwar's (2001) observations on a 'racialized somatic norm' within the British Civil Service. Alimo-Metcalfe's (1995) examination of leadership as a gendered construct provides a specifically feminist standpoint within the broader, diversity-related critiques already discussed. Together with Alban-Metcalfe (2005) she developed a 'transformational leadership questionnaire' which claimed to incorporate the different ways in which men and women lead in order to provide an 'ungendered' recruitment tool—these claims are examined, together with their underlying premise. More broadly, the already-mentioned Western bias in leadership writing is countered via a look at how leadership writers from other traditions—and specifically from China—understand and write about leadership issues.

Chapter 11: Strategic leadership: The 'perennially unfinished project'

In turning to strategic leadership, we are concerned with leadership *of* organizations rather than leadership *in* organizations. In contrast to more supervisory incarnations of leadership, what is explored here is the responsibility of senior executives—and specifically CEOs—for the performance of large organizations (Yukl, 2002). Thus Hitt and Ireland (2002) define the role of strategic leaders in terms of their responsibility for managing the resources and capabilities of the organization such as to create and maintain competitive advantage. To this end, this chapter presents an overview of the mainstream tools for strategy development available to the practising leader before offering a radical challenge to this perspective from a 'strategy as practice' perspective. Drawing on leading writers in this field, including Balogun and Johnson (2005) and Jarzabkowski (2005), the chapter develops Knights and Mueller's (2004) view of strategy as a 'perennially unfinished project'. Tapping into the authors' own research, it goes on to set out some of the leadership practices through which the strategy process is enacted by leaders on an ongoing basis.

Chapter 12: Authentic and ethical leadership: A return to morality?

This chapter explores the resurgence of more holistic views of leadership in the wake of the widespread disillusionment respecting transformational and charismatic approaches. The need to encourage workers to bring their 'whole selves' to work, combined with the return of a sense of morality in relation to leadership, has resulted in a number of 'new age' philosophies within the field. From ethical leadership (Ciulla, 2004), to servant leadership (Greenleaf, 1977), to spiritual leadership (Fry, 2003), the common theme here is a return to morality and a focus on the well-being of followers rather than the self-aggrandizement of leaders. Whilst all these approaches to leadership remain largely philosophical in their development, the chapter explores their implications for the practising leader, and locates them in the self-proclaimed 'root construct' of authentic leadership (Avolio and Gardner, 2005).

Chapter 13: Responsible leadership for a sustainable world

With issues of climate change, inequalities in social justice, an uncertain energy future, and a wide range of related world ills taking increasing prominence in the media and in people's minds in recent years, this chapter addresses the future of leadership in relation to how to integrate successful business practice with concerns for social, environmental, and ethical issues. It asks the question, what kind of leadership is needed to develop more sustainable societies, in the context of social practices and organizational systems that are highly resistant to change. Through an exploration of corporate social responsibility (CSR) and sustainability theories and practices relating to leadership and change for sustainability, and an engagement with systemic thinking and issues of power, politics, and diversity applied to such change it suggests ways in which concerned leaders can develop their leadership practice, understanding, and impact for the future. The aim of the chapter remains modest, however: to encourage readers to engage in the intellectual debates that reflect core issues and dilemmas with a view to becoming better leaders for the future rather than to suggest that leadership alone can solve the problems of the world.

Chapter 14: Leadership development

This chapter considers the process of becoming a leader, and the extent to which it can be taught versus learned. Clearly, a strong element of becoming a leader is the development of skills, knowledge, and behaviours that come with breadth and depth of experience. What, then, can be taught in relation to leadership, and how can leadership teaching be made to fit the needs of working practitioners? A distinction is made between leader development and leadership development, and various approaches attached to each of these ideas are explored. Some of the more popular approaches to developing leaders in their workplace are covered, including coaching and mentoring, and action learning. In addition we look at the use of outdoor education and experiential approaches to learning to lead.

Chapter 15: The mindful leader

This concluding chapter draws on innovative work which explores the need for 'mindfulness' in modern leadership. Mindfulness refers to the discipline of being completely in touch with and aware of the present moment, as well as taking a non-evaluative and non-judgemental approach to your inner experience. This forms the basis of the ability to challenge one's own perspective and assumptions as a precursor to frame-breaking learning, a prerequisite in an ever changing world. By combining a philosophical approach to learning to learn— underpinned by Aristotle's idea of 'practical wisdom' and the crucial importance of managerial judgement—with a focus on critical reflexivity in relation to personal experience, the chapter offers a counterpoint to the preceding chapters and a challenge for the future. In asking readers to be mindful of their collective and cognitive conduct (i.e. their mental demeanour) it suggests the importance of 'learning from action' as well as action learning.

Chapter summary

In this introductory chapter we have attempted to position the book in relation to the field, and suggest some of the benefits of studying leadership from a theoretical perspective. We have talked about the challenges of modern leadership and the ways in which leadership theory can support the development of improved leadership practice. We have said something of the format and features of the book, and how readers can best use it to support both their critical understanding of leadership theory and the development of their own leadership practice. We hope we have said enough to encourage you to embark on the fascinating and rewarding journey that is the study of leadership.

Further reading

Antonakis, John, Ashkanasy, Neal M. and Dasborough, Marie T. (2009) Does leadership need emotional intelligence? *The Leadership Quarterly*, 20 (2) 247–61.

Avolio, Bruce and Gardner, William (2005) Authentic leadership development: Getting to the root of positive forms of leadership. *The Leadership Quarterly*, 16 (3) 315–38.

Badaracco, J. (2002) *Leading Quietly: An unorthodox guide to doing the right thing.* Boston, MA, Harvard Business Press.

Barker, Richard A. (1997) How can we train leaders if we do not know what leadership is? *Human Relations*, 50 (4) 343–62.

Bryman, A. (1996) Leadership in organizations In S. Clegg, C. Hardy, and W. Nord (eds), *Handbook of Organization Studies*. London, Sage.

Greenleaf, R. K. (2002) *Servant Leadership: A journey into the nature of legitimate power and greatness.* Mahwah, NJ, Paulist Press.

Grint, K. (2005a) *Leadership: Limits and possibilities.* Basingstoke, Palgrave Macmillan.

Part 1

Key Themes in Leadership

2

Leadership, power, and influence: Defining the leadership construct

 Learning outcomes

On completion of this chapter you will:

- Understand the foundational ideas about the nature of leadership
- Discover how these ideas of leadership align with theories of power
- Know the sources of power and the possible use of these sources by leaders
- Appreciate the concept of influence and how this links to power and leadership
- Understand how a leader can develop and use influencing tactics to achieve results
- Gain a critical understanding of the theories of power and influence

Introduction

What is the essence of leadership? At its simplest, as Grint (2010a: 2) says, perhaps it is just 'having followers'. However, when we ask this question of executive or postgraduate groups the answer is often concerned with the ability to get things done. What they invariably mean by this is influencing, cajoling, encouraging, demanding, or forcing people (perhaps these same followers) to do something that is in line with the vision or strategy of the organization and, in extreme cases, is something that they would not otherwise do. One could surmise from this that the essence of leadership may purely be an attempt to influence the actions and behaviours of others through the exercise of power.

Critics of leadership literature have frequently noted the absence of discussion about the overlap between the theories of leadership and the concept of power. This chapter aims to address this by introducing the core leadership ideas that have been developed, and juxtaposing these with theories of power and influence. The leadership theories presented here will be explored in more depth in later chapters.

The leadership construct

Leadership is a contested subject. Gallie (1955–6) once described power as an essentially contested concept, a concept that is subject to endless disputes which never seem likely to be resolved. This would seem to be an appropriate term for leadership as well as power (Grint, 2005).

As such, leadership is a concept that is difficult for scholars to define. As far back as the early 1970's leadership writers were commenting on how every leadership scholar seems to have their own definition (Stogdill, 1974: 7; Bass, 1990). The use of the word leadership has markedly increased in the last forty years. Jackson and Parry (2008: 9) record that in 2007 they found 168,000,000 results on Google for a search on the word leadership. By June 2011 this had risen to a staggering 418,000,000 results! So one can assume that definitions of leadership will continue to multiply!

Whilst there are many definitions available, there do appear to be some main themes that can be determined in the academic literature about leadership. For some, leadership is vested in the individual. It is concerned with the characteristics or traits that an individual brings to the arena where leadership is exercised. This is an exclusive view of leadership. Those few with the characteristics or competencies can be leaders and those without them cannot. The leader here is seen as superior to the follower due to their possession of traits that give them an advantage.

Trait theories developed in the early twentieth century, and closely followed the idea that leaders were all 'great men'. The idea of traits theory was to examine what attributes or characteristics made these men great. For example, Kirkpatrick and Locke (1991), on reviewing the evidence for trait theory, claimed that the key leadership traits were as shown in Table 2.1. We will explore trait theories of leadership in more depth in Chapter 4.

In 1948, the psychologist, Ralph Stogdill, reviewed the research evidence on trait theory and concluded that 'a person does not become a leader by virtue of the possession of some combination of traits'. The evidence showed that the ability to lead was a combination of an individual's traits interacting with the situation at hand. As Stogdill (1948) said, 'It is not difficult to find people who are leaders. It is quite another matter to place these persons in different situations where they will be able to function as leaders.'

Stogdill's work started a new wave of leadership research which was focused on the situation or contingency that the leader faced. 'Great leaders' were able to quickly analyse and understand situations and adapt their leadership style to suit the person, or the problem, or the situation presented to them.

Fiedler (1974) was one of the key authors of the contingency theory approach. He suggested that leaders were prone to being either more task focused or more relationship focused. Good leaders could combine the two elements in order to achieve results. Fiedler proposed that the effectiveness of leadership depended on the combination of three things:

- the relationship between leader and follower;
- the structuring and clarity of the task to be achieved;
- the formal position that the leader occupies and the power that the leader possesses.

Table 2.1. Adapted with permission from Kirkpatrick and Lock (1991).

Trait	Description
Drive	Achievement, motivation, ambition, energy, tenacity, initiative.
Leadership motivation	Desire to lead; Seeking power as means to achieve desired goals (social power motive) rather than an end in itself (personalised power motive)
Honesty and integrity	Correspondence between word and deed; being trustworthy.
Self confidence	In decision making; assertive and decisive; emotionally stable
Cognitive ability	to analyse situations accurately; solve problems; make decisions; usually not genius; manage perceptions of others on intelligence
Knowledge of the business	Able to gather and assimilate extensive info about company and industry; necessary for developing suitable visions, strategies and business plans

When these three elements combine, favourable conditions for a successful leadership intervention are created.

Hersey, Blanchard, and Johnson (1996) were also key contributors in this field. They proposed a model of situational leadership that considered the response a leader should give to situations the leader faced. The response was determined by factors such as the competence, confidence, and motivation of followers and the complexity of task. A leader must understand:

- what goal is to be achieved;
- what task must be undertaken to achieve goal;
- who will be undertaking the tasks;
- what their development level is for each task.

And therefore:

- what style of leadership is appropriate.

We will consider contingency and situational approaches in more depth in Chapter 4.

Modern authors have conceived of leadership as more of a collective process, concerning relationships between individuals and between an individual, the leader, and a group. Northouse describes this in the following way:

> Leadership is a process whereby an individual influences a group of individuals to achieve a common goal. (Northouse, 2010: 3)

Northouse constructed this definition from the main themes running through the leadership literature. Breaking this sentence down, we see that leadership here is not power vested in an individual, but is conceptualized as a process involving the influence an individual has over a group. This influence has a direction as it is focused on the attainment of a goal that the group shares.

The key element here is influence. Northouse is strongly supported in the importance of influence by Yukl, who, after acknowledging that there is no one true definition of leadership, states that 'Influence is the essence of leadership' (Yukl, 2010: 141). House et al. suggest that as well as influence, an individual needs the ability to 'motivate' and 'enable others to contribute' to the success of an organization (House et al., 1999: 184). So the focus here is on an individual using their influence in a relationship with undefined others (they could be followers, subordinates, employees, peers, or even employers) to achieve organizational goals or objectives. In this sense, as Jacobs and Jaques state, leadership can be conceived of as 'a process of giving purpose (meaningful direction) to collective effort, and causing willing effort to be expended to achieve purpose' (Jacob and Jaques, 1990: 281).

Looking at the variety of different definitions of leadership, it would seem to be impossible for scholars to come to a final consensus on what this phenomenon actually is. The different contexts and cultures in which leadership is enacted, multiplied by the different approaches taken by scholars researching this subject would seem to ensure that a final definition will never be achieved. Grint (2005) took a view on defining leadership not from any consensus across the writing on this subject, but rather from the areas of dispute that he observed. This led to a conceptualization of leadership in four 'significantly different approaches' (Grint, 2005: 31):

- Leadership as *person*: is it WHO leaders are that makes them leaders? This draws on the trait research to leadership suggesting it is the character or personality of a leader that makes them a leader. We will further explore this in Chapter 5 when we consider the charismatic and transformational approaches to leadership.

- Leadership as *process*: is it HOW leaders get things done that makes them leaders? This comes from the assumption that leaders in some way act differently to others and it is this difference that sets them apart as leaders. The recognition of a leader through their processes will be very dependent on the context in which leadership is enacted and on the accepted cultural norms of what leadership is. For example, how a leader gets things done in an emergency or on a battlefield will differ entirely from how a leader gets things done in a call centre or a Board room. And how their actions are interpreted will differ from country to country. So there is no one process that could be claimed to be the way all leaders get things done, but different processes applied in different contexts and different cultures can be recognized as leadership.

- Leadership as *position*: is it WHERE leaders operate that makes them leaders? This is the most traditional conceptualization of leadership, and is the most common understanding of leadership voiced by MBA students whose management experience comes from working in developing economies. Here we find someone being described as a leader because of the hierarchical position they occupy. Of course, this position gives access to resources and allows for the use of these resources to influence, bringing us back to leadership being the exercise of power. If leaders are defined by their position, then they have the opportunity to exercise direction and control through the power that they possess, or are thought to possess, due to their position in a hierarchy. Believing that leadership is only about position denies the possibility that leaders can be distributed, existing at many levels within an organization, something we will discuss further in Chapter 7.

- Leadership as *results*: is it WHAT leaders achieve that makes them leaders? Grint points out that without a 'successful' result it is difficult to logically define someone as a successful leader, in other words 'without results there is little support for leadership.' (Grint, 2005: 23). However, Grint acknowledges that there is a lack of logic in this position as it is often difficult to directly attach the success of an organization to an individual leader's action. Rather it would seem that organizational success is the product of work

Discussion point: What is leadership?

Consider Grint's four descriptions of leadership individually.

- Think of a **person** you would describe as a good leader? Why are they a good leader? What is it about them that causes you to attribute good leadership to them?

- Does this person hold a **position** that contributes to you labelling them a leader? How much is your choice of person influenced by their position?

- Identify some **processes** that are used by this person in their leadership behaviour. What do they do that says they are a leader?

- Describe the **results** this person has achieved. How much has the perception that this person is responsible for delivering results influenced your opinion on them as a leader?

Discuss your thoughts with a colleague or friend who comes from a different country and culture to your own. How do your perceptions of what leadership is differ?

by a large number of people, thus making a causal link difficult, if not impossible. Grint uses imagery from Tolstoy's *War and Peace* to make this point. Tolstoy, he says, 'likens leaders to bow-waves of moving boats—always in front and theoretically leading, but, in practice, not leading but merely being pushed along by the boat itself' (Grint, 2005: 24). If this were true, then leadership as defined by results would be a myth! However, this would be a myth that society and the media would not accept, as they continuously attribute the success or indeed the failure of an organization to an individual, despite the lack of direct evidence to support this.

Person, process, position, and results can also be used to explore the concept of power. Is power vested in a person due to their personal characteristics—their force of personality? Or is it the way that someone operates that makes them powerful? Is it about their position, their access to resources in order to reward or punish? Or does the delivery of a result have to be present for people to acknowledge that someone actually does have power? We will begin to explore the relationship between leadership and power in the next section.

RESEARCH IN FOCUS: 'Wholes', 'pieces' and 'moments'

Donna Ladkin, in her wonderful book *Rethinking Leadership*, uses the phenomenological categorization of wholes, pieces, and moments, put forward by Sokolowski, to examine leadership from a new perspective. A 'whole' is described as a distinct entity which serves its own purpose without reference to something else, like a bridge or a bin or a table. 'Pieces' are individual elements that make up a 'whole'. For example, a table may be made up of wood, metal, plastic, and screws. All these are separate entities, but in relation to the table, they are all 'pieces' of the 'whole'.

The table will have a certain colour and weight. These are inextricably part of the table and indeed cannot exist independently from the table. As Ladkin says, 'their 'beingness' is dependent on the things of which they are part' (Ladkin, 2010: 25). Items, concepts that are dependent on things they are part of, are called 'moments'—something that is 'wholly dependent on other phenomena for its expression in the world'.

Ladkin proposes that much of leadership research makes an assumption that leadership is a 'whole', a distinct separate entity, and as such they study it outside of the context in which it has arisen. She argues that leadership cannot exist separate from the people who are engaged in leading, or from the context, organization, culture, nationality, community within which that leadership occurs. As such, Ladkin suggests that leadership is not a 'whole' but a 'moment', not a time related 'moment', but something that is so dependent and interconnected with a myriad of other entities that 'we can never arrive at the reality of leadership as separated from those particular contexts in which it arises'.

By defining leadership as a 'moment', Ladkin seeks to find an explanation for why there are so many different conflicting theories of leadership, and why it has been so difficult for academics and practitioners alike to come to an agreement on what leadership actually is.

Ladkin, D. (2010) *Rethinking Leadership: A New Look at Old Leadership Questions*. Edward Elgar

---

In the mainstream

Leadership and power

It is easier to talk about money—and much easier to talk about sex—than it is to talk about power. People who have it, deny it; people who want it do not want to appear to hunger for it; and people who engage in its machinations do so secretly. (Moss Kantor, 1979: 65)

A common theme in our discussion about leadership is that the ability to lead is dependent on relationships between people in organizational settings. Wherever there are relationships between people, there will be power present. As Linstead, Fulop and Lilley (2004: 183) point out 'Power is an indisputable part of everyday life, every social relationship imaginable, and one of the most controversial aspects of organizations.'

Moss Kantor's article acknowledges that power can be the product of social relationships, but rejects the view that a leader can have power because of some individual trait, or due to an ability to adapt to situations. Echoing one of Grint's perspectives on leadership, Moss Kantor argues that power is a product of the position one holds in an organization. Positions that have access to the resources, information and support needed to achieve a task, and have the authority to act quickly are powerful. Positions where access to these things is blocked or unavailable are powerless.

Powerful positions will be linked to both the formal and informal systems that operate in the organization. A powerful leader will have control over resources through a formal system, but may have to use an informal network to build the cooperation necessary for a decision to be enacted.

In keeping with this approach, Moss Kantor defines power as, 'the ability to mobilise resources (human and material) to get things done' (Moss Kantor, 1979: 66). Power can be seen through the results achieved by mobilizing such resources. The point is made here that coercive power which may use fear of punishment to achieve results does not make a leader powerful, as it serves to cut off information flows from the leader, thus leaving the leader to make bad decisions based on incomplete and biased knowledge.

Moss Kantor acknowledges that charisma may also give a leader power, but that this is also dependent on the use of resources and information to achieve results. A charismatic leader who does not do anything will soon run out of followers!

This focus on resources and information rather than the individual differs from later leadership writers. Yukl (2010), for example, describes power like this;

> the absolute capacity of an individual agent to influence the behaviour or attitudes of one or more designated target persons at a given point in time. (Yukl, 2010: 142)

Here power is described as an ability to influence individuals or groups. This is sometimes broken down and described as the type of power an individual can hold. At other times the focus is on power being a description of a relative relationship—A has more influence over B than B has over A. However, in each scenario, power is seen as a property that an individual can possess and exercise in some way over another. It is depicted as something that is tangible and so can be identified and used. This is convenient for leaders as viewing power in this way gives leaders the impression that they can take and use power in order to get results.

Yukl points out that when discussing power there has to be reference to the target at which power or influence is being aimed. In this he is describing power as a relative concept, conditioned by and dependent on the context in which the power or influence is being wielded. When the context changes, power can shift very quickly away from those previously thought of as powerful.

A case in point: Sepp Blatter vs Muhamed Bin Hammam

On 21 March 2011 Muhamed Bin Hammam, President of the Asian Football Confederation, announced his intention to run against Sepp Blatter for the Presidency of the world football body, FIFA. Blatter had been President for 13 years. Hammam expressed a desire to make FIFA more transparent after it had suffered several corruption cases. A struggle for power ensued, in which both men used their various forms of power to influence the outcome.

The FIFA President is elected by senior members of the organization. Two members were identified as key players by the Guardian newspaper, Jack Warner, President of Concacaf, the North & Central American and Caribbean section, whose members held 35 votes, and Michel Platini, President of UEFA, the European arm with 53 votes. Platini was widely reported to be planning to run for FIFA President in 2015, allegedly with Blatter's blessing. Should Blatter lose in 2011 a new President would have a strong chance of staying in post in 2015, thus potentially undermining Platini's ambition.

Patronage appeared to have a long tradition in FIFA. When Blatter was originally elected, he was supported by the previous incumbent, João Havelange. Havelange continued this support, writing to the members of the Conmebol, the South American arm, to secure their 10 votes.

Unsurprisingly, then, on 6 May 2011, UEFA declared itself in favour of Blatter. Blatter has also had an element of fortune, having been able to address a meeting of Concacaf on 3 May, whilst Bin Hammam could not attend the meeting due to visa problems. However, Bin Hammam and Warner organized a second meeting for 10 May. The newspapers still gave Bin Hammam a chance, increasingly calling his campaign 'well-funded'.

One week before the final election, Bin Hammam and Warner were suspended from their posts after allegations of bribery were made against them. Warner commented that, it was 'interesting to note the timing of these allegations and the hearing scheduled days before the FIFA Presidential elections'. Blatter was then also implicated in the bribery allegations, after Bin Hammam accused Blatter of having knowledge of the 10 May meeting and its financial 'arrangements'. On 29 May the FIFA ethics committee cleared Blatter of the charges, but suspended Bin Hammam and Warner. Bin Hammam withdrew from the Presidency race.

Despite calls for the election to be postponed to allow other candidates to come forward, FIFA duly elected the unopposed Blatter on 1 June 2011. It seemed that the power of position and reward had won the day!

On 12 October 2011 the *Telegraph* newspaper published video evidence that allegedly showed Jack Warner offering $40,000 each to the members of Concacaf in return for their votes in favour of Bin Hammam.

Sources: Guardian 21 March, 6, 10, 21, 25, 27, 31 May, 1 June 2011
Telegraph 25, 27 May, 1 11 October 2011
Financial Times 29, 30 May

A historical view

The relationship between leadership and power can be traced back throughout the history of leadership authors. One of the earliest texts commonly cited by business leaders and leadership writers is *The Art of War* by Sun Tzu (400–320BC). In this we get a particularly severe description of the power a leader can take over his people. In a part of the text entitled 'Nine Grounds', Sun Tzu is recommending how to set up for battle against an enemy. He advises that leaders should position their own troops so the troops have no obvious route of retreat. This being the case, the troops will 'die before fleeing'.

Sun Tzu recommends a ruthless use of power tactics to enforce a leader's will on followers. In this he is supported by another famous writer often cited in popular leadership texts, Nicolo Machiavelli (1993). Machiavelli describes the politics and the exercise of power that he has witnessed during his service to the state of Florence. He advises that it is better for a leader to be ruthless and violent when gaining or keeping power, than to be restrained by his morals. Machiavelli does appear to have a caveat on this, especially in his other work, *The Discourses*, where he suggests that the ruthless use of power should only be deployed in defence of the greater good of your community, and not for the individual leader (Grint, 2010b: 8).

Both Sun Tzu and Machiavelli are describing possible actions a leader can take that will ensure their influence over followers. In both cases there is a larger goal, to win the battle or to ensure peace and order in your city. The means to these ends are in the hands of leaders, who control situations and take actions to ensure that their will dominates. Power, then, is the ability to get others to do something they may not wish to, a view that has had a profound effect on the ideas that describe power, its constituent parts, and a leader's ability to use these parts to achieve a result.

The bases of a leader's power

A much cited work that comes from this perspective is the work on the bases of power by French and Raven (1959), who were examining the ability and potential of an influencing agent to secure a change in the belief, attitude, or behaviour of a person through the use of the resources available. These resources were defined as the six bases of power: Informational, Reward, Coercion, Legitimate, Expertise, and Referent.

Informational power is the ability to provide information about a subject or task in such a way that the recipient will accept that information and behave in the way the influencing agent is suggesting. Raven (2008) argues that this type of power can create socially independent change, change in a behaviour that continues even without future supervision or intervention.

Reward power and **coercive power** are both said to lead to socially dependent change. This is due to the dependence on the ability to reward (in terms of pay, promotion, extra leave, etc.) or to threaten (with disciplinary action, dismissal, etc.). Raven argues that where this type of power is used, the target is only compliant if they think the influencing agent is watching them, measuring them and so having evidence from which to reward/punish them. Hence, surveillance is necessary if a leader chooses to use this form of power. More recently Raven updated the Reward and Coercive Power idea to go beyond the obvious, tangible elements to more intangible ones, such as approval or rejection from a well liked boss.

Legitimate, expert, and referent power are all also classed as leading to socially dependent change, but Raven argues that this change would not require surveillance. *Legitimate power* means the person being influenced accepting that the influencer has the right to direct, request, or demand a change. This right is usually associated with the position of a person in the hierarchy, or with the job title that the person possesses. *Expert power* is where the agent possesses, or is believed to possess, knowledge or insights that are accepted as superior and therefore influence the target to change behaviour. Finally, *Referent power* is where the target holds the agent in high regard, admiring their behaviour and trusting their judgement, and so is happy to emulate them.

 Blog box

I once had a boss who was very overt in his use of power. The business was a seasonal one, and at the start of the season we would recruit just too many staff so that the boss could fire one or two within the first two weeks. This early demonstration of the owner's power was to ensure the others worked harder for fear of being sacked themselves. The result fits well with Raven's description of socially dependent change. When the boss was around, everyone ensured they were seen to be working very hard. When he was gone, everyone relaxed into a more sustainable pace of work. My lesson from this was that the use of coercive power may make you feel powerful, but requires a leader to drive the workforce rather than instilling the self-motivation needed to make a business great (CS).

These sources of power have also been grouped under two broad headings, positional power and personal power (Yukl, 2010 drawing on Bass, 1960 and Etzioni, 1979). Yukl (2010) states that position power includes the aspects related to a hierarchical position (legitimate, reward, coercive, and information power); whist personal power includes the aspects that an individual possesses themselves and can transfer between positions (referent and expert power).

RESEARCH IN FOCUS: Lessons from Aboriginal prehistory

Professor Karl-Erik Sveiby's research seeks to understand how ancient communities organized on a non-hierarchical basis, and how work can be organized without formally appointed leaders, a problem very familiar to UK MBA students engaged in group work during a one year MBA programme.

In his article Sveiby (2011) uses ancient law stories from Australian Aborigines, blended with anthropological studies of African forager communities to derive principles for leaders and followers. The stories come from the Nhunggabarra people, an Aboriginal people from south-east Australia. They provide a moral code presenting the norms or 'correct' form of behaviour for the Nhunggabarra people.

The article focuses on the story of the Black Swans, in which a tribal *wiringin* (shaman) called Wurunna, tells his people of a land of women where there are fantastic tools that he has traded for possum skins. Instead of further trading, Wurunna develops a plan to steal the tools. This involves a deception using a fire and his two brothers who have been turned into swans for the occasion. The plan worked, the tools were secured and the women began fighting with each other. However, Wurunna's brothers were punished by remaining as swans, and he, because of his arrogance, lost his *wiringin* power.

Sveiby quotes the work of Skuthorpe (2006) who derives twelve examples of bad leadership and excessive power use from the story. These include the leader using power for an ego-trip; the leader using fear of the unknown to gain the acceptance of the community for his venture; and the leader exploiting the community belief and trust in his knowledge to get what he wants, even to the point of using and discarding his own brothers.

Sveiby then uses the ontology of Drath et al. (2008) to analyse the interpretations of the story. This proposes a move away from a traditional leadership ontology of leaders, followers, and shared goals to one defined by three interacting elements: direction, alignment, and commitment (DAC). DAC is focused towards an understanding of leadership in modern contexts, where organizations increasingly focus on collaboration and flat structures create the need for peer-leadership.

The result of this interrogation using DAC is a set of 18 possible leadership beliefs which are formed into a power-symmetric collective leadership model, and discussed using French and Raven's forms of power.

Sveiby's article provides a welcome addition to the leadership and power literature, highlighting the importance of power-relationship issues in the leadership construct, and promoting the ability to learn from ancient communities the principles of viable collective leadership methods.

Sveiby, K. (2011) Collective leadership with power symmetry: Lessons from Aboriginal prehistory. *Leadership*, 7, 385–411

Daft (2010) groups the sources of power under the headings of hard and soft power. Hard power consists of power that comes with a position of authority. It is the power to coerce, to reward and to punish. It is legitimate power. Soft power, on the other hand, is personal; it is the expert power or the referent power. It is the ability to work relationships to achieve an end. Daft suggests that hard power leads to followers either complying or resisting. Soft power is more likely to produce the intended result and to generate commitment in followers. In keeping with this idea, Daft states that 'In today's world, soft power is, more than ever, the tool of the leader' (Daft, 2010: 327).

Yukl (2010: 153) adds to the French and Raven list an additional form of power—ecological power. This is the power to change the physical work environment through activities such as creating open plan offices or enforcing regular relocations of staff; with the power to change technology, say introducing hand-held computers that aid sales or repairs staff with appoint-ments, so reducing the need to return to the office; and the power to change the organization of employees' work, perhaps by grouping people around work activities. Yukl lists ecological power under the heading of position power as a leader would have to hold a position of seniority to achieve some of these changes.

There are strong links that can be made between this view on power being in the posses-sion of an individual, and the original trait theories of leadership. The leader has characteris-tics that people admire, and this gives them power; they have knowledge and expertise which makes them powerful; they have access to information and resources that confers power on them; they hold positions of power.

Discussion point: What power do you have?

Think about a situation where you are part of an organization. It may be one you work for, or a team you are part of. Consider the following questions individually and then discuss them with a colleague:

- Which of these sources of power do you have? How do you know?
- How could you make better use of these bases of power?
- Which of these bases of power are most used in your organization? How could you develop this for yourself?

Leadership and influence

> Leadership cannot be understood without knowing what influence is and leadership cannot be practised without using influence (Rost, 2008: 86)

Leadership authors tend to see sources of power being linked to the opportunity for leaders to influence others. Rost (2008) suggests that influence is when a great leader will use their ability to build good relationships and generate cooperative and collaborative strategies. In this sense, influence is seen as the exercise of personal power (expert and referent power) rather than positional power (coercion, reward, and punishment). Daft (2010) suggests that while power is an element that can be used to get things done or to achieve an outcome, influence is the impact of the use of power in terms of changes to attitudes, values, beliefs, and actions of others. A source or base of power is something that can be used to try to influ-ence others, but it will not do the influencing without being used in some way. For example, if through your position you are deemed to possess legitimate power, then making a request of a subordinate or colleague that is seen to be within your legitimate area of responsibility will usually be enough to influence that person to act.

Where a person fails or refuses to act because they dislike the request for some reason, then a leader may have to resort to other forms of influence. Yukl (2010) provides a detailed descrip-tion of research that has been done on different types of influence tactics that may exist, and on how effective these are when used by managers and leaders. The focus of this research has been on the types of behaviour leaders and managers adopt to influence the decisions of others.

Yukl describes eleven 'Proactive Influencing Tactics' that can be used (Table 2.2).

These behaviours can be seen to be tied in very tightly to the bases of power described above. For example, if a leader is using rational persuasion, it seems logical that a certain amount of

Table 2.2. Adapted from Yukl (2010) with permission.

Proactive Influence Tactic	Description
Rational Persuasion	Using facts, evidence and logic to persuasively argue that a plan or proposal will work.
Apprising	Persuading an individual by focusing on how the achievement of a task will personally benefit them in terms of their career, skills or profile.
Inspirational Appeals	To gain an emotional commitment to a task or plan. The appeal will usually be to an individual's values, ethics, hopes or ideals.
Consultation	To gain ownership by having the individual help develop the plan or task. The user of this tactic has already determined what the broad task will be, but consults on some details to influence others to support the plan.
Exchange	A transactional approach, offering something of value in return for support for a plan or work on a task.
Collaboration	A collaborative approach, offering resources and help to achieve a result in return for a willingness to carry out a plan or task.
Personal Appeals	A relational approach. A request for help based on friendship or personal loyalty.
Ingratiation	Complimenting and praising a colleague in order to solicit their help or support. Could be seen as manipulative.
Legitimating Tactics	Using position, policy, organisational rules or norms to make a request appear legitimate to a colleague.
Pressure	A coercive approach. Tactics used here could include threatening words and behaviour, micro-management and continuously demanding a response.
Coalition Tactics	Building a coalition of colleagues in order to influence a specific person.

expert power will enhance their ability to influence; or to successfully use an inspirational or personal appeal, a leader would presumably have some form of referent power. Yukl points out that there has been little research on the relationship between sources of power and successful influencing tactics. His discussion on the efficacy of tactics suggests that rational persuasion, inspirational appeal, consultation and collaboration are the most successful forms and the most likely to gain not just compliance but possibly commitment. At the other end of the scale the forms of coercion—pressure, legitimating, and coalition tactics, will at best gain compliance and may result in the 'target' becoming resistant to the influence attempt.

Cohen and Bradford (1989) offer a different approach to influencing. They suggest that influence is a process of reciprocity between allies. To be an effective influencer the leader must see others as potential allies in their quest. Understanding your allies' needs, wants, and interests allows you to know how to influence them. Critical to this process of exchange is a good understanding of what you actually want, something the authors claim that many leaders are not clear about before they start attempting to influence.

Leadership being the use of power in order to influence others fits well with the ideas about transformational and charismatic leadership that are discussed in Chapter 5. The transformational leader is a visionary who consults others, uses rational rather than emotional arguments, is inspirational, and persuades others to collaborate in the organization in order to bring about change. Interestingly the transformational leadership literature does not discuss the sources of a leader's power, but focuses heavily on the influence tactics the leader might use.

> ## Discussion point: What influencing tactics do you favour?
>
> We all favour certain forms of influence over other forms. We will be skilled at using some tactics more than others, and there will be some tactics that will work on us when used by other people. Consider the following questions individually and then discuss them with a colleague:
>
> - Which influence tactics do you most commonly use?
> - Which influence tactics work best when used on you—gaining at least your compliance and possibly your commitment?
> - Which tactics have caused you to resist the attempt to influence you?

In a very practical discussion of influencing tactics, Charles Handy (1993) describes the two categories of influence as overt and unseen.

Overt influence:

- Force—the blunt instrument of power. Usually linked with coercive power, with the person deploying this tactic having a large physical presence and perhaps control over resources. Bullying is an obvious example of this form of influence. Handy points out that it is most useful in one-off situations, where immediate compliance is needed. In longer-term situations the negative effects of using such a tactic out weigh the instant result.

- Exchange—similar to Cohen and Bradford's definition, this is a transaction which depends on one actor having something that the other actor values. This could take the form of a normal business transaction, a trade-off between senior managers or, in extreme cases, a bribe.

- Rules and procedures—the power behind these comes mainly from position and resource power, as the instigator and implementer of the rules must be seen to have both the accepted authority to introduce rules and the ability to reward and punish those who follow or break the rules.

- Persuasion—based on the skills of critical thinking (facts, logic, assumptions, inference, and argument) and on expert and personal power. Handy claims that this is the preferred method of influencing and the one most people try first, before resorting to others if necessary.

Unseen influence:

- Ecology—defined by the *Oxford English Dictionary* as the 'relations of organisms to one another and to their physical surroundings'. Handy uses this to highlight the potential of leaders to use the physical environment to influence the behaviours of many employees. By physical environment he means the office space and arrangement of people, the levels of heat, light, and noise, the organization of business processes and individual job descriptions, the structure of the business and its geographical spread, and other physical factors in the control of leaders such as the climate of the organization. Whilst ecology is an unseen means of influence, Handy believes that it 'sets the conditions for behaviour' (Handy, 1993: 138).

- Magnetism—derived from the personal power a leader may have. This is the acceptance of influence from someone we like, admire, trust, and respect. Handy warns that influence based on magnetism can be easily shattered, as once trust is broken it is difficult to recapture.

Blog box

Reflecting on your own experience of influencing others, jot down examples of when your influencing tactics were successful and when they were unsuccessful. Consider what led to success and what led to failure in your attempts to influence. Which of the overt and unseen categories described by Handy do you favour?

Rost (2008) summarizes the ideas surrounding influence as a post-industrial understanding of leadership. Here a leader does not rely on their position or the resources at their disposal, as suggested earlier by Moss Kantor. Rather a modern leader is one who has the ability to develop good relationships with peers, colleagues, and followers. The leader works through relationships to empower and engage the organization, generating collaborative approaches that focus on achieving a common goal. Leadership, then, is about developing the skills needed to build coalitions that will move an organization closer to its defined ends.

 Leadership in the media: Charlie and the chocolate factory

Roald Dahl's book *Charlie and the Chocolate Factory* presents the story of Charlie, a poor but very well behaved little boy, and his adventures in the amazing chocolate factory that belongs to the charismatic Mr Willy Wonka. The secretive Wonka publicly decides to allow five children to visit his factory and receive a prize of a lifetime supply of chocolate. These children will be the finders of five golden tickets that are hidden in Wonka chocolate bars. This prize leads to a global search for the tickets, meaning hugely increased sales of Wonka chocolate bars. The winners are five children, four of whom are caricatures of what the author sees as bad behaviour in children that is allowed by their parents—the greedy, obese child; the child who continuously chews gum; the spoilt, demanding child who always gets what she wants; and the child who does nothing but watch television. These behaviours are shown to lead to a bad end, with all four children leaving the factory early after a series of mishaps connected to their behaviour. Only the very well behaved Charlie stays the course and is rewarded by Mr Wonka who gives him the whole chocolate factory!

   The story could be seen as a morality tale, where the good are rewarded and the bad punished in order to encourage the readers to follow the path of Charlie. We can see Handy's concept of ecology at work here. Wonka does not directly punish the children, but leads them to places which trigger their worst behaviours. He has created the rules and procedures of the factory which have an impact on the children, but it is the behaviours of the children that get them the punishments they deserve! In the 1971 film version, *Willy Wonka and the Chocolate Factory,* we see this more obviously, with the children signing a contract on entering the factory, and losing their lifetime supply of chocolate due to their rule breaking.

   In Wonka we see the magnetism that Handy talks about, derived from his expert power as supreme chocolate maker, his eccentric behaviour, and the colourful legends told about him early in the book. However, this magnetism only appears to work on Charlie and his Grandpa Joe. The other adults and children ignore his rules and warnings and suffer the consequences. Wonka also influences the chocolate buying public through the reward of a factory visit and a lifetime supply.

   The book can be seen as Dahl's attempt to influence the parents and children who read the story. The obvious, if initially unseen, rewards for good behaviour, and the terrible fate that awaits the badly behaved are Dahl's means of influencing the behaviour of his audience. The charismatic behaviour of Wonka as the leader in the story can also be seen as a role model for leaders of the innovative and creative industries. He shows the traits of brilliance, energy, creativity, extraversion, and risk taking. He is also painted as a shrewd business man, a combination of traits we see in the more famous, charismatic business leaders of today.

From a critical perspective

The perspective on power put forward by French and Raven has dominated the subsequent research and writing on the subject of power and influence. Hardy and Leiba-O'Sullivan (1998) discuss how the 'mainstream' writing on power has been dominated by the assumption that power is a clearly observable phenomenon. One could also assume that influence tactics derived from these sources of power are also observable. However, the authors suggest that power can only be observed in situations where conflict is present, where there is conflict between what the leader wants and the differing opinions of followers, for example. In these situations a leader can exercise power through the control of scarce resources.

> On the surface, power is exercised through the mobilization of scarce critical *resources*, and through the control of decision-making *processes*. At a deeper level, power is exercised by managing the *meanings* that shape others' lives. Deeper still, is the suggestion that power is embedded in the very fabric of the *system*; it constrains how we see, what we see, and how we think, in ways that limit our capacity for resistance. (Hardy and Leiba-O'Sullivan, 1998: 460)

 Leadership in the media: I Claudius

In 1976 the BBC produced a television series that charted the early years of the Roman Empire, from the death of Marcellus in 23BC to the death of the Emperor Claudius in 54AD. The series follows the family of the Emperor Augustus, who after the death of Julius Caesar has managed to unite the empire and hold it in a fragile form of peace. Augustus, who is childless, seeks to find an heir whom he can groom to lead the empire, whilst at the same time setting a path to bring back the Roman Republic. Augustus's wife, Livia (Siân Phillips), uses her power, influence, and cunning to ensure that her son, Tiberius, becomes Emperor when Augustus dies.

The action is narrated by Claudius (Derek Jacobi) who guides the audience through the plots, schemes, murders, and politics of Imperial Rome, demonstrating how leaders can sometimes use power and influence in appalling ways to get what they want! In keeping with traditional views on power, conflict is present throughout, and the ability to appear powerless, linked with the availability and control of information through mostly informal networks, proves to be the successful strategy in Claudius's own rise to power.

Hardy and Leiba-O'Sullivan discuss four dimensions of power. The first three they take form the work of Lukes (1974), adding a fourth themselves. The first dimension of power contains the ideas of French and Raven set out above. Here power is in the hands of the individual who uses resources to influence decision making. The second dimension sees power being exercised through control of the processes of decision making. In this dimension access to decision making processes is deliberately limited and some are excluded, leaving power in the hands of others. This exclusion can be seen in the process of setting agendas for discussion, and in the use of organizational processes to create non-decision making—where decisions are delayed or not taken at all.

The third dimension describes how power can be used to avoid the need for conflict. According to this dimension, people can be educated, or cajoled into agreeing with the perspective of a leader, so much so that they do not think to question or challenge but merely accept decisions as they are made. This use of power could be seen as maintaining the status quo and has been linked to issues of class, and privilege. In organizations, this dimension of power is said to work through the management of meaning by 'dominant interest groups'. Drawing on the work of Pettigrew, the authors describe how the powerful defend and legitimize their positions to such an extent that others positions become unthinkable. Resistance to these positions is therefore avoided by the inevitability of the positions of the powerful.

The final dimension discussed by Hardy and Leiba-O'Sullivan draws heavily on the work of Michel Foucault. Foucault rejects the popular views of power being the possession of individuals through the control of resources and information. Rather he sees power as being 'a network of relations and discourses' that impacts on those deemed powerful and those deemed powerless in equal fashion. Power cannot be possessed. Instead it circulates amongst individuals and groups in organizations. Power is not the property of individuals or groups but manifests itself through knowledge and discourses, techniques and procedures which shape behaviours and control individuals.

From this perspective, although leaders may control the resources and direct them to achieve a desired end, they will not necessarily gain the outcomes originally planned. They are at once the exercisers and the recipients of power, held in a web that is difficult to escape. This web or network, acts to constrain what people think is possible, and thus the actions that are deemed desirable or effective. In proposing this view, Foucault is highlighting the limits of power that leaders may not even be aware of.

Considerations and negative issues

To conclude this discussion of power and influence we need to highlight some issues linked to power that are relevant for leaders. It would be both easy and convenient to subscribe solely to the view that power is in the hands of an individual; that through gaining access to information or resources, by using your charisma or your coercion, you as a leader can gain and exercise power over others in order to achieve results. Handy (1993) highlights three considerations for a leader who is seeking to gain and use power to influence others. The first is the relativity of power. Handy points out that if the power you attempt to use has no value for the person or group you are attempting to influence, then it will have no impact. In this sense power is relative and use of the same power source or influencing tactic will not work in every situation or with every group (Handy, 1993; Cohen and Bradford, 1989).

The second consideration is that power will never be one sided. There is always something that the target can do in response, or as Handy puts it, to balance the use of power. For example the more the British Empire tried to use coercive power to hold onto power in India, the more power Ghandi and his followers gained through the use of non-violent protest.

The third consideration Handy terms the domain of power. Here he points out that context is critical in the use of a power source and that not all sources of power are valid everywhere. In addition, there may be a view in the organization as to the limit of an individual leader's power, beyond which they do not have legitimate influence. A leader who attempts to use the power they believe they have to achieve something that is seen as beyond their remit will find themselves frustrated.

Handy also discusses a form of power that he terms 'negative power' (Handy, 1993: 131). This is the 'capacity to stop things happening, to delay them, to distort or disrupt them'. Handy points out that this type of power can be accessed by anyone in the organization; it is not dependent on one's position. Employees can delay answers to manager's questions, ignoring email requests or denying they have been received at all. A PA can ensure that some things do not get to the attention of the boss, or do not make it onto the agenda for a meeting. This brings us back to Moss Kanter, with employees using negative power to restrict the flow of information to a leader and hence potentially undermining a leader's power base. Handy points out that this type of power will not be used frequently, but perhaps is more obvious when employees have low morale or high stress, and lay the blame for this at the feet of their leader or manager. In this sense negative power can be said to be latent, waiting for the right moment to strike!

Case in point: The expenses clerk

James left University during the recession of 1991. Jobs were hard to come by, so James signed on with a temping agency that placed people in accountancy departments. One of the first placements he received was with a large technology and software company based near London. His job was to process the expense claims of the organization, checking receipts, entering the data into the system and printing out the claims. Claims came from all across the business, with the largest, usually from the senior management, running into thousands of pounds.

These large claims were often badly receipted, with the senior management deeming themselves too busy to follow the laid down rules and procedures. A delay in the payment of expenses and a request for receipts would usually lead to a fractious phone call from the senior person. James was frequently subject to managers using their position of power and control of resources to threaten punishment if expenses were not paid immediately.

However, even though he was only a 'temp', James had the power of rules on his side. Claims could not be processed unless they were in order. Angry claimants were sent up the line of authority, with the most senior eventually getting a dressing down from the Financial Director, who would demonstrate exactly who held the ultimate positional power in the organization. Even the CEO was subject to the rules of expenses.

By contrast, those managers who came to discuss their expenses and explore possibilities built relationships with the finance team that usually led to compromises on the payment of their expenses!

Chapter summary

In this chapter we have considered:

- Some foundational ideas about the nature of leadership
- How these ideas of leadership align with theories of power
- The sources of power and the possible use of these sources by leaders
- Influence and the links to power and leadership
- How a leader can develop and use influencing tactics to achieve results
- A critical appraisal of the theories of power and influence

Integrative case study: The search for a CEO

The following case is based on a real selection process for the new CEO of a European company. Whilst the names and some details have been changed to ensure confidentiality, the description of events, behaviours, and outcomes is accurate.

Chestnut Plc is a successful European company in the construction industry. It had achieved substantial growth over a number of years, during which time it had expanded its geographic reach whilst maintaining a fairly stable senior management team. The CEO, Donald Atkin, had been in post for 12 years, and had been fundamental in driving the growth of the organization. Donald had a national presence, sitting on several influential industry groups and meeting regularly with Government officials to advise on policy.

Chestnut Plc is structured in a similar way to many UK businesses. It has a Board responsible for the governance and strategic overview of the business. The Board is made up of experienced independent non-executives, and influential dignitaries. The Chair of the Board was a former politician, Peter Johnson, who had a long history of association with the construction sector and chaired the Board in a challenging way.

The company was run by a Senior Management Team made up of the CEO, the Deputy CEO and Director of Development Claude Beaumont, the Finance Director Julie Wilson, the Director of Operations Morten Worsley, the Director of Human Resources Frank Green, and the Director of Sales and Marketing Daniel Webster.

When Donald announced his retirement to the Board, the Chair instigated a search for his successor. Executive Search Consultants, McKinley & Backhouse, were appointed and the principle of the business, William McKinley, personally oversaw the work as this was a big client. Adverts went out in the industry publications, and the Executive Search firm began to politely enquire if people would be interested.

The senior team of Chestnut quickly fell into two camps, those who would 'throw their hat into the ring' and those who would not. The Deputy CEO, Claude, who colleagues said had been waiting for this opportunity for at least 6 years, declared his interest. The FD, Julie, and the Director of HR, Frank, quickly counted themselves out. The Director of Sales, Daniel, never revealed if he had applied or not.

Morten, the Director of Operations, took time to consider his options. By all accounts, Morten was a very strong candidate for the position. He had the experience, the ability, and the internal support to do the job. Morten had worked his way up through the organization and had proved himself to be a highly organized, professional manager. He was highly thought of by his peers, and direct reports from inside the organization and several individuals, including Julie the FD, encouraged him to apply for the position. Morten had also built up an excellent reputation externally with partners and customers. In the course of his normal meetings with these stakeholders he received numerous messages of encouragement and support. After much consideration, Morten put in an application.

With such a strong and well supported candidate now in the mix, Peter Johnson now had a quandary to sort out. Johnson had already decided that he did not want an internal candidate to become the new CEO. He believed that the organization needed a shake up and bringing in a new, dynamic CEO was the best way of achieving this. His position had been made clear in private discussions with William McKinley, from which a selection procedure was devised.

The first stage was the application vetting. This saw the removal of several candidates, bringing the field down to nine finalists who would have a first interview. This included the two internal candidates, two strong candidates who were already CEOs of other organizations, and two other applicants who looked weaker on paper than the other five candidates. The first interviews would be with the Chair and Executive Search consultant. The final round would be in front of a panel of the full Board, including client representation.

Morten found the interview both encouraging and challenging. The questioning initially focused on his ability to do the job and his vision for the business. He was challenged by some questions

(Continued...)

which implied that at his age he should already hold the most senior position in a business. Generally, though, he felt he had done well in the interview and got some encouraging feedback afterwards from William McKinley. He expected to have a final interview, where the support from the Board would make him an extremely strong candidate.

So it was a surprise when Morten got a call from Peter Johnson to say that he had not made the final cut. He later learned that Claude had also fallen at the first interview stage. Both Peter and William were glowing with praise about Morten's application, his experience and suitability for the job. The only fault seemed to be that he had not been a CEO before, but other candidates who did make the final cut were in a similar position, so this seemed to be a spurious reason for rejection. William admitted that Morten had been prevented from playing his best card by not being interviewed by the Board. A good performance at that interview, plus the support that Morten already had on the Board, may have made it difficult for Johnson to achieve his aim of a new CEO for the organization.

By carefully defining the process, keeping the first round closely under control, and influencing the key decision makers, Johnson gained the candidate he wanted, an experienced, dynamic new CEO for Chestnut Plc.

Case study questions:

- What sources of power does Morten have within the organization? How is he prevented from turning this power into influence?
- Using the ideas of Yukl and Handy, describe the influencing tactics employed by Johnson to ensure he gets his way. What sources of power does he draw on to be successful?
- Put yourself in Morten's position. How could you have used the influence you had to try and achieve a different result?
- Do you think the more senior a position you hold automatically means that you are more likely to be successful in influencing others?

Further reading

Ladkin, D. (2010) *Rethinking Leadership: A New Look at Old Leadership Questions*. Cheltenham, Edward Elgar.

Raven, B. H. (2008) The bases of power and the power/interaction model of interpersonal influence. *Analyses of Social Issues and Public Policy* 8 (1): 1–22.

Sveiby, K. (2011) Collective leadership with power symmetry: Lessons from Aboriginal prehistory. *Leadership* 7, 385–411.

3

The leadership/ management debate: Is there a difference and does it matter?

Learning outcomes

On completion of this chapter you will:

- Understand how 'leadership' and 'management' have been defined by theorists trying to explain them and how this is reflected in actual leadership and management practice

- Understand the mainstream view of leadership as being different from management, and as requiring different skills

- Be aware of the critique of this view, which challenges the usefulness of the 'leadership versus management' distinction

- Understand how the 'leadership versus management' debate is rooted in the historical origins of the leadership discipline, and how this underpins our understanding of each

- Be aware of the positions taken by key writers in the field and the basis for their claims

Introduction

Early leadership studies were based on the idea that one could identify a 'one best way' of being a leader and that the ability to perform in this way was based on a person's character traits. In more recent times leadership studies as a discipline has begun to align itself with business and management theories and models. This has led some to question the difference between leadership and management. For instance, a common argument is that leadership transcends the bureaucracy of management and is about 'doing the right things' rather than just 'doing things right' (Bennis and Nanus, 1985). Other authors (for example, Fullan, 2001) make the distinction between leadership as relating to such things as mission, direction, and inspiration, and management as involving designing and implementing plans, working effectively with people, and getting things done. Central to most attempts to distinguish between leadership and management has been the issue of orientation to change. For example, Kotter (1990) defines management as 'coping with complexity' and leadership as 'coping with change'. Despite the obvious appeal of the leadership/management distinction, there is still considerable debate as to whether the two can actually be distinguished in practice. The need for consistency, predictability (Rost, 1991), and a sense of continuity (Gosling and Murphy, 2004)—things normally associated with management rather than leadership—even in times of change, suggest considerable overlap between the two. Similarly, the ability of the same individual to progress from a 'management' role to a 'leadership' one—whilst still being the same person!—suggests that it may be more useful to conceive of leadership as just one of the many roles a manager undertakes (Mintzberg, 1975).

Rather than clarifying the definition of leadership, the continuing debate seems only to emphasize its complexity, leaving us with the feeling that 'leadership is like the Abominable Snowman, whose footprints are everywhere but who is nowhere to be seen' (Bennis and Nanus, 1985: 19). This chapter will present the 'leadership versus management' debate, and the competing viewpoints which underpin it, in more detail in an attempt—not to resolve the debate—but to help you decide your own position in relation to it. In so doing, we encourage you to reflect on when distinguishing leadership from management may be helpful, and when it may 'straitjacket' our thinking rather than improving our performance.

 Blog box

Personally, I tend to use the term 'leadership' for things I feel accountable for—taking a tough decision, such as making someone redundant or delivering bad news, such as a disciplinary interview—and 'management' for activities relating to organizing activities and tasks (which I find much easier). For me, there is a sense of 'stepping up' to leadership; that it is an activity that requires more of me than management, but this is not necessarily related to change (as the literature often suggests). I suppose I would agree to some extent with Bennis and Nanus that leadership is about 'doing the right thing', but not with the glamour or heroism that this is sometimes seen as implying. Leadership can be just as mundane—and just as much in the doing of detail—as management. For my PhD I spent a whole year following leaders around and asking them 'what are you doing?' and the answer was never as simple as 'now I'm doing leadership; now I'm doing management'. The difference is often in the intent rather than in the action, and in how it is received rather than how it is delivered. And sometimes we just fall into using the words interchangeably, without really thinking! I think we can only decide whether the distinction is useful and relevant on a case by case basis, depending upon what 'work' we want the words to do. (MIW)

Industrialization and the development of 'scientific management'

In the late nineteenth and early twentieth centuries, growth in demand for goods and services by a more affluent population (in the Western world, at least) led to a move away from craft-based production in favour of more mechanized methods capable of producing goods in greater quantities. Small craft shops gave way to larger factories—originally 'manufactories'— and the era of the deskilled production worker began. The core ideas of 'scientific management' which followed were developed by Frederick Winslow Taylor in the 1880s and 1890s, and were first published in his monograph *Shop Management* in 1903 and later expanded in *The Principles of Scientific Management*, published in 1911. Taylor had been working as a lathe operator, and later as a foreman, at the Midvale Steel Works in Philadelphia, Pennsylvania, when he noticed the natural differences in productivity between workers, which he attributed to differences in talent, intelligence, or motivation. In attempting to formalize these observations, he was one of the first people to apply scientific methods to the problems of production and manufacturing. As well as understanding why and how these differences existed, he wanted to devise a systematic method of analysing and synthesizing work processes that would enable him to develop 'best practices' that could then be generalized to other factories. He believed that working practices based on standardization would produce better quality outputs and more efficient production than the old craft-related 'rules of thumb' which he still saw operating around him. Putting this belief into effect, he instigated wide-ranging 'time and motion studies' to make careful study of how specific work tasks were accomplished most effectively, and he wrote detailed step-by-step procedures based on his findings. The application of these procedures—the bedrock of 'scientific management'—was contingent on a high level of managerial control over employee work practices, which necessitated a higher ratio of managerial workers to labourers than previous management methods. It also, over time, became a source of friction between workers and managers, and was the origin of the social tensions which came to exist between 'blue collar' and 'white collar' classes.

From this, we can see that the early remit of management was to control and administer 'unwilling' workers, with the emphasis very firmly on efficient production and task completion. Whilst Taylor had observed that some workers were more motivated than others, he did not suggest that managers should try to motivate them. Instead, his emphasis was on creating efficient step-by-step work processes that forced workers to operate at the required pace. These ideas were the early origins of 'Fordism' and the development of mass production lines that moved at a certain pace and required workers to keep up. By 'management' here, we are talking about little more than 'supervision'—a far cry from the complex role we would see as modern management. And large organizations—such as the Ford Motor Company—had 'owners' rather than 'leaders'. These were the people who invested the capital and extracted the profits, and saw their workers as just another resource in the production process. The recognition that workers were people too was yet to come!

 Leadership in the media: Modern Times

In 1936 Charlie Chaplin starred in and directed a silent film, *Modern Times*, which, although superficially a comedy, presented a sharp commentary on what he saw as the dehumanizing effects of mass production and industrialization. In the film, we see a poor, hapless worker completely at the mercy of the production line on which he works. In the early stages of the film, we see him frantically trying to keep up with the machine, tightening bolts which seem to make no difference to what the machine is doing. It is pointless work, and yet he is driven to do it. Later, he is selected for an experiment with an automatic feeding machine, but various mishaps lead his boss to believe he has gone mad, and Charlie is sent to a mental hospital...

This was Chaplin's last 'silent' film (although filled with mechanical sound effects), made when everyone else was making 'talkies'. The film depicts Chaplin's views of the dangers of industrialization, and the need for us to retain our humanity at all cost. Whilst clearly very dated in its format, it remains an iconic record of the times in which it was made.

The various attempts to implement scientific management, by Taylor and his followers, were not particularly successful, usually because they failed to account for several inherent challenges. Specifically, whilst recognizing that different people had different talents and skills, the principles of scientific management developed on the back of this observation failed to take into account the fact that the most efficient way of working for one person may be inefficient for another. At its most basic level, for example, asking a left-handed worker to perform a manual task in exactly the same way as a right-handed one is likely to produce poor results. The theory also failed to take into account that the economic interests of workers and management were rarely identical, and that this was likely to have an impact on how the new methods were viewed by each party. The measurement processes and the retraining required for Taylor's methods were frequently resented and sometimes sabotaged by the workforce, who—except through the limited impact of piece work—derived no benefit from them. Not surprisingly, workers felt they were being exploited by the owners of the business—who enjoyed the additional profits which resulted—and saw managers as the instrument of this exploitation. This was particularly galling when managers—as was so often the case—were promoted from the rank and file of workers, and were thus seen as 'turning traitor' on their own kind. Taylor himself recognized these challenges but was still unable to make a lasting success of any of his trials of scientific management.

In management literature today, the greatest use of the term 'scientific management' is to refer to the principles of the division of labour and step-by-step process specification which Taylor devised (though some of his other ideas are forgotten or attributed elsewhere—he is seldom credited with recommending more breaks for workers, for example). Whilst the dehumanizing effect of some aspects of scientific management led to its replacement by other forms of management, it is still recognized as a seminal contribution to our understanding of organizations. Today, task-oriented optimization of work activities is nearly ubiquitous in industry. The theory behind it has evolved greatly since Taylor's day, reducing the ill effects, leaving a legacy that is recognizable in business process management, business process re-engineering, lean manufacturing, and Six Sigma—all ongoing attempts to make the production process more efficient.

Discussion point: Can workers be self-managing?

- Taylor clearly believed that people will tend to do the least possible work that will not result in punishment, and that they therefore need to be 'managed' by others. Do you agree with Taylor's reasoning and, if so, what evidence do you have from your own experience that this is the case?

- Taylor recognized that participating in the benefits of more efficient work practices through 'piece work' was an important motivator for workers. What other methods of participation could he have considered?

- Where workers are promoted to supervisory or managerial positions over their own colleagues, what problems is this likely to cause, and how can they be minimized?

Taylor's disciples and the growth of management ideas

Amongst Taylor's co-workers at Midvale Steel was Henry Gantt. In addition to the Gantt chart—still an important project management tool today—Gantt left a number of legacies to production management which, to our modern way of thinking, appear more enlightened than those of his colleague by virtue of their more human approach to the workers upon which production depended. His 'task and bonus' system linked the bonus paid to managers to how well they taught their employees to improve performance whilst, more widely, he believed that businesses have obligations to the welfare of the society in which they operate—the forerunner of today's writing on corporate governance and corporate and social responsibility.

Henri Fayol, a contemporary of Taylor's though not a colleague, was a French mining engineer who, independent of scientific management, developed a general theory of business administration—often known as Fayolism—which became one of the most influential contributions to modern concepts of management. As defined by Fayol, business administration consists of the performance or management of business operations and thus the making or implementing of major decisions within an organization. In this context, 'administration' refers to the all-encompassing process of organizing people and resources efficiently so as to direct activities toward common goals and objectives—the origin of the present day Masters in Business Administration or MBA. As such, and in contrast with Taylor's more supervisory version, it is clearly recognizable as 'management' as we know it today. Fayol's was one of the first comprehensive statements of a general theory of management: it proposed that there are six primary functions of management, namely:

- forecasting
- planning
- organizing
- commanding
- coordinating
- controlling

Some writers—for example Daft (2003)—reduced these functions to four: planning, organizing, leading, and controlling, but they continue to cover much of the same ground incorporated in the original six. Fayol also proposed that there were 14 principles of management (Fayol, 1917), as summarized in Figure 3.1. These principles have, in the main, stood the test of time and are still widely taught and applied today.

Also a contemporary of Taylor's but with a very different perspective on matters relating to work was Max Weber, the German sociologist and political economist. Much of Weber's early work dealt with the rationalization and disenchantment he associated with the rise of capitalism and the modern methods of production which fed it. In his later works, Weber focused significant effort on the understanding of bureaucracy and on classifications of authority. The latter he divided into three types, which he referred to as legitimate, traditional, and charismatic. Here we have the first inkling of a sense of a difference between leadership and management, and the impending rise of the latter in importance both as a practice and an academic area of study. Weber defined charismatic authority as power which drew its legitimacy from the leader's exceptional personal qualities or accomplishments, which were such as to inspire loyalty and obedience from followers. In this definition we can clearly see the origins of charismatic leadership and the notion that a 'leader' is somehow more or different from a manager. There are echoes, too, of the 'great man' theory, made popular by Thomas Carlyle in the 1840s, under which it was said that most of history could largely be explained by

1. **Division of work or labour**: the premise that specialisation increases output by making employees more efficient.
2. **Authority**: managers must be able to give orders. Authority gives them this right and responsibility arises wherever authority is exercised.
3. **Discipline**: employees must obey and respect the rules that govern the organisation, and will be encouraged to do so by effective leadership, a clear understanding between management and workers regarding the organisation's rules, and the judicious use of penalties for infractions of the rules.
4. **Unity of command**: every employee should receive orders from only one superior.
5. **Unity of direction**: each group of organisational activities that have the same objective should be directed by one manager using one plan.
6. **Subordination of individual interests to the general interest**: the interests of any one employee or group of employees should not take precedence over the interests of the organisation as a whole.
7. **Remuneration**: workers must be paid a fair wage for their services.
8. **Centralisation**: the task is to find the optimum degree of centralisation (to management) or decentralisation (to subordinates) in relation to decision making for each situation.
9. **Chain of command**: the line of authority from top management to the lowest ranks represents the chain of command and communications should follow this chain, unless specifically agreed otherwise.
10. **Order**: people and materials should be in the right place at the right time.
11. **Equity**: managers should be kind and fair to their subordinates.
12. **Stability of tenure of personnel**: high employee turnover is inefficient and management should provide orderly personnel planning and ensure that replacements are available to fill vacancies.
13. **Initiative**: employees who are allowed to originate and carry out plans will exert high levels of effort.
14. **Esprit de corps**: promoting team spirit will build harmony and unity within the organisation.

Figure 3.1 Henri Fayol's Fourteen Principles of Management.

Sources: www.mindtools.com; www.citehr.com; http://managementinnovations.wordpress.com

the impact of 'great men' or 'heroes'—highly influential individuals whose personal charisma, along with other characteristics such as intelligence, wisdom, or Machiavellianism gave them a power that allowed them to have a decisive impact on historical events. As we shall see in a later chapter, the term 'great man' was later to be associated with a trait-based theory of leadership within which some of these same characteristics were viewed as being important. It is worth noting that it would be a long time before the notion that there might also be 'great women' would be voiced in leadership writing—although perhaps not so surprising when you consider the origins of organizational leadership writing in the largely physical working world of heavy industry.

It is important at this point to remember that the study of leadership per se has a much longer history than that of management. Aristotle was trying to understand leadership in a political context over 2,300 years ago, long before the advent of industrialized society—the context within which the study of management emerged—at the turn of the twentieth century. As we debate the relevance and characteristics of leadership versus management in this latter context, we should not forget the broader arena within which the former may be considered. So, for example, when Northouse (2010: 10) says that 'the overriding function of management is to provide order and consistency to organizations, whereas the primary function of leadership is to produce change and movement' it is implicit in this statement that management is about organizations whilst leadership can have a much broader focus. The same sense of leadership existing on a broader canvas than management is to be found in Rost's (1991) definition of management as an authority relationship between managers and subordinates to produce and sell goods and leadership as a multi-directional influence relationship between leaders and followers with a shared purpose to accomplish change. Not only does the former specify a commercial context which is absent from the latter, but also the definition of leadership acknowledges that influence can be exercised in the absence of hierarchical authority, another feature more usually associated with an organizational context. We should bear this fundamental difference of scope in mind as we proceed with our exploration of how organizational writers have compared—and contrasted—leadership and management in an organizational context.

In the mainstream

'Leadership is about change'

We have already seen Kotter's epigrammatic linking of management to complexity and leadership to change in the introduction to this chapter. More specifically, he maintained that:

> Management is about coping with complexity. Its practices and procedures are largely a response to one of the most significant developments of the twentieth century: the emergence of large organisations. ... Leadership, by contrast, is about coping with change. Part of the reason it has become so important in recent years is that the business world has become more competitive and more volatile. (Kotter, 2001: 86)

He thus attributes the rise of leadership in an organizational context to the change of pace and growth of uncertainty to be observed there. Early industrialists were focused on producing and selling goods in a relatively unchanging environment and with relatively little competition. Good management—to produce and sell products efficiently—was sufficient here. The advent of more competition between manufacturers, more demand from customers for novelty and innovation, and—most recently—the development of a 'global market', have resulted in the need for businesses to be in a constant state of change, bringing workers along with them. This has required leadership both to drive it and to deal with its consequences. This perceived division in relation to the kind of intervention required to meet the different situations being faced by modern organizations is expanded upon by Kotter (1990) when he sets out the functions served by leadership and management respectively in relation to directing the organization, developing employees, and implementing and achieving outcomes. So, for example, leaders establish direction, communicate vision and strategy, and energize people to overcome obstacles whilst managers decide action plans and timetables, develop policies and procedures, and take corrective actions against shortfalls. In each case, it can be seen that the more dynamic or exciting tasks fall to the leader, whilst the more mundane activities are the lot of the manager.

This qualitative distinction has been expressed many times by leadership writers (though, interestingly, less so by management writers!) So, for example, as early as 1977, Zaleznik was claiming that leaders are artists who use creativity to navigate their way through chaos, while managers are problem solvers dependent on rationality and control, and arguing that leaders and managers are actually different types of people. In a similar vein, Bryman (1986) saw leaders as catalysts focused on strategy whilst managers were viewed as operators/technicians concerned with operational goals. Similarly, Heifetz (1994) draws the distinction between 'technical work'—by which he means known problems that can be resolved through the application of known solutions—and 'adaptive work' where uncertainty or ambiguity in relation to problems require the application of a more imaginative process to create new solutions. A similar theme is developed by Grint (2005b), discussed in detail in a research in focus box in this chapter. What all these distinctions or definitions have in common is the sense that leadership is somehow more dynamic or creative than management.

A case in point: Ricardo Semler—'leadership by omission'

Ricardo Semler was 21 when he inherited his father's $4 million manufacturing business in Sao Paulo, Brazil, making industrial equipment and document management solutions. He immediately began asking questions about why things were done the way they were, and set about making radical changes. Semco group is now a leader in its field, and in 1993 (when Semler published his first book, *Maverick!*) had revenues of over $212 million. The company now has over 3,000 employees and is rated one of the best employers in the world. Employee turnover is less than 1% per year.

Semler—who describes his approach to participative management as 'leadership by omission'—has created a truly unique working environment in which all meetings are optional, employees set their own work schedules, candidates applying for jobs are interviewed by those who will work for them, strategic decisions are made by democratic vote (Semler himself has only one vote—the same as everyone else), the company's books are open to all employees and employees set their own salaries, and all employees are encouraged to job rotate regularly. There are no organization charts, no 5-year plans, no values statements, and no dress codes. Corporate leaders are elected and there is no formal hierarchy. It should come as no surprise, then, that when Semler was hit by a truck in 2005 and spent several months in intensive care, it was 'business as usual' at Semco and the company continued to be as successful as ever, notwithstanding the absence of its remarkable leader.

Source: Ricardo Semler (1993) *Maverick!: The Success Story Behind the World's Most Unusual Workplace.* Century. London; <en.wikipedia.org>; <www.project83.com>

Both Heifitz and Grint take an identity oriented approach to the leadership/management divide, seeing the relationship between the two as being a combination of the individual's own sense of identity (do they see themselves as a leader or a manager?), how these two roles have been socially constructed within—largely Western—society (managers are sound but dull; leaders are dynamic and take risks), and how the organizational context in which they occur is understood or constructed (does the organization operate in a fast changing environment or a largely static one, for example).

In writing about leadership and management from an identity perspective, Carroll and Levy (2008) saw management as the default identity—the baseline identity from which people in organizations begin—and leadership as an emergent and desirable identity to which they aspire. Being a good manager is possible on the basis of having good technical skills in the role from which one has been promoted, whereas being a good leader requires 'identity work'—changing the way one views oneself—as well as leadership development work.

RESEARCH IN FOCUS: What's the problem?

In one of his many contributions to the field of leadership, Grint concerned himself with 'the processes through which decision-makers persuade their followers, and perhaps themselves, that a certain kind of action is required' (Grint, 2005b: 1469). In considering this question, he draws on the distinction between management and leadership by suggesting that they represent different forms of authority, rooted respectively in certainty and uncertainty. As such, he sees them as being suited to addressing—drawing on Rittell and Webber's (1973) typology—tame and wicked problems. Tame problems are defined as complex, but resolvable through unilinear acts and, as such, requiring the application of appropriate processes (that is, management). Examples would include timetabling the railways, building a nuclear plant, and conducting heart surgery. By contrast, wicked problems are seen as intractable and with no 'right' or 'wrong' answer. They thus require someone to ask the right questions to enable the best possible alternative to be identified (that is, leadership). Examples given by Grint include developing a transport strategy or developing a strategy for dealing with global terrorism. The benefit of asking questions here, rather than trying to provide answers, is the initiation of a collaborative process which taps into the greatest possible range of skills, knowledge, and experience in arriving at a decision, at the same time as enhancing buy-in for whatever actions are finally agreed upon. In setting up this typology, it is Grint's contention that decision-makers give persuasive accounts of situations to followers that shape the nature of the situation in alignment with their own preferred style of intervention. If what they are good at is management, then every issue is constituted as tame: if they are strong in the arts of leadership, then wicked problems abound in their vicinity.

In this fascinating and challenging paper, Grint also postulates a third kind of problem—the critical problem, characterized by the need for rapid action—which requires commanding or authoritarian interventions by decision-makers. The premise here is that any decision is a good decision as long as it is made quickly and delivered with authority! What he doesn't say is how effective the subsequent interventions—management, leadership, or command—are likely to be. What happens if it is just not that kind of problem?

Source: Grint, K. (2005b) Problems, problems, problems—the social construction of leadership. *Human Relations*, 58 (11), 1467–94.

 Blog box

Write a description of yourself and your current job role as you see it—around 300 words would be good. Then read it back and assess the 'identity' it portrays: is it that of a leader or a manager? If the former, jot down your recollections of any specific 'identity work' you have undertaken to make the transition from manager to leader. If you still see yourself as a manager, reflect (in writing) on how you would have to see yourself differently to feel like a leader.

From a critical perspective

All part of being a good manager?

The idea that leadership is somehow more important or exciting than management in an organizational context, or that it takes precedence over it, is a relatively new perspective and reflects what Meindl (Meindl, Ehrlich, and Dukerich, 1985) referred to as the 'romanticization of leadership'—the 'hyping up' of leadership and leaders and what they can deliver to the extent that they are in danger of being perceived as the solution to all organizational ills (we will look at this view in more detail in Chapter 6). There is a more traditional, and moderate, claim for leadership which goes some way towards challenging the distinction we have been making so far. Whilst not doing away with the distinction entirely, it does 'demote' the role of leadership from that of the pre-eminent skill set to that of 'one among many'. Specifically, Mintzberg (1975) viewed leadership as just one of the many skills and abilities which an effective manager needed to possess. These include informational roles (such as being a spokesperson for the organization and/or disseminating information internally), decisional roles (including handling disturbances and allocating resources), and interpersonal roles (where being a leader sits alongside but is not superior to liaison and figurehead activities).

Mintzberg based this typology on his observations of managerial activities after a detailed study of the behaviours and activities of executives. He suggested that collectively the ten roles account for all of a manager's activities, and that any given activity may be encompassed by one or more role. Whilst all managers are likely to perform all of the roles at some time or another, their relative importance will vary from manager to manager. The pattern of roles will be largely determined by the nature of the managerial position, but there will be some flexibility around the individual's preferences and how they choose to handle various situations.

Not surprisingly, role conflict is often a problem for managers, either because two or more of the roles listed above might require different interventions in a given situation, or because the manager's perception of his role and what it requires him to do may differ from the expectations of others. This can be the case both in relation to the expectations of more senior managers and of subordinates. For example, difficult economic conditions may lead senior management to require a manager to make employees redundant: at the same time, it may be imperative for the organization that production continues at the same rate. A manager must reconcile these two conflicting expectations of him from the same source. Alternatively, subordinates might quite reasonably expect their manager to be open and honest with them—to disseminate the information that they are privy to about current operations and future plans relating to the organization. This might be no problem in relation to daily production targets or emerging quality issues, but impossible when there are redundancies being contemplated or an acquisition attempt in progress. In both these cases, confidentiality is likely to be important and the manager, as a figurehead and spokesperson for the organization, will be required by senior management to uphold the 'party line' until such time as the plans are ripe to become public knowledge. More generally, role conflict may arise in relation to differing priorities or the manner in which a particular role should be carried out. Issues of power are likely to be important here, since the manager may well resolve such conflicts by meeting the expectations of those with more power to influence outcomes relevant to the manager themselves. This is one explanation of why managers appear to be 'on the side of' senior management rather than of their subordinates!

The potential for role conflict is also reflected in what Korac-Kakabadse and Korac-Kakabadse (1997) have referred to as discretionary leadership, reflecting the role incumbent's ability to shape the scope and identity of their role through the choices they make in relation to the issues and colleagues with whom they engage. Whilst some aspects of their role are likely to be prescribed, others offer scope for involvement or abstention depending upon the interests and skills of the role incumbent. In making choices about what is encompassed within their role, leaders also delineate the parts of the organization for which they are accountable and the operational or strategic level at which they are seen to operate. This ability to exercise discretion within the executive role is seen as having potential to result in significant disparity of choices between different role incumbents, particularly at times of fundamental change within the organization. This can result either in disputed territory or in some issues dropping off the agenda completely. Kakabadse and Kakabadse (1999) see dialogue—the process through which agreement is reached in disputed areas—as the opposite side of the coin to choice: taken together they are said to constitute the practice of leadership. In exercising discretionary leadership, through which the scope and identity of an executive role is established, leaders can also be said to be presenting themselves as either leaders or managers. The issues they choose to engage with, and the dialogues they enter into, are likely to form a pattern of activity which others would see as falling into one or other of these categories.

 Blog box

Look at the job description for your current role, and write a commentary of about 300 words on how you have chosen to interpret the scope of the role and your identity within it. You might reflect back to the preceding blog box entry as a starting point for this exercise. Where have you chosen to take on responsibilities not really within your remit? Where are you shying away from specific tasks or activities you should be undertaking? How are these choices a reflection of how you see yourself as a leader/manager?

In Mintzberg's framework, we can clearly see the way in which how we use language plays an important part in the leadership versus management debate. We can see, for example, that the 'disturbance handler' role—designated by Mintzberg as part of management—bears

 Leadership in the media: How the media presents leaders

Choose three or four newspaper clips or business journal articles on the same topic but from different newspapers/journals. This could be the departure of a CEO, the announcement of a company's annual results, a political or other leadership appointment, or any other news item in some way related to leadership.

Assess the pieces for the following factors:

- Political or other bias. Certain newspapers have known political or class-related leanings, cultural or religious biases or other 'filters' through which they present the news—can you see this reflected in the way they describe the topic or the leaders involved? For example, is a CEO justly well rewarded for good results or a 'fat cat'?

- Use of sensationalist language. Does the piece use lots of superlatives or other 'over the top' adjectives? Are words like 'crisis', 'disaster', 'desperate', and 'dire' really reflective of the situation or just designed to sell newspapers?

- Provision of supporting evidence. What evidence, and from what sources, does the article provide to support the claims it makes? For example, does it include quotes from reputable and relevant interviewees or figures from rigorously conducted research? Or just the unsubstantiated opinions of the author?

Based on what you have read, how realistically do you think leadership is presented? On a scale of one to ten, how much faith would you put in articles from each newspaper/journal in future?

a strong resemblance to what Grint referred to as 'dealing with wicked problems' and hence requiring leadership by way of intervention. Similarly, the symbolic activities encompassed by the 'figurehead' role come very close to some of the work we would now associate with leadership, such as disseminating a vision.

> ## Discussion point: Leadership in the media
>
> - How are political and business leaders presented on TV and in the press? What language is used to describe their activities and the results they produce?
> - Are leaders presented differently from managers, and if so, how? What claims are implicitly made for leadership in the way leaders are presented? Are these claims greater than for managers?
> - What can we as viewers/readers do to find corroborating evidence for the ways leaders are presented?

Running counter to this perception of language confusion surrounding the words 'leadership' and 'management' is an explicit examination of the leadership discourse—the ways in which the language, and particularly the metaphors, we use in describing it give power to the notion of what it is and what it can do. Research work by Alvesson and Sveningsson (2003) lead them to conclude that many managers who are engaged in leadership work find it easy to articulate the abstract ideals of what leadership is (presenting a vision, motivating and inspiring employees, building commitment, and so on) but find it much harder (if not impossible) to say what they actually do to deliver on these ideals on a day-to-day basis. Their everyday work seems to consist of holding meetings, sending emails, making decisions, reading documents, and other activities which seem too mundane to constitute leadership. Yet talk about leadership remains a powerful aspect of how they and others see their role. It is also widely viewed as vital to any organization hoping to be successful in the modern world. As Carroll, Levy, and Richmond (2008) observe:

> Leadership has more power as a discourse and identity, giving practitioners enhanced self-esteem, significance and 'positive cultural valence' (Alvesson and Willmott, 2002: 620) rather than a specific or distinctive set of practices or interventions in organisational life. (Carroll, Levy, and Richmond, 2008: 372–3)

In a similar vein, Chia (2004) suggests that in the academic domain, the leadership discourse has now become so pervasive that when practitioners are asked about their leadership behaviours and skills, they frame their answers in terms of the theory without really relating this narrative to what they actually do on a day-to-day basis. As Chia (2004: 30) puts it, 'they are likely to "conceal even from their own eyes the true nature of their practical mastery" (Bourdieu, 1977/2002: 19)'. This suggests that 'leadership' may have become a post hoc rationalization of some of the activities which managers undertake, rather than a genuine portfolio of practices in their own right. The readiness with which 'practitioners willingly provide quasi-theoretical accounts of their own practices' (Chia, 2004: 30) in the language of leadership is also suggestive of the extent to which managers now feel they 'ought' to be doing leadership. A powerful discourse indeed!

Leadership in the media: Remember the Titans

By the early 1970s, suburban Virginia schools had been segregated for generations, notwithstanding their proximity to the nation's capital, home of the claim that all men are born equal. As the backdrop to the film *Remember the Titans*, one black and one white high school have been closed and the students sent to T.C. Williams High School under federal mandate to integrate. The year is seen through the eyes of the football team where the man hired to coach the black school is made head coach over the highly successful coach from the white school. Based on the actual events of 1971, the team becomes the unifying symbol for the community as the boys and the adults learn to depend on and trust each other.

There is definitely more to this film than meets the eye. What looks as if it is going to be a fairly straight-forward film about American college football is made rich and uplifting by being set in a context of the fight against segregation. From a leadership versus management perspective, it also provides a fascinating case study of how these different roles can be played out: how they are different and how they can be the same. Watch out for examples of differing styles and behaviours from the two coaches (Herman Boone and Bill Yoast) and from the two team captains (Julius Campbell and Gerry Bertier). Decide for yourself who is leading or managing and when.

Alvesson and Sveningsson (2003) found that one leadership practice which practitioners could specifically identify was listening—listening in meetings, listening to subordinates raising issues, listening to senior managers' priorities, even listening to personal problems. Whilst this is clearly a very ordinary activity in itself—and one that we all do all the time—Alvesson and Sveningsson saw it as taking on particular significance when being performed by someone whom others look to as a leader. They described this phenomenon as the 'extra-ordinarization of the mundane' and suggested that it was the sense of leadership which conferred significance on the listening rather than the listening that, in itself, constituted leadership.

 Blog box

Reflecting on your own experience of leadership, jot down examples of when an otherwise mundane act took on leadership significance because of who performed it or the circumstances in which it occurred. What made those on the receiving end orient to it as leadership? How did they recognize it as such? How does this 'mundane' view of leadership stand up against more 'romanticized' views and which do you find more convincing in practice?

This idea that leadership is actually made up of a wide range of mundane skills and activities—somewhat like management?—rather than some kind of unique or superhuman feat, is a prominent feature of what is called the 'practice turn' in the study of leadership. The emphasis here is not on 'big picture' models and frameworks, but on the day-to-day practices through which the work of leadership is accomplished. So, for example, Samra-Fredericks (2003) conducted a detailed empirical investigation into the everyday routines and interactions of strategic leaders, and isolated six practices common to all. She described these as:

> The ability to speak forms of knowledge; mitigate and observe the protocols of human interaction (the moral order); question and query; display appropriate emotions; deploy metaphors and finally, put history 'to work'. (Samra-Fredericks, 2003: 144)

Most of these would be fairly recognizable to us all as mundane skills and practices. Such activities constitute the 'practical wisdom' of actually *doing* strategic leadership—or, arguably, any kind of leadership—and seem a far cry from the calls to 'be charismatic or transformational', to 'create a vision', or to 'lead change' which are often used to characterize leadership within the mainstream of academic writing.

A case in point: Picking up litter as leadership

Steven Hunter is the Principal of a large further education college in the South of England. He wouldn't describe himself as a charismatic leader, and he prefers speaking to staff one-to-one wherever possible, rather than making visionary speeches. But notwithstanding his 'quiet' approach, everyone in the college is very clear about what he wants for his students, in terms of quality education and an inclusive learning experience. And everything he does can be seen to exemplify the beliefs he holds and the standards he sets for the college. So, when staff see him picking up litter in a college forecourt, this act is interpreted in the context of those beliefs and standards. Thus what would rightly be seen as a mundane act when undertaken by the janitor, becomes an act of leadership when performed by the college Principal. Done by a leader known to hold certain views and to prescribe certain standards of behaviour (including, say, respect for the environment), it takes on symbolic significance in terms of 'setting an example' or 'walking the talk' which is inseparable from its situated occurrence, rather than being a property of the act itself. On this view, leadership is only leadership because the members of a particular setting agree to see it that way!

Source: This is a real incident, observed during the author's PhD research, although the names have been changed to preserve anonymity.

Lakomski (2005)—author of *Managing without Leadership: Towards a theory of organisational functioning*—goes further when she states very clearly that organizations can and do operate successfully without leadership and suggests that academic writing on the subject is nothing more than a post hoc rationalization of how organizations work. She contests the idea that leadership is 'the right'—or even 'an'—explanation of organizational phenomena and sees a marked discrepancy between the ways in which members believe their workplaces operate and how theories of leadership account for organizational functioning. In talking about her ongoing research into the fine-grained properties of contextualized organizational practices, she critiques the work of leadership writers as follows:

> Advocates for the existence and necessity of leadership assume more than they can deliver given their own theoretical resources, and given that organisations seem to manage perfectly well to accomplish their goals regardless of who is at the helm, the causal nexus between leadership and organisational practice is hard to sustain. The move to studying how we think and act in practice, and how we learn, promises a better empirical understanding of how organisations accomplish their goals. (Lakomski, 2005: preface)

Finally, in an attempt to draw this debate to a close, consider Nienaber's (2010) view that a careful study of the content of each concept—leadership and management—reveals nothing unique about leadership that isn't already covered by the concept of management. On this view, we are all just victims of the 'hype' which has surrounded leadership in recent years.

Discussion point: A useful distinction to make?

Based on the various perspectives presented in the chapter, consider the following questions:

- In what circumstances do you think it might be helpful to make a distinction between leadership and management? When might this not be the case?

- When would you personally use each of the two terms, and how does your understanding of each align with the theory? How has this understanding changed as a result of what you have read?

RESEARCH IN FOCUS: Shared territory?

Frustrated by the lack of clarity in how terms like 'leadership' and 'management' are conceptualized in the academic literature, Hester Nienaber (2010) undertook a synthesis review of 80 works within the field in an attempt to compare the content of the two constructs and their respective roles in delivering business success. Her study included work that reported on the content of leadership or management, the tasks or activities leaders/managers perform, what they actually do, differences and similarities between them, and the history/origins of the two concepts. She identified twenty-five distinct tasks: for example, 'determine priorities', 'understand the business environment', or 'determine what constitutes customer value', which were regularly discussed by either leadership or management writers and mapped them according to which group of authors claimed them to be part of their discipline. Whilst some tasks appear in the 'management' space and many in the space where 'management' and 'leadership' overlap, there are no tasks which appear in the 'leadership' space alone. As Nienaber (2010: 669) notes, the fact that leadership has no distinct tasks within its boundaries 'warrants the question whether leadership is indeed a separate and exalted concept in relation to management'. She goes on to suggest that management is a more comprehensive concept than leadership and that, given the integrated way in which the constituent tasks are performed, it adds no value to attempt to carve out a unique space for leadership.

Finally, she suggests that whilst there may be some value in reserving 'leadership' as a term for the distal activities of senior executives and applying the term 'management' to the more proximal activities of shop-floor supervisors, overall little has really changed since Fayol categorized the activities of managers as planning, organizing, command, coordination, and control in 1917. These five headings are still sufficient to describe the work of those seeking to deliver the goals of organizations, whatever title we give them.

Source: Nienaber, Hester (2010) 'Conceptualisation of management and leadership', *Management Decision*, 48 (5), 661–75.

Chapter summary

In this chapter we have considered:

- How organizational leadership has developed as a separate discipline from management, but has its roots much longer ago and in the far wider field of political leadership

- How key writers in the field have defined leadership and management, and the distinctions they have sought to make between the two

- The tendency to associate leadership with dynamic, visionary activities such as change, and to see management as relating to more mundane activities such as dealing with familiar (if complex) problems

- Alternatives to and critiques of this mainstream perspective, including the view that leadership is just one of the many roles an effective manager has to play

- More radical critiques of the mainstream position, which question whether the leadership/management distinction is a useful one to make, and whether we could actually 'see the difference' if we were to follow a leader/manager around over a period of time

- How this distinction is applied in the real world of organizations, and what practical purposes it might serve

 Integrative case study: Safety leadership or safety management?

Carillion plc is a leading integrated support services company with a substantial portfolio of Public Private Partnership projects and extensive construction capabilities. The Group had annual revenue in 2010 of £5.1 billion, employs around 50,000 people and operates across the UK, in the Middle East, and in Canada. This case study (originally conducted in 2007 and with supplemental information from 2011) focuses on its road maintenance and construction operations, which cover a wide range of activities from the design and build of major motorway networks through to the repair of small potholes in minor roads. Notwithstanding this extensive remit, the setting involves largely mundane technology, and often fragmented working environments. So, for example, individual operatives may be using pneumatic drills, grass strimmers, or petrol-driven compactors rather than operating large pieces of machinery, and may be part of small gangs working in dispersed locations. Even in relatively large scale construction projects, the equipment used—cranes, pile drivers, mechanical diggers, etc.—is relatively unsophisticated. The risks involved in its operations often have distal consequences—for example, the delayed onset of health problems as a result of exposure to noise or vibration—and failures in safety result in frequent, minor risk outcomes rather than one-off disasters. Nonetheless, according to recent figures from the Health and Safety Executive website (<www.hse.gov.uk/statistics/industry/construction.htm>) there were 77 fatalities in the UK construction industry in 2006–7, and approximately 90,000 cases of self-reported work-related illness, making the issue of safety an important one.

The wide range of health and safety hazards which occur in the construction industry are all subject to risk assessment procedures by companies such as Carillion, who are also required to put in place appropriate mitigating measures—either through the wearing of personal protective equipment (PPE) or through the application of written method statements for safe working. The risks relate to the environment in which work is carried out, the tools and equipment used by operatives, the physical activities undertaken, and the safety of members of the public as well as of those working in the industry. Whilst everyone in Carillion recognizes that safety is a serious issue, different contract managers go about implementing safety rules and procedures in different ways and have differing attitudes to the underlying risks. This case study compares the approaches to safety issues taken by contract managers (the leaders on the ground in this context) from different contracts.

'Newbuild' is a six mile long construction site, running down both sides of a high-speed two-lane highway, with the purpose of expanding it to a three-lane motorway. Workers here consist of well-qualified tradesmen and graduate engineers, equipment used is large scale (for example, pile drivers and excavators), and the proximity to fast moving traffic and high speed trains makes safety a high profile issue. Although workers tend to work in small gangs, they are often in close proximity to other gangs and are in frequent contact with supervisors and managers in the course of the working day. The contract manager takes every opportunity to introduce safety into every work-based exchange with colleagues, recruits supervisors based on their safety record and attitude, publicly rewards safety suggestions from operatives, and provides workers with high quality personal protective equipment, after first consulting them on what would best meet the requirements of the job. Speaking of the company-wide 'Target Zero' campaign for eliminating accidents at work, he saw it as a good—if abstract—aim, but one which required to be translated into genuine commitment to be effective: 'you don't do safety in an office; it happens out there—we all know that!'

This approach generates safety initiatives at all levels across the contract, and the active engagement of operatives to devise safer ways of working. As the following example illustrates, this could even entail a willingness to go against company rules and to defend the decision to do so to clients as well as to senior management. Hand-arm vibration is a serious risk attaching to the use of held-held tools, and can lead to potentially debilitating health conditions. In order to reduce the amount of time spent using pneumatic drills, workers on the contract changed the way they poured and finished the concrete for foundation piles on the site. Rules say concrete piles should be dug down to bedrock, and the casing filled with concrete to 1.2 metres above ground level: this is to ensure you have good concrete at ground level. The excess is then removed with a pneumatic drill. By using a new 'overspill' method—technically, a rule violation—to produce the necessary clearance without the need for trimming with a pneumatic drill, they reduced the exposure to vibration from drill usage and made a significant contribution to safety. This new technique has now been approved for general use across the company.

By contrast, 'Oldmaint' is a maintenance contract previously operated under the auspices of local government and covering minor and local roads across a wide area. Many workers have transferred from the previous contractor and are low-skilled 'old-timers'; newer workers also have limited qualifications and skills. Equipment used consists mostly of hand tools (such as pneumatic drills and compactors), and gangs are small and work with minimal supervision. There is a widespread operative distrust of management and little dialogue relating to safety: rules perceived as poor or ineffective tend to be ignored rather than proactively challenged.

Safety here is handled through a strong reliance on personal protective equipment and rule compliance. Whilst the contract manager is very diligent in monitoring compliance, and believes that this is the most appropriate approach given the past history of the workforce, he does recognize that there is a danger that operatives will develop a concern with being *seen* to be compliant rather than with whether compliance will be generative of safety. Thus he acknowledges that preoccupation with rule-following could be potentially detrimental in terms of reduced attention paid to actual safety. Some supervisors on the site recognize this risk, and see it as a function of the safety culture created by the manager. They are very positive about the fact that Carillion has strict rules about safety, and enforces them, but feel that this sometimes creates a fear of punishment for violating the rules rather than a healthy mindset in relation to safe behaviour. As one supervisor said, 'I want the lads to be relaxed at work, because when you're relaxed, you're more conscious, you're more aware. All you're worried about now is, have I put the signs out right, is my lorry clean, is my plant looked after. ... The guy who's out at the sharp end working in the most dangerous environment is now more worried about his signs being clean and upright and that, and not concentrating on the traffic and stuff.'

Safety leaders on different contracts could be characterized as, at one extreme, intermediaries for the delivery of company policies on safety to, at the other extreme, initiators of locally relevant safety practices and drivers of strongly participative safety cultures. Those who act as intermediaries for policies initiated by senior management are characterized by a tick-box, outcome-oriented approach which tends to replicate a relatively static approach to safety. Their occurrence within Carillion tends to coincide with more mundane, maintenance-related settings (for example, Oldmaint), worked by low-skilled, change- and authority-resistant operatives. The phrases 'we've always done it that way' (frequently heard from operatives) and 'method statements are put in place to tell you how to do things safely' (said by a member of management as part of the induction procedures for new employees) could be used to summarize the resultant safety culture in which managers tend to be focused on enforcing safe working practices in a complex and dangerous environment. At the other end of the scale, charismatic, pro-active initiators of locally relevant safety practices create strongly participative safety cultures by translating company initiatives into relevant, localized practices which

(Continued...)

incorporate localized expertise and knowledge. Safety leadership in these contexts tends to be more dynamic, and to be strongly associated with the personal commitment of the leader. This type of leader tends to be found in more dynamic, fast-moving settings (such as Newbuild), and in relation to better qualified, more engaged, or responsive operatives. The emphasis here is on improving safety procedures through a process-based view of safety which allows for evolution in the face of experience and is characterized by the phrase 'preparing method statements makes you think about the issues; once prepared the statements have done their job' (a statement by the Newbuild contract manager).

Case Study Questions

- The case study seems to be showing us a clear case of 'safety leadership' versus 'safety management', but to what extent do you think each contract manager was just responding appropriately to the skills, abilities and attitudes of the workers on the contract?
- Do you think 'leadership versus management' is a useful distinction to make in this situation? If so, why?
- Do you think it should be part of the contract manager's role to create a particular safety culture within the contract, or should this be a company-wide initiative, led from the top?
- What are the risks attaching to each of the approaches to safety leadership/management illustrated in the case study? How might these be replicated in relation to other leadership/management issues?

Further reading

Kotter, J. P. (1990) What leaders really do. *Harvard Business Review*, May–June, 102–11.

Alvesson, M. and Sveninsson, S. (2003) Managers doing leadership: The extra-ordinarization of the mundane. *Human Relations*, 56 (12), 1435–59.

Bryman, A. (1996) Leadership in organizations. In S. Clegg, C. Hardy, and W. Nord (eds), *Handbook of Organization Studies*. London, Sage.

4

Born versus made: Early approaches to understanding leadership

 Learning outcomes

On completion of this chapter you will:

- Understand the collection of theories that surround a leader being defined by their personal characteristics or traits
- Be aware of how these ideas developed into behavioural theories of a leader
- Be aware of how the situational/contingent approach grew from a critique of trait theories
- Understand situational theories of leadership
- Understand critical perspectives on these theories
- Appreciate the links between these approaches to understanding leadership and modern competency frameworks used in recruitment and selection activities

Introduction

Do you believe that leaders spring fully formed from their mothers' wombs? Do they possess an innate ability to influence in order to achieve organizational goals, an ability that they have not picked up from studying, but one that is inbuilt into their character? Can only some gifted people be leaders?

Or do you believe that leaders have learned to lead? That through study, experience, or both, they have developed the characteristics of a leader. Can anyone be a leader?

Or is it something in between—that some people are born with the gift, but have developed or honed this over time to form the abilities and characteristics that are recognized as leadership and are applicable in many situations?

This is a common question asked on leadership courses and by academics setting exam questions—are leaders born or made? It is not a new question. In the fourth century BC the philosopher Plato wrote his views on leadership in the book *Republic*, which explored the structure of life in an ideal state or society. This book considers many different issues, one of which is the inherent features or qualities of a leader. For Plato, leaders must be 'philosopher-kings'. They should possess knowledge and a form of wisdom that can discern truth from mere speculation or opinion. They should have a keen instinct for morality, in modern business terminology they should possess and demonstrate integrity, which includes the ability to control their own desires and only to take action that is for the common good. Finally, and most essentially, a leader should possess the necessary character to be able to rule effectively. For Plato a leader's character is not one that desires power, but one that, through the acquisition of knowledge, can exercise control, and see the world in a rational light, enabling better decision making (Takala, 1998; Williamson, 2008). Summarizing the traits evident in Plato's work, Antonakis (2010) identifies intelligence and personality as being the most important for the leader of a city state. Plato's original insights bear an uncanny resemblance to modern thinking and research on what it takes to be a leader in the twenty-first century, something we will explore in this chapter.

This chapter will examine the theories that have been used on either side of this debate. We will look at some of the original ideas that influenced the study of leadership in the early twentieth century, especially the 'Great Man' theory and the way this launched a search for the traits that were thought to be core to a leader's being. We will trace how this search for traits led to a change in thinking that took the focus away from the innate traits and redirected it to the obvious behaviours or style of a leader. We will look at how the trait theories were challenged by an appreciation that the situation or context may play a part in the competencies needed by leaders. Along the way we will consider some of the psychological literature that has been used to support the claims of trait, behavioural, and situational theorists.

In the mainstream

Trait theories

Whilst Plato may have laid the philosophical foundations for trait theories, the credit for examining the lives of successful men to determine key characteristics of leadership is frequently given to Thomas Carlyle. Carlyle (1795–1881) was a Scottish writer and historian, a contemporary of the economist Karl Marx and a friend of the writer Ralph Waldo Emerson and the philosopher John Stuart Mill. Carlyle's book, *On Heroes, Hero Worship, and the Heroic in History* (1846) gave rise to the study of 'Great Men' and their qualities or characteristics. It would be a mistake to think that Carlyle had a completely romantic view of the great men of history. He fully appreciated that all men were fully human, and were subject to their own failings, and it was the reaction of great men to situations where these failings surfaced that particularly interested Carlyle.

The Great Man theory that sprang from Carlyle's work has a founding premise that people are different, and only some people have what it takes to become great. True to Carlyle, this view looks not only at who leaders are, but the effect that they had, what they caused or set in motion. Carlyle said 'the Great Man was always as lightning out of heaven; the rest of men waited for him like fuel, and then they too would flame' (Carlyle, 1846).

Underlying the idea of the Great Man theory was an assumption that the qualities or characteristics evident were inherited, that leaders were born, and not just that but born to a certain societal class and to a certain gender.

The ideas ascribed to Carlyle gave rise to the largest body of research into leadership that exists today. Scholars sought to determine what made these leaders great, whether there was anything that could be learned from the personalities of these great men that could help in determining who had the elusive ability to lead and who did not. This research moved away from the assumption that leaders were born, but merely sought to examine the general characteristics, psychological, biological, and behavioural, that differentiate leaders from followers or non-leaders. In other words, trait theory was born!

It is easy to understand why trait theory became so popular amongst researchers in the early twentieth century. It offered a scientific way to investigate the difficult concept of leadership. If one could identify a number of possible individual characteristics that could be related to leadership performance, then one could test this hypothesis using quantitative, scientific research methods. For this to hold true, traits would have to be observable to such an extent that they could be measured. This measurement would recognize that there would be obvious differences between individuals, in other words people could hold the same characteristic, but to a greater or lesser degree. To be able to observe and so measure traits, they would need to regularly occur in certain similar situations, in other words, they would need to be predictable. And for a trait to be linked to leadership then it would have to be linked to an outcome. Trait theory, therefore, supposed that measurement and statistical analysis of large study groups would give us a general understanding of what it is to be a leader (Antonakis, 2010).

These early trait studies were analysed by Stogdill (1948) in his seminal review of trait theory research. Stogdill acknowledges that these studies were methodologically flawed and that their results could be due purely to the selection of subjects or method of study. However, having analysed 124 studies, Stogdill compiled a list of factors associated with leaders, which he summarized as capacity, including intelligence, judgement, and communication skills; achievement, both physical and mental; responsibility, being dedicated and dependable as well as having a drive to succeed; participation, social skills valuable in group situations; and status, both actual position and popularity.

Stogdill concluded that the research did not support the view that just possessing a certain set of traits made a person a leader. Whilst acknowledging that there were characteristics that distinguished a leader from a non-leader, he also observed that the situation plays as much a part in a person's ability to lead as does their innate character traits.

A second survey by Stogdill published in 1974 analysed 163 new studies. Here he developed the view that traits were associated with leadership, in combination with situational and other factors. However, Stogdill's legacy is mostly associated with the view from the 1948 study that a person may not be a leader in all situations, in other words, their traits alone will not necessarily enable them to lead in every situation. This legacy is generally cited as discrediting the trait theories of leadership, but this does not seem to have been Stogdill's intention. Instead, he builds on trait theories by highlighting the impact of the situation on one's ability to lead, and the evidence for patterns of leadership behaviour being 'persistent and relatively stable' (Stogdill, 1948: 65). Stogdill also recognized a factor that features in modern writing by trait theorists. He found that it was not just individual traits that made one a leader, but a combination of these traits acting in a complex way with the characteristics and desires of followers and the dynamic nature of situations faced by the leader.

> Thus, leadership must be conceived in terms of the interaction of variables which are in constant flux and change. (Stogdill, 1948: 64).

It is perhaps the very number of 'variables' and the continuous 'flux and change' of organizational situations that has made it so difficult for trait theorists to come up with a definitive list of characteristics associated with leadership, although many have put forward their own lists. Indeed, when comparing lists of traits that theorists have argued have best relationships with leadership effectiveness or leadership emergence. Judge et al. (2002) found that only self confidence has appeared in the majority of lists that they reviewed.

An often cited list of leadership traits was put forward by Kirkpatrick and Locke (1991). They argue that whilst traits alone are not a predictor of leadership in all situations, they are an essential element in the leadership mix. In other words, someone cannot be a leader unless he has the potential to be a leader, and traits give you that potential.

> Leaders ... do need to have the 'right stuff' and this stuff is not equally present in all people. (Kirkpatrick and Locke, 1991: 59)

 Leadership in the media: The Matrix

The Matrix is a science fiction film that depicted a world where humans had become a source of power for a machine dominated world. To keep the human population controlled the machines developed a virtual world that all humans were plugged into, a huge virtual-reality game that was so life-like that few people realize they are prisoners in a computer game.

The lead character, Neo, is taken out of this world, and is depicted as a saviour for the human race, the One, someone who has the attributes required to take control of the virtual game and defeat the machines. Neo doubts that he is the One, and so he and his colleagues visit a character called the Oracle, who has the insight to predict people's future.

The Oracle tells Neo 'Well, you got the gift, but you seem to be waiting for something.'

In other words, the traits are there, Neo has the characteristics of the One, he has the 'right stuff', but he needs the right situation to bring these traits into play.

For Kirkpatrick and Locke the traits that matter are drive, a desire to lead, honesty and integrity, self confidence, cognitive ability and knowledge of the business (Kirkpatrick and Locke, 1991: 49). In keeping with modern trait theories, each of these traits is not an individual item, but rather a combination of traits and motives. For example under the trait of drive they list a greater than average need for achievement, ambition—a competitive desire to get ahead in terms of work and career, long-term mental and physical energy, tenacity—similar to Stogdill's persistence and initiative, the ability to be pro-active. The importance is the combination of these characteristics, recognizing that a long list of individual traits has not been a successful predictor of leadership, but rather that leaders combine several trait characteristics together to enhance their ability to lead.

Traits and personality

The investigation and categorization of personality traits is a subject that has been long debated in psychological literature. Goldberg (1990) summarized this debate and concluded that there was evidence to suggest that personality could be generalized into five main factors (Goldberg, 1990; Judge and Bono, 2000):

- Surgency (or extraversion)—being outgoing and assertive, possibly even a thrill seeker
- Agreeableness—being trustworthy, gentle and warm

- Conscientiousness (or dependability)—including both the desire for achievement and the ability to be dependable
- Emotional stability (versus neuroticism)—usually defined by the neuroticism elements of anxiety, depression, and mood swings as these are more easily measured
- Openness to experience (or intellect)—being creative, imaginative and thoughtful

Whilst these factors are still being debated, they are widely accepted by researchers into personality (Judge and Bono, 2000). This Five-Factor Model of personality traits has been adopted by trait theorists and used to establish whether there is a link between these traits and theories of leadership, or between these traits and the leader's performance. Judge and Bono (2000) used the Five-Factor Model to examine the relationship between personality traits and the key elements of transformational leadership. Their study did not give definitive evidence of a link, but showed that of the five personality traits, agreeableness correlated most strongly with transformational leadership, followed by extraversion and openness to experience. Neuroticism and conscientiousness were found not to have a strong correlation with transformational leadership.

However, in a meta-analysis study on the Five-Factor Model and leadership, Judge et al. (2002) found that agreeableness had a very weak correlation with leadership, whilst extraversion had the highest correlation, followed by conscientiousness, neuroticism, and openness to experience. Judge et al. concluded that their research showed strong support for the trait theory approach to leadership, so long as the traits were organized along the lines of the Five-Factor Model approach.

One criticism of linking the Five-Factor model with performance has been that the majority of studies only use self-reporting as evidence. Oh, Wang, and Mount (2011) set out to correct this by asking observers to rate an individual's performance against the Five-Factors Model. Their research has found that personality traits are a strong predictor of the performance of an individual in the eyes of an observer.

Interestingly, Shoa and Webber (2006) followed the same research method as Judge and Bono (2000) to establish whether there was a correlation between the Five-Factor Model and transformational leadership in China. This showed a negative correlation, suggesting that the Five-Factor Model of personality traits and the link between this and leadership may not hold across different international cultures.

Current trait approaches

The personality approach to trait theory is evidence of the desire amongst trait theorists to move beyond the original ideas based purely around lists of attributes and into a broader understanding of the traits possessed by leaders who are effective. Zaccaro (2007) is a prominent proponent of this view of trait theory. Zaccaro's definition of leadership traits fall into three distinct elements. First he argues against the perception that traits are a list of individual items, each of which is possessed by an individual and utilized to have an effect. Instead Zaccaro argues that traits should be observed as 'integrated constellations', and that 'leadership emerges from the combined influence of multiple traits', thus agreeing with Stogdill's (1948) view of leadership as a complex integration of variables. For Zaccaro, it is how an individual works different characteristics together in certain situations that makes them a leader.

Secondly, Zaccaro describes how modern views on trait theory have moved from a narrow definition of attributes, to a much broader understanding of what differentiates leaders from non-leaders. This understanding includes personal qualities such as motives, values, knowledge and expertise, and skills such as social skills and problem-solving skills.

This leads to a model of leadership traits that is defined by the integration of several sets of attributes:

- Cognitive capacities—including intelligence, creativity and cognitive complexity
- Personality attributes—for example extroversion and openness to experience
- Motives and values—including a desire to achieve and the motivation to lead
- Social capacities—negotiation and persuasion skills as well as social and emotional intelligence

Discussion point: Traits?

Look around your class or workplace. Who are the leaders? Write their names down and put this paper to one side.

Make a list of your colleagues and rate them against the following criteria:

- Who is the most extrovert?
- Who is the most engaged, open to all elements of your course?
- Who is the most ambitious or driven?
- Who makes decisions based on their values?
- Who can persuade or negotiate most effectively?

Now compare this list with your list of leaders. Do they correspond? Meet up with a colleague and share your lists. Have you observed the same traits in your colleagues? Have you identified the same leaders? If not why do you think that is?

The third point is a counter argument to Stogdill's view on traits alone not allowing leaders to lead in all situations. Zaccaro states that traits or attributes have an enduring quality, making them applicable in more than one situation. The key point here is that traits can have relevance in different situations so long as they possess an element of stability. This idea of stability or coherence agrees with the evidence from psychological research on personality traits, which have established that certain personality traits have a coherence that is observable across numerous situations.

In summary, the trait perspective originated with ideas of great men, which assumed these men had inherited attributes that could be studied and measured. The theory about inheritance, leaders being born, was quickly discarded, and attempts to define and empirically measure individual traits continued in earnest until Stogdill's landmark paper. Whilst this turned the research of leadership away from traits to a focus on situational aspects, trait theory continued to influence the thinking of leadership scholars, showing particular relevance to ideas such as charismatic and transformational leadership, something we will cover in the next chapter. The adoption of models of personality and the broadening of an understanding of traits to cover morals and values has seen a resurgence of interest in trait theories, and has brought the ideas full circle to Stogdill's original 1948 findings on the interaction of traits, the complexity and variability of what can be counted as traits, and the influence of the situation.

The work of Stogdill (1948) is credited for initiating two streams of leadership research, one into the actual behaviours of leaders, and the other into the importance of the context or situation for leaders. We will look at each of these in turn.

RESEARCH IN FOCUS: Traits, evolutionary psychology and behavioural genetics

'The bright and dark sides of leader traits: A review and theoretical extension of the leader trait paradigm', an article by Judge, Piccolo, and Kosalka published in *The Leadership Quarterly* in 2009 attempts to review trait theory from a conceptual perspective, and examine it alongside theories coming from very different areas of research. The focus here is on leadership effectiveness and leadership emergence, two areas that are informed by ideas from evolutionary psychology and behavioural genetics.

The authors argue that psychological attributes associated with leaders, such as extraversion and conscientiousness, may have developed to give certain individuals an advantage from an evolutionary perspective. This advantage is connected to the idea of the 'fitness' of an evolutionary concept taken from the hypothesis that the evolution of species is driven by both adaptation to a changing environment and a battle for the survival of the fittest.

Leaders, the authors speculate, develop psychological attributes that enable them to gain an advantage in evolutionary fitness. This advantage would include greater opportunities for procreation and a better position from which to gain an advantage in terms of the availability of nourishment. With more opportunities to feed and procreate, the attributes that gained a leader these advantages in the first place could be passed down the genetic line, thus making leaders, to a certain extent at least, born.

Behavioural genetics research is used to reinforce the hypothesis that traits are inherited. The authors quote studies which show that approximately half of personality traits are inherited, whilst the others emerge through interaction with an environment, although the authors are keen to point out that inherited genes may mean people self select themselves into particular environments that then develop their inherent traits. The authors use this hypothesis to create a conceptual model of leader trait emergence and effectiveness, which links natural selection processes with genetic mutation to produce the 'bright and dark sides' of leader traits such as extraversion, agreeableness, conscientiousness, emotional stability, openness, core self-evaluation, intelligence, charisma, narcissism, hubris, dominance, and Machiavellianism.

Judge, T. A., Piccolo, R. F., and Kosalka, T. (2009) The bright and dark sides of leader traits: A review and theoretical extension of the leader trait paradigm, *The Leadership Quarterly*, 20, 855–75.

Behavioural theories

Rather than seeking to determine the innate characteristics or attributes of a leader, the behavioural approach sought to measure the observable characteristics that leaders demonstrated on an everyday basis. This can be seen as part of a shift in research methods in the area of psychology, which led to the creation of the Five-Factor Model described above. The intention here was to uncover leadership behaviours that could be applied in many different situations, thus building on Stogdill's work (Fleishman, 1953).

The most famous studies on leader behaviour came from the Universities of Ohio State and Michigan. The Ohio State studies asked subordinates to evaluate their leaders against 150 criteria contained in the Leader Behaviour Description Questionnaire (LBDQ). Subordinates were asked to comment on how often a leader actually demonstrated the described criteria. The results were analysed and categorized, giving rise to two main dimensions:

- Consideration—a focus on relationships and feelings in which the leader seeks to support and involve followers, valuing open communications, team work, and mutual trust. A leader scoring highly on this element had a correspondingly high satisfaction rating from subordinates

- Initiating structure—a focus on task in which the leader is focused on the goals of the organization, and on planning, controlling, and criticizing, all to ensure the delivery of this goal. A leader scoring highly on this element was considered more effective, but if they did not also score highly for consideration, they experienced higher discontent from employees shown by higher grievance and absentee levels (Fleishman, 1953; Korman, 1966)

 Blog

My wife and I met on an MBA programme. Prior to the course she was a project manager for a consulting company, and I was general manager of a tourist attraction. She was one of the most focused members of our MBA cohort. If there was a piece of coursework to do, that was the sole focus of her days, and she would not be distracted. My approach, on the other hand, was to combine the work with social activity such as having lunch with friends or playing sport. My MBA day would mostly finish in the college bar, whilst she would have to be persuaded to join us for a drink! Our different preferences for task or relationship were quite apparent, and they are something that now makes us a great team. (CS)

What about you? In your group work are you focused on task, or do you take time for relationships as well? (CS)

The consideration dimension can be seen as a direct ancestor of Individualized consideration, one of the characteristics defined by Bass (1985) in his description of Transformational Leadership (see Chapter 5).

At the same time, researchers from the University of Michigan were examining the effect a leader's behaviour had on small groups. The Michigan studies also found two main categories of leadership behaviour:

- Employee orientation—a focus on 'human relations', on trust, respect, and participation in the workplace

- Production orientation—a focus on the production and technical aspects of the job, on using employees primarily as a means to an end (Bowers and Seashore, 1966)

This study originally saw the employee and production orientations as being at each end of a spectrum. This meant that leaders who were more interested in achieving the goal were automatically less interested in employee relations. As the Ohio State work had shown that a leader could score highly on both task and relationship aspects, this categorization was later reconceptualized into two independent dimensions.

Following the initial research from Ohio State and Michigan, leadership researchers spent many years attempting to find empirical evidence for the existence and effectiveness of the leader behaviours of consideration and initiating structures. These studies have broadly confirmed the original conclusions of both Ohio State and the University of Michigan (Vecchio, Hearn, and Southey, 1996: 481–6). Studies focused on examining the intersection of the two approaches relating to the effectiveness of a leader have been at best inconclusive, and attention has now moved away from this approach to a more refined view of behaviours that views the complex interaction of behaviours as being more relevant to leadership effectiveness (Yukl, 2010).

Discussion point: Task or relationship

- The Ohio State and Michigan studies both discovered the focus of leaders favouring either tasks or relationships. Do you agree that when working in a team you are more focused on the task to be completed than on the relationships?

- Blake and Mouton saw the task focus and the relationship focus as being interdependent; when the focus of one changed there would be an equal change in the other. Does this idea fit with your experience? Or have you experienced these as separate, independent variables?

Task/relationship approaches

Blake and Mouton's Management Grid was one of the approaches that developed from the original research into employee and production orientations. Underpinning this approach is the belief that 'there is one consistently sound style for exercising leadership across different situations' (Blake and Mouton, 1981: 440). The Grid utilizes two variables, a concern for people, which draws on the description of an employee orientation, and a concern for production, which draws inspiration from the description of the production orientation. Blake and Mouton view these variables as interdependent, that at their point of connection, they cease to be separate variables and combine to create something new. This implies that if a leader's score on one variable should change, it will have an impact on their score on the other variable.

The original Grid depicted four main areas of intersection to which a fifth was added later by Blake and McCanse (1991) (Figure 4.1):

- 1,1 Low concern for people and production = Impoverished Management: expending minimum efforts to get the very basics of the job done

- 9,1 High concern for people and low concern for production = Country-Club Management: achieving a great working environment, whilst sacrificing the speed of task completion

- 1,9 High concern for production and low concern for people = Authority-Compliance Management: gaining a good, efficient, tempo of work by minimizing the relational aspects

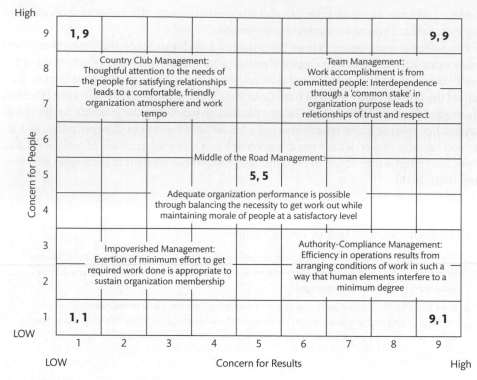

Figure 4.1 The Leadership Grid© figure

Source: Robert R. Blake and Anne Adams McCanse (1991) *Leadership Dilemmas—Grid Solutions*, Houston: Gulf, p.29.
Copyright © 1991, by Scientific Methods, Inc. Reproduced by permission of the owners

- 9,9 High concern for people and production = Team Management: commitment of leaders and employees who all have clarity over the task and are recognized for their work
- 5,5 Middle concern for people and production = Middle-of-the-Road Management: balancing enough task focus with enough people focus to move the organization along in an adequate manner

With a score of 1, 1 the Impoverished Management leader will only do the minimum to get the job done. They do not interact often with employees, and could be seen as apathetic when concerned with the task at hand.

On the other hand, with a score of 9, 9 the Team Management leader is very pro-active, being highly involved with both the employees, to whom is given trust and responsibility, and in the task. This is Blake and Mouton's one best leader for all situations, someone who offers clarity of purpose and approachability to employees.

In using the Grid for organizational development and training interventions, Blake and his colleagues found that leaders could switch between styles without integrating the two styles. They identified the paternalism/maternalism leader who would use 1,9 and 9,1 styles, being focused on the task one minute, and on the person the next, but always separating out the two. In other words, to coin a phrase used frequently by Donald Trump in the television series *The Apprentice*, 'it's not personal, it's just business'!

The authors also recognized that for some leaders, the main task was their own advancement, and that these leaders would use any of the five styles as long as this style would advance their own personal ambitions in some way. This style was termed opportunism, but equally could be termed psychopathy as you will see from the research in focus section.

RESEARCH IN FOCUS: Corporate psychopath

It is easy to mistake psychopathic traits for specific leadership traits. (Babiak, Neumann, and Hare, 2010: 190)

In light of frequently occurring corporate scandals, for example cases of fraud, insider trading, or just the excessive risk taking that caused the recent financial crisis, Babiak, Neumann, and Hare (2010) sought to investigate whether the prevalence of psychopathic traits in the behaviour of corporate executives was higher than in wider community samples. The authors used the Psychopathy Checklist-Revised (PCL-R) to study 203 managers and executives who were participating in a management development programme.

The PCL-R looks for evidence against four main dimensions or traits:

- Interpersonal—defined by glibness, superficial charm, high sense of self-worth, pathological lying, conning/manipulative behaviour
- Affective—defined by a lack of remorse, a shallow affect, a lack of empathy, and a failure to accept responsibility for actions
- Lifestyle—defined as a need for stimulation (i.e. prone to be bored), parasitic lifestyle, a lack of realistic long-term goals, impulsivity and irresponsibility
- Antisocial—defined as poor behavioural controls, early behavioural problems, juvenile delinquency, revocation of conditional release, and criminal versatility

Promiscuous sexual behaviour and many short-term relationships also contributed to the total PCL-R score. An individual would have to display all four of these features chronically and consistently over time to be considered clinically psychopathic.

The study found that there were nine people in the survey (4.4%) who scored close to or above the common research threshold for psychopathy. This was higher than samples from the community. The highest scores were on the Interpersonal dimension, characterized by glibness, superficial charm, lying, and manipulation. No correlation was found between the level of seniority and the level of psychopathy, although of these nine people, two were vice presidents, two were directors, and others were considered to be high potential candidates, supporting the author's speculation that 'some psychopathic individuals manage to achieve high corporate status'.

There was a correlation which associated psychopathy and a perception that the people identified above had slightly better communication, strategic thinking and creativity skills, but these same people had worse managerial skills, scored badly in appraisals and were considered to be poor team players. Babiak et al. (2010) speculate from this and other research that the skills of communication and manipulation seem to override the performance evidence, and the psychopathic traits such as charm, manipulation, and visioning can be mistaken for self-confidence, influencing skills and a lack of realistic goals respectively.

the very skills that make a psychopath so unpleasant (and sometimes abusive) in society can facilitate a career in business even in the face of negative performance ratings.' (Babiak et al. 2010: 191)

Babiak, P., Neumann, C. S., and Hare, R. D. (2010) Corporate Psychopathy: Talking the Walk, *Behavioral Sciences and the Law*, 28:, 174–93.

Table 4.1 The System 4 Approach (reproduced with permission.)

System 1: Exploitative authoritative

A dictatorial approach from autocratic leaders. Delegation and involvement in decision making is minimal. People are motivated through punishment or fear of punishment.

System 2: Benevolent Authoritative

Delegation and involvement in decision making is still minimal. People are motived through rewards.

System 3: Consultative

Information is shared and subordinates are involved in the decision making processes. Some teamwork is in evidence and there is more trust than under systems 1 & 2.

System 4: Participative

Subordinates are actively involved in decisions. There is open communications at and between all levels. The involvement of people leads to high levels of trust.

A second approach related to the research on task and relationships was developed by Rensis Likert. Likert headed up the Institute for Social Research at the University of Michigan. The Institute conducted over 500 studies on more than 350 companies, surveying 20,000 managers and some 200,000 subordinates. After analysing the results, Likert noted that there were patterns of managerial behaviour and its effect emerging from the research. He grouped these patterns into the Four System model shown in Table 4.1.

Likert found that the closer a company's management and leadership were to System 4, the higher the productivity of the company and the greater their potential earnings (Likert, 1979). This increase in productivity was reported as being between 10–40 per cent, whilst at the same companies the levels of employee satisfaction, health, and labour relations were also good.

In a similar way to the Blake and Mouton work, Likert was a key proponent in the search for one best way of leading that was relevant across all situations. In contrast to this, the next section looks at the contingency or situational theories that advocated that there was no one best way, but lots of best ways which should be applied in each different situation.

Contingency/situational approaches

In a similar way to behavioural approaches, contingency theories were developed from the two variables originally discovered by the Ohio State and Michigan studies. The production and relationship variables were the basis on which Fiedler (1974) developed his initial contingency theory. Fiedler used a survey that asked subordinates to describe the manager or leader that they had least enjoyed working for. The person was rated against a series of bipolar adjectives, for example friendly–unfriendly, and in this way they were judged to be relationship or task focused. The results of this survey became known as the Least-preferred Co-worker (LPC) scale. Leaders with a low LPC score were thought to be more task focused and leaders with a high score relationship focused. Those with a low score would achieve the task without consideration of the people and this could be accentuated in situations of great stress. Those with a high score might perform poorly under pressure due to the focus being more on the people than the task.

Fiedler's hypothesis was that rather than adjusting their personality or motivation to suit a situation, it is easier for a leader to adjust the situation to suit their own style (Fiedler and Mahar,

1979). In fact, Fiedler goes on to advocate that in some circumstances it may be best to change the situation, the leader, or both, to get the best result for the organization (Fiedler, 1974).

Fiedler found that there was a complex relationship between group performance and situational favourability, in other words, some situations were better for some leaders. This led Fiedler to analyse situations and leadership styles against three criteria which he felt allowed a leader to assess the favourability of a given situation:

- Leader–member relations—being associated with the quality of relationships and the presence of trust and respect
- Task structure—being associated with the clarity with which the task has been described, designed, and structured
- Leader power position—being similar to the position power of French and Raven (1959) in that the formal position and the ability to reward and punish are important here

Those leaders who favoured a task orientated approach over a relationship orientated approach tended to lead best in situations where they had a high degree of control and influence, or where they had a low degree of control and influence, whilst those who favoured the relationship orientation were best in situations where their level of control and influence was neither high or low.

Discussion point: Favourability

Consider the last team or group situation you faced. Preferably where you were the leader. How favourable was the situation for you to lead?

- What position power did you have?
- Was the task clearly defined, structured, and understood by the team?
- How low or high was the quality of the relationships between you and the members of the group?

Reflect on the success of the group in completing its task, and on your success in leading this group. How much influence did the three variables above have on the outcome?

Situational leadership

Whilst Fiedler believed that it was difficult for leaders to adjust to situations, Hersey, Blanchard, and Dewey, (1996) believed that leadership behaviour could change not just for each situation, but specifically for each subordinate. Their model was based on the belief that leadership required three main competencies:

- *Diagnosing*—the cognitive ability to understand complex and dynamic situations, seeing them as they are now and as they reasonably could be in the near future
- *Adapting*—the behavioural ability to change the way you behave as a leader to match the situation as you have understood it
- *Communicating*—defined as a process skill, knowing how to get your message across to individual employees in any given situation

A key belief here is that individuals can improve their ability to understand situations, to adapt and to communicate through study, experience, and training. In other words, from a situational perspective, leaders can be made (Hersey et al., 1996: 120). A second key belief is that there is no one best way of leading that is appropriate for all situations. A leader must learn to understand situations, and then adapt their leadership style to match that situation.

Case in point: Flora Sandes

Flora Sandes was the only British woman to fight as a soldier in the First World War. She had originally joined up with the St Johns Ambulance service as a nurse and had been sent to Serbia to help in the humanitarian crisis there. In Serbia she joined the Serbian Red Cross, and worked in the ambulance unit of the Serbian Army. She was separated from her unit and enlisted in a Serbian Army unit for safety, rising through the ranks of Corporal and Sergeant-Major to Captain. Having been injured in hand to hand combat in 1916, she left the front line to run a hospital. She received the highest Serbian military honour for her service.

   As a child Flora was said to enjoy and excel at riding and shooting. One report says that she wished she had been born a boy. It is possible that Flora had all the natural attributes that would make her a good soldier, but until the situation arose to utilize these attributes, they remained hidden.

Sources: Sandes (1916); Wheelwright (2004); Hazen (2006)

Hersey and Blanchard initially took the two dimensions of task and relationship and viewed these as separate entities, not interdependent as Blake and Mouton had viewed them (Blake and Mouton, 1981). These were plotted on two axes, with low to high task behaviour on the horizontal axis and low to high relationship behaviour on the vertical axis. This created four basic styles of leader behaviour:

- Style 1: high task and low relationship behaviour
- Style 2: high task and high relationship behaviour
- Style 3: high relationship and low task behaviour
- Style 4: low relationship and low task behaviour

To this matrix they added a third dimension of effectiveness. In their model the task or relationship describes the actual style of the leader as observed by employees. The behaviour is only effective if it is suitable for the situation faced by the leader. They called this the Tridimensional Leader Effectiveness Model (Hersey et al., 1996: 139). Here they argue that a leader can show consistent behaviour by adapting their style to suit different situations. The leader that sticks with the same style in every situation is labelled an inconsistent leader as their style will be seen as inappropriate by their subordinates.

   From this original idea, Hersey and Blanchard developed their Situational Leadership model whilst working at the Centre for Leadership Studies. The model was further developed by Blanchard and colleagues in his private company, Blanchard Training and Development. The model is again focused on the behaviour of the leader towards others. It examines the interrelationships between the amount of task focused direction given by a leader, the amount of relationship focused support given by the leader to the subordinate, and the readiness of the subordinate to deliver their task.

Hersey and Blanchard's definitions of task and relationship are very similar to the definitions given earlier in this chapter. Task involves telling people what they are supposed to do with great clarity, including how, where, and when to do the task, and whose responsibility the task is. The relationship aspect is measured by the way a leader communicates to both individuals and groups, and how well they listen to and support their people.

The readiness of the subordinate is made up of their ability (knowledge, experience, or skill) and willingness (confidence, commitment, or motivation) to do the task. It is more a measure of how prepared the subordinate is to do the task, rather than of any traits or attributes. In a similar way to dividing the leader's style into four elements, the authors divide readiness into four variables, each of which is backed by observable behavioural factors so that leaders can judge where their employees are on this scale:

- R1: unable or unwilling or insecure
- R2: unable but willing or confident
- R3: able but unwilling or insecure
- R4: able and willing or confident

The Situational Leadership Model suggests that the leader's style needs to change in relation to the readiness of the employee for any given task. For example, for a low level of readiness there needs to be a directive leader style; for a high level of readiness, the appropriate style may be more hands off. Blanchard, Zigarmi, and Zigarmi (2000) suggested the readiness element contained development levels. Each development level was made up of two elements: competence and commitment—essentially the same as the original ability and willingness. The four development levels are:

- D1 *Enthusiastic beginners*—motivated and committed but lacking competence, in need of direction and supervision
- D2 *Disillusioned learners*—some competence but lacking commitment having become disillusioned about their ability to be effective, in need of some direction, but also encouragement and support
- D3 *Reluctant contributors*—fully competent but lacking motivation, needing very limited direction, but perhaps a lot of support and encouragement
- D4 *Peak performers*—competent and committed, needing to be left to make decisions and be given space to perform

The development levels assume that an individual will develop along a fairly structured path in their work, and that this will be determined by both their competency in and their commitment to the job. This implies that people may be at different development levels for different elements of their work, and that the leader must know this in order to adapt their leadership style accordingly.

In summary, contingency/situational theories raised the importance of a leader's understanding of the details of each situation they are faced with, from the wider environment, to the specifics of each task and the motivation of each employee. There were criticisms of this approach, which we will look at in the critical perspective section.

Leadership in the media: Saving Private Ryan

In the film *Saving Private Ryan*, after storming the beaches of Normandy in the Second World War, Captain John Miller and his unit are sent on a mission behind enemy lines to find and extract an American soldier, Private Ryan. On their journey they encounter a machine gun emplacement, and this becomes the backdrop for Miller to demonstrate an ability to adapt his leadership to different situations.

First the need to storm the emplacement is contested by the troops, and Miller uses his positional power, and his communication skills to force the completion of the task. During the action a member of the team is killed, leading to arguments after the event between the soldiers, first on what to do with a German prisoner they capture, and secondly on whether they will follow Miller again after he decides to release the prisoner. In an emotionally charged scene, Miller appeals to the troops in a relational way, describing his job before the war, and how he wants to return there knowing he has done the right thing. The difference from the first task-focused approach to the second relationship-focused approach is stark. The task itself can be seen to change, and with it the degree of relationship-focus needed by the leader.

The underpinning premise of the trait, behavioural, and contingency approaches is that elements of a leader (characteristics, behaviours, situations faced) can be measured. This idea has led to the core ideas about leadership from these approaches being translated into assessment tools and competency frameworks developed by organizations to allow them to select and develop their personnel. We will briefly look at competency frameworks in the next section.

Competency frameworks

One of the original authors on competencies, White (1959), made a direct link to the work of trait theorists by defining competencies as human traits. McClelland (1973) took this idea and argued that the testing that existed at the time, based on testing intelligence, was not sufficient and organizations should consider testing for a range of competencies such as communication, patience, goal setting, and ego development.

Boyatzis (1982) developed this idea within the framework of organizational effectiveness. He sought to discover those competencies that improved the effectiveness of the organization. These competencies included traditional ideas from trait theory, but also looked at other elements such as skills, knowledge, behaviours, and motives. In keeping with the idea that leaders are qualitatively different from non-leaders, Boyatzis found that the competency models had revealed a difference between effective and less effective managers. Effective managers demonstrate traits such as a strong work ethic and concern for task completion; a strong desire for power including evidence of assertive behaviour; high self-confidence; and a strong belief in their ability to create a desired result. Effective managers demonstrate better communication and networking skills, as well as stronger critical thinking and conceptual skills.

This focus on competencies has led the Human Resources industry to focus on using competency frameworks to assess leaders and managers in increasing numbers (Soderquist et al., 2010). Competency frameworks have moved from assessing the individual attributes needed to perform a specific job or task, to the capabilities of the person doing the job or task, in other words, from what is needed to complete the task, to how the task is achieved.

Soderquist et al. (2010) outline three distinct perspectives on competencies which they bring together in a competency typology.

- *Generic versus organization-specific competencies*—competencies for a specific job or job family, or a specific job in a specific organization
- *Managerial versus operational competencies*—competencies for a specific role. Managerial competencies tend to include more interpersonal skills
- *Competencies as skills versus competencies as behaviours*—competencies that are learned and observed as behaviour, or are inherent and influence how an individual does a job

From this we can see a strong link to the various theories discussed in this chapter, and how they are being operationalized in HR practice. As we will see in the next section, there are some fundamental questions that have been raised about these approaches and their uses.

From a critical perspective

To a great extent the theories and models presented in this chapter can be seen as critiques of each other. The theory of the Great Man was shown to be flawed as it denied the leader the ability to develop themselves through either experience or training. It also denied women the chance to assume leadership positions, something that has been shown to be mistaken throughout history. From ancient female leaders like Boudicca, Queen Nefertiti, Cleopatra, Catherine the Great, Empress Wu Zetian, to modern figures such as Margaret Thatcher, Aung San Suu Kyi, and Mrs Rajashree Birla, there are numerous examples to disprove the theory of great men!

As we have seen, trait theory was critiqued for not coming up with a definitive list of traits, despite years of empirical research, and for not taking into account the impact of the situation on a leader. Kets de Vries (1994) found that whilst there were commonalities amongst the findings of trait studies (conscientiousness, extroversion, dominance, self-confidence, energy, agreeableness, intelligence, openness to experience, emotional stability), each of these is in itself a contested word, contested in terms of the meaning of its and in terms of its applicability. Kets de Vries takes a psychoanalytical and family systems approach to understanding why leaders behave in the way they do, rather than relying on a psychological approach as most theories in this chapter have done. This approach sees leaders as having been made by their life experiences, rather than being born as leaders.

The re-emergence of the trait perspective, tied into the idea that the big five personality traits may tell us something about the effectiveness of leaders, has also been called into question. Andersen (2005), in a review of the research on personality and leadership, found that whilst a relationship between personality and leadership behaviour existed, there was very limited evidence to support any relationship between personality and leadership effectiveness. He also found that on purely scientific ground no traits had been discovered that were universally related to leadership and as such leaders' traits cannot explain organizational effectiveness. Andersen sums up by saying:

> What we know is this: it is not that leadership is unimportant. Leadership appears to have, however, far less impact on organizational effectiveness than commonly believed. (Andersen, 2005: 1089)

In defence of trait theories, Zaccaro (2007) points to studies that question the assumption that traits cannot be applicable across situations. He supports the view that leaders can adapt to situations, but argues that this ability to adapt is actually a combination of traits, including cognitive complexity and flexibility, social intelligence, metacognitive skills, emotional intelligence, openness, and tolerance for ambiguity.

> Simply put, persons who emerge as leaders in one situation also emerge as leaders in qualitatively different situations. (Andersen, 2005: 13)

A case in point: Jonny Wilkinson

Jonny Wilkinson is one of the greatest rugby players to have played at international level. He has won domestic, national, and international success with both club and country, including winning the Rugby World Cup with England in 2003. Playing at number 10, or fly-half, means that he is one of the key leaders and decision-makers on the pitch. He is also the first-choice goal-kicker, a skill that has contributed to him becoming the second highest points scorer in test history.

His book, *Jonny—My Autobiography*, describes the attributes that helped Jonny become such a phenomenon in rugby. From an early age he set himself the goal of playing for and captaining England, of winning a world cup, and of being the best player in the world. This ambition was matched with his obsession for being the best, showing he was better than other players in training and on the field, and for perfection in his kicking. He describes an ability to switch into a zone where he gets the energy needed to push himself as hard as it takes to become fitter and better than the rest. He also describes an obsession with getting his kicking perfect, that leads to endless kicking sessions at all hours of the day and night.

These traits bring huge success, but they are described as a combination of natural abilities and learned skills. Jonny is naturally a player who likes to run the ball, with running, passing, and tackling being his key attributes. Kicking, the skill for which he is known world wide, is something he develops through training with great coaches, and literally hundreds of thousands of hours of practice.

We also see the negative side of these traits. The overtraining and over kicking lead to numerous injuries that blight his career. His obsessive personality that has brought so much success, does not allow him to recover from injuries, and even causes injuries that could have been avoided. The complete focus on the drive for success brings problems of mental illness. The inability to adjust to situations as they arise off the field because of the strength of the traits Jonny has, work against him, and it takes a while to adapt to these situations.

Contingency theories have been criticized in a similar way to trait theories. There are different approaches within contingency theories, creating different variables and methods. These variables (e.g. supportive, task, relationship, etc.) are often not explained or justified in sufficient detail. The notion that a leader of a company can at any one time hold in their mind the detail of each and every task to be done by her immediate subordinates, plus the competence and commitment of those subordinates to each and any of those tasks at any one time, and can correlate these sufficiently to adapt their style in any given moment seems difficult at best and impossible at worst. As Grint (2010) points out, by the time the leader has gained sufficient detail on the situation to think about adapting, it is likely that the situation will have changed!

Intuitively attractive models, like the Managerial Grid or the Situational Leadership Model, whilst popular with management development and training programmes, have been criticized for the lack of empirical research data to support their underlying assumptions. Indeed the authors of these two models have critiqued each other's work, with Blake and Mouton insisting that task and relationship are interdependent, while Hersey and Blanchard see them as independent (Blake and Mouton, 1981). Neither has produced convincing empirical evidence to back their claims.

Of course, all the approaches in this chapter are based as much on the empirical methods of the researchers as they are on the actual behaviour that these methods uncovered. It is possible that the very methods used are the reason that leadership has not been fully defined by either the trait or contingency approaches. If one entertains Ladkin's (2010) view that leadership is a phenomenon that exists only in a moment, then the empirical approach to the measurement of leadership becomes the wrong tool for the job.

Chapter summary

In this chapter we have considered:

- Original theories that leaders are great men, or possess inherited attributes that define them as leaders
- An approach that sought to define leaders by their behaviour and models used in training and development that sprang from this approach
- Leadership traits as complex collections of leadership attributes, behaviours, values, and morals
- The impact of personality characteristics on possible leader traits and behaviour
- The idea that leadership is dependent on the situation faced by the leader, and that a leader should be able to adapt to different situations
- Theories that have sought to bring these ideas together
- How theories of trait and contingency have been developed into competency models used by business today

 Integrative case study: Nelson Mandela

Nelson Mandela is possibly the person most people would quote as the example of a great leader. When one looks at his achievements, leader of the African National Congress (ANC) Youth movement, founder of the military wing of the ANC, freedom fighter/terrorist turned political prisoner, first black

(Continued...)

president of South Africa, Nobel Peace Prize winner, he would certainly qualify as one of Carlyle's great men.

This raises the question of whether Mandela was born this way, or whether he made himself into the leader the world now acknowledges. He was born into a royal family, his father being Chief of the Tembu Tribe. Genetically, then, he could be said to have been born with genes that have evolved through natural selection to give him an advantage. It certainly gave him the natural physical features that are commonly described by people who have met him: his height, his erect stance, his large hands, his warm, engaging smile, and his regal bearing, even when dressed in prison clothing. These physical features caused Kobie Coetsee, the South African Minister for Justice during the last years of Mandela's incarceration, to comment that he was a born leader.

His genetic make up may also have given him the prodigious energy that he is credited with. As a regular routine that Mandela held even before being imprisoned, he would wake at 4.30a.m. and proceed to do an hours exercise before sunrise. Prior to being in prison this was a run to help in his training as an amateur boxer. Even in prison this did not prevent him from initially running on the spot and later, when in a larger cell, from running circuits for an hour. In later life this routine was maintained with an hour's walk before sunrise.

He was also said to possess a keen intellect and a thirst for knowledge. Whilst in prison Mandela realized that an armed struggle could never succeed, and that any lasting solution in South Africa had to involve all South Africans, black and white. Mandela realized he needed to understand his enemy and so set about learning the Afrikaans language and history. Frequently he showed an ability to recall the facts he had learned and he did not hesitate to try out his knowledge of the Afrikaans language on his guards. In fact, throughout his life there is plenty of evidence to suggest Mandela was clever and willing to take risks.

When people recall their first meetings with Mandela they generally relate how comfortable he made them feel. Mandela seemed to have a knack of making people feel welcome, from the people he met in the street, to his prison guards and the leaders of the far right white supremacy parties. His secret is said to be that he is willing to meet friend and foe alike and that he gives and expects respect. It is said that Mandela assumes that he will like the people he meets and that they will like him. His open and honest style helps in this respect- and trust-building exercise.

This relational approach came from great preparation Mandela put in before meeting key people. For example, before meeting the head of Pollsmoor prison, Major van Sittert, Mandela learned everything he could about rugby and on his first meeting with Sittert in a prison corridor he launched straight into a discussion about rugby entirely in Afrikaans!

Again, before his first meeting with P. W. Botha, then president of South Africa, he prepared meticulously for the meeting over a period of days, learning facts about the person as well as preparing to discuss the situation. He focused on the similarities between the Afrikaans people's struggles throughout history and the African people's struggle against apartheid, an argument he could carry due to his knowledge and his sincerity.

Stories that are told about his respect for others include his apologising to maids around the world for making his own bed, a habit he developed in prison and that never left him. He is also said to have stood every time the Afrikaans lady who served tea to his guests when he was President came into the room, and to remain standing until she left.

All the while, through this use of personal relationships, through his clever and beguiling style, Mandela was always focused on the task: to kill apartheid and unite his nation. He understood that this could only happen in a bloodless way if people put aside old prejudices and learned to trust each other. In the end the relatively peaceful transition of South Africa from apartheid state to modern democracy is testament to his understanding, patience, focus, and ability to bring people along with him.

Sources: Carlin (2008); Mandela (1995); Sampson (2000).

Case study questions

- Nelson Mandela was clearly born with some genetic advantages, but do these account for all his success as a leader?
- How much do you think Mandela's reputation as a great leader is down to his hard work and intelligence, and how much to his attributes?
- If you were to place Mandela on Blake and Mouton's Managerial Grid, where would you place him and why?
- Do you think his characteristics and behaviours depicted in this case would have allowed him to lead in other circumstances? How transferable do you think his leadership attributes and skills are and why? What is your evidence?

Further reading

Carlin, J. (2008) *Playing the Enemy: Nelson Mandela and the game that made a nation*. London: Atlantic Books.

Hersey, P., Blanchard, K. H., and Dewey, E. J. (1996) *The Management of Organizational Behaviour: Utilizing human resources*, 7th edn. Englewood Cliffs, NJ: Prentice Hall.

Judge, T. A., Piccolo, R. F., and Kosalka, T. (2009) The bright and dark sides of leader traits: A review and theoretical extension of the leader trait paradigm, *The Leadership Quarterly*, 20, 855–75.

Zaccaro, S. J. (2007) Trait-based perspectives of leadership, *American Psychologist*, 62 (1), 6–16.

Transformational and charismatic leadership: Vision and values at the top?

Learning outcomes

On completion of this chapter you will:

- Understand the historical origins of the lure of transformational and charismatic forms of leadership

- Have a critical understanding of how transformational and charismatic leadership have been defined, the areas of overlap between the two, and the moral dimensions of each as a key differentiator

- Have an understanding of how transformational leadership contrasts with transactional leadership and its role within a 'full range' leadership model

- Be familiar with the mainstream exponents of each approach, and how they have explicated their leadership models

- Be aware of the limitations and pitfalls of each approach, as well as the evidence that exists for their effectiveness

Introduction

One of the most popular approaches to understanding leadership at the present time is that of transformational leadership. Since it came to prominence in the 1980s there has been considerable conceptual and empirical research around the 'new leadership' paradigm (Bryman, 1992) of which it is a part. The term 'new leadership' refers to a collection of approaches which all share a number of common themes relating to the emotional and symbolic aspects of leadership. Compared with previous, largely behavioural, approaches they place more emphasis on the charismatic and affective elements of leadership and draw extensively on intrinsic motivation and follower needs as the underpinnings of effectiveness. As such, they seem to signal a new way of conceptualizing leadership, and of researching and practising it. Within this paradigm, a number of different strands have emerged, with different writers placing emphasis on different aspects of how this 'new leadership' can be characterized. So, for example, writers such as Bass and Avolio (1990, 1994, 1997), Tichy and Devanna (1986), and Alimo-Metcalfe and Alban-Metcalfe (2001) have developed perhaps the most central idea of transformational leadership. House (1976) and

Conger and Kanungo (1987, 1998) wrote about charismatic leadership, often with considerable overlap appearing between these two typologies. Also within the genre are writers on visionary leadership—such as Sashkin (1987) and Westley and Mintzberg (1989)—and those, including Bennis and Nanus (1985), Kotter (1990), and Kouzes and Posner (1987, 1998, 2002), who claim the word 'leadership' should only be used to refer to this new instantiation of the phenomenon. Collectively, these strands within the paradigm share a conception of the leader as someone who defines organizational reality for those who follow. Through the articulation of a vision—a new idea in the 'content' of the leadership proposition—leaders are said to significantly shape followers' perceptions of their situation, the goals to be strived for, and the ways in which they are to be achieved. They are, as described by Smircich and Morgan (1982), 'managers of meaning' for employees willing to put aside their own interpretations of events in favour of interpretations created for them by those who are designated or emerge as leaders. Similarly, by marking out the key priorities and aims for the future, they enable followers to interpret information and events in an ambiguous and uncertain world, sifting out meanings which are inconsistent with the whole and adopting those which make sense in relation to the bigger picture. This view of leadership as 'sense-making' was articulated by Karl Weick (1995) and has been developed more recently by Annie Pye (2005).

RESEARCH IN FOCUS: Leaders as managers of meaning

In 1982, Smircich and Morgan wrote a seminal article in which they described leaders as 'managers of meaning'. What they meant by this was that, when faced by a credible leader, followers were willing to forgo their own interpretation of situations and events in favour of one provided by the leader. Thus framing and defining the reality of others was seen as an emergent process of organization: one which became a right or even an obligation once an emergent leader was placed in a formal position of authority.

On this basis, individuals emerge as leaders because their structuring and interpretation of the experience of others is perceived as meaningful, and as framing what would otherwise be ambiguous and chaotic experiences in a manner which provides a viable basis for action. It is this sense of viability and purpose which makes followers willing to be complicit in the leader's decision to define reality in a particular way.

Followers may still reject or rebel against that which is defined, however. When this occurs, followers both accept the reality as defined (in that it is something which exists to be fought against) and reject it (as a reality that is unsatisfactory or unsustainable) at the same time. And also at the same time, alternative leaders may present counter-realities and engage in political activities to win over the right to define 'the' organizational reality. In this context, leadership itself is seen as being inherently dialectical such that it is shaped through interaction and negotiation between leader and led. When this dialectical process becomes institutionalized in formal leadership roles, the right to define reality becomes an obligation, and leaders are held accountable for the situation 'really' being the way they have defined it. When the expectations thus created are unfulfilled, the leadership which defined them is said to be ineffective and the leader is often replaced.

In this idea of leaders as managers of meaning we can easily see the importance of images or patterns of thinking which form the basis of organizational visions. At the same time, we can see how leaders are—or become—the embodiment of organizational values and purpose.

Source: Smircich, L. and Morgan, G. (1982) Leadership: the management of meaning. *Journal of Applied Behavioural Science*, 18, 339–58.

It has been suggested by Bass and Riggio (2006) that one of the key reasons why new leadership—and transformational leadership in particular—has become so popular is because it has resonance with our own increasing desire for self-actualization through work. Work is less about the transactional exchange of effort for pay than it was in early industrial times and more about opportunities for job satisfaction and personal development, with what we do for a living becoming a central part of our identity. And it appears as a natural corollary of our greater expectations of our working lives that we have increased expectations of our leaders too. Followers are now seeking a more inspirational form of leadership that not only achieves organizational goals but brings out the exceptional in them, enabling them to achieve beyond even their own expectations. This is seen as self-actualizing for the followers as well as producing higher levels of performance for the organization. This being the case, we could argue that transformational leadership represents a return (at least partially) to the days of trait theory and the 'great man'—leaders are once again expected to be larger than life and to bring superhuman characteristics to their role in order to transform the lives and beliefs of those who work for them.

Taking a more global perspective, the interest in 'new leadership' can be seen as a response to the changing economic and political environment within which businesses are called upon to operate. The rise in the 1980s of the Asian economic powers such as Japan and the Little Dragons, as well as stronger, more coordinated competition from Europe, undermined the previous market dominance of North American companies. At the same time, initiatives aimed at restoring competitiveness usually involved significant restructuring and downsizing, with the result that employee morale and commitment were often seriously damaged. Old psychological contracts between employees and employers—based on loyalty and long-term security—were broken and new ones—in which both sides recognized a more independent, self-reliant relationship—had yet to emerge. Thus companies were challenged by the need to orchestrate major change programmes at a time when their major resource—that is, employees—were less than committed to the organization and its goals. It is hardly surprising, then, that an approach to leadership developed which placed greater emphasis on the role of senior leaders as change agents and that the mechanisms of motivation and morals were suddenly seen as important.

 Blog box

In the late 1980s, I was a young treasury manager, working in the Treasury Department of TI Group, previously Tube Investments, a UK-based engineering company. It was an exciting time for TI—they had recently moved their head office from Birmingham to London and were in the process of turning themselves from a broad-based engineering and consumer white goods conglomerate (owning such brands as Russell Hobbs and Creda) into a much leaner specialist engineering company. Under CEO Chris Lewington (Sir Chris Lewington as he is now) the company was going through an exciting period of disposals and acquisitions, involving a fair amount of long hours and hard work! Chris was a master at selling the vision of TI's future to those at the coal face, but he was also a hands-on leader who was always there when his management team were pulling all-nighters to get a deal signed off and in the bag. It was not unknown for him to appear late at night with burgers and cola for those hard at work, handing them out personally to members of the team. Although I was on the periphery of much of this activity, I still remember Chris as one of the rare charismatic leaders I have ever worked for and, like a good magician, you could never see how he did it! He was just a natural presence that one couldn't help but be drawn to—he was where the action was, and everyone wanted to be there too—even in the early hours of the morning! (MIW)

The term transformational leadership was first coined by Downton (1973) although it is more usually credited to political sociologist James McGregor Burns (1978) whose classic work entitled *Leadership* first brought it to prominence. In linking the roles of leadership and followership through the mechanism of motivation—leaders were described as those who tapped into the motives of followers with the aim of achieving the shared goals of both—Burns put forward the concept of 'transforming leadership' later to become transformational leadership. He saw it as 'a relationship of mutual stimulation and elevation that converts followers into leaders and may convert leaders into moral agents' and which occurs when 'one or more persons engage with others in such a way that leaders and followers raise one another to higher levels of motivation and morality.' Burns was writing about political leadership, so it is perhaps not surprising that he saw it in terms of values and morality, but it took a major shift in academic and practitioner thinking to bring this 'new leadership' to its current prominence in organizational contexts. As we shall see later in the chapter, the main proponents of transformational leadership have been Bernard Bass and Bruce Avolio. In 1994 they wrote that:

> the goal of transformational leadership is to 'transform' people and organizations in a literal sense—to change them in heart and mind; enlarge vision, insight and understanding; clarify purposes; make behaviour congruent with beliefs, principles or values; and bring about changes that are permanent, self-perpetuating, and momentum-building. (Bass and Avolio, 1994: 3)

Like Burns before them, they contrasted transformational leadership with transactional leadership, which treats the relationship between leaders and followers in terms of an exchange, whereby followers are given rewards that they value (pay, promotion, etc.) in return for what the leader desires (most commonly the achievement of organizational goals). For Burns, the former appeals to the moral values of followers in an attempt to raise their consciousness about ethical issues and to mobilize their energy and resources to reform institutions. In non-political contexts, this translates into building on the individual's need for meaning and to transcend the day-to-day trials of organizational life. In practical terms, it does this through the alignment of structures and systems with values and goals, attempts to design jobs that are meaningful and challenging, and which release human potential, and the placing of day-to-day work in the wider context of mission and strategy. By contrast, transactional leadership (again, according to Burns) motivates followers by appealing to their self-interest: in return for work effort, it offers pay and status. Thus it is more task-oriented, involves a focus on short-term goals and tactical issues underpinned by structures and systems that support 'the bottom line' of efficiency, and is mired in the daily issues of power and politics, perks and position.

Arguably, this can be seen as an oversimplification of the ethical foundations of these two types of leadership, suggesting that one is somehow more ethical than the other. Kanungo (2001) posits instead that transformational and transactional leadership should be judged to be ethical based on two different sets of values, motives and assumptions. Transformational leaders, he would claim, have an organic world view and moral altruistic motives grounded in a deontological perspective (concerned with the duties and rights which shape our actions), whereas transactional leaders have an atomistic world view and mutual altruistic motives grounded in a teleological perspective (concerned with the consequences of our actions). Thus, whilst different influence processes may be at work in the two kinds of leaders and their relationship with followers, each can be conducted in an ethically sound (or unsound) way.

As already noted, the basic principles of transformational leadership are being revisited in modern leadership writing in terms of visionary leadership, ethical leadership, and so on. In this context transactional leaders are seen as persuading followers to undertake prescribed tasks in pursuit of established goals: a far more circumscribed activity on both sides than that contemplated by its transformational counterpart. Whilst the latter is based on the generation of commitment through influencing and inspiring followers to give of their best to improve organizational performance, the former depends largely on compliance in achieving its more limited aims. Given that transactional leaders see their followers in terms of trade, swaps, or bargains whilst transformational leaders are charismatic individuals who inspire and motivate others to perform 'beyond contract', it is not difficult to see why some writers equate transactional methods with management and transformational methods with leadership.

Northouse (2010) offers an interesting commentary on the moral component of transformational leadership and the manner in which it can be said to transform both leaders and followers. He offers Mohandas Gandhi as a classic example of a leader who 'raised the hopes and demands of millions of his people and, in the process, was changed himself' (Northouse, 2010: 172). Less well known, perhaps, but no less relevant is the example of Ryan White, the American teenager who raised national awareness about AIDS. In the process, he became a spokesperson for increasing government support for AIDS research, a life-changing role for him and for the AIDS sufferers he was seeking to help. Northouse goes on to highlight the potential for leaders to be negatively transformational, and the inappropriateness of casting such leaders as Adolf Hitler and Saddam Hussein in the transformational mould. This is arguably one of the fundamental differences between charismatic and transformational leaders—that one can be charismatic without being moral or having uplifting goals, but that to be transformational is to be explicitly moral. To address this apparent ambiguity in the notion of transformational leadership, Bass (1998) coined the term pseudo-transformational leadership to refer to those leaders who transform others but do so in pursuit of their own goals and in a manner that is self-consumed, exploitative, and power-oriented, underpinned by warped moral values (Bass and Riggio, 2006). This is a personalized form of leadership, in contrast to authentic transformational leadership, which may be said to be socialized in that it transcends individual interests in favour of the interests of others (Howell and Avolio, 1993). This distinction between authentic and pseudo-transformational leadership was further developed by Bass and Steidlmeyer (1999), who delineated four components said to constitute authentic transformational leadership and contrasted them with their counterfeits in pseudo-transformational leadership. Underpinning these components is the requirement for truly transformational leadership to be grounded in moral foundations.

Discussion point: The morality of leadership

We are all aware of the high-profile corporate scandals that regularly appear in the media: for example, accounting fraud at Enron in America, obtaining contracts by bribery at BAE Systems in Saudi Arabia, and large-scale financial fraud at Satyam Systems in India. And we are equally aware of the small-scale frauds we let pass every day of our working lives—using the photocopier for personal documents or spending company time on the telephone to a friend or relative. But should we expect better of our leaders? And how far up the organization do we have to be before we count as leaders ourselves in this context?

- Should leaders be morally driven? If they aren't, why should others follow them?
- Where should we draw the line in terms of what 'counts' as immoral behaviour? Does photocopying a personal document count, or only large scale fraud?
- What about the 'softer' moral issues, such as discrimination, equal opportunities, and distributive justice?

Roughly in parallel with Burns' work on transformational leadership, House (1976) and others were developing the theory of charismatic leadership. 'Charisma' is a Greek word—meaning 'divinely inspired gift'—which was first used by the early sociologist Max Weber (1947) to describe a form of influence based on follower perceptions of leader extraordinariness rather than on formal authority or tradition. House took this term to refer to leaders who act in unique ways and have specific personality characteristics which have a strong influencing effect on their followers. As we will see later in the chapter, House included strong moral values as being amongst the personality characteristics exhibited by charismatic leaders—thus drawing a parallel with transformational leadership—but this component was not universally accepted. A closer reading of House suggests how this apparent similarity between charismatic and transformational leadership—which we believe to be significantly different—can be understood. Whilst House would claim that charismatic leaders have a strong sense of their own moral values, he does not go so far as to suggest that the aim of their leadership is to morally transform others: this, we would suggest, is the basis of the difference between the two strands of 'new leadership' and why charismatic leaders can pursue aims and goals which most of us would recognize as being immoral or, at least, amoral.

 Blog box

To what extent to you think leaders act morally in their day-to-day activities and decision making? Reflect on specific leaders you have worked for and, in not more than 300 words, reflect upon how they faced up to the challenge of upholding moral standards in the face of the numerous pressures they faced in the fulfilment of organizational goals. Did they even think of their role in these terms? Was pragmatism the accepted order of the day? How has your view of what it is to be a leader been influenced by your observation of others in this respect?

In the mainstream

Transformational and full range leadership

The main proponents of transformational leadership in an organizational context have been Bernard Bass and Bruce Avolio. Although their conceptualization of the components of transformational leadership evolved over time, the most mature version (Bass and Avolio, 1990) is that commonly referred to as 'the Four Is'. This framework identified four factors (all conveniently beginning with the letter I) which together constitute the practice of transformational leadership, namely:

1. *Idealized Influence*—the articulation of a mission or vision for the organization. This is also sometimes referred to as charisma (we can see how this might cause confusion in relation to rival theories), and requires leaders to act as strong role models for followers and, as such, to embody high standards of ethical and moral conduct

2. *Inspirational Motivation*—the motivation of others through the communication of high expectations, such as to inspire them to put organizational interests before self-interest. In practice, leaders will use symbolic language and emotional appeals to build employee

commitment and to persuade them to buy in to a shared vision of the organizational future

3. *Intellectual Stimulation*—the encouragement of creative and innovative behaviours through the presentation of a challenge to see what they are doing from new perspectives. This challenge should include an exploration of their own beliefs and values, as well as those of the leader and the organization

4. *Individualized Consideration*—the development of others to their highest levels of ability through the creation of a supportive climate in which they listen closely to follower needs and provide coaching and advice as necessary. The aim here is to allow followers to self-actualize at the same time as tapping into this self-actualization in the furtherance of organizational goals.

It is a fundamental principle of transformational leadership that this type of leadership practice will produce an augmentation effect (Waldman, Bass, and Yammarino, 1990) in performance terms over merely transactional leadership. But here we come to a conceptual difference between Burns' original specification of the transformational/transactional divide in leadership, and Bass and Avolio's development of it. Burns saw transactional and transformational leadership as opposite ends of a spectrum, and hence saw leaders as being either one or the other. For Bass the two were conceived as separate dimensions which could be practised either together or separately. Based on this conceptualization, Bass extended the original model to include a third approach to leadership, which he called laissez-faire, and combined the three elements into the full range leadership model. This model comprised seven factors and is illustrated in Figure 5.1.

We have already outlined the four factors which constitute transformational leadership. Let us now look at the remaining three factors which make up transactional and laissez-faire leadership. Transactional leadership differs from transformational leadership in that it does not individualize the needs of followers and is not concerned with their personal development. Its primary aim is the achievement of pre-determined organizational goals through the exchange of things of value to each party. The transactional leader's tools are:

- *Contingent reward*—the distribution of specific rewards in return for directed effort. There is an implicit negotiation or trade-off in this leadership factor, with the leader gaining agreement from the follower to perform certain tasks in exchange for an agreed reward, usually in the form of pay.

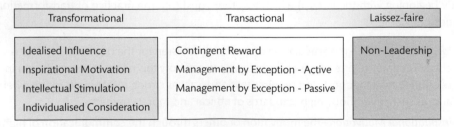

Figure 5.1 The Full Range Leadership Model

Source: Avolio, B. J. (2010). *Full Range Leadership Development* Second Edition, Sage Publications Inc. Adapted with permission

- *Management by exception*—this type of leadership involves corrective criticism, negative feedback, and negative reinforcement activities by the leader in response to follower activities. It can take two forms: active and passive. Active management by exception requires the leader to watch followers closely for mistakes, rule violations, and other shortcomings and to take corrective action on each occasion. Passive management by exception occurs when the leader intervenes only after certain standards have not been met or certain goals have been missed, with smaller or less significant contraventions being allowed to pass uncorrected.

- *Laissez-faire leadership*—effectively the absence of leadership, representing behaviours that are non-transactional such as abdicating responsibility, delaying decisions, giving no feedback, and so on. The name comes from the French phrase meaning 'hands off' or to let things ride, and hence this kind of approach is unlikely to result in the meeting of organizational goals or the development of individuals within the organization.

A case in point: Aung San Suu Kyi

Born in Rangoon in 1945, Aung San Suu Kyi was the third child of Aung San, commander of the Burmese Independence Army, and Daw Khin Kyi, senior nurse at the Rangoon General Hospital. Her father was assassinated when she was two years old, and her childhood years were spent watching her mother become a prominent public figure: she travelled with her to New Delhi in 1960, when Daw Khin Kyi was appointed Burma's ambassador to India. After the death of her mother, and following the resignation in 1988 of General Ni Win, Burma's military dictator since 1962, her political career began. The popular uprising which followed Win's resignation, and was greeted by violent military suppression, prompted her first overtly political act—an open letter to the government, calling for the formation of an independent consultative committee to prepare the way for multi-party elections. She went on to form the National League for Democracy (NLD) with a policy of non-violence and civil disobedience. Despite a ban on political gatherings of more than four people, Suu Kyi toured the country speaking to large audiences with the result that in the following year she was prohibited by the ruling SLORC (State Law and Order Restoration Council) from standing for election. She was later placed under house arrest, without charge or trial—an act which failed to prevent the NLD from winning the election held that year with 82 per cent of parliamentary seats, a result which the SLORC refused to recognize.

In 1995, after six years of detention, the SLORC released Suu Kyi from house arrest, albeit her movements and communication channels remained heavily restricted. In 2011 incoming President Thein Sein began a wave of political reforms aimed at establishing international legitimacy for the administration. In this context, persuading Aung San Suu Kyi's party to rejoin politics after it boycotted the 2010 election was a key turning point in the government's campaign for the lifting of the Western economic sanctions imposed during military rule. The outcome of the April 2012 by-election was a resounding victory for the NLD, with the party winning almost all of the 45 seats contested. Whilst this has been seen as a major step towards reconciliation after decades of military rule in Burma, Suu Kyi's fight for democracy is far from over. She and the other newly elected NLD MPs boycotted the opening of the new parliament because they objected to the oath saying they must 'safeguard the constitution' when in fact they want to amend the constitution to reduce the military's power. Whilst the process of democratization in Burma will no doubt continue for some time, no one can doubt the truly transformational nature of this woman's leadership.

Sources: Aung San Suu Kyi, in *Current Biography*, February 1992. Clements, Alan and Kean, Leslie (1994) *Burma's Revolution of the Spirit: The Struggle for Democratic Freedom and Dignity*. New York: Aperture. Mirante, Edith T. (1993) *Burmese Looking Glass. A Human Rights Adventure and a Jungle Revolution*. New York: Grove. Victor, Barbara (1988) *The Lady: Aung San Suu Kyi: Nobel Laureate and Burma's Prisoner*. London: Faber & Faber.

Whilst this format has become the dominant formulation of transformational leadership—and the one for which the most empirical evidence has been generated—there have been other formulations and perspectives which have also contributed to our understanding of this leadership phenomenon. So, for example, Bennis and Nanus (1985) identified four common strategies used by leaders in their attempts to transform their organizations. These were:

1. Having and communicating a clear *vision* of the future state their organization needs to achieve. This vision needs to present an attractive, believable, and attainable future state that followers can commit to and put their effort behind

2. Acting as *social architects* for their organization by creating for organizational members shared meanings which create a sense of identity around shared values and norms

3. Creating *trust* in the organization through their own practices of honesty and transparency, and by creating a sense of predictability and reliability even in the face of ambiguous and uncertain events

4. Effectively deploying a positive sense of self or *positive self-regard* as the basis for emphasizing their own strengths and not dwelling on their weaknesses. This basic sense of competence allows them to operate effectively in difficult times, rather than being distracted by self-doubt, at the same time as generating confidence in followers.

In addition to these four strategies, Bennis and Nanus found that the leaders in their study, all of whom had successfully transformed their organizations, were committed to continual learning both for themselves and their organizations.

Another model of transformational leadership is presented by Kouzes and Posner (1987, 2002), based on interviews conducted with 1,300 middle and senior managers in both private- and public-sector organizations. They identified five fundamental practices which enable leaders to get extraordinary things accomplished and backed up these practices of exemplary leadership with commitments or strategies said to be needed to put them into operation. The five practices are:

1. model the way
2. inspire a shared vision
3. challenge the process
4. enable others to act
5. encourage the heart

Unlike the other models described, the Kouzes and Posner practices have an emphasis on behaviours (rather than motives) and are somewhat prescriptive in nature. It also differs from the other approaches we have seen in suggesting that these practices are available to anyone and are not the outcome of special abilities or personal characteristics.

Measuring transformational leadership

There have been a number of attempts to measure transformational leadership. The first of these, and the one most consistently applied in subsequent empirical research, is Bass and Avolio's (1997) Multifactor Leadership Questionnaire (MLQ). This was derived from Bass's early work in operationalizing the full range leadership model, and their consistent work to refine it: even so, the factor structure remains the subject of debate. In 1990, Podsakoff et al. produced an alternative instrument which measured six transformational leadership factors (articulates vision, provides appropriate role model, fosters acceptance of goals, communicates high performance expectations, provides individualized support, and intellectual stimulation) together with four factors representing contingent and non-contingent reward. Both of these measures are concerned with proximal leadership and incorporate both transformational and transactional elements. In contrast, measures by Kouzes and Posner (1998) and Alimo-Metcalfe and Alban-Metcalfe (2001) focus exclusively on transformational leadership and can be applied to more distal leaders.

Leadership in the media: Amazing Grace

The film *Amazing Grace* tells the story of William Wilberforce's 25-year struggle to abolish the British slave trade. As a popular and ambitious member of the British parliament in 1782, Wilberforce is persuaded by a group of friends, including William Pitt (later to become Prime Minister), to take on this potentially damaging issue. With mentor John Newton (an ex slave ship captain turned priest who wrote the well known hymn *Amazing Grace*) and freed slave turned author Olaudah Equiano, Wilberforce fights both vested business interests in London, Bristol, and Liverpool (ports whose wealth and prosperity are derived from the trade) and public indifference at great cost to his own career prospects and health. Continuing to battle against the odds, it is not until 1807 and after many attempts to introduce the necessary legislation that he is eventually responsible for a bill being passed through Parliament which abolishes the slave trade in the British empire forever. This inspiring and moving film provides us with a fascinating opportunity to measure the tenets of transformational leadership as presented in the literature against the acts of one very determined man.

Charismatic leadership

As already noted, the development of charismatic leadership theory ran roughly in parallel with that of transformational leadership albeit on a less smooth course. Also different, is the absence of a clearly defined 'winner' in the attempts to delineate the components and mechanisms underpinning this complex psycho-social phenomenon. There are three competing approaches, all of which have a degree of currency in the literature. These are the behavioural approach (most commonly associated with the work of House), the attributional approach (articulated by Conger and Kanungo), and the follower self-concept approach (a conceptual approach attributable to Boas Shamir). We will look at each of these approaches in turn.

Although House (1976) saw charismatic leadership as being underpinned by certain personality characteristics (see Figure 5.2), it is with the types of behaviours exhibited by such leaders that he is most concerned. These behaviours are centred around competence and role modelling, articulating goals and communicating high expectations, and encouraging, motivational interaction with followers. As Figure 5.2 illustrates, these behaviours are seen as producing trust, affection, and obedience towards the leader and increased confidence and performance in the follower.

As noted in the introduction to this chapter, House's inclusion of 'strong moral values' as one of the personality characteristics underpinning charismatic leadership does not translate

Personality Characteristics	Behaviours	Effects on Followers
Dominant	Strong role model	Trust in leader's ideology
Desire to influence	Shows competence	Belief of similarity
Self-confident	Articulates goals	Unquestioning acceptance
Strong moral values	Sets high expectations	Affection towards leader
	Expresses confidence	Obedience
	Arouses motives	Identification with leader
		Emotional involvement
		Heightened goals
		Increased confidence

Figure 5.2 House's model of charismatic leadership

Source: Northouse, P. G. (2010). *Leadership Theory and Practice* Fifth Edition, Thousand Oaks, CA: Sage. Adapted with permission.

directly into moral behaviours or objectives. Since other formulations of charismatic leadership omit this component, we believe there is strong reason for maintaining the existence or otherwise of a moral underpinning as a significant distinction between transformational and charismatic leadership.

Attributional approaches to charismatic leadership

In putting forward their attributional theory of charismatic leadership Conger and Kanungo (1987, 1998) were more concerned with the mechanism through which such leadership operates than with the behaviours or character of the leader themselves. They proposed that the attribution of charisma by followers was dependent on a combination of leader behaviours and aspects of the situation. Thus the presence of individual behaviours might vary between leaders, and their relative importance to followers in attributing charisma would depend in part on how those followers perceive the situation in which they are exercised. Nonetheless, Conger and Kanungo identified five behaviour/situation combinations that were most likely to lead to the attribution of charismatic leadership. These were as follows:

1. Advocating a vision that is markedly different from the *status quo*, but is not so radical as to be unrecognizable to followers

2. Acting in unconventional ways in order to achieve the vision

3. Taking personal risks and being willing to make personal sacrifices in order to achieve the vision

4. Appearing confident, both in themselves and in the success and expediency of their vision

5. Using visioning and persuasive appeals to engage followers, rather than relying on either authority or participation

> ### 🖥 Blog box
>
> Think of a leader you would describe as charismatic. In no more than 300 words, write a description of what it is about them that leads you to see them in this way. Is it specific things they do or say? Is it something about their personal presence? When you have written your description, compare it with the attributional behaviour/situation combinations set out by Conger and Kanungo—how aligned (or otherwise) is what you have written with what they suggest?

The initial statement of the theory was not explicit concerning the influence processes through which charismatic behaviours led to follower attributions, but in 1989 Conger conducted additional research designed to fill this gap. His findings showed that personal identification with the leader—and hence a desire to please and imitate them—was the primary mechanism here. Through this mechanism leader approval is said to become a powerful measure of self-worth for followers and to lead to the internalization of the leader's values and beliefs.

Follower self-concept and charismatic leadership

The third approach to the understanding of charismatic leadership is that of Boas Shamir, and builds on the work of House. Shamir, House, and Arthur (1993), whilst acknowledging the personal identification mechanism identified by Conger and Kanungo, saw the social identification, internalization, and augmentation of self-efficacy mechanisms (collectively designated the self-concept theory) as being more significant. They postulate that charismatic leaders are able to harness followers' self-concepts—their sense of identity—to the goals and aspirations of the organization, and to bring about the internalization of these organizational goals both collectively and individually in followers. They identify four mechanisms through which this motivational change is brought about, namely:

1. Changing follower perceptions of the work itself, to make it appear more valuable or worthy

2. Offering an appealing vision of the future, of which followers feel a part

3. Developing a deep collective identity among followers, such that they are willing to put this before their own individual identity

4. Heightening both individual and collective self-efficacy, such that followers believe in their ability to deliver on demanding goals

Internalization occurs when followers see the attainment of organizational and collective goals as an expression of their own values and social identities. As a facilitating condition for this to occur, it is suggested that some degree of congruence between the leader's vision and the existing values and identities of followers is necessary, as is the ability of the leader to frame task goals in ideological terms. One of the authors of the current text remembers vividly being told the (probably apocryphal) story of the US politician visiting NASA in the early stages of the moon missions and asking various workers what they were doing. The answers included 'designing the guidance system', 'building the propulsion unit', and so on. Then the politician asked the man sweeping the hangar what he was doing. The reply: 'I'm helping to send a man to the moon.' A tribute, perhaps, to the charismatic leadership of John F. Kennedy in creating a believable vision of lunar travel.

Discussion point: Can anyone be charismatic?

As we have seen, views on the sources of charisma in leaders vary, but what are the implications of this for those seeking to lead?

● Based on the three approaches to charismatic leadership discussed above, do you believe it is possible to learn to be charismatic as a leader? Are there behaviours and techniques which can be used to persuade followers to see a leader in this way?

● Do you agree with the proposal made by the authors, that transformational leadership has a moral component whilst charismatic leadership may not? What are the implications of this for which model of leadership we should adopt for the future? Is it reasonable to expect leaders to be morally driven in a far from moral world?

Articulating a vision and the 'rhetoric arts'

Both charismatic and transformational leadership are strongly associated with the idea of articulating and communicating a vision. Before looking at some of the criticisms of these two types of leadership, let us briefly digress to consider what really constitutes a 'vision' and how it can be successfully communicated. Research (Nanus, 1992; Zaccaro and Banks, 2001) suggests that a leadership vision must incorporate a picture of change which is worth trying for and which, whilst challenging, is not unattainable. In communicating this vision—in representing the picture—it has been suggested that there are a number of 'rhetorical arts' through which the leader might sell his ideas to others such that they choose to 'buy into' it as their own. Such rhetorical arts might include:

● Communicating the vision by *adapting the content* to suit the audience
● Highlighting the *intrinsic value* of the vision by emphasizing how it represents ideals worth pursuing
● Choosing the right language—*words and symbols*—to make it motivating and inspiring
● Using *inclusive* language that links people to the vision and makes them feel part of the process

---

A case in point: Yes, we can!

Few of us can have escaped hearing—either at the time or via the internet since—Barack Obama's now famous 'Yes, we can!' campaign speech during the New Hampshire primaries, prior to his election in 2008. It was a rousing call to the people of America to acknowledge the many problems they faced and to meet them head on. It was also a confident claim by Obama that he was the right person to lead them through the difficult times ahead. In the course of the speech, he created a number of vivid pictures of how key issues within the country's economic, domestic, and foreign policy would be different if he were to be elected, and gave clear indications of how he (and the American people) would need to go about achieving these changes. He drew constantly on a sense of shared values and used language that was strongly resonant of the American self-image. Not surprisingly, it produced a powerfully positive reaction in supporters. Listen to the speech again and deconstruct the 'rhetoric arts' through which Obama conveyed this powerful message.

Source: http://www.youtube.com/watch?v=Fe751kMBwms

The essence of these arts—and of conveying a vision—is the ability to make a message delivered to a large number of people feel very personal and individual: not too difficult perhaps in a single organization but far more challenging across a whole nation.

From a critical perspective

A number of criticisms can be levelled at 'new leadership' generally, with varying degrees of accuracy for the different formulations we have seen. For many, the apparent focus on senior and formally appointed leaders excludes the significant amount of leadership activity going on in middle management and in informal or emergent situations. For others, the somewhat generic, often prescriptive nature of the approaches seems to ignore necessary elements of organizational context. There have also been complaints that insufficient attention has been paid to the underlying influence processes which are at work here and/or the specific behaviours entailed. We would suggest that all of these criticisms have some truth in them but—as will be evident from the preceding sections—they are less true than they were and much work has been done to fill in the gaps. Perhaps a more worthy challenge relates to the somewhat rosy view the literature seems to have of transformational and charismatic leadership, and the insufficiency of work to identify the negative effects which each approach can generate.

RESEARCH IN FOCUS: New managerialism's 'disciplinary gaze'

In an article that is critical of what they call 'new managerialism' Ball and Carter (2002) use the ideas of Foucault to call attention to the 'normalizing' or 'disciplinary gaze' which they suggest is shaping how managers behave and how they seek to be perceived. In coining the phrase 'new managerialism' Ball and Carter draw attention to the number of highly popular new initiatives (TQM, BPR, lean, six sigma, and so on) which have been promulgated within organizations since the 1980s. They claim that what they all have in common is an increased emphasis on organizational culture and a consequent need for charismatic leadership to drive them. They also note the rigour with which such initiatives are presented as the current 'best practice', acting as what Foucault (1972) referred to as a 'regime of truth'. Using Foucault's archaeological and genealogical methods, they argue that 'new managerialism' has become a discourse on a grand scale (that is, one which delimits a field of knowledge) as well as occurring in everyday talk and text. It is through taking on 'archaeological' or grand-scale status that a discourse is said to become institutionalized into organizational thinking and beliefs and to exert a normalizing effect on managers' behaviours and—perhaps more significantly—on their sense of their own identities. Thus constructing one's identity as a charismatic leader is seen as being key to achieving perceived dominance, control, and good practice within one's own organizational domain. Ball and Carter identify a number of 'interpretive repertoires', all of which are said to align with ideas within the new managerialism discourse, which managers were found to use in constructing such identities for themselves and presenting themselves to their followers. Through a series of case studies, they explore how these repertoires are utilized to build power relations and legitimate the manager's own position. In a return to Foucault, they contend that the 'relations of power' thus created offer further evidence of the way in which these discourses serve to restrict or shape the practice of everyday management.

Source: Ball, Kirstie and Carter, Chris (2002) The charismatic gaze: everyday leadership practices of the 'new' manager. *Management Decision*, 40 (6) 552–65.

In relation to transformational leadership, it has been suggested that despite the significant amount of empirical support for some measures of the model (in particular, Bass and Avolio's Four Is) there is a lack of conceptual clarity. Research by Tracey and Hinkin (1998) showed substantial overlap between each of the four Is (idealized influence, inspirational motivation, intellectual stimulation, and individualized consideration), which would suggest that these dimensions are not clearly delineated. Rafferty and Griffin (2004) suggest there is also a lack of empirical support for the hypothesized Four Is model and suggest an alternative five factor model, consisting of vision, inspirational communication, intellectual stimulation, supportive leadership, and personal recognition. Whilst they go on to test the associations between the various factors and specific follower outcomes, and offer confirmatory factor analysis for their proposed factor structure, they acknowledge that the limited scale of their research can allow for only modest claims for this alternative model. It is certainly insufficient to resolve the previous lack of clarity. Also, as pointed out by Bryman (1992), there is considerable overlap between the dimensions of transformational leadership models and those of other leadership models, bringing into question whether it is truly a 'new' conceptualization.

The measurement of transformational leadership is also seen as problematic, with the validity of the MLQ having many doubters. The high correlation between the factors here (as found by Tejeda, Scandura, and Pillai, 2001) is an unsurprising corollary of the conceptual confusion already noted. At a more fundamental level, it is also questioned whether transformational leadership should be considered as a personality trait or personal predisposition rather than as a set of behaviours which can be learned. Again, the overlap with charismatic leadership serves to muddy the waters here. Its potential to be elitist and antidemocratic—and to suffer from a bias towards 'heroic' forms of leadership—has been noted by its main protagonists, Bass and Avolio, and refuted by them on the grounds that leaders can be simultaneously directive and participative, democratic and authoritarian. We would suggest that this refutation—that transformational leaders can be all things to all followers—is somewhat flimsy and fails to address what appears to be a valid question in relation to this highly acclaimed leadership 'solution'. The potential for abuse through—and indeed, the underlying ethics of—a form of leadership which advocates changing followers' values in the process of moving them to a new vision has also been raised, hitting at the heart of Burns' original conception of leadership as creating a relationship of 'mutual stimulation and elevation' with followers.

Turning to charismatic leadership, one of the major problems here has been recognized as the transitory nature of the phenomenon, which is based on personal identification with an individual leader who is perceived to be in some way extraordinary. When the leader departs or dies, a succession crisis is likely, and many organizations founded on charismatic leadership fail to survive this crisis. Characterizing this problem as the 'routinization' of charisma, Yukl (2002) suggests three methods by which organizations (and/or the departing leaders themselves) can attempt to perpetuate the leader's influence on the organization:

1. By transferring charisma to a designated successor through *rites and ceremonies*. The problems here are that it is seldom possible to find an equally extraordinary successor for an extraordinary leader and that the existing leader may be unwilling to identify a strong successor early enough to ensure a smooth transition

2. By creating *administrative structures* that will continue to implement the leader's vision. This can be difficult to sustain when a vibrant, living vision is replaced by a bland,

bureaucratic set of rules. It can also strangle the organization as the vision becomes tired through lack of personal renewal

3. By perpetuating the leader's vision by *embedding it in the organizational culture*. This requires followers to be persuaded to internalize the vision and feel empowered to implement it. Of the three, this approach is probably the most likely to be successful, though it is not without its pitfalls and limitations, not least of which is the fact that sooner or later a new leader with ideas of their own is likely to be required.

In addition to issues of sustainability, charismatic leadership has also been attacked on the grounds that its proponents overemphasize the potential for positive consequences. The 'dark side' of charisma is now emerging as a topic in the literature and refers to such issues as the dependency relations which may be created and the potential for narcissism. The former is said to inhibit followers from making suggestions or challenging ideas, to lead to the acceptance of risky projects and the denial of problems or failures, to prevent the development of individuals who could be potential successors, and to create an illusion of leader infallibility. The other side of this relationship is the tendency for narcissistic individuals to be drawn to positions of high power and influence in order to feed their need for adoration and praise, potentially with disastrous results. The weak self-control, indifference to the needs and welfare of others, and lack of emotional maturity which form part of this syndrome can cause leaders to articulate impossible goals and require them to be met at all costs.

A case in point: Steve Jobs—a hero of our time?

Steve Jobs was undoubtedly a charismatic and highly successful leader. As co-founder and CEO of Apple he became a byword for innovation and great design. As one-time head of Pixar he helped to launch one of the most creative and successful movie companies of the modern era. But almost as famous as his charisma and talent are his narcissism, near-legendary temper, and tendency towards very public *faux pas*. This combination of the negative and positive elements of charismatic leadership make him an interesting study for practitioners and academics alike. And with Jobs' habit of making the keynote address at nearly every significant Apple event, many of which can be viewed on YouTube or similar media, there is plenty of material to examine. Look out for the obvious stage management, production, backdrops, props, lighting, etc. which collectively support and maintain the identity which Jobs has created as the personification of Apple. What do you think would have been the benefits and costs of working for this undoubtedly charismatic man?

Sources: http://en.wikipedia.org/wiki/Steve_Jobs; http://allaboutstevejobs.com/bio/bio.php

---

Finally, a number of studies have considered the transferability of transformational and charismatic leadership models to non-Western cultures. Given the presentation of new leadership as a universal panacea in much of the Western literature, this is important research and has produced some interesting results. Walumbwa and Lawler (2003) noted that previous cross-cultural research in this area had focused on replicating the augmentation effects of transformational over transactional leadership. They chose, instead, to examine the moderating effects of culture on the relationship between transformational leadership and work outcomes, with particular attention being paid to collectivism versus individualism. Their study was conducted in China, India, and Kenya and suggested that, whilst transformational leadership is effective across cultures, it can be expected to impact differently on measures of job satisfaction, organizational commitment, and withdrawal behaviours dependent upon the cultural context. In collectivist cultures, the emphasis placed on collective goals and the transcendence of individual goals by transformational leadership is likely to be more culturally aligned than in individualist (largely Western) cultures, leading to a higher acceptance of this type of leadership. These findings were replicated by Jung, Yammarino, and Lee (2009) in a study of followers' attitudes in the USA and Korea. In a study of Japanese and British followers, Fukushige and Spicer (2011) examined leadership preferences against Bass and Avolio's full range leadership model. They found that, in relation to transformational leadership, British followers preferred idealized influence, inspirational motivation, and individualized consideration, whereas Japanese followers more positively endorsed intellectual stimulation. In relation to transactional styles, both contingent reward and management by exception were more highly favoured by Japanese followers.

In relation to charismatic leadership, there have been studies to test the factor structure of Conger and Kanungo's model of charismatic leadership in China (Lian et al., 2011) and comparisons between Gandhi and US presidents who were considered charismatic—specifically, Theodore Roosevelt, Franklin D. Roosevelt, John F. Kennedy and Ronald Reagan (Bligh and Robinson, 2010). The former study found that, whilst the factor structure was replicated, some specific behaviours were not attributed as charismatic and were less effective in China. In the latter, comparable themes were found in the leaders' speeches of articulating an intolerable present, appealing to values and moral justifications, an emphasis of similarity to followers and statements of followers' worth. In contrast, Gandhi was found to use more collective themes in his rhetoric, and to show more variation in his use of active, aggressive language. Bligh and Robinson suggest that some of these differences may relate to issues of collectivism, but are cautious in generalizing across cultural settings. As they rightly conclude, there remains a vast amount of research to be done in this complex and important area.

Chapter summary

In this chapter we have discussed:

- Three formulations of the transformational leadership model as put forward by different authors
- The full range leadership model, which includes transformational, transactional, and laissez-faire leadership as an additive framework
- Some of the criticisms which have been levelled at these models and, in particular, the difficulties of measuring transformational leadership
- Three perspectives on charismatic leadership, and some of the problems associated with it
- The emergence of these forms of 'new leadership' in the wake of the restructuring and redundancies of the 1970s and their frequent perception as a universal panacea
- Some of the cultural variations and limitations which have been explored in relation to the application of transformational and charismatic models of leadership

Integrative case study: Bombay Electric—transformational by design

Priya Kishore is the founder and Creative Director of one of the most dynamic fashion outlets in Mumbai: in the eight years since it first opened, Bombay Electric has become a beacon for the city's creative elite and received recognition around the world. Its founder has taken her own love of jewel colours and quirky design and turned it into big business. She has still managed to keep the personal touch, however, often taking time to talk customers through the finer nuances of the current designer collection. When the idea for Bombay Electric was first conceived, there were relatively few luxury brands in India, and much of the 'fashion' revolved around traditional wedding outfits. The idea of ready-to-wear fashion was almost unheard-of, as was any outlet for designer talent within the country. For Kishore, this represented an irresistible opportunity to offer discerning clients international brands with an emphasis on design rather than labels. Bombay Electric quickly developed a cult following, driven almost entirely by word-of-mouth and a high degree of brand loyalty, and now has its own private label. In the process, Kishore has brought over 70 emerging designers from across India into the public eye, providing a platform for innovation and shaping the burgeoning retail and design industries.

Located in a unique heritage building just around the corner from the Taj Mahal Palace Hotel, in Mumbai's Colaba Causeway district—the Bond Street of Mumbai—the flagship store has been described as 'a tavern of intoxicating aesthetics' and is symbolic of the dynamic fusion of modern and traditional influences which permeate the city itself. It carries established Indian designers such as Manish Arora and Rajesh Pratap Singh, as well as having a reputation for spotting rising new talents. It also buys in international brands known for their strong focus on design, such as Comme des Garcons, Surface 2 Air, and United Nude. Kishore chooses ranges that can be worn anywhere in the world, and often encourages designers to produce collections themed around a single colour or texture. And in addition to a unique shopping experience, the space—together with its palm-tree lined courtyard—is also used to host everything from book readings, to craft exhibitions, and photography shows. At the other end of the cultural scale, the store has showcased a collection of hand-woven items—created in collaboration with Women Weave, an NGO set up to develop global markets for rural Indian crafts and create a market for sustainable fashion and design within India—honouring the life of Mahatma Gandhi.

Continuing her ground-breaking approach, Kishore has now opened Pocket Electric—India's first guerrilla store, located in New Delhi. Says Kishore, 'we've taken occupation of a space at the Garden of Five Senses and I'm quite excited about the result. We see Pocket Electric as Bombay Electric's rebellious kid sister—an espresso shot of the best of the flagship's collections, but with a distinctly new edge from our new collaborations.' These collaborations include India's most progressive photographer, Bharat Sikka, and the celebrated tabla player and father of modern Asian electronic music, Talvin Singh. In 2009, Kishore's creative genius won her the Young Fashion Entrepreneur of the Year Award and as friend and colleague, designer Gaurav Gupta says, 'she knows how to push boundaries to get what she wants.' She is also renowned for her eye for detail and creative vision, and fellow designer Sonam Dubal described her as a 'style icon' in her own right.

So what lies behind Kishore's vision for Indian fashion? Born in the UK, she has an international education having studied philosophy, politics, and economics at Oxford and anthropology and international relations at the University of Chicago. She was a speech writer at the British House of Commons and hosted a radio talk show in America. On returning to London, she worked for advertising agency DDB, reporting on macro-trends in international markets, and it was here that the seeds of the idea for Bombay Electric were sown. Says Kishore, 'while the creative sector was slowing in the West, there was a creative renaissance about to happen in India.' Her response was to move to Mumbai and thrust her design ideas into its energy-filled midst. 'Mumbai is a new city every two months,' she says. 'Bombay Electric mirrors old school Bombay with the electric new Mumbai.' As a modern woman who still holds strong traditional values, Kishore loves the cultural and spiritual richness of India and sees it as the perfect base for her own blend of talents and vision. She has personally formulated the brand identity of her store, its positioning in the market and the company's communication strategy, with her success resulting in more than 80 publications across 24 countries.

(Continued...)

Still going strong despite the economic downturn elsewhere, Bombay Electric has become a key player in the dramatic change in Indian consumer tastes. Says Kishore, 'the Indian consumer remains very discerning, even our wealthiest customers consider their choices greatly. They do not think as Western consumers, nor do they have similar tastes—recognizing this is the key to success for luxury brands in India.' With her combination of an international business mindset and an innate understanding of Indian culture, it is no surprise that Kishore now advises the board of Indian fashion week and is a panel member for a range of design and cultural events. Where next, one wonders?

Sources: Amed, Imran (2006–2011) The Business of Fashion. www.businessoffashion.com accessed 6 June 2011. Malhotra, Purvi *India Today*, 8 May 2009) www.yatedo.com biography accessed 19 September 2011. Shah, Gayatri R. (29 September 2009) *Bombay Electric: Buzzing with the best Indian fashion design.* www.cnngo.com accessed 19 September 2011. Zakaria, Namrata (posted Friday 11 June 2010) www.indianexpress.com accessed 19 September 2011.

Case study questions

● How would you describe Priya Kishore's leadership of Bombay Electric? Is she best described as a charismatic or a transformational leader and why?

● Many of Kishore's initiatives involve collaboration with others and cultural/artistic sidelines: do you think she is morally motivated in these activities or do you think she sees them as 'good business'?

● The Bombay Electric and Pocket Electric concepts have clearly had a major impact on Indian fashion retail. What do you think motivated Kishore to move in this direction and what do you think it would be like to work for her?

Further reading

Avolio, Bruce J. and Bass, Bernard M. (2002) *Developing Potential across a Full Range of Leadership.* New York: Psychology Press.

Bass, B. M. and Riggio, R. E. (2006) *Transformational Leadership* (2nd Edition). Mahwah, NJ: Lawrence Erlbaum.

Pye, Annie (2005) Leadership and organising: Sense-making in action. *Leadership*, 1 (1) 31–50.

Tourish, D. and Vatcha, N. (2005) Charismatic leadership and corporate cultism at Enron: The elimination of dissent, the promotion of conformity and organisational collapse. *Leadership*, 1 (4) 455–80.

6

In the eye of the beholder: Leadership as a social construction

Learning outcomes

On completion of this chapter you will:

- Understand the main follower-centric approaches to leadership and how they stand in relation to more mainstream views
- Understand the notion of the 'romance of leadership' and how this influences our construction of leadership as a phenomenon and our assessment of practising leaders
- Be aware of the role of implicit leadership theories in shaping our response to the leadership of others
- Understand the role of cultural factors in shaping our ideas of leadership and our willingness to follow particular styles of leadership
- Have considered how practising leaders construct ideas of success and failure in relation to their own practice

Introduction

Whilst most mainstream writing discusses leadership from the perspective of the leader—their traits, their behaviours, their vision—the socially constructed view of leadership explored in this chapter acknowledges the key role of followers and followership. Drawing on the seminal work of Meindl, Shamir, Uhl-Bien, and others, the socially constructed view of leadership contrasts a view of followers as passive recipients of leadership influence with that of active constructors of leaders and leadership. On this view, what counts is how the actions of would-be leaders are perceived rather than what their intentions were in performing them: the response of potential followers rather than the intentions of those seeking to lead. Underpinning this response—this willingness to follow—will be the followers' understanding of what constitutes leadership and whether the actions of the putative leader conform to these views. Thus how we construct our ideas of leadership is fundamental to the establishment of a leader–follower relationship.

The chapter will explore the implications of this thesis for our understanding of leadership, and some of the specific theories to emerge will be outlined and critiqued. As a corollary to the notion that leadership is 'in the eye of the beholder' the chapter will also critique its current status in both popular and academic thinking via Meindl's thesis of 'romanticization'—the idea that both in practice and in the media the whole notion of leadership is 'hyped-up' to produce undeliverable expectations and beliefs.

Follower-centric approaches to leadership

Traditional writing on leadership tends to see followers as passive recipients of leadership influence. They are written about as a homogeneous lump, just waiting to do the bidding of 'effective leaders', with no real agency of their own. All the focus here is on the traits and behaviours of the leaders themselves—this is what determines leadership, this is what makes leaders effective, we are told. It came as a radical departure from this viewpoint when writers began to consider the role of followers in constructing ideas of leadership and choosing when and whether to follow others based on the extent to which they lived up to these ideas. This 'socially constructed' view of leadership sees it as being 'in the eye of the beholder'—that is, followers within a particular setting agree what constitutes leadership and hence who they are prepared to follow. They orient to particular behaviours as leadership and see other behaviours as 'management' or 'interference' or 'coercion' as the case may be. It is implicit in the idea of a group of followers agreeing what, for them, constitutes leadership that this will vary from group to group and setting to setting. We can recognize the appeal of this idea when we think about what leadership we might want as a soldier going into battle, compared with what might be appropriate if we were a social worker dealing with a sensitive case. What we want and need from our leaders—how we want them to interact with us—is likely to be very different in these two situations, as is what we view as 'leadership'.

> ## A case in point: mundane acts as leadership
>
> In Chapter 3 we saw the case of Steven Hunter, Principal of a large further education college in the South of England, and the way in which college staff interpreted even his most mundane acts—such as picking up litter from the college forecourt—as leadership because of the consistency with which they reflect the beliefs and standards which are integral to their shared constructions of leadership. Followers in that context have constructed an understanding of leadership which includes such behaviours as setting an example, living by the standards one sets for others, focusing on details as well as the 'big picture', and so on. Whilst many of the staff were familiar with ideas of charismatic leadership and the need for a vision or mission for the college, these mundane acts were more meaningful to them in terms of what leadership actually looked like, and how it achieved its objectives. This understanding of leadership might not have been shared by the higher education college in the same town or the school down the road but it was shared by the members of this setting—leaders and followers alike—and was thus effective in shaping both leader behaviours and follower responses.

The result of this new stream of leadership writing is a collection of follower-centric approaches which have collectively been referred to as 'socially constructed leadership', and which derive from the work of James Meindl. We will look at Meindl's specific thesis—in relation to what he called the 'romanticization of leadership'—in a later section, but first let us consider the work of a group of writers who sought to pay tribute to Meindl (who died in 2004 at the peak of his career) by putting forward five 'follower-centred perspectives on leadership' (Shamir et al., 2007). They saw followers in the following roles:

- as recipients of leader influence
- as moderators of leader impact
- as substitutes for leadership
- as leaders
- as constructors of leadership

The first two roles are what we would recognize from the traditional, mainstream leadership literature. 'Followers as recipients of leader influence' represents the early trait theories and later charismatic/transformational views of leadership, where the follower is seen as a passive recipient of whatever the leader is or does. 'Followers as moderators of leader impact' is recognizable in approaches such as situational or contingent leadership theories where the leader is required to adjust their behaviours to suit different individuals or situations, but the followers are still largely passive recipients. 'Followers as substitutes for leadership' is exemplified by the work of Steven Kerr and John Jermier (1978) which argues that under certain conditions, the influence of a leader over a follower may be neutralized or even substituted. For example, where the task at hand is very routine or straightforward (such as a worker on a production line) and thus there is seen little need for leadership. Similarly where the job is intrinsically satisfying, such as a paramedic or member of the clergy, and hence no need for the operative to be externally motivated to do it or praised afterwards. Seeing 'followers as leaders' is a slightly odd perspective here: whilst it is usually taken to refer to distributed leadership and its variants, it is more accurately neither leader- nor follower-centred; rather it attempts to do away with the distinction between the two. The suggestion is that any given individual will both lead and follow within the exercise of the duties of a given role, and that the distinctions between the two are thus less than might be supposed.

It is when we come to 'followers as constructors of leadership' that we truly move into the territory of socially constructed leadership, and where Shamir et al. (2007) made their real departure from what had gone before. By drawing attention to how followers make or construct ideas of leadership—and specifically how they construct and represent leaders and leadership in their thought systems—they were turning the field on its head. The emphasis was no longer on the leaders as creators of their own leadership practice, but on followers as arbiters of construct content.

Discussion point: leaders and followers

- What evidence do you see in your own experience of the different roles played by followers in determining what we understand by the term 'leadership'? How important are the views of followers in the leader–follower relationship?
- Where do your own ideas of what constitutes leadership come from? Leaders you have seen? Media representations? Cultural expectations? Training courses? The views of peers?
- If followers play an important role in determining what constitutes leadership—and hence effective leadership—what are the implications of this for leaders? How should they go about creating followership in their subordinates and team members?

Attribution theory and leadership

Linked to the idea of leadership as a socially constructed phenomenon is the role of attributions in leadership processes. Attribution theory per se is usually said to originate in the work of Fritz Heider (1958) and his proposal that:

> attributions are the result of the fundamental cognitive processes by which people ascertain cause and effect so that they can solve problems and become more efficacious in their interactions with their environments. (Martinko, Harvey and Scott, 2007: 562).

Thus Heider saw people as 'naïve psychologists' trying to understand the causes of positive and negative events in their lives and to attribute these events to other people or circumstances in a way that makes sense to them and helps them to make decisions about how to live their lives. Kelley (1971, 1973) worked on the 'front end' of this process by considering what kind of information people used in making attributions—for example, consensus, consistency, and distinctiveness were all shown to be important in the attribution process. Weiner (1986) focused instead on the consequences of the attributions actually made in terms of their emotional and behavioural impact.

Most early attempts to apply attribution theory to leadership focused on the attributions of leaders in relation to followers. So, for example, Green and Mitchell (1979) suggested that different behaviours by team members or followers produced informational cues which leaders used to make attributions which, in turn, influenced the leadership behaviours they directed towards these members/followers. They also recognized that there were a number of factors (such as the mutual expectations of leader and followers, their personal characteristics, and boundary conditions such as organizational policies) which moderated this attribution process and its affect on leader behaviours. By contrast, Calder (1977) proposed that 'leadership exists only as a perception' and hence that the attribution of leadership to an individual by followers is the very essence of the construct. He makes the distinction between the 'first degree constructs' of everyday life and experience and 'second degree constructs' which are the abstract, theory-laden conceptualizations of 'scientists', and emphasizes the importance of the former in producing recognizable theories of leadership as well as the role of follower perceptions in producing and articulating this kind of knowledge. He goes on to suggest a process model by which followers as 'naïve psychologists' define leadership as a first degree construct through their observation of leader behaviours.

In an intriguing case study of a German beer producer, Schyns and Hansborough (2008) investigate the operation of the fundamental attribution error—the tendency to discount situational factors as causal explanations in favour of the internal characteristics of actors involved in the situation—in relation to leadership. They agree with Pfeffer's (1977) argument that the attribution of leadership acts as a simplification of complex problems and is routinely undertaken as part of the sense-making process within organizations with organizational leaders thus appearing in the roles of symbols and scapegoats. This latter attribution is particularly evident in political and other public contexts (for example, the 2011 scandal over phone-hacking by the British news media and the consequent resignation of the Chief Constable of the Metropolitan Police Force, which was implicated in the investigations) and often disguises an unwillingness to uncover the deeper, systemic causes which may have contributed to the failure. They also suggest that it is part of the perceived social role of leaders to be responsible for mistakes.

Blog box

Think of an organizational success that has been celebrated recently within your own organization—this could be a major new piece of business, a rise in profitability, or a significant innovation. To what extent is that success attributed to the organization's leaders—either by employees or by the media? Write a list of all the other factors (internal and external) and all the other people who actually had a hand in bringing the success about. Then reflect, in around 300 words on why you think people prefer to attribute successes (and failures) to individual leaders.

Drawing on the work of others in the field, Yukl (2002) summarizes the various types of information followers may use in making attributions about their leaders, and considers the external factors which may influence these attributions. He suggests there are five interrelated factors which determine how followers assess leader effectiveness and arrive at attributions of success and failure by leaders:

1. *Performance indicators/trends*—The leader is more likely to be seen as effective if their unit or team is doing well than if it is failing, whatever the external circumstances within which they are operating.

2. *Leader actions*—Followers will look for specific actions by the leader which could explain the observed outturn, with direct or highly visible actions being given more weight by followers than indirect or less visible ones.

3. *Uniqueness of action*—Actions perceived as unique to the leader are more likely to be perceived as leadership per se than actions that anyone could have taken.

4. *Situational information*—Followers are found to take situational information into account in making attributions in relation to leadership success or failure, in particular the degree of power or discretion available to the leader in relation to government or industry regulations, for example.

5. *Leader intentions*—Finally, followers will make judgements concerning the degree of intentionality in determining a leader's underlying competence, as well as making qualitative judgements as to whether their intentions were good.

As a criticism of attribution theory Lord and his colleagues (Cronshaw and Lord, 1987; Lord and Maher, 1990; Lord and Smith, 1983; Phillips and Lord, 1986) wrote a series of articles expressing and exploring the concern that the 'cognitive labour' required to make rational attributions precludes the use of such processes to explain everyday occurrences, and makes it likely that they will only 'kick in' for disappointing or surprising outcomes when they will be consciously engaged in. As a consequence of this criticism, it is suggested that people are most likely to attend to and use information cues that are salient to their own interests and to use pre-existing scripts and heuristics when forming behavioural responses to everyday events, thus 'short-circuiting' the rational decision making processes implied by attribution theory. As such, this criticism doesn't invalidate the existence or use of rational attributional processes per se but rather suggests a boundary condition—that of important or surprising circumstances—for their use.

Implicit leadership theories

Not mentioned in Yukl's list of determinants, but also with a key role to play in the making of leadership attributions are the follower's implicit leadership theories, which act as a frame of reference within which to assess observed leader behaviours. Implicit theories of leadership are the common sense ideas we develop about what it means to be a leader. These ideas arise from our own experiences and are underpinned by shared social values and the taken-for-granted cultural context in which we find ourselves. Such views therefore owe something to the stereotypes and prototypes which are common within these contexts, but are refined and personalized through reflection on the specific encounters we have. It is inevitable that such implicit theories will influence the expectations we have of people we view as leaders—and, indeed, *who* we view as leaders—and will shape our responses to them.

 Leadership in the media: Mona Lisa Smile

After graduating from a State University, Katherine Watson has accepted a position teaching art history at the prestigious, all-girls, Wellesley College. Watson is a very modern woman, particularly for the 1950s, the period for the setting of the film, *Mona Lisa Smile*, and is keen to instil intellectual freedom in her students as well as to teach them art history. Whilst there are some pockets of free thinking amongst both staff and students, in the main the repressive mores of this highly conservative college seem set to guide students down a predetermined path of biding their time until they find a suitable man to marry. Whilst a strong bond forms between Watson and her students, in the end her views are incompatible with the dominant culture of the college: her leadership style is at odds with the implicit leadership theories held by her peers and her superiors and she leaves Wellesley disillusioned and diminished. This is a stylish period piece which subtly illustrates the power of culture and deeply-rooted implicit ideas.

In a challenge to what he sees as the mainstream tying of the leadership construct to 'prevailing structural assumptions of hierarchy and power (Biggart and Hamilton, 1987)' and its consequent role in 'offering ideological support for the existing social order' Bresnen (1995: 499) draws on the idea of implicit leadership theories to explore the role of follower agency in the formulation and interpretation of the concept of leadership. In a study of practising managers in the construction industry Bresnen observed the premium that all the managers interviewed placed on patterns of behaviour which resembled traditional leadership-related ideas, such as initiating structure, consideration, and participatory styles, as well as noting that the managers articulated their views of leadership in alignment with well-known contingency approaches by recognizing that a leader needed to change their style or behaviour to meet the needs of the people or situations they faced. In most cases, however, this perceived need was justified by reference to illustrative personal stories or vignettes rather than with reference to theoretical frameworks. It was also clear from the study that individual differences play an important part in how people construct implicit theories of leadership: thus shared experiences might still produce different implicit theories as they were translated via the individuals' own cognitive frames of reference. In terms of the specific content of implicit theories, Bresnen found a number of shared

presumptions underpinning all the accounts of what leadership meant to the study participants, as follows:

- Managerial authority was seen as a necessary (if not sufficient) condition for the exercise of leadership. Put another way, they felt that 'leadership' finds its expression in the perceived effective exercise of legitimate management authority.

- Leadership was viewed from the 'transactional' perspective of getting things done, making decisions, managing objectives, etc. Given the roles of study participants—as junior and middle managers in the construction industry—this is hardly surprising, but it is in contrast to much current writing on leadership which emphasizes the 'transformational' elements of instilling a vision, articulating values, providing motivation, and so on.

- Leadership was seen as residing in the personal attributes—whether innate or learned—of the individuals seen as leaders, but with the understanding that these attributes might find expression in very different ways.

While these findings were clearly contextual to the study setting and to the level of seniority of the participants involved, they offer an interesting insight into the 'grass roots' understanding of leadership which many of us would subscribe to: in so doing, they raise interesting questions about the validity and contribution of much of the more ambitious theories of leadership currently achieving popularity!

According to Schyns and Schilling (2010) much of the research into implicit leadership theories—including that by Bresnen—implies that the image of a leader in general reflects the image of an effective leader: this, they say, runs contrary to leadership research in general where the more negative aspects of leadership are fully acknowledged. Their qualitative research—in which 76 Dutch retail workers were asked to name six attributes of a leader in general and to rate these characteristics on effectiveness—suggests that our implicit leadership theories are actually composed of effective and ineffective attributes and are thus not as completely romanticized as had previously been suggested. They used 15 dual categories to analyse participant responses and found evidence of both favourable/unfavourable and effective/ineffective statements.

 Blog box

Before looking ahead to the findings of Schyns and Schilling's study, reflect for a moment on your own implicit theories of leadership. Make notes on the characteristics you would associate with the idea of leadership. Where do these ideas come from? What experiences or individuals have shaped them? Do they include negative elements or are they essentially images of effective leadership? Capture your reflections in no more than 300 words.

Significant elements (based on frequency of occurrence) in the participants' implicit theories included pleasantness, communicativeness, strength, being a team player, charisma, devotion, tyranny, and being organized. Note that some of these—in particular being a team player (opposite subcategory: individualistic) and tyranny (opposite subcategory: participative)—were significant in both their positive and negative forms. In addition to noting the relatively small size of their study, the authors also noted the potentially significant cultural influences on their results and that Ling, Chia, and Fang (2000) conducted a similar study with Chinese participants and arrived at very different relevant categorizations.

Discussion points: Implicit theories of leadership—how do you see it?

● The studies by Bresnan (1995) and Schyns and Schilling (2010) both suggest some of the features which practising managers may see as important in relation to the role or behaviours of a leader. Would you agree with the features suggested by these authors? What others would you add based on your own experiences?

● In forming your own implicit theories of leadership, what experiences have been most important and why? How have social and cultural norms influenced the theories you hold? In what circumstances would you be prepared to challenge these norms?

● How might an awareness of the implicit leadership theories you hold help you to be more effective as a leader? How might it influence your attribution of leadership qualities to others?

In the mainstream

The romance of leadership

As already outlined in the introduction to this chapter, the 'followers as constructors of leadership' strand of writing focuses on how followers individually construct and represent leaders in their thought systems, and how they collectively, inter-subjectively agree what is meant by the term leadership in any given setting. A significant area of theory within this strand of writing is around the 'romance of leadership', which is based largely on the work of James Meindl, and is an exploration of the tendency (both within the literature and in organizational settings) to overestimate the significance of leadership and its impact on organizational success. The strong emphasis on leadership in organizational research literature is seen as both mirroring and perpetuating the hyped-up and often unrealistic expectations that are routinely placed on real leaders, most particularly in the arenas of business and politics. First introduced by Meindl, Ehrlich, and Dukerich in 1985, the phrase itself—'the romance of leadership'—refers to the tendency to attribute responsibility for company performance to organizational leaders and to disregard other factors which might have had a part to play in the achievement of a successful outcome, and denotes 'a strong belief—a faith—in the importance of leadership factors to the functioning and dysfunctioning of organised systems' (Meindl and Ehrlich, 1987: 91). It is a fundamentally constructionist approach in that it is concerned with how people—and specifically followers—explain the complex processes which underpin organizational performance.

Paying tribute to Meindl's work, Bligh and Schyns (2007: 343) describe the tendency to 'overuse and glorify leadership as a causal category' as being 'due primarily to a psychological need to make sense of complex organisational phenomena': as a result, they say, 'the concept of leadership has been elevated or inflated to an unwarranted status and significance'. In effect, Meindl and his followers suggest that the construct of leadership acts as a simplified, biased, and attractive way to make sense of organizational performance, and note that this 'romantic tendency' seems to have the greatest sway in times of extreme success or extreme failure. Meindl also coined the phrase 'social contagion' to denote the way in which the understanding of what was leadership and who was a leader was socially constructed through the 'spontaneous spread of affective and/or behavioural reactions among members of a group'. Since its inception as a radical leadership perspective, the effects of the romanticization of leadership have been studied within a number of different social science disciplines and in eleven different countries. Notable examples of the cultural range of the phenomenon can be found in Awamleh's (2003) research in Jordan and Shamir's (1992) research in Israel. The scope of this strand of research has also been extended to consider the role of the media in the process of contagion, and the manner in which the media develop

> ... constructions of leadership regularly and widely for our consumption... These images feed and expand our appetites for leadership products, appealing not only to our collective commitments to the concept but fixating us in particular on the personas and characteristics of the leaders themselves. (Chen and Meindl, 1991: 522)

The work of Chen and Meindl has been influential in highlighting the significance of the media in shaping our beliefs and ideas about leaders and leadership, and in drawing attention to how media images of 'celebrity CEOs' influence our views of the reputation and legitimacy of the firms they are seen to represent. On this basis, charismatic relationships between leaders and followers are understood as existing in the minds of followers and can be seen as a by-product of inter-follower processes and activities rather than as a function of the dynamics between leader and follower.

RESEARCH IN FOCUS: The construction of leadership images in the popular press

Building on Meindl's 'romanticization of leadership' thesis, this classic article by Chen and Meindl used content analysis of image descriptions and metaphors to explore the construction and reconstruction of leadership images that takes place in the popular media. It is a basic premise of this work that the media operate not purely to deliver us factual information, but to transmit what the authors call para-ideological messages—that is, messages which are indicative of the confluence of cultural conceptions and beliefs, both shaping and reflecting the views of the society in which they operate. In the case of the business media, their role is not just to report facts and information about organizational performance, but to transmit deeper messages about the role and function of organizations, and the part played by their leaders. Chen and Meindl identified four forces at work in the popular press, namely (1) anti-determinism—the belief that individuals determine the fate of organizations; (2) the effects of performance cues and attribution history on the leadership image construction process; (3) the professional values and ideology of news organizations as a reflection of culture; and (4) the role of organizational routinization in constraining and defining the constructions which come to be made.

Taking as a case study the dramatic fortunes during the 1980s of People Express Airlines Inc and their founder and chairman Donald Burr, the authors demonstrated the strategies used by the press to maintain consistency with previous constructions of leader identity, at the same time as plausibly accounting for dramatic changes of organizational fortune. Over a period of six years, the organization grew from nothing to being hugely successful before being acquired by a rival whilst on the point of collapse. Throughout this period, Donald Burr was at the helm and frequently in the press both for his radical humanistic management practices and as the perceived architect of organizational outcomes. Chen and Meindl's fine-grained analysis of how Burr was portrayed over this period offers a fascinating insight into the ease with which we are sold images of leaders and leadership, and how these are manipulated in the face of changing times.

Source: Chen, Chao C. and Meindl, James R. (1991) The construction of leadership images in the popular press: the case of Donald Burr and People Express. *Administrative Science Quarterly*, 36(4) 521–51.

Meindl was very clear that his perspective was not intended to be 'anti-leadership' but should instead be seen as complementary to existing leader-centric approaches in that it 'embraces the phenomenological significance of leadership to people's organisational experiences' (Meindl, 1995: 330). Implicit in this phenomenological perspective is the concept of leadership as an emergent—rather than a hierarchical—phenomenon and the potential for multiple constructions to emerge from the same setting or pattern of behaviours. As Meindl (1995: 331) phrased it, 'any given behavioural exertion of "leadership" by the leader can be associated with a wider range of constructions, and imbued with a wider range of meanings, than is otherwise assumed'.

A case in point: Steve Jobs and Apple

Set out below are just three of the thousands of media quotes that even a cursory internet search produces about cult figure Steve Jobs: these were accessed a few days after he stepped down as CEO of Apple, but there has seldom been a time in recent years when a similar haul could not have been found.

'Steve Jobs rescued Apple from near oblivion and turned it into a byword for quality, production values and beauty.' John Naughton, *Guardian*, 27 August 2011, 'What made Steve Jobs a giant amongst the world's greatest communicators'.

'Insanely creative Apple chief transforms a multi-billion dollar industry every few years.' Forbes 'world's billionaires' profile, March 2011 (accessed 28 August 2011).

'because we like to be seduced' Robert Cringely, *Inc Magazine*, 1 April 2004, 'America's 25 most fascinating entrepreneurs'.

This kind of media treatment of successful leaders is a graphic illustration of what Meindl referred to as the 'romanticization of leadership' and how it serves to inflate both our future expectations of leaders like Jobs and our perceptions of what 'leadership' consists in.

Psychoanalytic theories of leadership

Another strand in the literature looking at how ideas of leadership are constructed draws on psychoanalytic theories in emphasizing the importance of our early experiences in shaping and defining our individual leadership philosophies. Derived from the work of Sigmund Freud and Carl Jung, this approach highlights the centrality of our family origins and upbringing in understanding our behaviour as a leader or a follower. Thus, models of leadership we have from our parents, teachers, and other influential figures we encounter in our youth are likely to influence our understanding of what leadership is as well as our choice of whether to lead or to follow.

Based on these formative psychodynamic experiences, we might react to a leader in a dependent, counter-dependent, or an independent manner (Stech, 2004). Thus we might look to the leader for emotional and practical guidance in everything, rebelliously reject the leader's directives, or objectively assess the leader's directives and decide if they are ethical and reasonable before choosing how to act. In explaining why followers construct leaders in a dependent way, Shamir et al. (2007) point to the psychodynamic processes of projection and transference. Projection is when we attribute to another person our ideals, wishes, desires, and fantasies—for example die-hard fans of a pop star or movie star tend to see an idealized version of them rather than seeing them 'warts and all'. Transference is when we respond to another person as if that person were a parent or other significant figure from early childhood, for example by being subservient or showing undue admiration. These processes can be particularly salient during periods of crisis or threat, when people feel confused, helpless, or insecure. Their idealization of the leader is in no way related to the leader's actual abilities or any special characteristics. Nonetheless, through these psychodynamic processes leaders are seen as providing a means by which followers can reduce their level of anxiety and obtain a measure of psychological safety in an increasingly dynamic and ambiguous working environment.

It has been suggested (Popper, 2011) that these and other approaches to understanding the psychology of followers are actually key to understanding the influence leaders have over followers and the attraction that specific leaders—even poor ones—can have for them, either individually or *en masse*. So, for example, this approach can explain why followers sometimes allow or tolerate the creation of 'toxic leaders'—leaders who manipulate their followers' ordinary human needs and exploit their natural fears for their own advancement. Cult leaders or religious fundamentalists might fall into this category: but to a lesser extent 'management gurus' such as Peter Senge or Stephen Covey might be said to exercise a similar influence over followers seeking a miracle cure for their organizational problems. Over the decades, we have seen numerous management fads—just in time, business process reengineering, the learning organization, to name but three—promulgated as the way forward. Where do we draw the line in deciding whether these philosophies are really in our best interests or are just commercially successful manipulations of our desire to be more effective leaders?

 Leadership in the media: The Magnificent Seven (or The Seven Samurai)

In an American remake of the classic 1954 film *The Seven Samurai*, *The Magnificent Seven* tells the story of a Mexican peasant village, oppressed by bandits, who offer what little they have as payment to American gunfighters to come and defend their homes. The seven who eventually come to the villagers' aid all come for their own reasons and bringing their own 'baggage' but within the group are some fascinating portraits of psychodynamic theory at work. Foremost amongst these is the relationship between Chico—from a peasant home himself but trying desperately to deny his origins—and Chris, the leader of the seven, whom he admires and tries to emulate. In this relationship we see both the projection of all of Chico's leadership ideals onto Chris, and his counter-dependent reaction to Chris when he feels belittled by the tests he is set by the older, more experienced man. In another interesting relationship, we see Bernardo—a fatherly figure amongst the gun-fighting group—adopted by the peasant village children. Less glamorous than most of his compatriots, he at once represents a recognizable image of leadership and provides a contrast with the children's own fathers whom they view as cowardly for not having stood up to the bandits before. Again, we see the complex psychodynamic origins of their understanding of leadership played out in this touching relationship. All-in-all this is a film that goes far beyond the 'shoot 'em up' genre to which it is often seen as belonging.

Social identity theory of leadership

The previous section dealt with psychological constructions of leadership at the individual level. In this section, we consider the individual in their social context and the manner in which social identity theory has been applied to leadership. Under this theory, it is suggested that the selection or acceptance of a leader is based on their prototypicality or representativeness within the group (Van Knippenberg and Hogg, 2003), where Hogg defines prototypicality as 'a fuzzy set of features that captures in-group similarities and intergroup differences regarding beliefs, behaviours and feelings' (Hogg, 2005: 56). This theory builds on the idea that 'like attracts like' but suggests that the followers choose the leader rather than the reverse. As such, it sees leadership as a structural feature of in-groups, such that 'leader' and 'follower' are inter-dependent roles embedded within a social system which is bounded by common group or category membership. Leadership dynamics are thus likely to be significantly affected by the social cognitive processes associated with group membership—processes relating to self-categorization, assimilation, and depersonalization—and the possession of the prototypical or normative characteristics of a psychologically salient in-group may be at least as important for leadership as being charismatic or fitting a particular leadership stereotype. Although essentially an emergent view of leadership, the theory can also be applied to enduring or structurally designated leadership situations when group membership salience is particularly elevated (for example, in times of organizational merger or acquisition, or in the face of team restructuring or underperformance).

The social influence process through which a leader is selected or acquires support within this approach is said to occur in three broad phases (Hogg, 2005):

1. *Prototypicality*—within a salient group, a group member (or appointed leader) is perceived as occupying the most prototypical position as a result of best embodying the behaviours to which others aspire to conform. This results in an embryonic role differentiation into followers and leaders.

2. *Social attraction*—the person occupying the most prototypical position may acquire the ability to actively influence other members of the group because he or she is viewed as socially attractive, such that they will eventually be imbued with prestige or status within the group. The prototypical person is thus able to exercise leadership by having his or her ideas accepted more readily or more widely than the ideas of others.

3. *Attribution and information processing*—group members begin to attribute the success of their leader to that person's special personality rather than because of their prototypicality. Thus the prototypical member begins to exercise active leadership and to become less prototypical in the process: at the same time, members begin to attribute the leader's success to internal or intrinsic leadership ability thus constructing a 'charismatic' leadership persona.

Social identity theory can be helpful in making sense of a number of contemporary issues in leadership. For example, research has shown that in Western societies, demographic minorities (for example, women and ethnic minorities) find it difficult to attain top leadership positions. If organizational or wider cultural prototypes (such as modes of speech, dress, attitude, and interactional style) are socially cast so that minorities do not match them, then this theory would explain why they are unlikely to be endorsed as leaders, particularly under conditions when organizational prototypicality is important: that is, when organizational identification and cohesion are high, such as in times of uncertainty or crisis.

From a critical perspective

Followers as co-producers of leadership

Originally promulgated by Shamir et al. (2007), 'followers as co-producers of leadership' is advocated as a critical alternative to the five roles we have looked at so far, and propounds the notion that leadership is a relationship based on mutual exchange between leaders and followers. Thus in opposition to the traditional view of leadership as a downward influence process, authors such as Hollander (1958) have suggested that leadership is a two-way influence and social exchange relationship in which leaders and followers influence and respond to each other. Similarly, Messick (2005) describes leadership as a mutually beneficial relationship predicated on psychological exchange in which leaders and followers each receive benefits that are valued by them. So, for example, leaders provide followers with vision and direction, and protection and security, whilst followers provide leaders with commitment and effort, cooperation and sacrifice, and respect and obedience. Not surprisingly, given the idealized nature of these exchanges, it is pretty rare that either side actually delivers all these things to the other! Nonetheless, in an effective leader–follower relationship there is a sort of 'implicit contract' between leaders and followers that assumes good intent on both sides and ensures that while a broad-based equilibrium between the needs and expectations of each is maintained, leadership will be sustained.

Leader member exchange theory

The dynamic co-production of leadership has, perhaps, been best operationalized in the form of Leader–Member Exchange theory, or LMX (see, for example, Graen and Uhi-Bien, 1995). Leader–Member Exchange theory is centred on the interactions between leaders and followers, in terms of dyadic, 1:1 relationships. It sees these relationships as the focal point of the leadership process—differing from traditional theory which focuses on leaders and considers followers *en masse* as passive recipients—and sees leadership itself not as hierarchical but as occurring through the relational dynamics throughout the organization. As such, this approach focuses on the processes of meaning-making in relation to leadership, rather than the content of the leadership construct itself. To this end Uhl-Bien (2006) claims that LMX—and the more general typology of relational leadership theories to which it belongs—should be viewed as an overarching framework for the study of leadership, which itself should be seen as a social influence process through which emergent coordination and change are constructed and produced.

Early studies referred to LMX as 'vertical dyadic linkage theory' and looked at the linkages leaders formed with each of their subordinates, identifying two general types—those that were based on expanded and negotiated role responsibilities (described as 'in-group') and those that were based on the formal employment contract (called the 'out-group'). Within an organizational unit, subordinates became part of the in-group or the out-group based on how well they worked with the leader and how well he/she worked with them (Graen, 1976). Subordinates who are interested in negotiating with the leader what they are willing to do for the group could become part of the in-group. These negotiations involve exchanges in which subordinates take on activities that go beyond their formal job descriptions, and the leader, in turn, does more for the subordinate such as sharing more information with them, giving them more interesting work or opportunities for advancement, etc. If the subordinates are not interested in taking on new and different responsibilities, they remain part of the out-group.

In later studies, the focus moved to how LMX theory was related to organizational effectiveness, and in particular, how the quality of leader–member exchanges was related to positive outcomes. These studies found that high quality leader–member exchanges resulted in less employee turnover, more positive performance evaluations, higher frequency of promotions, greater organizational commitment, more desirable work assignments, better job attitudes, greater participation, and more attention and support from the leader.

Findings from these studies were the impetus for current research in LMX, around how exchanges between leaders and members form the basis for leadership making. This prescriptive approach to leadership suggests that a leader should develop high-quality exchanges with all of their subordinates rather than just a few, with the aim of making every employee feel as if they are part of the in-group in order to maximize the performance benefits shown to accrue to this group. Graen and Uhl-Bien (1991) suggest that leadership making develops progressively over time in three phases:

1. *Stranger or role-taking phase*—interactions are generally rule-bound and rely heavily on contractual relationships similar to those experienced by out-group members. The subordinate is generally compliant to the influence of the leader, and exchanges are fairly low quality. Both sides are motivated largely by self-interest.

2. *Acquaintance or role-making phase*—one side or the other makes an offer for improved, career-oriented social exchanges, such as sharing more resources and personal or work-related information. This is a testing period for both sides to assess whether the subordinate is interested in taking on more roles or responsibilities and the leader to provide more challenges and support. Exchanges improve in quality and move away from purely rule-driven interactions.

3. *Mature partnership or routinization phase*—exchanges are of high quality, the relationship is mutually negotiated, and benefits are reciprocated. The relationship has been tested and found to be strong and trustworthy and now has marked in-group characteristics. Where a number of these relationships exist, the result is a strongly cohesive team or group.

These phases are summarized in Figure 6.1, which also shows the different elements of the leadership making process.

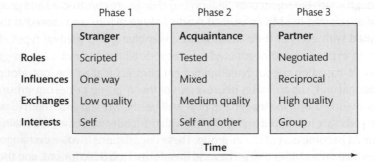

	Phase 1	Phase 2	Phase 3
	Stranger	**Acquaintance**	**Partner**
Roles	Scripted	Tested	Negotiated
Influences	One way	Mixed	Reciprocal
Exchanges	Low quality	Medium quality	High quality
Interests	Self	Self and other	Group

Time →

Figure 6.1 Leader–member exchange theory—phases in leadership making

Source: Graen, G. B. and Uhl-Bien, M. (1995) Relationship-based Approach to Leadership: Development of Leader–Member Exchange (LMX) Theory of Leadership Over 25 Years. *The Leadership Quarterly* 6 (2) 219–47. Adapted with permission.

Blog box

Bringing everyone in one's team into the 'in-group' may be good for performance, but it isn't always easy to achieve! As Director of an Executive MBA programme, I have a number of colleagues within my teaching and administrative team, all with different motivations and different views of how the programme should be run. One member of the teaching team is near to retirement and, although he is keen to do the best he can for his students, he isn't interested in taking on more responsibility or in taking an innovative stance towards programme pedagogy. Another member of the teaching team is keen to develop as an academic, but places a lower value on teaching responsibilities. Within the administrative team, some members are lifelong professionals, whilst others see their role as a stepping stone to other things or as a 9–5 job which they will happily leave when they start a family. As a leader, I try to develop and maintain quality one-to-one relationships with all members of the team, but that doesn't necessarily mean that high performance will result! Sometimes members of the group will simply have different personal goals and a degree of compromise within the team will be inevitable. (MIW)

The strengths of LMX theory are that it is strongly descriptive, in that people can easily relate to the characteristics of the different phases, it is unique in leadership theory in focusing on dyadic relationships, and also noteworthy in the attention it focuses on communication in leadership. There is also substantial research providing evidence of correlation between high-quality leader–member exchanges and a range of positive organizational outcomes. On the downside, it can be criticized for running counter to basic human values of fairness—in that it produces in-groups and out-groups—although this was not its aim. It can also be argued that the theory has yet to be fully developed—for example, it currently fails to explain *how* high-quality leader–member exchanges are created (only the order of phases, not how to move from one to the other).

Whatever its shortcomings, LMX offers a broadly sympathetic approach to the creation of meaningful leader–follower relationships at a micro-level. This is in stark contrast to the work of Gemmill and Oakley (1992)—fierce critics of the leadership construct at the macro-level—who propound the view that leadership is an alienating social myth that functions to reinforce the existing social order. This radical critique of the leadership construct as it is constructed at the societal level underpins a raft of standpoint and emancipatory sociological perspectives which continue to this day—though rarely so powerfully expressed. This radical critique of leadership is discussed in more detail in Chapter 11.

A note on 'failed' leadership

Throughout this chapter we have been looking at how the notion of leadership is socially constructed by followers. Implicitly, we have been talking about how *successful* or *effective* leadership is constructed, since implicitly we tend to discount leadership that is ineffective or produces poor results, often saying that it does not constitute leadership at all. It is worth noting, however, that our constructions of successful leadership must inevitably contain the seeds of their opposite—failed leadership. Whether we consider this in terms of the outcomes produced or the ways in which the act of leading is performed, followers—and leaders—attribute success and failure as an integral part of the social construction process. We saw this in Schyns and Schilling's (2010) work earlier in the chapter. This theme of how success and failure in leadership are constructed—by both leaders and followers—is also explored in the case study which concludes the chapter.

Cultural differences and the construction of leadership

We have already seen that the idea of leadership as a socially constructed phenomenon leads us to the potential for leadership to be constructed in different ways in different settings or by different groups of people. If we take this to its natural conclusion, then we would expect different national groups to have different constructions of leadership based on their different cultural heritages and characteristics. Of course we are all familiar with common national stereotypes and how these might lead us to construct leaders from particular countries (what would a stereotypical leader from your country be like?) but there has been considerable research into the genuine differences between nations and how this might impact on what constitutes effective leadership around the world. The classic research in this field was conducted by Hofstede (1980) who undertook a cross-cultural study of 116,000 employees of the same multi-national company located in 40 countries. Figure 6.2 outlines the four dimensions of cultural difference identified by this study.

Power distance: Extent to which an unequal distribution of power is accepted by members of a society	
Low power distance—managers and employees expected to work more cooperatively together, fewer levels of hierarchy and devolved decision-making (e.g. Australia, Denmark, Sweden, Austria)	High power distance—more hierarchical levels and more fixed roles and responsibilities (e.g. Mexico, India, Philippines, Malaysia).
Uncertainty avoidance: Extent to which members of a society feel threatened by ambiguous situations and have created beliefs and institutions which try to avoid these	
Low uncertainty avoidance—tolerance for ambiguity in structures and procedures, weak loyalty to employer and short average duration of employment (e.g. UK, USA, Denmark, India, Singapore)	High uncertainty avoidance—value job security and strong procedural support (e.g. Greece, Portugal, Japan, France, Peru).
Individualism/collectivism: Tendency to take care of oneself and one's family versus tendency to work together for the collective good	
Tendency towards individualism—individual achievement is what counts, limited concern for the wider community (e.g. USA, UK, Australia, Canada)	Tendency towards collectivism—collective achievement is prized, individuals see themselves as part of the wider community (e.g. Taiwan, Mexico, Greece, Venezuela)
Masculinity/femininity: Extent to which highly assertive masculine values predominate versus extent to which collaborative feminine values predominate	
Masculine values predominate—acquisition of money at the expense of others, live in order to work (e.g. Japan, Australia, Italy, Mexico)	Feminine values predominate—showing sensitivity and concern for other's welfare, work life balance (e.g. Thailand, Sweden, Denmark)

Figure 6.2 Hofstede's dimensions of cultural difference

Source: Hofstede, G. (2003) *Culture's Consequences: International differences in work-related values* (2nd Edition). London. Sage. Adapted with permission.

Whilst work of this nature must inevitably contain oversimplifications (for example, within the Spanish nation, the Catalan sub-culture is quite distinct from Castilian Spanish culture) it served to provide a point of departure for understanding how leadership practices which worked in one country might not work in another. So, for example, a manager moving from Canada—where the culture is individualist in nature—to Taiwan—where it is much more collectivist—might get a poor response from his team if he tried to motivate them via the introduction of performance measures based on individual performance. Adopting measures which recognize the input of the whole team, or place achievements in the context of the benefit to the community as a whole are likely get a more positive response and see the leader rated as more effective by subordinates and superiors alike. Later work by Hofstede and Bond (1988) led to a fifth dimension being added, relating to long-term versus short-term orientation. This concerns the ability to pursue long-term and general goals versus the need to focus on short-term gain or advantage. Hofstede and Bond suggested that China, Japan, and South Korea were examples of cultures with a long-term orientation, whilst Canada, Pakistan, Nigeria, and the UK tended to focus much more on the immediate future.

A decade later, Trompenaars (1993) had a different way of looking at cultural differences. Coming from a consultancy background, he took a more practical approach to helping managers work effectively in cross-cultural environments. The findings of his survey of 15,000 respondents from a range of organizational settings are shown in Figure 6.3 and contain seven dimensions of culture.

Interestingly, only one of these dimensions—individualism versus collectivism—coincides with those identified by Hofstede. Since these two pioneers, the cultural aspects of leadership and followership have become popular research territory. Most notable, perhaps, amongst

Universalism—culture is driven by rules and prefers rational and logical approach (e.g. Canada, UK, USA)	*Particularism*—culture is based on relationships and encourages flexibility in interpretation of rules (e.g. China, Thailand)
Affective cultures—emotions are revealed more openly (e.g. Italy)	*Neutral cultures*—people may find emotions difficult to handle (e.g. Japan, Germany)
Specific cultures—managers separate their work relationships from other relationships (e.g. USA, UK)	*Diffuse cultures*—relationships at work influence relationships outside work (e.g. Malaysia)
Achieving culture—status is considered to be achievement based (e.g. USA, Scandinavia)	*Ascribing culture*—status is due to age, education, gender, etc. (e.g. Hong Kong, Argentina, Egypt)
Time as sequence—suggests a rational linear approach to issues based on present performance and short-term relationships (e.g. USA)	*Time as synchronisation*—suggests there could be parallel activities and sense of the past with long-term relationships (e.g. France)
Inner directed—belief that individuals should seek to control the natural and human environment; they are masters of their fate (e.g. USA, Switzerland)	*Outer directed*—sees world as more powerful than individuals and needing to be in harmony with nature (e.g. China)

Figure 6.3 Trompenaars' dimensions of national culture

Source: Trompenaars, Fons and Hampden-Turner, Charles (2012) *Riding the Waves of Culture: understanding diversity in global business* (3rd Edition). Nicholas Brealey Publishing and McGraw Hill Education. Reproduced with permission.

their successors is House et al.'s (2004) GLOBE project—standing for Global Leadership and Organizational Behaviour Effectiveness. Developed on the back of Robert House's observation that charismatic leadership behaviours, which have been studied in a wide array of cultural settings, might be universally acceptable and effective, the project aimed to explore followers' perceptions of prototypical leaders around the world. The study, which involved 127 investigators from 62 cultures, and interviewed 17,300 middle managers from 951 organizations, identified nine major attributes of culture, namely:

Future orientation	Institutional collectivism
Gender egalitarianism	Permanence orientation
Assertiveness	Power concentration/decentralization
Humane orientation	Uncertainty avoidance
In-group collectivism	

Four of these attributes (albeit renamed) align with Hofstede's original dimensions, whilst others represent concerns that appear more characteristic of modern society. Notwithstanding the existence of these core dimensions across the globe, the study found wide variation in the values and practices associated with them. The programme has had many critics (including Den Hartog and Dickson, 2004; Peterson and Castro, 2006; Dansereau and Yamminaro, 2006) but perhaps the fundamental flaw remains, as noted by Jackson and Parry (2008: 78), that its 'theoretical base is still firmly rooted in American soil'.

Chapter summary

In this chapter we have discussed:

- The notion that ideas of what constitutes leadership are socially constructed by followers, rather than inherent in the intentions or characteristics of leaders
- Meindl's proposition that, both in academic writing and in the media, the idea of leadership—and the results it can produce—are 'romanticized' to a degree that is unrealistic and not representative of actual practice
- Psychoanalytic and social identity theories of leadership which explore different aspects of how leadership identities are individually and socially constructed, and the implications for leaders
- Perceptions of failed leadership, as a counter to the tendency—both in the literature and in practice—to focus exclusively on effective or successful leaders
- How cultural differences may impact on the constructions of leadership that arise in different parts of the world, and the implications of this in an increasingly mobile and international working environment

Integrative case study: Accounting for failure—a Principal's perspective

Whilst the notion of a failing college tends to be seen as encompassing a range of academic and financial outcomes, success or failure for a college principal can be understood (and felt) in much more localized, personal terms. In the case study outlined below, there were respects in which Catherine viewed herself as having failed despite the fact that Wentworth College, of which she was Principal, consistently produced good results, both for students and in terms of Ofsted inspections. For her, the notion of failure was about the poor relationship which existed between herself and her Vice Principal, Ted, and to a lesser extent her concerns about the lack of coherent leadership currently being provided by the senior management team (SMT).

Singing from the same hymn sheet?

Despite good Ofsted inspections, an external consultancy report has recently identified a lack of shared management priorities within the college and the tendency for members of the SMT to 'go their own way' by pursuing often competing initiatives. Catherine herself has some concerns around this issue and her inability to align her team around a shared agenda, which she feels may be the result of poor communication and weak leadership. So, for example, when Catherine asks John (Assistant Principal for Teaching and Learning) if he is going to the 'blue sky' strategizing meeting with their ICT consultants concerning the development of a new management information system for the college, he says he hasn't received any information about the purpose of the meeting, and so has decided not to go. In a further attempt to ensure appropriate attendance at the forthcoming meeting (which has already had to be cancelled once) Catherine then asks the same question of Ted (her Vice Principal and a key player) who informs her that the post-inspection action plan takes priority and hence he won't be attending either. Although Catherine has repeatedly made the case for the importance of the meeting, her message doesn't seem to be getting through to her senior team.

Clearly, this is an issue for Catherine herself, who feels she has been put on the back foot in her communications with her SMT, and that the messages she is trying put across don't appear to carry much weight. When the 'blue sky' meeting does finally take place, John takes the lead in terms of liaising with the ICT systems consultants and ideas put forward by Catherine appear to be as much for consideration by her colleagues as by the consultants. As the meeting progresses, one of the consultants comments that: 'What I don't understand is who's driving this within the college.'

Despite these warning signs, Catherine's concern in relation to the SMT is still mild and she is reluctant to step in with a 'uniting vision' of the college for fear of suppressing what she views as the SMT's undoubted talent and ability. She continues to believe that 'light touch' leadership will eventually win them round without killing off creativity and initiative, and that as long as Ofsted results continue to be good the communication issues which lead to such incidents shouldn't be given too much weight.

Who is failing who?

Catherine would be the first to admit that she has a difficult relationship with her Vice Principal, Ted, but her assessment of why and how the relationship is 'failing' is open to interpretation. So, for example, when Catherine calls a pre-meeting to talk about their strategy for a forthcoming funding meeting with the Learning and Skills Council, the funding body to the further education sector, Ted holds a side conversation with John and makes 'laddish' jokes. When Catherine briefly leaves the room, Ted settles into a serious conversation about questions the LSC might raise and how they might address them, but stops as soon as she returns. When Catherine tries to focus the meeting's attention on the need for planning and preparation, Ted is back to joking again: 'Don't worry, we're good at winging it, Cath!'

(Continued...)

Catherine feels powerless to prevent herself being undermined by her Vice Principal in front of other senior colleagues or to effectively assert her authority or challenge his unprofessional behaviour. Ted further undermines Catherine by presenting himself as 'the real leader of the college' in public meetings: a presumption in which she often colludes by making herself 'invisible'. In the absence of a strong lead from her, it is easy for him to step in and fill the gap. At the same time, Catherine has doubts about Ted's capabilities in the VP role, and his failure to share the burden of leadership with her. A rational assessment of Ted's performance would include his inability to use ICT effectively, his failure to complete staff assessments, and the impact of his frequent mood changes on staff working with him. There are also numerous instances of unprofessional conduct on his part—for example refusing to participate in meetings, saying outrageous and inappropriate things whilst representing the college, and making one department within the college a 'no go area' for Catherine by an attitude of extreme possessiveness towards it. Despite all these indications of under-performance and blatant disrespect, Catherine sees the difficulties within the relationship as being her failure rather than Ted's. She believes that if she were more supportive of him, he could become a fully performing member of the team at the same time as accepting her as a leader. In this instance, her constructions of success and failure are entirely personal and from the perspective of one individual feeling responsible for the well-being of another, rather than as a Principal responsible for the delivery of quality provision to her students and needing to hold her VP accountable for the responsibilities he has within that role.

Note: All the people and incidents in this case study are real but names have been changed and the case study itself has been invented as a composite of the experiences and feelings of three 'failing' principals encountered in the overall study of leadership in the UK Learning and Skills sector.

Case study questions

- Catherine's college is clearly successful, but should we attribute that to her leadership, the work of others within the college (including the SMT) or other factors not discussed within the case study?
- Do you think Catherine is justified in down-playing the issues within her senior team? Do you believe the college can continue to be successful without a 'uniting vision'?
- Would you agree with Catherine's view that she 'failed' as a leader in her relationship with her Vice Principal, and if so, how? How would you have dealt with his underperformance and lack of respect?
- If you had been a teacher or middle manager in this college, what constructions of leadership do you think you would have put on the behaviours you observed within the senior team?

Further reading

Shamir, B., Pillai, R., Bligh, M. C., and Uhl-Bien, M. (2007) *Follower-centred Perspectives on Leadership: A Tribute to the memory of James Meindl.* Charlotte, NC: Information Age Publishing.

Chen, Chao C. and Meindl, James R. (1991) The construction of leadership images in the popular press: the case of Donald Burr and People Express. *Administrative Science Quarterly*, 36(4) 521–51.

Uhl-Bien, Mary (2006) Relational leadership theory: Exploring the social processes of leadership and organising. *The Leadership Quarterly*, 17, 654–76.

Popper, Micha (2011) Toward a theory of followership. *Review of General Psychology*, 15 (1) 29–36.

Leaders and leading: Everyone is a leader now!

 Learning outcomes

On completion of this chapter you will:

- Know the critique of traditional leadership theory that led to the development of ideas of shared and distributed leadership
- Understand the core concept of distributed leadership
- Be familiar with ideas that share the basic premise of leadership not being solely the property of the individual such as shared, collective, and collaborative leadership
- Be aware of the research evidence linked to distributed leadership
- Appreciate the limits of the distributed concept and the main criticisms of this approach to leadership

Introduction

This chapter describes a radical attempt to redefine the very idea of leadership, moving it away from the belief that leadership is the preserve of a single individual. As charted in earlier chapters, leadership has been thought of as the preserve of 'great men', of individuals who either possess certain attributes, or who have the ability to be flexible in certain situations. Either way, it is the individual who is seen as a leader, positioned at or near the top of an organization, creating the vision, setting the direction, and taking the decisions. The individual with the position has been seen as the one who influences in order to achieve the purpose of the organization.

This belief in the individual leader has spawned a leadership research agenda that has taken the individual as the single unit of analysis and places a great emphasis on the ability of the individual to have an all-pervasive influence on the organization. Thorpe, Gold, and Lawler (2007) note that while there is a large amount of anecdotal evidence of the importance of the individual leader, there is very little empirical research evidence that backs the idea that an individual leader actually has such a great level of influence.

Distributed leadership challenges this belief in the individual as leader. It proposes that leadership may actually be the result of people collectively performing acts of leadership in close collaboration with each other, with a shared understanding of desired outcomes. From this perspective, leadership becomes an interdependent process that occurs between people which results in an outcome that may be observed as collective leadership behaviour.

Authors writing on distributed leadership generally see this collective leadership as beneficial to organizations. The concept has its origins in the education sector and the existence of distributed leadership in schools has been linked to improvement in learning outcomes for students. It has also been said to improve the leadership capacity of an organization, and give employees a wider understanding of how interdependent organizations actually are (Harris, 2008).

In this chapter we will consider the concept and origins of distributed leadership. We will explore distributed leadership as a response to the changing nature and form of our organizations. The distributed leadership literature will be examined, starting with Gronn's critique of leadership and his work developing this concept. Finally, we will consider the critique offered against the concept of distributed leadership.

In the mainstream

There are various theories about when distributed leadership was first developed as a concept. Harris (2008) suggested that the idea of a form of leadership that was not solely focused on the individual can be seen as early as the 1920s and probably existed earlier than this. Gronn (2000) cites the first author to use the term explicitly as being Gibb (1954), who said that leadership was 'probably best conceived as a group quality, as a set of functions which must be carried out by the group' (Gibb, 1954, cited by Gronn, 2000: 324). Gibb was investigating influence across different formal and informal groups. He described the influence that could clearly be seen as attached to an individual as 'focused' influence, and that which seemed to move between individuals in a group as they gained influence in a particular moment as being 'distributed' influence.

Gronn (2002) took on these concepts of focused and distributed approaches to develop the initial theory of distributed leadership that will be explored in this chapter. Gronn's notion of distributed leadership seeks to see leadership as the product of multiple hands across an organization, resisting the desire to privilege the actions of an individual and so bestow on them the term of sole leader.

A distributed view of leadership stems directly from the critique of the concept and study of leadership made by Gronn (2003). After studying leadership for over 20 years, Gronn identified six areas of concern with the predominant views of leadership in the mainstream research and indeed more generally held across Western society. We will briefly cover each of Gronn's areas of concern in turn.

Critique of traditional leadership theory

The relationship between leadership and management

The concern here is with the favouring of the terms leader, leading, or leadership over manager, managing, or management. Gronn (2003) points out that these terms are generally ascribed to a person by colleagues, observing the actual behaviour of the leader/manager in question. This definition of a person due to the tasks they perform can mean that essential management tasks, and thus management in general, begins to be seen as dull, mundane, and dreary, when in fact it is essential to running effective organizations. Gronn's concern is that people who are attributed the title of leader are somehow privileged over those who are attributed as managers. Leaders are seen as greater, more able, rarer, and more exceptional than managers (Alvesson and Sveningsson, 2003). For a more detailed discussion of the distinction between management and leadership see Chapter 3.

Leadership, influence and power

Gronn (2003) questions whether the term leadership should in practice hold a special place above concepts such as power and influence. He points out that there has developed a hierarchy in which people think about these concepts, with the ideas of power and influence, along with those of authority, coercion, and manipulation, being subsumed into the concept of leadership. In part, this elevation of leadership has been driven by the difficulty in determining exactly how these three terms relate to each other.

The majority of research and discussion on the concept of power has taken place between academics from the political sciences. This has included examination of the concentrations and distributions of power in government, political, and social areas. This type of examination, along with the majority of this research into power, has not been transferred into the literature on leadership to any great extent (Gronn, 2003). If power can be considered distributed across political and social societies, then leadership, which is so intimately bound up with notions of power, influence, and authority, can surely also be considered from a distributed point of view, rather than it being purely the possession of an individual. For a more detailed discussion of the relationships between power and leadership see Chapter 2.

Other explanations for what we believe to be leaders or leadership

Gronn describes leadership as having a 'privileged explanatory status' (Gronn, 2003: 277). The causal nature of individual leadership is questioned here, and Gronn suggests that there are several activities normally associated with leadership that could be explained in other ways. Leadership has become a default explanation for a number of work activities or practices that may be explained by examining the type of task or person doing the task rather than the impact of a leader on the outcome of the task. In this way, leadership has been preferred to other explanations, allegedly before those other possibilities have been considered. It is the preference for leadership as an explanation that concerns Gronn most, and the desire to see leadership as one element amongst others of equal value that drives his critique of leadership theory.

Leadership and the division of labour

Here we come to a key criticism of leadership ideas—the conceptualization of leadership being defined by having followers. The implicit assumption in the leadership literature is that leaders must have followers, and the simplistic belief is that all members of an organization must therefore fit into one of these two categories, thus creating a binary division of labour. Gronn's concern is that this binary definition prescribes a set of relationships rather than describing what these relationships are actually like in reality. As anyone who has been in a position of authority would acknowledge, you are always reporting to someone, and thus the exclusive juxtaposition of leader and follower can be seen to be a myth.

Blog box

As a non-executive Board Director of a company, I see the myth of the leader/follower divide on a regular basis. The CEO, nominally defined as the leader of the organization, has to bring all major changes and decisions to the Board, and follow the lead of the Board once these decisions have been discussed. He may try to lead the Board, but will at times have to follow the Board's decisions. However, the Board itself is subject to followership as well, having to follow standards set out by the standards committee, regulations laid down by government, charity and accounting bodies, and measures set out by the lenders.

Being a progressive organization, our governance structure includes a good deal of involvement from customers. There are times when customer voices have led the discussions in meetings, and the executives of the business have had to follow this lead, thus clearly demonstrating that we are all simultaneously leaders and followers despite the lofty job titles we may hold! (CS)

The division of labour in modern organizations rarely creates situations where there is a single authority figure with a number of followers doing the bidding of the one. Rather it has become a coordinated activity where a number of people come together to achieve a desired outcome. This coming together usually involves a process to be followed, of which a leader may be part, but will not necessarily be the most important part. It is becoming increasingly clear that modern organizations, with their focus on flat hierarchies and flexible working practices, can no longer claim to divide labour between the leaders and the followers, but rather need to reconceptualize this binary definition to better reflect the actual practice of getting work done.

Discussion point: Is everyone a follower?

Reflect on a leadership position you have held.

- Did you do this alone?
- Where you totally in charge, or did you have to liaise or report to someone else?
- Have you ever occupied a leadership position where you were not a follower at some stage?

The cult of exceptionality

The fifth concern of Gronn (2003) is the monopoly of the individual when it comes to research into leadership. From the original trait theories (Chapter 4), to the transformational and charismatic theories (Chapter 5), we see an assumption that leadership is the preserve of individuals who are exceptional in some way. By conceptualizing leaders as exceptional, followers—and perhaps also managers—are automatically conceptualized as unexceptional. Gronn rightly points out that this conceptualization is unhelpful at best, and at worst can create a culture of 'learned helplessness and disempowerment' (Gronn, 2003: 282) that could lead to employees becoming demotivated and disengaged with the primary activities of the organization, and indeed with the desire to take on a leadership position. A self-belief that says that leadership is for the exceptional, and a humility that leads a person to assume that they are not themselves exceptional, could lead to perfectly equipped employees not seeking senior positions.

Case in point: Perceptions of leadership on a development course

Leadership for Housing was developed in 2005 by Lancaster University Management School in partnership with the National Housing Federation (NHF). Research from the NHF showed that employees in the housing sector were 70 per cent female and/or from ethnic minorities. However, the majority of housing association CEOs were white males. The Leadership for Housing programme was created in part to address this issue, and to give women and people from ethnic minorities the confidence to get the senior level jobs.

Leadership for Housing has completed six cohorts at the time of writing. What has come through very clearly is an assumption made by some delegates on the programme of what embodies leadership. This assumption has been defined by numerous delegates in their reflective assignments as 'charismatic white men'. Delegates on the programme came to realize that this was a 'shadow belief' (Cashman, 2008), a belief about leadership that held them back from seeking to progress to the most senior jobs because they were not white, or not charismatic, or not male. In other words they did not fit with what they believed leadership looked like.

Having gained an understanding of their 'shadow belief' and a broader knowledge of leadership, delegates found themselves in a better position to decide whether or not they wanted and indeed could attain the top jobs in the sector. A number of alumni have done this, gaining the position of Managing Director or CEO of UK housing associations.

Standards-based leadership

Gronn's final concern is linked to the previous point of exceptionality, and the assumption of the increased causal influence that leaders are assumed to have over organizational outcomes. This has led to the development of standards for leaders, a design that recruiters of leaders can follow to get the right people, and which people in senior positions will follow to be seen to be leaders. This 'designer-leadership' can be seen as a state, company, or regulatory body attempting to create the type of leaders it wants, and by doing so develop a form of cloning mechanism for all leaders across a particular sector which serves to normalize leaders' behaviours by favouring one set of data on what is considered a good decision or good behaviour by a leader over a different set of data.

These six concerns of Gronn's led him to try to conceive of distributed leadership, which was more in line with a political science view of the distribution of power. It is a view on leadership that rejects the assumption that leadership is the provision of exceptional individuals, and suggests that cooperation or coordination between individuals has a greater impact on outcomes than the actions of an individual alone.

Leadership in the media: Harry Potter and the Philosopher's Stone

The denouement of the first book and film of the *Harry Potter* series sees the main characters, Harry, Ron and Hermione, attempting to reach a fabled philosophers stone by tackling several seemingly insurmountable tasks. The first is a giant three-headed dog, which, in the book, they sneak past while Harry plays a flute to keep him asleep. The second is a plant called Devil's Snare which tries to trap them. This requires Hermione to take the lead using her knowledge of plants and her wand to direct the others to safety. Third is a test of skill on a broomstick and Harry comes to the fore here, working with the others to grab the exit door key and get out of the room alive. Fourth is a live game of wizard chess. Here Ron takes the lead having the greater knowledge and expertise at chess. He employs his knowledge of the rules and moves of the game to win, although at some cost to himself. The film then moves to the end point, with Harry alone facing the final danger, whilst the book describes several more tasks that are completed by the three close friends working together and taking the lead when their gifts or skills were most relevant.

In this example we can see the three main elements of distributed leadership known collectively as conjoint activity (described below): spontaneous collaboration, intuitive working relationships, and institutional practices. The interdependence described by authors of collective, collaborative, shared, and distributed leadership is evident, as is the high level of trust and mutual concern described as important aspects that enable distributed leadership to occur.

Distributed leadership

Distributed leadership is a commonly perceived and commonly misunderstood phenomenon. As Gosling, Bolden, and Petrov (2009: 303) state 'It is not really obvious what it refers to, and yet everyone seems to know what it means'.

At the heart of ideas of distributed leadership is the belief that leadership is not the preserve of a single individual, but is a concept that is more fluid, moving between coordinated and collaborating sets of employees in an organization. The focus of distributed leadership is on the relationships and interactions between members of an organization, and their interaction with the situational context within which they are working. Thus it is a richer, more complicated perspective on leadership than the traditional view of individual leaders.

Whilst at its core distributed leadership questions the assumption that leadership is the sole prerogative of an exceptional individual, this does not mean that it is a proposed replacement for the type of individual leadership discussed in previous chapters. As Spillane, Halverson, and Diamond (2001) point out, 'While individual leaders and their attributes do matter in constituting leadership practice, they are not all that matters.' Distributed leadership examines what else might be involved in the practice of leadership and offers a description of how numerous leaders in an organization combine their individual effort to produce a desirable result (Gosling, Bolden, and Petrov, 2009).

The definition of distributed leadership has some similarities with others, all of which share a common belief about leadership as a process that happens between individuals, rather than being the possession of one. We will briefly outline some of these similar concepts.

Similar concepts

Shared leadership

Shared leadership is described by Pearce and Conger as:

> a dynamic, interactive influence process among individuals in groups for which the objective is to lead one another to the achievement of group of organizational goals or both. (Pearce and Conger, 2003: 282).

This is done through the creation of practices that can be used by employees at all levels of the organization. Shared leadership clearly sees leadership as emerging from the inter-dependencies created at group level. To enable this, there is a focus on the creation of the conditions, skills, and abilities needed to enable collective learning (Currie and Lockett, 2011). Pearce and Conger suggest that when shared leadership has been enabled, there will be a flow of influence that is both horizontal and vertical in an organization, with leaders influenc-ing across peer groups as well as up and down the institutional hierarchy.

The case made by Pearce and Conger for shared leadership includes a view that modern corporations are moving away from the traditional top-down hierarchies, with more flat-tened structures that require leadership to become a process of influence rather than relying on positional power. They make the point that creating the vision for an organization is no longer the job of a single leader, rather it is the job of many employees to jointly create shared visions for an organization, and to share in the motivation of staff towards achievement of these shared visions. However, they are keen to clarify that shared leadership is not a rejec-tion of leadership as an individual activity, but rather an attempt to integrate the individual as leader with the concept of leadership being a social process shared across an organization. In this they differ from distributed leadership, which imagines leadership emerging organically, rather than being planned or having the involvement of a hierarchical leader.

Collaborative leadership

Kramer and Crespy (2011) offer a description of a collaborative leadership method which ac-knowledges the importance of the role of the hierarchical leader in creating the conditions for collaboration to occur. This includes the leader framing or describing issues in an accessible way, mobilizing the talent in the group to act, using dialogue as a tool to reduce the perceived difference in power between group members including the leader, and giving away decision making power to the group. The authors envision collaborative leadership being generated through the relationships that are built within the group. These will be both between the group members themselves and between the group and the leader, meaning that collabora-tive leadership is in essence a co-constructed phenomenon (Kramer and Crespy, 2011).

Participative leadership

Participative leadership is a method of enabling employees to make a greater contribution to the work process. It consists of a set of behaviours or actions that a leader could take to improve the participation of followers. This might include giving followers more information, control of resources, discretion, or increased attention and support. The aim is to include

followers in decision making processes, including consulting widely in an organization before taking decisions (Vroom and Yago, 1998). Participative leadership has been widely used
by global corporations when developing new businesses in different geographic locations,
although it is unclear whether it is a suitable leadership method in cultures where there is
usually a great distance in power relations (Huang et al., 2006).

Leaderful practice

Leaderful practice is a democratic approach to the issue of leadership. It offers another
alternative to the traditional idea of leadership being vested in an individual. The focus of
leaderful practice is on how leadership is enacted in different social settings and contexts,
on leadership as a process and as a practice. Leadership here is a shared process, collaborative in nature, and there is an assumption that many in an organization can be involved.
Raelin (2003) outlines four tenets of leaderful practice, namely collectiveness, concurrency,
collaboration and compassion. Collectiveness examines how many people can be a leader;
concurrency explores how many people in a unit are leading at the same time; collaboration
looks at the co-creation work done by a group; and compassion focuses on the attitudes of
group members towards each other. Raelin suggests that leaderful communities will be defined by 'people talking together, acting together, and thinking together' in order to co-create
the solutions to their issues (Raelin, 2011: 207).

RESEARCH IN FOCUS: Participative leadership and Chinese state-owned enterprises

The study by Huang et al. (2006) looked at the impact of Western participative leadership behaviours on
the workforce of Chinese companies. They suggest that a participative style of leadership has become increasingly used in both the sino-foreign joint ventures and in state-owned businesses as well. The authors
were investigating whether this type of leadership empowered the workers and led to higher levels of employee commitment, as is suggested by some of the Western literature reviewed in this study.

Huang et al. point to a number of studies that suggest this style of leadership may not be suitable or appropriate for the cultural norms of China. Employees traditionally have been used to a top-down style of
leadership, defined by a Confucian style of parental authority and a command style of leading, although
they also quote some recent evidence that modern Chinese workers are becoming amenable to more
Western styles of leadership.

After researching 173 Chinese state-owned companies, the authors found that there was evidence of
the participative style of leading having a positive effect on the employees who had only been working
at the organization for a short time. The main impact was to improve workers' perceptions of their own
competence in the job, thus increasing their self-confidence. Unfortunately, this style of leadership had
less of an effect on those employees who had been with the organization for a long time.

It is interesting to note that the former assumptions of Chinese management practices and the expectation from workers for a strongly authoritarian leadership style may be changing more quickly than previously thought. This study concludes that Western leadership practice, and in particular the notion of
participative leadership, is having a positive effect on the Chinese workforce.

Huang, X., Shi, K., Zhang, Z., and Lee Cheung, Y. (2006) The impact of participative leadership behaviour on psychological
empowerment and organizational commitment in Chinese state-owned enterprises: the moderating role of organizational tenure. *Asia Pacific Journal of Management*, 23, 345–67.

Collective leadership

Collective leadership has been defined by Friedrich et al. (2009) as:

> a dynamic leadership process in which a defined leader, or set of leaders, selectively utilize skills and expertise within a network, effectively distributing elements of the leadership role as the situation or problem at hand requires. (Friedrich et al., 2009:)

The authors suggest that collective leadership is much more formal and dynamic than distributed leadership, describing it as leadership which 'pops up' at critical moments. The leaders that surface to deal with issues as they arise can come from any area of a business, although there is some formality in this as their involvement depends on the information they possess and the expertise that is needed to deal with the issue. In this way, leadership is not limited to the members of the senior management team, as has been suggested by some writers on distributed leadership (Wallace 2002), nor is it limited to those whom the leader chooses to involve, as suggested by the participative or collaborative leadership theories. Rather it is a dynamic process, drawing in different people as different expertise and knowledge are needed to deal with an issue.

Collective leadership also takes an external perspective into account, considering the impact of external actors, policy makers, and the like, on the focus of leadership within the organization (Currie and Lockett, 2011).

Friedrich et al. (2009) clarify that collective leadership does not mean that the traditional role of leader is obsolete, as they acknowledge that someone has to be accountable for the outcomes and for the creation of a team, network, or process to deal with an issue.

Having considered some of the concepts that share a similar understanding of the process of leadership, it becomes clear that distributed leadership appears to have emerged as a catch-all term for the concepts of leadership mentioned above, along with others such as co-leadership (Heenan and Bennis, 2000) or democratic leadership (Gastil, 1997). All these ideas question the conventional wisdom that leadership is the exclusive possession of an individual, and favour the view that leadership emerges out of interactions within groups or networks and as such it can be widely distributed across members of an organization. Unfortunately, grouping different concepts under the heading of distributed leadership may have generated some misconceptions of what distributed leadership actually is. For example, delegates on leadership programmes frequently misconceive of distributed leadership as a multi-plethora of leaders in an organization, and they question this on the basis that if everyone is trying to lead, who is actually directing this leadership activity towards a purposeful outcome? Distributed leadership has also been misused to describe any type of team-based activity or shared leadership event (Bolden, 2011; Edwards, 2011; Harris, 2008).

The key elements of Gronn's theory of distributed leadership are the emergence of leadership activity caused by the interaction of individuals who have been brought together formally or informally to work on issues for the organization. It is the interaction and the product of that interaction that has been termed distributed leadership. As Bolden (2011: 251) puts it, distributed leadership is 'conceived of as a collective social process emerging through the interactions of multiple actors'. In this sense it is a more holistic, systemic approach to investigating the concept of leadership, which was one of the original aims of Gronn, who desired to give a new unit of analysis that could be used to understand leadership from a more collective perspective. What Gronn wanted to measure was how leadership drifts across a group, a process he described as concerted action (Gronn, 2002).

There are three forms of concerted action that can be examined to find evidence of distributed leadership: spontaneous collaboration, intuitive working relations, and institutionalized practices.

Spontaneous collaboration carries an assumption that leadership is a practice of interaction that is extended over the whole organization, not just in the formal regular rituals of an organization, such as meetings, but in the informal social interactions and in the resolution of immediate issues as well. In coming together to discuss an issue or solve a problem, the interaction that results can be termed spontaneous collaboration, where different people lead at different times.

Intuitive working relations are those that can be observed between people who have developed a close working partnership. This can be seen in the high levels of trust that exist between colleagues who have learned to work closely together and have developed an intuitive understanding of the others' working practices. Gronn describes a blurring of roles between people who work closely, with leadership emerging from this blurring.

Institutional practices refers to the formal structures of an organization that can be either designed or can emerge as an organization adapts to new circumstances and demands. Gronn see the creation of practices that involve close interaction of people on an equal footing as those that would generate distributed leadership.

A case in point: Winning the Rugby World Cup

In 2003 England won the Rugby World Cup. In the last play of the game, deep in extra time, a clear example of distributed leadership could be seen. England needed a field position from which to score a drop goal. They had a line out (throw-in) in their own half and chose a throw to the back of the line—the longest and most difficult throw, requiring acts of leadership from both Thompson, the thrower, and Moody, the catcher. From the successful line out the ball was distributed to the England backs, and Catt, who had just come on as a replacement, received the ball with a clear, institutionalized practice to enact. He had to run straight and hard at the Australian defence, knowing he would get tackled hard, and had to ensure the ball came back on England's side. This put England in the right place and in range for a drop goal, but only just. There followed a moment of spontaneous collaboration, where the scrum half, Dawson, saw a small gap in the Australian defence and ran through it, supported by several England players who made sure the ball stayed with England when Dawson was tackled. England were now within distance and in the right position, but their best passer of the ball, Dawson, was at the bottom of a pile of players. In an example of intuitive working relations, the England captain, Johnson, and his long-term team mate, Back, who was acting as scrum half in Dawson's absence, knew they had to take the ball on in order to get Dawson back in the game. Back passed to Johnson, who ran and was tackled, Back helped the ball to come back to Dawson who passed it to Wilkinson for the final act of leadership—kicking the drop goal that won the world cup.

This final play involved the whole team. It was a move no doubt practised many times on the training group, allowing for institutional practices to be developed and intuitive working relations to be formed. But at the moment when it counted most, it was spontaneous collaboration to solve an immediate issue that had arisen in the moment that enabled England to win the World Cup.

The case in point feature provides an example of how the combination of the three elements described above can be regarded as 'conjoint agency' (Gronn, 2002: 431), where the players are creating a synergy from the synchronization of their individual activities which build on each other to achieve the outcome desired by the whole team, a process termed reciprocal influence.

The case also demonstrates several key properties of distributed leadership including interdependence, coordination, and trust. For any sports team these elements are essential. In the workplace this requires people to move from a mindset that says they are autonomous, masters of their own destiny, to a more humble position where leaders understand that they are dependent on others for the success that may then be attributed to them alone.

This understanding of dependence is rooted in ideas of successful team leadership. Katzenbach and Smith (1993) describe the highest performing teams as being defined by interdependence and an interest in the development of others, rather than a focus on the self. Kets De Vries (1999), in a study of pygmy society, identifies seven lessons that can inform the development of effective teams, and thus enable distributed leadership:

- respect and trust for team members
- collective support and protection
- open communication defined by dialogue rather than debate
- a strong common goal
- common values and shared beliefs that are strongly held
- team objectives put first, personal objectives second
- an acceptance of distributed leadership—no one leader; everyone empowered to take decisions

Kets De Vries argues that companies need to create an environment that will allow these elements to develop, including senior leaders adopting an authoritative approach that will allow a distribution of power alongside the distribution of leadership.

Discussion point: Exceptional individuals or shared interdependence?

Consider Gronn's critique of traditional theories of leadership and discuss the following questions:

- Do you think leadership is an act or acts done by an exceptional individual, or can it be defined as a collective act of conjoint agency?
- Does the binary description of leaders and followers exist in your experience of a work situation?
- How much influence does the context of the workplace have on the type of leadership that is apparent?

Evidence for distributed leadership

Distributed leadership has been criticized for being merely a descriptive idea that is useful as a foil for more individualistic forms of leadership. It has been suggested by Gronn himself that a system of distributed leadership will not necessarily make an organization more effective, and indeed, there is little evidence to suggest that different patterns of distributed leadership have a great impact on the achievement of organizational goals (Harris, 2008). On the positive side, Harris suggests that there is some evidence that distributed leadership can be a positive influence on organizational development and in organizational change initiatives (Harris, 2008: 183). The empirical research to support distributed leadership has been largely focused on leadership in the education sector, and more specifically on trying to understand how leadership is distributed across organizations, rather than whether distributed leadership is a good thing in itself. This is largely due to the very nature of distributed leadership being situated in a process or activity, hence research being focused on how leadership is distributed, and whether there are some forms of distribution that are more effective than others.

One well-cited study was carried out by Spillane, Halverson, and Diamond (2001, 2003, 2004). This research assumed distributed leadership as a unit of analysis, meaning the study had to be focused on leadership practice at a group or institutional level, rather than at an individual level. Spillane and colleagues defined distributed leadership slightly differently from Gronn, drawing on ideas from distributed cognition and activity theory to broaden out the concept.

- Distributed cognition takes the view that the mental process of acquiring knowledge is intimately linked to the social, physical, and cultural context in which this process occurs.
- Activity theory sees human activities being affected by the whole social system within which they take place. It seeks to understand how activity is influenced by elements such as culture, artefacts, environment, and history. Fittingly for distributed leadership, activity theory rejects the individual as an appropriate unit of analysis, focusing instead on the interaction of many elements that make up human activity.

For Spillane it is the interaction of people in coordinated activities, the interaction of people with tools (such as technology and language), and the interaction of people with artefacts and cultures which all combine to make up distributed leadership which can be said to be described as 'stretched over the school's social and situational contexts' (Spillane, Halverson, and Diamond, 2001: 23). From this definition a framework for studying distributed leadership was developed which focused on four central elements: leadership tasks and functions, task enactment, the social distribution of task enactment, and the situational distribution of task enactment (Spillane, Halversdon, and Diamond, 2004: 5). Thirteen schools were studied over a four-year period and the study suggested that there was evidence that in the narrow field of instruction, the function of leadership was apparent in the work of a number of individuals who were interacting on a particular task or tasks (Spillane, Halverson, and Diamond, 2003). In achieving the task, different people took on the role and mantle of leader at different points. The authors argued that situation and context were a prime consideration that must be taken account of when analysing leadership. For them the situation was an essential part of leadership practice, without which the practice of leadership could not be fully understood. Thus distributed leadership could only be observed by studying the interactions between leaders, followers, and situations. The study produced a complex framework for the study of distributed leadership, and anecdotal evidence that this concept of leadership exists in the practice of school leaders involved in the instruction of students.

In a more recent study, Leithwood et al. (2007) studied the school environment to chart patterns of distributed leadership, what the functions of leadership were and who performed them, and what enabled or limited the development of distributed leadership. They extended Gronn's description of conjoint activity in the following way:

- *Planful alignment*—similar to institutionalized practice, where thought has been given to what the leadership tasks or functions actually are or should be for that organization, and which source of leadership is best suited to take on each task.

- *Spontaneous alignment*—similar to spontaneous collaboration, where there is little thought or planning given to what leadership tasks are or who should do them, but instinctively the right tasks end up with appropriate people, hence remaining aligned with organizational goals.

- *Spontaneous misalignment*—little thought or planning to the tasks means that they end up in the hands of inappropriate organizational sources which has a detrimental effect.

- *Anarchic misalignment*—leaders actively rejecting the influence of others in the organization on what is perceived to be their 'turf'. This can be observed in independent behaviour and competition for resources by such leaders.

The study hypothesized that planful alignment would be the most effective pattern of distributed leadership observed in terms of the productivity of the organization. This was found, but mainly when observing the most important issue or project that a school was dealing with. Planful alignment was less obvious with lower priority issues.

 Blog box

Think about a time when you have come together with colleagues to solve an important issue or deliver a piece of work. How did this happen? Did you consider what kinds of leadership might be needed to complete the task? Was there a deliberate attempt to distribute leadership, did distributed leadership emerge, or was the group led by a single individual?

Write a 300-word blog on your personal experience of working on this issue with colleagues.

The implication of Leithwood's work is that someone has to consider the issue to be dealt with and facilitate employees to come together around this issue in a planned way in order to create distributed leadership. In other words, focused leadership by an individual at the top of an organization may lead to planful alignment, thus linking distributed leadership ideas back to the original theories that Gronn was criticizing. Distributed leadership, it appears, still needs leaders to lead it!

This study also suggested that the idea of distributed leadership in itself was not necessarily a good thing. When leadership was found to emerge around less important issues this did not improve efficiency or the quality of the outcome. What matters more is the specifics of how leadership is distributed, and the importance of understanding the context or situation in which leadership is being distributed.

Overall, the research that has been done into distributed leadership seems to suggest that there are benefits in terms of learning outcomes for students in education

(Harris, 2008: 173). However, as the majority of this research has taken place in the educational sector it is unclear whether these ideas can be transferred to the wider business community.

From a critical perspective

Distributed leadership by its very nature is a critique of the belief and assumptions that underpin the mainstream research and theory of leadership developed during the twentieth century. The core beliefs that pervade Gronn's work are those of equality and a sense of fairness towards all within the workplace who contribute to the success of a venture, and a reaction against the privileging of individuals over the collective.

We began the discussion on distributed leadership with one of the most frequent criticisms of the concept; that it seems easy to comprehend, and yet is a difficult term to define. Gosling, Bolden, and Petrov (2009) cite research involving 152 managers from the higher education sector who were asked about distributed leadership in their organizations. Very few of these individuals asked for a definition of this term, suggesting that they had an idea of what was meant by this term and that is was something that was congruous with their experience of leadership in their organizations.

Gosling, Bolden, and Petrov question what value the concept of distributed leadership brings to theorists and practitioners alike. They see four functions that the idea could serve:

- as a description that best captures how influence is actually exerted by individuals in collective activity
- as a correction to the former ideas of leadership, moving this from the individual focus on exceptional people to a more collective understanding
- as a means for empowering people across an organization to take on leadership responsibilities and actions
- as a rhetorical term that can be used to support or to challenge forms of authority that develop within institutions

Gosling's study of higher education looked for evidence of each of these functions, and concluded that within this sector distributed leadership did not describe the reality of leadership in the institutions studied. As a concept, they appreciated its role as a tool to examine how leadership flows between people over time, but thought that returning to examining the focus and distribution of power may be more relevant. They did find that where the term distributed leadership is used as rhetoric to describe how an organization should make decisions, then this may enable empowerment of people across the organization. The rhetoric also allowed for the establishment of widely distributed leadership development programmes, but that does not mean it allowed for distributed leadership to actually occur. Finally, as a rhetoric function the authors see that distributed leadership presents a persuasive account of a type of collegial leadership that would be acceptable to academics in the higher education sector, who tend to oppose the implementation of mechanistic management practices and favour a traditional system of democratic and collegial decision making processes (Gosling, Bolden, and Petrov, 2009).

A second frequent critique of distributed leadership is that it is a specialized idea that mainly belongs to the education sector. Indeed, the main authors used for the description of distributed leadership in this chapter have written on distributed leadership in the context of the emergence of leadership in schools, colleges, and universities that are located in the Western world, mostly North America, the UK, Australia, and Denmark. Almost half of all articles written on the subject originate in the USA, whilst 68 per cent can be found in education or educational management journals (Bolden, 2011). As mentioned above, perhaps the reason for this is that the concept appeals to the traditionally collegial nature of educational establishments in the Western world. It is questionable whether the concept could transfer successfully into the corporate world more generally, especially with the dominance of the belief that exceptional individuals make the difference to companies evidenced by the relentless rise in senior executive rewards over the last thirty years.

A further criticism is that distributed leadership is actually bad for teams and organizations. Harris (2008) cites work from the 1950s that suggested that where there are fewer leaders, there is clearer communication, better coordination, and people feel more highly valued. Harris also highlights the work of Melnick and Bryk. Melnik (1982) included distributed leadership as one of six limits of good team performance. He sees distributed leadership as a fluid, emergent process where individual team members become unsure as to who holds responsibility to act at any particular time. He is supported in this view by Bryk (1999) who believes that distributing leadership can create confusion in an organization, especially when people want to lead in different directions from the official company line.

Discussion point: How applicable is distributed leadership in different cultures?

Seek out colleagues from different nationalities and cultures and discuss the following questions:

- From the perspective of your country, what is leadership?
- Would a distributed style of leadership work with companies in your country?
- Can you envisage your political leaders leading in a collaborative, participatory, or collective manner?

Whilst leadership may be distributed, authority or power does not always get distributed along with it (Hatcher, 2005). Hatcher sees distributed leadership in the UK schools system as a tool that has been promoted by government to help push through an agenda of change across the schools system. It is a method for controlling head teachers, increasing managerialism in the sector, and controlling staff through an idea that teachers may instinctively be drawn to. He is critical of the separation of leadership and power in Gronn's work. Gronn speculates that leadership is open to all in an organization as all are able to influence others. Hatcher disagrees, suggesting that only those in authority, at the top of an organization, can really have influence, and it is these leaders who will agree the direction of that influence and back it with some form of power and resources. 'Thus, officially sanctioned "distributed leadership" is always delegated, licensed, exercised on behalf of and revocable by authority' (Hatcher, 2005: 256).

What is interesting about Hatcher's critique of distributed leadership is that it mirrors Gronn's critique of traditional leadership theories. Both highlight the fact that writing on leadership does not deal with the concept of power, nor does it adopt the political science view of power being at once focused and distributed. Distributed leadership, like the individualist theories before it, seems to have ducked the issue of how theories of leadership interact with the theories of power.

Finally, it is increasingly being appreciated in the literature that distributed leadership is not a simple thing to achieve. There appear to be significant barriers to the adoption of this as a leadership style across an organization, many of them tied up with the relinquishing of power by those in positions of authority. Harris (2008) identifies several issues that may make it impossible for modern global organizations to adopt this style of leadership:

- *Distance*—distributed leadership requires high levels of interaction between colleagues for a high level of interdependence to be created. It remains to be seen whether new technologies that facilitate communication over long distances will be sufficient to create the close bonds and trust needed by distributed leadership.

- *Culture*—this must move away from a top-down control model to one that is comfortable with higher levels of risk, uncertainty, and spontaneous motion, and potentially a slower pace of delivery of outcomes. This invariably means a loss of direct control for those at the top, something that would seem an anathema to many senior managers.

- *Structure*—organizations adopting distributed leadership would need to move away from functional organizational structures and create more flexible, cross-functional team-orientated structures. Again this has proved difficult within most organizations due to the vested interest of those whose identity and previous success is bound up with their functional area.

Harris puts the onus on formal leaders to create the conditions and structures necessary for distributed leadership to develop. In a sense this might be seen as similar to 'turkeys voting for Christmas'. If distributed leadership takes hold in an organization, then why the need to laud and highly reward those at the top? This is perhaps the biggest barrier to the development of distributed leadership. Those at the top and those aspiring to be at the top may not want to share the power or rewards more equally across an organization, especially as the responsibility and accountability for outcomes will still remain with the head teachers and CEOs. Gronn suggests that distributed leadership is an idea whose time has come. Perhaps this is true, but it may also be an idea that is so challenging to the conventional wisdom of how organizations actually work that it will remain a descriptive term of how leadership occurs and a lens for studying the process of leadership, rather than becoming a normative term of how leadership should be enabled and allowed to develop in organizations.

Leadership in the media: Apollo 13

Apollo 13 tells the story of the ill-fated attempt to put a third US team of astronauts on the moon. The film follows the account of the Apollo 13 flight, from the initial explosion in the oxygen tanks, through the various issues that had to be overcome by the crew and experts at NASA, to the eventual successful re-entry and safe return to earth of the crew.

There are a number of clips in this film which could be used to show elements of distributed leadership. In one scene the NASA team are discussing how to safely return the crew to earth. Several different problems are identified as the main issue, and teams form to deal with each problem. The critical issue of power is identified by one of the youngest members of the team, John Aaron, whose expertise and knowledge clearly show him that the spacecraft will run out of power if they do not shut it down immediately, and he then has to create a means of turning the power back on later in the flight to enable the computer to successfully bring the command module back to earth. In investigating how to power up the spacecraft, we see leadership and influence shift round the team, from the engineers to Ken Mattingly, the astronaut working on the flight simulator.

At other points in the film we see teams formed to address issues such as the creation of new air filters for the landing module when the team realize that the spacecraft is suffering a potentially lethal rise in carbon dioxide levels. In each case leadership shifts around the ground team, with different expertise and knowledge coming to the fore in a way that would fit the description of collective leadership.

However, it is clear throughout the film that accountability for the safe return of Apollo 13 rests on the shoulders of one man, the lead flight director, Gene Krantz. At all points it is clear that Krantz takes the decisions. He consults widely, he gives space for others to lead in their own area, but he makes the final decisions. The film depicts lots of exceptional individuals coming together to solve a complex problem. These individuals always work in a group, and these groups are sanctioned by the leader, Krantz. In the process of bringing the astronauts home, we can see leadership emerging to meet different needs, but all the while are aware that it is Krantz who leads on the ground and Lovell who leads in the spacecraft.

Apollo 13 clearly shows leadership as a group process with people emerging as leaders to meet different needs. It also clearly shows leaders as exceptional individuals, who make difficult decisions and use their abilities to understand and solve complex problems, making a clear difference to the outcome. The practice of leadership is a process distributed across groups, but it is practised by leaders!

Chapter summary

In this chapter we have considered:

- A critique of previous leadership theory that questions the exceptionalism of individuals
- Different ideas of how leadership might be a process that emerges from interdependent groups
- The core concept of distributed leadership, its foundations, and main principles
- Research evidence into how distributed leadership may be enacted
- The criticism of distributed leadership and the need for leaders as well as leadership

Integrative case study: Semco

Semler and Company was a mixer and agitator supplier based in São Paulo, Brazil. In the early 1980s the company was focused on industries that were declining, especially the ship building industry. This focus was a source of conflict between the CEO, Antonio Semler, and his son Ricardo Semler, who disagreed on which markets the business should be in, and how the business was run.

The arguments between father and son came to a head when Ricardo threatened to resign. Instead of losing his son to the business, Antonio Semler resigned himself, and promoted Ricardo to CEO at the age of just 21 years old. True to his beliefs, Ricardo set about transforming the leadership of the organization in a radical way, initially by sacking 60 per cent of the senior managers in one afternoon, and seeking opportunities to diversify the companies business. He also tried to manage the business using a matrix style organizational structure.

By the age of 25 Semler had succeeded in diversifying the company, but the speed of change and the method in which it was done had alienated employees and stressed him to the point of collapse. He re-evaluated how he wanted to run the company in a simpler, more natural way, doing away with rules and measurement that were unnecessary, and were alienating for his staff.

The ideas for re-inventing leading a company took shape when Semler hired Clóvis da Silva Bojikian to be his HR director. Bojikian was an ex-teacher who had been fired for encouraging faculty and students to think for themselves and question authority. Semler and Bojikian together conceived of an organization where employees were involved in decisions, making them more motivated to achieve company targets.

Delegating power through the organization started small, allowing employees to take over the running of the cafeteria, choose the colour of their uniforms or the paint on the walls. This democratic style of leadership was similar to definitions of participative or distributed leadership, and included little formality in terms of hierarchy within the business, but a lot of respect for all workers as individuals. It also means that employees have substantial freedom within their jobs to achieve the best they can.

Ricardo Semler introduced a set of principles that the company follows, which have enabled the creation of a more democratic style of leadership to emerge in the business:

1. To be a dependable and reliable company

2. Value honesty and transparency over and above all temporary interests

3. Seek a balance between short-term and long-term profit

4. Offer products and services at fair prices which are recognized by customers as the best on the market

5. Provide the customer with differentiated services, placing our responsibility before profits

6. Encourage creativity, giving support to the bold

7. Encourage everyone's participation and question decisions that are imposed from the top down

8. Maintain an informal and pleasant environment, with a professional attitude and free of preconceptions

9. Maintain safe working conditions and control industrial processes to protect our personnel and the environment

10. Have the humility to recognize our errors and an understanding that we can always improve.

Of particular importance to the culture created at Semco are the last five principles: encouraging creativity, questioning and participation, an environment where employees feel safe and valued, and a humility that encourages others to lead. The attitudes that create this culture are outlined in the Semco Survival Manual, a comic book which serves as the only rule book in the company. Here the importance of earning respect as a leader is emphasized. Employees are encouraged to be informal, to express their opinions openly and honestly both internally and externally, and to rotate in their jobs, allowing the opportunity to bring teams together around specific ideas that will develop the business. Even the role of CEO is rotated amongst the senior team. There is a strong emphasis in this document on participation, honesty, and openness, and on hierarchy being less important than harmony.

This leadership style has increased employee involvement in the business. In the late 1980s a small group of engineers suggested that the business set up a Nucleus of Technical Innovation (NTI) where new businesses and new product ideas could be investigated. The NTI structure allowed those with knowledge or experience to try out new ideas, and this structure proved very fruitful, with eighteen new ideas in the first six months. From this Semco developed a business unit based structure that allowed greater responsibility to the individual managers and business units to pursue their ideas and new businesses. This structure was to become the core generator of new business for Semco, growing it from a US$4 million firm in 1982, to a US$212 million firm in 2003.

Semco became a business defined by innovation, creating new business in environmental consultancy, facilities management, real estate consulting, inventory services and mobile maintenance services. It is now a global market leader in the industrial equipment sector and the document management industry.

Semco workers are empowered to effectively work for themselves. They can decide on when they work and even in some cases how much they get paid and who they are supervised by. Employees can vote on key decisions, and every employee, including Semler himself, has only one vote.

The core belief about the respect of individuals has allowed Semco to form successful partnerships with a number of other global companies. The core value of respect underpins the Semco approach to partnering with businesses and this has allowed successful, lasting partnerships to be sustained.

In 2005 Ricardo Semler was severely injured in a car accident. He spent many months in intensive care and recuperation, but during this time Semco continued to run as a successful business, in spite of his absence. Semler puts this down to the structure and culture he has created, one that makes the business flexible and able to meet unforeseen demands and challenges.

Not everyone is a fan of this style of leadership. Semler has been accused of undermining the traditional authority of managers, and surprise has been expressed at the amount of power he has allowed to be distributed throughout his business. Semler's response to this is that he is questioning some long-held myths about authority and structure that have arisen predominantly in Western culture, so it is not surprising that the proponents and advocates of these systems question his approach. He speculates that others have not followed his lead due to two main elements—the inability to give up power, and the disbelief in the trustworthiness of other human beings. It would appear that the methods adopted at Semco need leaders comfortable with these two elements, and able to charismatically and persuasively argue for this form of participatory management.

Case study questions

- Do you believe people are generally trustworthy or generally untrustworthy?

- Think of a business you have worked in. What would happen if you allowed the employees to set their own hours, participate in their pay settlements, rotate in their jobs, and participate in major decisions such as hiring senior management?

- As a leader, how comfortable are you with the notion of giving power to all the empoyees in your organization?

Sources:

Semler, R. (2001) *Maverick! The success story behind the world's most unusual workplace.* London: Random House Business.

(Continued...)

Semler, R. (2004) *The Seven Day Weekend: a better way to work in the 21st century.* London: Random House Business.

<http://www.semco.com.br/en/content.asp?content=1> accessed 29 August 2012.

<http://en.wikipedia.org/wiki/Ricardo_Semler> accessed 29 August 2012.

<http://www.strategy-business.com/article/05408?pg=0> accessed 29 August 2012.

Further reading

Bolden, R. (2011) Distributed leadership in organizations: a review of theory and research. *International Journal of Management Reviews*, 13, 251–69.

Gronn, P. (2002) Distributed leadership as a unit of analysis. *The Leadership Quarterly* 13, 423–51.

Gronn, P. (2003) Leadership: who needs it? *School Leadership & Management* 23, 3, 267–90.

Pearce, C. L. and Conger, J. A. (2003) *Shared Leadership: Reframing the hows and whys of leadership.* Thousand Oaks, CA: Sage.

8 Leading teams: Delivering team performance

Learning outcomes

On completion of this chapter you will:

- Understand how the focus on teams developed out of the human relations movement, and how leadership has been closely associated with team performance throughout its history

- Be aware of the most frequently used frameworks for considering team formation and team performance, and the ways in which such frameworks draw together the team and leadership literatures

- Understand why team leadership constitutes a separate topic area from leadership per se and be familiar with mainstream approaches to understanding leadership within teams

- Be aware of more recent thinking in relation to teams, in particular the idea of 'teaming' as a response to fluidity in team situations and 'X teams' as a recognition of the interconnectedness of modern organizations

- Understand the concepts of self-managing teams and virtual teams and the role of leadership in these types of teams

Introduction

This chapter taps into the links between organizational behaviour and leadership to explore the leader's role in delivering team performance. As a starting point, it will consider why 'team leadership' constitutes a separate topic area in its own right and is not merely synonymous with leadership per se. As a preliminary to exploring models of team leadership, it will consider processes of team formation and measures of team performance. This is necessarily a brief overview of a field that is vast in its own right and could also include issues such as organizational culture, the development of team norms, patterns of communication, and why teams can be dysfunctional. The main thrust of the chapter is then a discussion of two mainstream models of team leadership, with issues relating to self-managed and virtual teams providing the alternative, critical perspective. Some recent developments in thinking about teams—specifically the ideas of 'teaming' and the need for 'connectivity' are also introduced.

Katzenbach and Smith (2005: 162) define a team as 'a small number of people with complementary skills who are committed to a common purpose, performance goals and approach for which they hold themselves mutually accountable'. Key elements here are around mutual accountability and shared goals, although the question of how small is 'small' continues to be much debated. In an organizational context, teams now abound, taking many forms and serving many purposes. McShane and Von Glinow (2009) suggest the following typology of teams:

- departmental teams
- production/service/leadership teams
- self-directed teams
- advisory teams
- task force (project) teams
- virtual teams
- communities of practice

Katzenbach and Smith contrasted their definition of a team with that of a 'work group' which they saw as being a 'small number of people working in a collaborative style with individual input and accountability, for example a seminar group at a university' (Katzenbach and Smith, 1993). The key difference here is that the actual work of groups—or the work product—tends to come about individually and that there is no direct pressure on groups to cohere or to be accountable to each other. They may work quite separately and only come together when they need to—they may not like each other or like working together and, depending upon their goals, this may not be a problem.

In recent years, teams have become a buzz-word—talked about as if they were the solution to all organizational ills—but how has this come about? The influences resulting in the rise of teams have been structural across the whole of the economic landscape and have included increased competition, increased complexity, a faster pace of work, and the cutting of over-heads though organizational delayering. The resultant team structures have required a different skills structure, different patterns of leadership, and different organizational monitoring and control mechanisms.

In research terms, the historical roots of interest in groups and teams began in the 1920s and 1930s as part of the human relations movement. In contrast to the scientific management theorists—who focused on individual activity and outputs—this movement was interested in collaborative effort at work and recognized the importance of such issues as motivation, job satisfaction, and social contact in raising performance. Whilst the human relations movement moved away from the entirely ratio-economic prescriptions of its scientific predecessor, it did so without significantly changing the dominant views of leadership which prevailed at the time: or rather, the focus was on employees rather than followers, and hence leadership was not an explicit area of interest. By the 1940s, the focus of attention had shifted to group dynamics and the development of a theory of social science. Group dynamics is the study of the processes which occur within groups (as opposed to random collections of individuals) and what happens when two or more people are connected to each other by social processes such as interaction and influence. The sorts of processes studied under this heading include group norms, roles, relations, need to belong, social influence, and the effects of all these processes on behaviour. This type of study became an important underpinning to various aspects of organizational development (OD) consultancy, still an important area of activity in modern organizations. It was only in the 1950s that the importance of leadership in groups came to the fore as a research topic, and by the 1960s and 1970s the use of OD interventions for the development of on-going teams and the promotion of leadership effectiveness became widespread. As a term, OD is used to refer to a conceptual, organization-wide effort to increase an organization's effectiveness and viability. As such, it usually involves interventions in the organization's processes, using behavioural science approaches, organizational reflection, systems improvement, planning, and self-analysis.

By the 1980s, the spread of Japanese management practices around the globe had led to research—as well as operational—interest in quality teams, benchmarking, and continuous improvement initiatives. This focus on quality continued into the 1990s as industry took on a more global perspective and increasing competition drove the need for increased efforts to maintain competitive advantage. It was these competitive pressures—and the organizational restructuring and delayering they produced in the drive to cut costs—which led to the real hey-day of teams as a panacea for industry's woes, arising from the belief that flatter organizational structures gave the faster response capabilities which were required by the increased pace of change which a highly competitive world generated. True multi-skilling—often self-managing—teams were the result. Research into the effectiveness and drawbacks of teams continues to the present day, with more recent studies becoming more complex, focusing on more team variables, and with interests beyond mere team performance (see Ilgen et al., 2005). Specifically, team processes—affective, cognitive, and behavioural—and their contribution to team success and viability have become a strong area of research interest, as have the role and impact of mediating processes such as trusting, bonding, planning, adapting, structuring, and learning.

There has also been a burgeoning literature which attempts to bring together the fields of organizational behaviour and leadership by attempting to understand the role of leadership in team performance. Stagl, Salas, and Burke (2007: 172) assert that '[n]ot surprisingly, the totality of research evidence supports this assertion; team leadership is critical to achieving both effective and behaviourally based team outcomes'. Whilst we would want to counter this somewhat dogmatic position—for example, by reference to the growing literature on the effectiveness of self-managing teams—it is nonetheless true that leadership can have an important role to play in delivering team performance or conversely (Stewart and Manz, 1995) in bringing about team failures.

So how is team leadership different?

Which brings us to a key question: when we talk about 'team leadership' what is it that we are referring to that is different from leadership per se? Most leaders lead teams in one form or another, whether it be a functional head leading their organizational department or a Prime Minister leading their Cabinet, it is likely that those reporting to the leader need to act as a team to some extent. So why does this topic deserve a chapter in its own right? What can we expect it to add to the theories of leadership expounded elsewhere in this book? To answer this question, we need to step back for a moment and examine the fundamental characteristics from which team performance is derived. According to Zaccaro, Rittman, and Marks (2001), these characteristics are:

- The existence of team processes which successfully integrate individual actions into a collective whole

- The ability to use these processes to operate in complex and dynamic environments
- The definition of team goals and the structuring of team activities to accomplish these goals through some form of leadership, either individual or shared

Given these characteristics, they go on to say that:

> Previous leadership theories have tended to focus on how leaders influence collections of subordinates, without attending to how leadership fosters the integration of subordinate actions (i.e. how leaders promoted team processes). (Zaccaro, Rittman, and Marks, 2001: 452)

It is this emphasis on the fostering of team processes that makes 'team leadership' a subtly different species within the leadership genus, and one which produces a different type of leadership theory.

A case in point: Team leadership on the field

Leading a sports team is, perhaps, the classic example of team leadership. If we consider Zaccaro, Rittman, and Marks's characteristics of team performance, we can see how these apply to, for example, the game of rugby, and how leadership in this context fosters the integration of subordinates' actions rather than just influencing a collection of individuals. In rugby, the goals of playing are well known to team members, and require no definition by the captain—the goal is to win! Instead, team leadership is about co-ordinating action on the field, in the face of fast moving play, in order to meet this goal. This means ensuring that the processes which make up the rules of play—forwards competing for the ball in line outs, wingers scoring tries, and backs operating as 'safe hands' to field kicks—all come together to enable the team to beat their opponents. It is the structuring of team activities—activities which are already well understood and well rehearsed but which occur differently every time they are performed—to produce a winning performance that constitute team leadership in this context. This is different from motivational leadership or situational leadership—although these may be occurring as well—and contributes to collective performance in a different way. The unit of analysis here is the team, rather than the individual.

How groups become teams

We have seen that to say a group of people are a team implies certain things about how they act and what they can achieve. But how does a group become a team? What processes need to occur within the group for a degree of cohesion and collectivity to develop? The classic work in this field was conducted by Bruce Tuckman and, despite the fact that his theory of team development dates back to the 1960s, it is still widely accepted today. Although Tuckman's original findings were based on a meta-study of research papers relating largely to therapy groups, T-groups, and experimental groups in laboratory settings, it can also be seen as having applicability to naturalistic groups in organizational settings, and much subsequent research has been conducted to validate and extend his original findings. Tuckman suggested four general stages of development which spanned both task and relational realms of integration. In the social or relational realm, the four stages he identified were those of testing dependence, conflict, cohesion, and functional roles, which he believed occurred sequentially. In the task

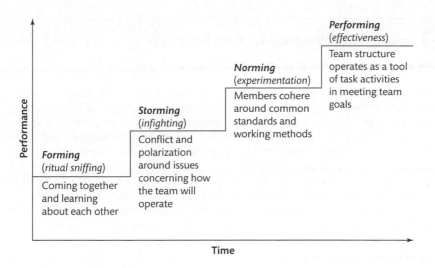

Figure 8.1 How groups become teams

Adapted with permission Tuckman, Bruce W. (1965) Developmental sequence in small groups. *Psychological Bulletin*, 63 (6) 384–99. Adapted with permission.

realm, the parallel sequence related to orientation, emotionality, relevant opinions exchange, and the emergence of solutions. Taken together, these four stages are more commonly referred to as Forming, Storming, Norming, and Performing. The four stages are summarized in Figure 8.1.

Each stage has implications for who does what, how they communicate, who makes decisions, and so on. In particular, the way in which leadership is exercised, and the response it generates, is suggested to be an important feature of the different developmental stages, moving from directive, through supportive and consensus building, to shared leadership by the time the team is performing effectively. Later work by Tuckman and Jenson (1977) identified a fifth stage often encountered by project teams and other groups with a limited lifespan: Adjourning—or Mourning, as it was also called—refers to a reflective stage often encountered by groups in the run-up to disbanding, when performance may drop off and team members start to distance themselves emotionally from each other in preparation for actual separation. Tuckman's stage theory can be criticized on a number of levels—the mismatch between its field of development and its field of application, problems with stage theories in general, and the potential for such a purportedly universal theory to overreach itself to name but three. Our own experience of teams may also suggest occasions when it is not necessary to travel through all four stages, or when the stages occur in a different order from that posited by Tuckman. We might also note that constant changes to the members of a team might suggest that a more cyclical model would more accurately reflect the ebb and flow of team life. Notwithstanding these many criticisms, the model has one over-riding advantage: it has so entered into the language of team development as to be almost ubiquitous. As such, it provides a shared language for those who seek to consciously improve the process of team formation for themselves or others.

Leadership in the media: Cool Runnings

Based on the true story of the first ever Jamaican bobsleigh team trying to make it to the Calgary winter Olympics, *Cool Runnings* is a classic example of a group of ill-assorted individuals finally developing into a close-knit and high performing team. It starts when Derice Bannock, son of Olympic sprinter Ben Bannock, fails to qualify for the 100-metre sprint due to a stupid accident. He hears that Irving Blitzer, disgraced Olympic bobsleigh gold medallist and old friend of Derice's father, is also living in Jamaica. Derice decides he will go to the Olympics anyway—as a bobsledder—and persuades Irving to coach the scratch team of misfits he manages to bring together. In the freezing weather of Calgary, Derice, Sanka, Junior, and Yul are laughed at by their fellow competitors and derided by the judges, but late-developing team spirit and a strong sense of national identity lead to a few surprises when they manage to qualify for the Winter Games.

This at once humorous and deeply touching film is a great example of how individuals eventually cohere into a team, but do they pass through Tuckman's four stages of team development to do it? You decide.

High performance teams

Is it enough to be a team? Katzenbach and Smith (1993) would say no—you need to be a high performing team. In cataloguing the alternatives, Katzenbach and Smith distinguish between groups who don't need to be teams (working groups) and groups that try to be teams but fail (pseudo teams). The latter group recognize the performance benefits associated with being a team, but fail to pull it off. Potential teams—collections of individuals who recognize that they could be more effective and are taking steps to develop methods and skills to do this—are a step up from pseudo teams but achieve only average performance levels. It is only when teams become what are referred to as real teams, whose members' skills are complementary and who have become committed to a common purpose and common working methods, that performance benefits start to emerge. The ultimate goal—that of becoming a high-performing team—is rarely achieved in practice, say Katzenbach and Smith. In those instances when it is, it is characterized by teams that have all the features of real teams but in addition show commitment to the personal growth of members and perform beyond the expectations of those around them. The performance levels associated with these different types of teams can be seen in Figure 8.2.

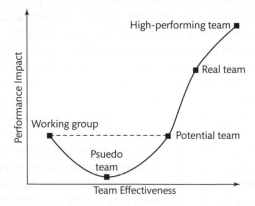

Figure 8.2 High performing teams

Katzenbach, Jon R. and Smith, Douglas K. (1993) *The Wisdom of Teams.* Boston, MA: Harvard Business School Press. Reproduced with permission.

Underpinning this framework are what Katzenbach and Smith refer to as the critical conditions for performance, namely, recognized performance need; personal commitment; mutual accountability; shared trust; and the effective operation of leadership roles. On this view of team performance, the issue of how leadership contributes to the creation and maintenance of effective team processes, and how these in turn lead to effective performance, will be crucial for any team leader to consider.

 Blog box

In my personal experience, high performing teams are rare and are hard to sustain. Back in the 1980s I was a member of such a team when I worked as Treasury Manager for TI Group plc, a UK-based specialist engineering company. As a team of five collectively responsible for treasury operations across Europe—including liquidity management, currency hedging, and longer-term funding issues—it was important that we worked effectively together to ensure the company's financial obligations were met and their financial risks minimized. In practice, we needed to share information, trust each other's judgement, and rely on each other to deliver on delegated tasks. At a more 'human' level we liked and respected each other, had a lot of fun, and worked extremely hard! I think what made the difference, though, was that we really did feel mutually accountable for the outcomes generated by the department, and for ensuring that the team was well regarded across the organization. There was a lot of loyalty between us and when TI moved its head office and the team broke up, the strong bonds we had formed made us supportive of each other in seeking new jobs and staying in touch. It is hard to really pin down what enabled us to be high performing—although motivational leadership certainly played a part—but I remember that time as one in which I was able to perform at my best, and in which I felt part of a team that was doing the same. (MIW)

In the mainstream

Models of team leadership

J. Richard Hackman has been a leader in the field of understanding teams and team performance since his early work on job enrichment schemes and their role in motivating superior performance. His approach to understanding team leadership reflects the nuanced complexities of what each side brings to the relationship. Teams have more collective talent, experience, and resources than individuals—but so often prove less effective. Leadership behaviours are often seen as a primary cause of team effectiveness—but so often backfire and produce mediocre results. Hackman (2002, 2009) suggests that the true role of a leader in a team context is that of putting in place the key conditions which then enable the team themselves to succeed. By instigating these conditions—irrespective of their own leadership style or skill—the leader can structure, support, and guide the team in such a way that:

- the social processes essential to collective working are enhanced
- the shared commitment, skills, and coordination strategies required by the task in hand are developed

- team members are able to take advantage of emerging opportunities and can identify and resolve developing problems
- individual experience and knowledge can be captured and shared across the team

Based on extensive research, Hackman concluded that to be effective, teams needed (1) to be real teams; (2) to have a compelling sense of direction; (3) to be possessed of an enabling structure; (4) to be operating within a supportive organizational context; and finally (5) to have access to expert coaching.

Each of the five key conditions is explicated through a number of features which, when present, enable the team to exceed expectations, grow in capability over time, and contribute to the learning and personal fulfilment of individual members. Thus being a real team rather than a team in name only—the first of Hackman's conditions—is dependent on four features: having a team *task*, clear team *boundaries*, clearly specified *authority* to manage their own internal work processes, and *stability* of membership over a reasonable period of time. Setting a compelling direction for the team's performance aspirations has the purposes of energizing team members, orienting their attention towards a shared goal, and engaging their talents in collective activity. Establishing an enabling structure is perhaps the most difficult for the would-be team leader, since many of the components of this condition may not be within their control: in organizational life we often inherit a team or a situation and can do little to modify it. Where we can, however, Hackman emphasizes the importance of intrinsically interesting work roles, meaningful degrees of autonomy, a climate in which feedback is given and received positively, norms of conduct which support active engagement with the working environment, and a team size and composition of members that promotes positive social interaction and a good mix of skills.

 Blog box

In no more than 300 words, reflect on the extent to which your current team (or one you have recently been a part of) fulfils the conditions set out by Hackman. If you are the leader of the team, in what ways does your leadership contribute to supporting effective team processes? How is this distinct from other forms of leadership you are called upon to exercise?

Collectively, the three conditions discussed so far are said to constitute the basic platform for competent teamwork. But teams do not work in an organizational vacuum, so the organizational context can be either supportive or destructive of the team's efforts. Important factors here are the reward system (by which is meant all forms of recognition and reinforcement, not just pay), information systems, needed to deliver the right amount and kind of information to inform the team's goals and activities, and educational systems, through which training and technical support are delivered. The final condition required for team effectiveness is the availability of expert coaching, either directly by the leader or through facilitated interventions by external professionals. The aim here is to enhance group processes in order to maximize the team's ability to use their collective resources in accomplishing the required work of the team as a whole. These processes relate to the distribution of effort amongst the team (high shared commitment or social loafing), the existence of performance strategies for accomplishing known and unknown tasks (reliance on routines versus innovation), and how members are called upon to contribute their skills and knowledge (shared and distributed or unevenly weighted). All of these processes can benefit from team coaching, helping the team members to work effectively with what they've got and with each other.

Whilst Hackman doesn't advocate a particular style of leadership—and, indeed, suggests that too much emphasis is often placed on the role of leaders in producing team performance—he does suggest the following 'execution skills' (Hackman and Walton, 1986) as being necessary if a team leader is to be effective in creating the key conditions discussed above:

- *Envisioning skill*—the ability to envision and articulate desired states
- *Inventive skill*—the ability to be creative in solving problems and seeing beyond the obvious
- *Negotiation skill*—the ability to work persistently and constructively with others to secure resources or support
- *Decision making skill*—the ability to make sound choices even in the face of limited information or uncertainty
- *Teaching skill*—the ability to support team members' learning either through direct teaching or through the provision of supportive experience
- *Interpersonal skill*—the ability to use a range of communication skills and styles to work constructively with others, even in difficult situations
- *Implementation skill*—the ability to get things done, at all levels of complexity

Hackman also emphasizes (Wageman, Fisher, and Hackman, 2009) the importance of timing when it comes to effective leadership interventions: team leaders need to know when a team is *predictably* ready for an intervention (type I timing)—for example, at its launch, as a mid-point progress review, and to harvest lessons learned at task completion—as well as knowing when to address the *unpredictable* nuances of group dynamics (type II timing). The key to the latter is said to be 'diagnosis on the fly'—that is, the ability to quickly diagnose team problems through the observation of the team doing its work, together with an ability to craft effective interventions in real time.

An alternative approach to team leadership is that of Susan Kogler Hill (2002). The founding premise here is that the team leader is in the driving seat of team effectiveness and that Hill's framework provides a 'road map' to help the leader diagnose team problems and take appropriate, corrective action. As such, a key element of the model is the requirement for the leader to take decisions about when to act and when to simply monitor what is happening. Once the decision to act is made, the type of action required must be determined as either task or relational and as either internal to the team or external. Figure 8.3 provides a summary of the decision points and underpinning factors as set out in Hill's 'road map'.

The model draws on a number of sources in providing a top-down view of team leadership, whereby leadership decisions are seen as prompting leader actions which, in turn, are said to bring about team effectiveness. The model has as its starting point the leader's mental model of the situation, bearing in mind the environmental and organizational constraints and resources (Zaccaro, Rittman, and Marks, 2001). It recognizes the need for behavioural

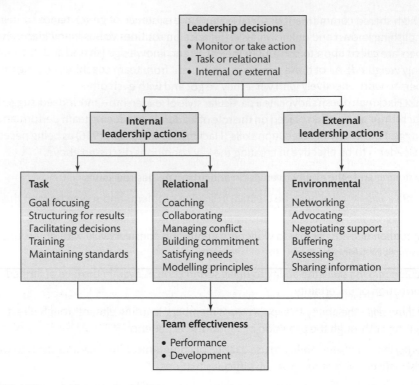

Figure 8.3 Hill's model for team leadership

Hill, Susan K. (2010) Team leadership. In Peter G. Northouse, *Leadership Theory and Practice.* Thousand Oaks, CA: Sage. Reproduced with permission.

flexibility (Barge, 1996) by the leader, underpinned by a wide repertoire of skills and behaviours to match the complexity of the situation. At the same time, a functional approach to leadership places the responsibility for guiding team-based problem solving in the hands of the leader (Fleishman et al., 1991). Most fundamentally, the framework adopts McGrath's (cited in Hackman and Walton, 1986) critical leadership functions of monitoring versus taking action and internal group issues versus external group issues as key to the role of an effective team leader. Together with a further sub-division of possible actions into task and relational, this process of decision making defines, according to Hill, the role of the effective team leader.

As Hill herself notes, the model is not without its weaknesses, not least of which is the lack of empirical support for its claims. Its complexity can also be seen as a double edged sword: good in that it is representative of the complexities of the real world but bad in that it makes the model hard to apply in real time, real world situations when a leader may be expected to produce solutions 'on the hoof'. It is also hard to see how the model translates into practical solutions for a range of everyday situations; as Hill puts it:

> What should you say to a team member who is crying? How do you deal with team members who are screaming at each other? What do you do when the organisation refuses to reward team performance? The team leadership model does not provide much guidance in everyday interactions and complications of team management. (Hill, 2010: 259)

What it does do is attempt to provide an overarching framework for the integration of a number of different aspects of leadership work, and to draw a boundary around leadership as it relates to teams and the support and development of team processes.

 Leadership in the media: Invictus

This powerful film shows us team leadership in its purest form: that of a national sports team. It depicts how Nelson Mandela, in his first term as the democratically-elected South African President, initiates a unique venture to unite the apartheid-torn land and quell the inevitable resistance to the radical change this represents. Mandela chooses the unlikely instrument of the Springboks—the national rugby team, previously denounced by him as emblematic of white supremacy in South Africa—to unite the country and give it a shared sense of national identity and pride. With the help of Springbok captain, Francois Pienaar, he sets the goal of winning the 1995 World Cup with a mixed race team. Mandela tries to inspire Pienaar to lead by example, by taking the radical step of introducing white security guards into his own (previously black) security team. Whilst the story is one of political skill and national triumph, it is Pienaar's leadership journey, and his ability to bring the team along with him, that most catches the attention. His success as a leader is clear—if we measure it by the success of the team in winning the tournament—but more interesting to consider is his impact on the team *as* a team: on their view of themselves and their sense of their own identity in a newly developing 'rainbow nation'.

A functional perspective on leadership in teams

We have already mentioned McGrath's reference to the critical functions of team leadership, relating to monitoring versus action and internal versus external issues. More broadly, McGrath proposes a functional approach to team leadership under which he suggests that the leader's 'main job is to do, or get done, whatever is not being adequately handled for group needs' (McGrath, 1962, as cited in Hackman and Walton, 1986: 5) Within this approach, the leader is seen as being effective to the extent that they are able to ensure that all the tasks and functions critical to team success are satisfactorily performed, either by themselves or by other members of the team. Building on this approach, Fleishman et al. (1991) saw team leadership as being a dynamic process of social problem solving accomplished through a range of generic problem solving skills which could be grouped under the headings of (1) information search and structuring; (2) information use in problem solving; (3) managing personnel resources; and (4) managing material resources. Zaccaro, Rittman, and Marks (2001) explicate this idea of functional leadership as a lens through which to understand leader–team dynamics, placing emphasis on the existence of reciprocal influence relationships whereby both leadership and team processes influence each other. Similar to Hackman's framework, they argue that leadership processes influence team effectiveness by their effects on four sets of team processes, namely cognitive, motivational, affective, and those relating to coordination, and that these effects are moderated by a number of characteristics of the environment, organization, and team within which they operate.

RESEARCH IN FOCUS: A functional model of team leadership

In their meta-analytic paper *What type of behaviours are functional in teams?* Burke et al. (2006) attempt to integrate Fleishman's functional approach with Hackman's key conditions (both of which we saw earlier in the chapter) to produce a function-based model of how leadership can impact on team performance. This integrated framework requires team leaders to search the environment for relevant clues and integrate the information obtained into their existing knowledge base and problem solving approaches in order to guide the team's problem solving processes. These processes should then produce a course of action. The leader needs to provide compelling direction to the team, in order that the courses of action chosen are collaborative and in line with collective team goals. This shared sense of direction then provides the underpinning rationale for the allocation of human and material resources. The provision of an enabling team structure and expert team coaching provide further support to team processes and ensure the generation of successful outcomes. Overall, the whole mechanism requires a supportive organizational context, in terms of rewards, training, and technical support, if it is to flourish. Whilst the resultant framework makes explicit use of the distinction between task focused and people focused activities as an organizing framework for leadership behaviours (as well as borrowing language from Transformational and Situational leadership theories), the internal versus external dimension is subsumed within the other layers of the framework. Overall, the resultant framework is an interesting attempt to integrate two different approaches to understanding team leadership, but there are some inconsistencies in its explication by Burke et al. which, we would suggest, stem from its attempt to do too much: to take too many typologies and squeeze them into one neat model. For example, in establishing the components of the model, they refer to the three categories of task focused leadership which have been empirically examined in teams, namely transactional, initiating structure, and boundary spanning. Whilst the latter two are clearly and usefully incorporated in their meta-analytic framework, the former—transactional—seems to disappear. Suggesting that this may form 'one mechanism that leaders may use during the provision of expert coaching' (Burke et al., 2006: 291–2) though equating it with the giving of feedback seems to us to be a bit of a stretch!

Source: Burke, CS, Stagl, KC, Klein, C, Goodwin, GF, Salas, E, and Halpin, SM (2006) What type of leadership behaviours are functional in teams? A meta-analysis. *The Leadership Quarterly*, 17, 288–307.

Discussion points: Is functional leadership really leadership?

- Based on the definition of functional leadership given in this chapter, to what extent do you think it is 'leadership' in the sense that it has been defined elsewhere in this text? Are the kinds of functional activities it is said to entail really about leading or just about getting things done?

- If we accept functional leadership as 'real' leadership, what skills and attributes would most qualify a potential team leader for fulfilling this role? How do they differ from those required for other forms of leadership?

- What challenges might arise for a team leader attempting to work in this way? How might they be viewed by (a) team members, (b) professional peers, and (c) organizational superiors?

- What kind of team situations or types of teams would be most amenable to this type of leadership? Where might it not work so well, and why?

From a critical perspective

Challenges to the integration of team and leadership theory

Whilst recognizing that team leadership now constitutes a discipline in its own right a number of challenges have been identified for those wishing to develop it either as a science or as a practice. Day, Gronn, and Salas (2006) discuss these challenges—which they also admit might constitute opportunities—under the following headings:

Multi-level issues

Day, Gronn, and Salas suggest that current attempts to understand what constitutes team leadership and how it can most effectively be practised need to do more—both conceptually and empirically—to ask questions about whether team leadership looks the same at team level as at individual level (isomorphism) or whether there are different looks at different levels (discontinuity). In the context of attempting to integrate the field, they suggest that this will clarify issues associated with how team-level leadership can transcend but not completely replace the contributions of individual leaders in building overall leadership capacity (Day, Gronn, and Salas, 2004).

Cross-level effects

Much of the extant literature on team leadership takes a 'top-down' approach by considering how team leaders can impact on team processes and performance. But what about 'bottom-up' effects whereby the team exerts influence or has an impact on the team leader? This is seen as an under-researched aspect of team dynamics, and it is suggested that research should consider a more dynamic approach 'in which the leader's behaviour towards the team changes as a function of the team's collective ability or capacity to set its own direction or provide for its own support' (Kozlowski et al., 1996, cited in Day, Gronn, and Salas, 2006).

Design, methods, and measurement issues

Whilst methodologically and theoretically sound research is always at a premium, and never easy to achieve, the difficulties of achieving this when examining team leadership at the team level of analysis are manifold. Sampling a sufficient number of teams to achieve statistical significance, being clear of the appropriate level of analysis in situations which are multi-level and dynamic, and developing appropriate measures to capture the cognitive, affective, and behavioural processes involved in team leadership are just some of the challenges to be addressed here.

Studying team leadership in context

Related to the previous issue is that of studying team leadership in context. Teams do not operate in a vacuum, nor are all teams similar in composition and type. A wide range of contextual and organizational factors will impact on the role a team leader is required to play and how they are required to exercise their leadership in order to be effective: the need for wide ranging field research is thus paramount if the largely conceptual models we have seen to date are to be empirically validated or new theories developed.

Hybrid leadership forms

Lastly, Day, Gronn, and Salas (2004) draw our attention to the need for more flexible conceptions of leadership to serve the many forms and functions of teams that require 'team leadership'. Distributed and emergent forms of leadership may need to be considered alongside more traditional, formally designated leaders to take account of virtual and self-managed teams, or other non-standard team formats.

Answers to a number of these challenges are starting to emerge, some of which we will explore in the remainder of this chapter. We start by considering a reversal of the influence process normally associated with leadership, which considers leadership as an outcome of team processes rather than a director of them.

New kinds of teams for new kinds of situations?

Traditional models of teamwork and team leadership place significant emphasis on the stability of team membership and lengthy processes of team development, at the same time as acknowledging that many teams do not enjoy the luxury of stable membership over time. A number of writers have considered the issues of team fluidity—together with the rapidly changing situations teams are often required to address—as the basis for a new take on what it is to be a team and how leadership can ensure effectiveness. So, for example, Edmondson (2012) proposes the concept of 'teaming' to describe a format in which people collaborate in fluid groups that emerge and dissolve in response to needs identified as work progresses. This 'teamwork on the fly' can be brought into effect to solve unique problems or to address situations where unexpected events require a rapid change of direction. The role of the leader in such teams becomes that of inspiring and enabling the teams rather than composing and managing them. Edmondson suggests that in modern organizations, it may be necessary to work in multiple teams with shifting membership and moving goals, and that team leaders will need to embrace principles from project management to make it work. She sets out a range of 'hardware' (technical issues relating to scoping, structuring, and task sorting) and 'software' (behaviour management in relation to emphasizing purpose, building psychological safety, embracing failure, and putting failure to work) related challenges which the leader of such teams will need to address.

Seijts and Gandz (2009) cover similar ground with their idea of 'one teaming', although the emphasis here is on the requirement for people to be selected for and trained in team skills *before* the advent of crisis situations brings a team into existence in order to form effective teams faster. The authors draw on literature relating to high reliability organizations and disaster situations, such as the Apollo 13 mission and the 1996 Everest expedition, in suggesting that the four themes which consistently underpin the ability to 'one team' are team leadership, team composition, extensive practice, and clear norms of communication.

Bushe and Chu's (2011) notion of 'fluid teams' specifically considers the issue of unstable team membership, and recognizes the conditions under which it may be necessary to operate in this way. So, for example, upsizing or downsizing within an organization, or high staff turnover, may result in frequent changes in team composition. So too may the require-ment for different team skills at different stages during a project, the need to offer career de-velopment opportunities, or the desire to promote vigilant communication in high reliability work settings. They suggest that the resultant fluidity creates problems around loss of indi-vidual knowledge from the team, lack of shared mental models, low individual commitment to team goals, and a lack of team cohesion. The proposed solutions to these problems focus on two areas: increasing efficacy—for example, through the creation of generalized roles and prescribed processes and the reduction of task interdependence—and increasing belonging—for example through designing peer transparency into work and building stable pools of formal expertise. Even with these measures, Bushe and Chu take the view that fluid teams will always be necessary rather than desirable, and that there is no substitute for traditional processes of team formation or for effective team leadership.

Also prevalent in traditional literature on teams and team leadership is the focus on inter-nal team processes. Ancona, Bresman, and Caldwell (2009) challenge this focus by suggesting that today's interconnected world requires teams to have an external orientation: to reach across boundaries to forge the dense network of connections needed to enable them to quickly understand complex problems. They call such teams 'X-teams' and set out three key principles which underpin their effectiveness:

- They make external activity their normal modus operandi
- They have a flexible membership and leadership structure
- They move through three distinct phases of exploration, exploitation, and exportation in understanding problems, utilizing resources available in solving them, and sharing their knowledge with others

X-team leadership is, not surprisingly, said to be based on a distributed leadership model and requires leaders to model the above principles as well as choosing team members for their networks rather than their functional skills; using internal processes to facilitate external work; and helping to focus the team on activities relating to scouting for information, ambassador-ship for their solutions, and task co-ordination. The idea that we are in a 'connective era' is echoed by Lipman-Blumen and Leavitt (2009), who suggest the need for 'hot groups'—said to be a state of mind rather than a type of team—led by 'connective leaders' to combat the com-peting demands of interdependence and diversity in the modern world. Hot groups are said to live in a 'task bubble' with their sole focus being on doing whatever it takes to solve the problem—be this commandeering resources, being rampant individualists, or sidestepping social and political norms. Team members share a sense of excitement and ennoblement, and are admitted to membership on the basis of perceived contribution. Whilst such groups are likely to be internally democratic, they still need leadership if they are to be effective. Lipman-Blumen and Leavitt see connective leaders as falling into three main types—'conductors'—who are hands on and have task related expertise; 'patrons'—high level executives who act as ambassadors to the rest of the organization; and 'keepers of the flame'—who act as a thread connecting sequential hot groups. What they all share are characteristics of seeing connec-tions, building shared visions, having ethical political savvy, creating a sense of community at the same time as remaining stubbornly accountable, sacrificing anything to attain the desired goal, and seeing themselves and their team as part of a noble enterprise. What emerges from these new forms of team, designed to respond to increasingly complex problems and operating environments, is the continuing emphasis on leaders and leadership to ensure their effectiveness. There is a suggestion that everyone—team members and leaders alike—need to step up a gear to meet the increased challenge of the modern world.

Self-managing and virtual teams—going against the flow?

The notion of self-managing teams may be seen as posing a challenge to the supposedly well-established role of leadership in teams, by suggesting that teams can operate without leadership—or, at least, without a leader—to guide them. They can be seen as representing a radical departure from more traditional, leader-led teams in terms of how work is organized within the team and how responsibility is distributed. As such, the team is empowered to assume responsibility for the whole of the task or function it exists to deliver and to exercise decision making authority to an extent traditionally reserved for management.

A case in point: Langdale and Ambleside Mountain Rescue

Langdale and Ambleside Mountain Rescue Team (LAMRT) is one of twelve semi-autonomous mountain rescue teams in the Lake District area of England existing under the umbrella of a regional association. Members of the team are all volunteers, who give up their time to help lost and injured walkers and climbers, and to assist the local emergency services. LAMRT members respond to over 100 incidents a year, ranging from twisted ankles, through lost or overdue walkers, to climbing fatalities. They are a self-funding charitable organization and the 'professional volunteers' come from all walks of life and go out in all weathers, providing a 24/7 service. When the call comes through from the local police, team members are paged and attend incidents on a best efforts basis. The response could require just a few members, or could involve co-ordination with adjacent teams and emergency services. Whilst all members will be competent fell-walkers and have first aid training, individual members may be experts at navigation, remote wilderness first aid, rigging rescue ropes, or working with search dogs. For any given incident, any combination of team members could be on scene, and the 'team' will form into an effective unit based on what needs to be done and who is best qualified to do it. There is no formal leader, but everyone has both the authority and the responsibility to make decisions as they arise and to take actions as they are required: a true example of a self managed-team.

Sources: <www.lamrt.org.uk>.; <www.facebook.com/pages/Langdale-Ambleside-Mountain-Rescue-Team-LAMRT>; <www.ldsamra.org.uk>.

Mounting evidence in the literature suggests that self-managed teams, when working well, can enhance work–life quality, customer service, and productivity (e.g. Cohen and Bailey, 1997; Emery and Fredendall, 2002), although it has also been observed that self-managing teams can vary considerably in effectiveness. Millikin, Hom, and Manz (2010) claim to have identified a broad range of self-management competencies exercised by members of self-managed teams which aggregate to form a collective construct that influences the productivity of the networked team. These competencies, which they categorize as behaviour-focused strategies, natural reward strategies, and constructive thought strategies, are said to constitute 'self-leadership' and hence to operate as a substitute for traditional leadership for the team.

All three competency categories contain elements that would normally be provided by a team leader—so, for example, constructive thought strategies include 'imagery of successful outcomes' and 'positive self-talk' whilst behaviour-focused strategies include 'self-set goals' and 'self-reward'—but in self-managed teams these are provided from within. Whilst the aim of Millikin and his colleagues' work was to explore what made self-managing teams effective, we think their findings can also be interpreted as suggesting that—far from being leaderless—self-managed teams develop their own brand of self-leadership to meet this apparently enduring need.

Discussion points: Self-managed teams—do they really exist?

- Based on your own experience of working in teams, do you agree with Millikin et al's (2010) findings that so-called 'self-managing' teams will actually develop substitutes for leadership, or do you think they can be genuinely leaderless?

- In what situations might self-managed or empowered teams be most effective? When might this be a risky or ineffective structure to adopt?

- If you were tasked with recruiting members to a self-managed team, what skills and characteristics—apart from any task-specific ones—do you think it would be important to incorporate into the team? How would these need to be distributed amongst team members?

The advent of virtual teams—and an increasing capacity for distance or virtual working within more traditional teams—has been an inevitable corollary of advances in technology. Such teams, whose members are geographically disbursed and cross-functional and yet are frequently called upon to work on highly inter-dependent tasks and to be accountable for shared outputs, present another type of challenge to the traditional model of team leadership. Research in this area has tended to focus on two main questions: (1) how does virtual leadership differ from face-to-face leadership and (2) how can leaders use the technology which divides them from their team as an effective tool to bring the team together?

Taking the latter first, Malhotra, Majchrzak, and Rosen (2007) identified six leadership practices of effective leaders of virtual teams, three of which turned explicitly on the effective use of technology to bridge the gap between being a physical team and being a virtual one. Addressing the first question, Zimmerman, Wit, and Gill (2008) considered how the degree of 'virtualness' of a team impacted on the relative perceived importance of task-oriented and relationship-oriented leadership behaviours by members when compared with face-to-face teams. Whilst there were some observed differences in the balance required between the two types of behaviours, the overall finding was that virtual team members needed more of both to be effective as a team. Cascio and Shurygailo (2003) produced a typology of 'virtualness' in teams—based on the number of locations and the number of managers involved in the situation—and mapped how the key processes of organizing and conducting virtual meetings and adapting one's communication style were addressed by leaders across the different types.

Key issues for virtual team leaders centred around establishing home/work boundaries for their team members, establishing norms and procedures, instilling processes for archiving team knowledge, encouraging emergent leadership, and promoting cooperation. Cascio and Shurygailo suggest that project management and project planning skills are of particular importance for leaders of virtual teams. Similarly, Zaccaro and Bader (2003) draw attention to the potential for 'process loss' within virtual teams, and the need for leaders to focus their efforts around activities which enable team members to identify who has the knowledge or skill required in a particular situation, and to combine these resources in the most effective and appropriate way.

Other research has focused on how specific leadership models translate to a virtual context with transformational leadership seeming to be a particularly popular choice here. So, for example, Balthazard, Waldman, and Warren (2009) explore the emergence of transformational leadership in virtual teams: when compared with transformational leadership in face-to-face teams, this is seen to rest less on personality dimensions such as extraversion and emotional stability and more on linguistic quality in written communications. In another study, Purvanova and Bono (2009) concluded that transformational leadership behaviours had a stronger effect and produced better team performance in virtual teams which used only computer-mediated communications than in face-to-face teams using traditional forms of communication.

Discussion points: Virtualness in teams

- How has the advance of technology impacted on your own working practices and on the 'virtualness' of teams you have been a member of? What influence do you believe this has had on how the teams were led?

- How feasible do you think it is to translate traditional forms of leadership—for example, transformational leadership—to virtual contexts? Or is a new, distinct form of leadership needed here? If so, what would be the important characteristics of such leadership?

- What characteristics do you think would be needed in virtual team members for them to work effectively as a team given that they rarely, if ever, meet each other?

On a final note, in considering the environmental factors which mediate the effects of leadership in team contexts, it is worth drawing special attention to cultural influences. In an increasingly global economy, leaders may need to lead across national boundaries and teams may be comprised of members from different cultures, with significant implications for the style of leadership adopted and the level of performance generated. Early exploration of this topic has mapped directive and supportive styles of leadership against the cultural dimension of individualism–collectivism with interesting results. In individualistic societies, managers tend to use less directive and less supportive leadership behaviours (i.e. less leadership overall) than in collective societies. Whilst team cohesiveness is negatively/positively associated with directive/supportive leadership behaviours respectively, it does not appear to be directly related to the individualism–collectivism of the host society. This is a new field of study within the literature, but one that can be expected to grow in the coming years.

Chapter summary

In this chapter we have considered:

- How team leadership differs from leadership per se in its emphasis on the coordination of team processes as the means to achieving organizational goals rather than as it impacts on a collection of individuals
- Team formation processes and the factors which impact on team performance
- The historical developments which led to an emphasis on teams as an important means of delivering organizational goals
- Two mainstream models of team leadership and the manner in which they are said to impact on team processes and team performance, including functional and relational views of leadership
- How self-managed and virtual teams provide a counter-point to the view that leadership is vital for team performance, either through their ability to operate without leaders or through the different ways in which technology requires leaders to lead their teams

 Integrative case study: Teamwork in China: a cultural challenge?

HighTech Solutions Limited is a UK-based niche technology manufacturing company, providing IT solutions to a wide range of industries. Over the last ten years, the company has expanded into Europe and the USA, with R&D and production facilities in twenty-one locations across seven countries. Having been with the company during the whole of this period, you have been instrumental in setting up three of the overseas locations—in Spain, Germany, and the USA—and are currently general manager of a large and successful plant, with R&D capability, on the outskirts of Madrid. The Board of Directors are now in the process of acquiring a competitor company based in Southern China, and have singled you out as the appropriate person to take on the role of general manager at the newly acquired company and to integrate it into the HighTech organization. As part of this integration process, the Board want you to introduce the practice of team working which is common throughout the rest of the organization. You have been asked to investigate the issues which this change of structure and style might raise and to present your implementing plan to the Board in three weeks time. As a starting point, you have begun to investigate the experiences of other companies, mostly from the USA, who have invested in China and attempted to introduce Western team-working practices.

Your research has suggested that traditional Chinese culture may present competing influences in relation to teamwork. On the one hand, the collectivist orientation of Chinese culture seems likely to support some of the core aspects of teamwork, such as common purpose, task interdependence, and group orientation. This orientation would also make it likely that workers would be willing to suppress individual interests for the good of team goals. On the other hand, the rigidly hierarchical nature of Chinese society, emphasized by Confucian principles, is likely to mean people feel uncomfortable with the fully autonomous and flexible working required of effective teams. Whilst the introduction of Western management styles and practices by a number of Western-invested enterprises (most notable being Motorola) may be having a cumulative effect on the traditional Chinese management system and on employee orientation, there is still a widespread suspicion of Western HR practices generally, which may impact on workers' perceptions of team working. This said, the younger generation Chinese are developing new attitudes as a result of more contact with the West: they are generally more individualistic and less political than the older generation and tend to be more receptive and adaptive to new ways of working.

(Continued...)

Considering some of the cultural aspects in more detail, your research suggests that collectivism may not be as supportive of team working as you had at first thought, since the focus of Chinese collective feeling is the family or clan, rather than work groups. This said, where US companies have introduced ideas of teamwork, and provided training in teamwork practices, Chinese employees have been found to develop a sense of identity with their functional department. The notion of power distance has also been found to be important: the hierarchical nature of traditional Chinese organizations has been reflective of an acceptance of uneven power distribution, with consequent expectations of job titles and status, appropriate behaviour to supervisors, and accepted patterns of responsibility and decision making. The degree of responsibility and participation required for true team working may run counter to these expectations and take workers out of their traditional comfort zones.

Motorola Inc. is one company that has effectively introduced team working to its pager manufacturing plant in Tianjin, China. Even here, however, your research suggests that team working is seen more as a general principle or 'spirit' rather than as specific integrated practices. More generally, research has shown that whilst the idea is gaining some appeal for Chinese workers, the actual practice of Western team working may prove less satisfying than they expect. Team working in this context is also circumscribed by strong, appointed leaders and exists within the more traditional framework of conformity, maintenance of face, and managerial authority. The more truly independent self-directed teams found elsewhere in the world may still be a long way off for China.

In investigating how you might implement team working in China, you have found some useful material to guide your efforts. This suggests that convincing workers of the interdependence of the tasks they need to perform will be important in creating a strong teamwork orientation. Also, workers are more likely to be willing to work in teams where their personal and professional evaluations of co-workers are positive—this could have significant implications for the composition of teams. These work situation factors may be more important in generating effective team working than broader cultural factors. Building a pattern of more open communication will also be important in strengthening mutual trust. Finally, given the importance of maintaining face, dealing with issues of poor performance at team level will present a cultural challenge. Giving feedback on poor performance and offering peer coaching are likely to be very uncomfortable for Chinese workers, so may require a different approach. The Chinese practice of simply working round the underperforming colleague and trying to minimize the damage they can cause will need to be rooted out sensitively and with care.

Sources: Chen, X. and Barshes, W. (2000) To team or not to team? *The China Business Review*, March–April; Bishop, James W., Chen, Xiangming, and Scott, K. Dow (1999) What drives Chinese toward teamwork? A study of US-invested companies in China. Paper presented at the Southern Management Association annual meeting, Atlanta, 27–30 October; Luo, Yue-er, Duerring, Erik, and Byham, William C. (2008) *Leadership Success in China: An Expatriate's Guide*, Development Dimensions International. Thanks also to our postgraduate students from China, who shared their own experiences and views of team working with us.

Case study questions

- How would you advise your Board of Directors in relation to their desire to introduce team working into their plants in China? What do you think would be the benefits and challenges of such a move?

- As the proposed expatriate general manager of the Chinese plant, how would you go about introducing teams and team working to the plant? What would you want to know about the employees and about current working practices before making the change?

- How would you practise 'team leadership' in this context, and how might this differ from team leadership in a more individualistic culture? More generally, how transferable do you think this style of leadership is to other cultures?

Further reading

Hackman, J. Richard (2002) *Leading Teams: Setting the stage for great performances.* Boston, MA: Harvard Business Press.

Hill, Susan K. (2010) Team leadership. In Peter G. Northouse, *Leadership Theory and Practice.* Thousand Oaks, CA: Sage.

Katzenbach, Jon R. and Smith, Douglas K. (1993) *The Wisdom of Teams.* Boston, MA: Harvard Business School Press.

Lencioni, Patrick (2002) *The Five Dysfunctions of a Team: A Leadership Fable.* San Francisco: Jossey-Bass.

Part 2

Hot Topics in Leadership

9

Leading change: Leadership's natural habitat?

 Learning outcomes

On completion of this chapter you will:

- Be familiar with the different types of change undertaken in organizations and the main approaches to planned change
- Understand the difference between linear, 'n-step' models of change and their contextualized counterparts
- Have considered the role of leadership in organizational change, and how this differs from the management of change
- Be aware of how and why employees resist change, and the approaches open to leaders in combating such resistance
- Understand how different approaches to leadership—in particular transformational and charismatic leadership—have come to be associated with change.

Introduction

If we accept the distinctions discussed in Chapter 1 in relation to leadership versus management, then change presents itself as the leader's natural habitat: it is in changing situations that leadership is most needed to show direction, provide inspiration, and solve problems. This chapter considers the change process in organizations, from both micro and macro perspectives, and the role of leadership in successful change implementation. The importance of this topic cannot be overestimated in the current fast-moving, global economic climate—not for nothing is the subject of leading change the first of our 'hot topics' in this text. New technology, increasing competition, changing customer demands, a constantly shifting regulatory environment, and the far-reaching impact of globalization make change the only constant for most organizations. Strategic change is accepted as a requirement of survival—of the need to keep up with external developments outside the organization's control. Whether it be physical restructuring (centralizing to cut costs or decentralizing to promote flexibility), cultural change (becoming more customer focused or embedding quality/efficiency initiatives such as Lean), the adoption of a new competitive strategy (quality rather than cost, or niche rather than general), or any of a myriad of other changes which organizations may seek to implement, what underpins them all is the need to survive: the recognition that just continuing to do what you have always done is likely to be a recipe for disaster in an environment that is very tough on organizational dinosaurs. Why then do we seem to hear so much about the failure of strategic change initiatives? If change is so important to organizational survival, why are organizations not better at it? It has been claimed that 'the capacity to manage change is an essential characteristic of executive leadership' (Taylor-Bianco and Schermerhorn, 2006: 458) and yet success rates for organizational change programmes seem to be remarkably low. For example, Appelbaum et al. (2008) suggested that between 55 and 75 per cent of planned change initiatives do not achieve the majority of their intended goals. Gilley, Dixon, and Gilley (2008) summarize research into this issue by saying that between a third and two-thirds of major change initiatives are deemed to be failures, while some actually make the situation worse. They draw on the work of Cope (2003) in claiming that some research would put the failure to deliver sustainable change through planned change programmes as high as 80–90 per cent. Interestingly, they also report on an empirical study they conducted which suggested that 'employees at all organizational levels hold a somewhat negative perception of their leaders' ability to effectively implement change' (Gilley, Dixon, and Gilley, 2008: 164) and that nearly 76 per cent of their respondents 'reported that their leaders never, rarely or only sometimes effectively implemented change'. Whilst this is only a small study—a drop in the ocean of research into change and change leadership—it does reinforce the strong association between leadership and change which we have already noted in the leadership literature.

Discussion point: Why change fails

From your own experience of organizational change initiatives, what are the key factors which determine their success or failure?

- What role does leadership play in implementing change? Who needs to be involved and what do they need to do?
- How does the initial introduction of change need to be followed through? What is the role of middle management at this stage?
- How do those on the receiving end need to be involved? Is communication enough, or will only consultation build the required commitment?
- In your experience, what is the biggest or most frequent barrier to effective organizational change?

It is no surprise that research suggests that those organizations that did best at implementing change appeared to have strong leadership that was closely involved with the change process. Driving change was not handed over to external consultants or initiated from the top but then left to run its course: instead the expertise to lead change was embedded in the functional capacity of the organization and involved at every stage of the process. This brings us to one of the fundamental issues we will be grappling with in this chapter: the difference between leading change and managing change. The change models presented below are all framed in terms of 'managing' a planned change process, with the emphasis being on stages to be gone through or factors to be considered. Thus the emphasis is on change processes rather than on who undertakes them. There is a different literature, however—which we explore in the critical perspective—which considers how different leadership approaches dovetail with the requirements of successful change. In particular transformational and charismatic leadership have often been associated with change and, in this chapter, are considered from a change rather than a leadership perspective. This literature recognizes the role of figure heads and role models in putting a personal face on the change process and influencing people to buy into the need to change their behaviour and to strive for new goals. Perhaps Caldwell (2003) sums it up best when he says that change leadership is about creating a vision of change whereas change management is about translating that vision into agendas and actions. This begs the more fundamental question, which we will also touch on later in this chapter, concerning the possibility of planned change versus an acknowledgement of its more emergent characteristics.

 Blog box

In my personal experience, it is easier to diagnose what needs changing in an organization than it is to make it better. Some years ago, I worked as a training consultant for an educational trust working with vulnerable young people and subsidising their work through training consultancy with corporate clients. The disconnect between the background/experience of the youth trainers and those of the corporate trainers—and the way in which each group was rewarded—caused considerable tension within what was a relatively small and close-knit organization, with a knock-on effect on commitment and staff retention. Like most of the corporate trainers, I was working for a lower than commercial salary because I believed in the work the organization was doing. I was still earning more than the youth trainers, however, who often dealt with situations that would have terrified me (young people acting out against anyone they saw as being in authority, for example, often violently) and exercised considerable skill and courage in doing so—and who were receiving the 'market rate' for this kind of work. What was needed was to identify creative ways of rewarding both teams—recognizing the value of development opportunities, increased autonomy and responsibility, and opportunities for the two teams to work together, for example—and to build on shared values to reduce tension and dissent. To my lasting regret, I became 'part of the problem' by repeatedly articulating the structural problems which underpinned these tensions rather than 'part of the solution' by creatively trying to find ways of improving them by bridging the gap between the corporate and youth training teams. I wasn't resistant to change, but nor was I proactive in seeking it. (MIW)

Role of leadership in change

So what is the role of leadership in change, and is it always the same? In their critical text entitled *Managing Organisational Change*, Palmer, Dunford, and Akin (2009) suggest that, as leaders, we form an image of change that determines how we see our role. They go on to suggest that there are six dominant images of change each suggesting a particular change leader/manager's role: these roles are director, coach, navigator, interpreter, caretaker, and nurturer. They see these different roles as arising from two key images of managing—as either controlling or shaping—and three key images of potential change outcomes—intended, partially intended, and unintended. Collectively, these produce a matrix of different activities and capabilities which a change leader brings into play in choosing what interventions to make in bringing about change. The views of management are likely to be inherent in the manager themselves, and part of their leadership identity and past experience. The change outcomes may be a function of the environment in which change occurs, the organizational culture, and the clarity with which the goals of the change initiative have been delineated. The resultant role images thus range from that of the *director*—who takes a controlling stance and sees the desired outcomes of the change as being wholly achievable—to that of the *nurturer* who recognizes that even small changes may have a big impact on an organization and that management is unlikely to be able to control all the outcomes of any given change, thus seeing their role as enabling positive self-organizing by organizational members. This framework offers us an insight into the complexity of change and of the role(s) of individuals in bringing it about. Nadler and Tushman (1990) offer a different typology, dividing change into a 2×2 matrix depending upon whether it is incremental or strategic and anticipatory or reactive, and suggest three components of the leadership role required—in different measure—to bring about different types of change, namely envisioning, energizing, and enabling. Whilst Nadler and Tushman claim that special kinds of leadership are required to bring about organizational change, Morrison (1994) reminds us that getting change to work is still about the basic need to understand and influence people either one-to-one or in groups. This is leadership at its most fundamental. Similarly, when Galpin (1996) states that effective leaders possess six attributes for leading change—namely creativity, a team orientation, good listening and coaching skills, a sense of accountability, and an appreciativeness for others— these skills are such as we would expect most effective leaders to display. We could take this as confirmation that change is truly the natural home of leadership—as the title of this chapter suggests—but as we shall see later, this could be a mistake: leadership may be just as necessary in resisting change or supporting stability and change may actually be hindered by an over-ambitious approach or the wrong kind of leadership.

Resistance to change

So far, we have talked about change from the perspective of those initiating it and, whilst we have not suggested that this in itself is simple, we have overlooked one of the major barriers to successful change implementation—that of resistance by those on the receiving end. We will look at this from a situational or contingency perspective later in the chapter—when we consider the work of Kotter and Schlesinger (2008) in setting out strategies for addressing different kinds of resistance—but the idea of resistance also represents an important micro level perspective on change, and one which requires an understanding of fundamental human emotions. At an organizational or macro level, change requires the mobilization of effort in a new direction, the adoption of new behaviours to achieve the change objectives, and the embedding of new ways of working into the organizational culture. These three stages need to be paralleled at an individual or micro level as employees learn to let go of their past ways of work and expectations, adapt to new ways of working, and to gradually learn to see these as a good thing and 'the way we do things around here'. Whilst some of us are more open to change than others, research suggests that all of us go through broadly the same stages of reaction to changes that are likely to affect us. Work in relation to individual reactions to organizational change has its origins in the work of Kübler Ross (e.g. Kübler Ross, 1969; Kübler Ross and Kessler, 2005) and others who investigated people's responses to personal loss (particularly to bereavement) and suggested a five-stage model of how they come to terms with what has happened to them and are gradually able to move on. Corporate authors observed

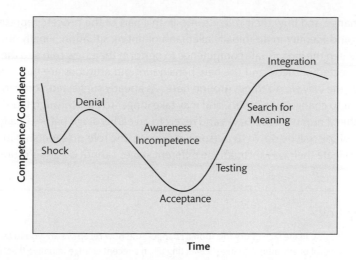

Figure 9.1 The transition curve

Adams, J., Hayes, J., and Hopson, C. (1976) *Transition: Understanding and Managing Personal Change*, London: Martin Robertson & Company. Reproduced with permission of John Wiley & Sons Inc.

a parallel between situations of personal loss and the potential losses employees may suffer in the advent of organizational change. Thus skill sets they have relied upon may become obsolete, objectives they are committed to may be replaced, team members they trust, like, and respect may be made redundant, and their own identity as it relates to a particular role may be threatened. Similar to the 'bereavement curve' developed by Kübler Ross—setting out the bereavement stages of disbelief, yearning, anger, depression, and acceptance—the transition curve (Adams, Hayes, and Hopson, 1976) maps the confidence and competence of employees dealing with change over time. The curve, as shown in Figure 9.1, suggests that individuals undergoing change pass through seven stages.

Initially, as the need for change is forced upon them, they suffer a feeling of shock as they realize that their own skills may become obsolete and their behaviours will have to change. The curve predicts that they will experience a drop in self-confidence as a result. After this initial reaction, there is likely to be a period of denial, when they either convince themselves that the proposed changes will not happen or that their own behaviour will not need to change. This process of rationalization leads to a return of their self-confidence, but actually prevents them from moving forward in the ways required to meet the changing needs of the situation. Thus they may attempt to perform new roles or fulfil changed job requirements by performing in the same old way and hence will not perform well. Over time, awareness of this underperformance will be forced upon them—either through their own rising self-awareness or as a result of feedback from the change initiators—leading to a further drop in confidence accompanied by feelings of inadequacy or deskilling. In parallel with this awareness is likely to come an acceptance of the necessity for change, both in themselves and in the organization as a whole, together with a willingness to let go of past behaviours and attitudes and to adopt new ones. Gradually, as they test out new behaviours and find them effective in generating improved performance, their confidence will be rebuilt. Through trial and error, they will discover which behaviours work and which do not, and will start to make sense of the overall pattern of change and how their role fits into it: this part of the process represents a search for meaning and identity in an initially alien and daunting situation. Finally, there ceases to be a gap between the individual's competence to perform their new role and the level of performance expected of them, and the new behaviours and attitudes are fully integrated into their sense of 'the way we do things around here'. As already suggested, some individuals are more resistant to change than others, and may take longer to pass through these stages—they may even suffer a number of setbacks and revert to an earlier stage before finally moving on. Whilst some of this will be down to personal resilience, the role of leadership in helping employees to navigate their way through the different stages cannot be underestimated.

 Blog box

How resilient are you in the face of organizational change? And how receptive are you to the need for personal behavioural or attitudinal change? Reflecting upon a recent change initiative that has occurred in your organization, jot down your reflections on these two questions in no more than 300 words. If you now recognize that you were slow to adapt to or accept change, what could you have done differently to make the transition smoother for yourself and more effective for the organization?

In the mainstream

Normative models of change

In 1995, John Kotter wrote an article in the Harvard Business Review entitled *Why Transformation Efforts Fail*. In it, he outlined eight 'errors' which he had observed that companies make in attempting to implement major change initiatives. This empirical piece—based on collating data from organizations such as General Motors, British Airways, Bristol-Myers Squibb, and Eastern Airlines—was to form the basis of his 'eight stage' model of change, later to become a successful book (Kotter, 1996). Kotter's was one of a number of normative models that suggested that successful change required the change process to go through a linear series of stages and that each stage needed to be completed in order to generate the desired outcomes. Most basic of these is Kurt Lewin's (1958) 'unfreeze-move-refreeze' model. The initial stage—unfreezing—is about preparing people in the organization for change by making them dissatisfied with the status quo and aware of the need for change. It is about creating a readiness for change at all levels within the organization by bringing people to a point where they feel that the pain and disruption which change often causes is worth enduring in order to overcome perceived problems. Next comes the actual change phase—referred to as moving by Lewin—in which the required changes are implemented through the introduction of new systems and policies, and through training and development to promote new behaviours and attitudes. In the final phase—refreezing—these new behaviours and attitudes are embedded through celebrating successes, rewarding desired behaviours, and other forms of positive reinforcement to prevent people from relapsing into the old ways.

   Whilst this model is still widely used, one of the main criticisms levelled against it is that in the modern world—where change is ongoing—this is a very static model. Recognition that refreezing will almost inevitably be followed by a further unfreezing and moving has resulted in the initial phase often being referred to as mobilizing and the third phase being renamed institutionalizing. This amendment fails to do away with the fundamentally 'synoptic' nature of this theory of planned change, and indeed most similar theories. It continues to rely on the idea of a 'snapshot' of where the organization is at a particular point in time, and to propose the intentional changing from one snapshot to another by means of an intentional intervention. As Ladkin, Wood, and Pillay (2010) observe, this type of thinking is based ultimately on Enlightenment ideas of cause and effect, which also underpin the largely Western tradition of leadership writing. As early as 1977, Pfeffer questioned whether the attribution of causation to individual social actors—and in particular, leaders—actually meets the necessary requirements for a causal explanation, and yet this approach to understanding leadership and change remains a prevalent theme. We shall return to this issue in the critical section of the chapter.

Other so-called 'n-step' models (Collins, 1998) have included Kanter, Stein, and Jick's (1992) 10-step model, Nadler's (1998) 12 'action steps', and Pendlebury, Grouard, and Meston's (1998) 'ten keys' to change. All of these are variations on the same idea: that change requires a sequence of stages to occur in a linear fashion if it is to be successful. Taking Kotter's 8-step model (illustrated in Figure 9.2) as representative, let us examine the stages in more detail.

If we examine these eight stages, we can see the parallels with Lewin's process of unfreezing, moving, and refreezing. Hickman (2010) categorizes stage 1 as unfreezing, stages 2 to 7 as moving or change, and stage 8 as refreezing: we would suggest that there is more preparatory work to be done and that the first four stages are about letting go of the past and preparing people for change, the middle two stages are where change actually happens, and the final

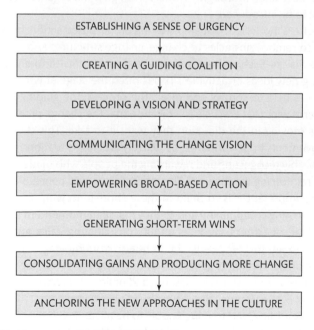

Figure 9.2 The eight stage process of creating major change

Kotter, J. P. (2012) *Leading Change*, with a New Preface by the Author, Harvard Business Review Press. Reproduced with permission.

two stages are about refreezing around the new behaviours and attitudes (although argu-ably stage seven is both about moving and refreezing). In establishing a sense of urgency, the change initiator should, according to Kotter, examine the market and competitive realities relevant to the sector in which the organization operates and, based on the information thus gathered, identify the potential crises or opportunities which can be used to create a percep-tion of the need for change. With this information under their belt, it will then be important to form a guiding coalition by bringing together a team of colleagues with enough power to spearhead the change. The third stage of the process is for this group to create a vision of what the changed organization will look like in order to provide direction to the change effort, and to develop strategies for achieving that vision. Only then are they ready to start communicat-ing with the wider organization. In communicating the vision—stage four of Kotter's model—it is said to be important to take every opportunity and to use every communication channel available to repeatedly communicate both the vision and the supporting strategies to others. Under-communicating—stating the vision once and then assuming you've finished—is one of the most frequently cited reasons for why change initiatives fail: people don't get the message because they don't see it consistently and frequently repeated.

Palmer, Dunford, and Akin (2009) observe that the opposite problem—information overload—can also be detrimental to effective change, and draw on Clampitt, DeKoch, and Cushman's (2000) typology in suggesting that it is not just the amount of communication but the type that is crucial. At the same time, the guiding coalition needs to role model the behav-iours expected of employees—another common reason for change initiatives to fail is when employees get mixed messages because senior managers say one thing and do another! Only once these stages have been thoroughly worked through is the organization said to be ready for actual change to be introduced.

Stage five of Kotter's model is about empowering broad-based action, by which he is refer-ring to the need to remove obstacles to change, change structures and systems that under-mine the change vision—such as inappropriate reward systems—and encourage people to take risks in trying new ideas or activities. This is often the stage at which unintended out-comes can arise. To help to control and direct the process, the guiding coalition needs to generate short-term wins that are a clear indication that the change process is working; that is, that change is moving in the direction they want it to take. This stage entails planning for visible improvements in performance by actively creating situations in which these can occur, and then visibly recognizing and rewarding the people who made those wins possible as an important reinforcing mechanism. The more major—and hence often long-term—the change, the more important it is to build in these short-term wins, to give people visible evidence that something is happening and to thus maintain momentum for the long haul.

The seventh stage of Kotter's model is about consolidating gains and producing more change—as noted above, this represents the transition from moving to refreezing in Lewin's terms. By building on the credibility generated by the short-term wins, the change leaders can progressively change all the systems, structures, and policies that don't fit the transformation vision and/or don't fit the changes that have already been implemented. This stage will in-clude recruiting, promoting, and training people to be aligned with the vision and who have the skills and abilities to carry forward the implementation process—and probably getting rid of those who do not. It is a harsh truth of any change initiative that there will always be a few who get left behind because they either cannot or will not change, and that it is often necessary to remove them from the organization if the change is not to be, at best, severely hampered or, at worst, completely sabotaged. Over time, the ongoing change process must be repeatedly reinvigorated by the introduction of new projects, additional strands to the vision, and the energy of new change agents. Finally, the new approaches thus developed must be anchored in the organizational culture. Key elements here will be the development of future leadership through succession planning and the regular articulation of the connections between the new behaviours and organizational success.

As we will see when we turn to contextual approaches to change, the complexity of the environmental factors underpinning any change initiative make it highly unlikely that such a linear, prescriptive process will be appropriate to every change programme. Indeed the idea of programmatic, planned change can itself be called into question (Beer, Eisenstat, and Spector, 1990) with many acknowledging that organizational change can be 'dynamic, emergent, and non-linear' (Balogun, 2006: 30) and that unanticipated outcomes can either reinforce or run counter to the intended ones. Also open to question here is the balance between leading change and managing change: Kotter makes the claim that successful change requires 70–90 per cent leadership and only 10–30 per cent management and that most modern organizations are over managed and under led. This being the case, one can challenge whether this ratio is actually supported by his process model—or rather by the whole notion of planned, programmatic change as represented by n-step models generally.

 Leadership in the media: Moneyball

The 2011 film *Moneyball* traces the true story of Billy Beane—general manager of the Oakland A's baseball club and his successful attempt to reshape the club on a limited budget by employing computer-generated analysis to acquire new players. In 2001, the Oakland A's lose to the Yankees in the World Series playoffs, then lose three of their star players to other clubs. Beane is faced with the challenge of rebuilding a competitive team with a salary budget that is less than a third of that enjoyed by the richer teams he must compete against for talent and then play against in the league. To the consternation of his scouts—who traditionally drive the player selection process through a combination of instinct, networking, and experience—Beane hires and listens to Peter Brand, a recent Yale graduate who evaluates players using an entirely statistical approach. Beane assembles a team of 'no names' who, on paper, can get on base and score runs, but which his scouts tell him are complete no hopers. He experiences further resistance to his ideas when his manager, Art Howe, won't use the players as Beane wants. Even without an understanding of the intricacies of American baseball, this film is a fascinating exploration of what it takes to make an organization change, and the tactics the change leader must employ to get people to see beyond the way they have always done things. Consider, as you watch it, to what extent Beane's change process resembles that outlined by Kotter.

Contingency models of change

Arguably more sophisticated than the n-step models of change we have considered so far are contingency models. These recognize that change is not a 'one size fits all' process and that different responses are required in different situations—much like contingency models of leadership. They are still focused on the process of change itself however, in contrast to the contextual approaches we will see later. Within the change process, there are different contingencies that different authors suggest need to be taken into account. The two most fre-quently cited models are those of Dunphy and Stace (1988, elaborated in Stace and Dunphy, 1993) and Kotter and Schlesinger (2008 reprinted from 1979).

Kotter and Schlesinger (2008) focus on the causes of resistance to change and offer a sys-tematic approach to selecting appropriate strategies to dealing with it. This is a micro-level model—in line with the transition curve considered earlier—which considers human responses to organizational change efforts and how they can best be addressed when they run counter to organizational goals. Kotter and Schlesinger observed that individuals and groups can react very differently to change, from passively resisting it, to aggressively trying to undermine it, to whole-heartedly embracing it. They identified four common reasons for resisting change, as follows:

- The desire not to lose something of value: also described as parochial self-interest, this is where individuals—not unreasonably—focus on their own best interests rather than the wider goals of the organization.

- The misunderstanding of the change and its implications: it can often be the case that the relative costs and benefits of proposed changes are misunderstood, leading to resistance to what is actually likely to be a beneficial change.

- The belief that the change does not make sense for the organization: if employees assess the need for change differently from managers, and thus do not believe that the proposed changes are needed or are likely to be effective, then this is another reason for resisting change.

- Low tolerance for change: the final reason for resisting change is simply the fear that one will not be able to adjust—to develop new skills and new ways of working that will be required by the proposed changes.

In dealing with these different types of resistance Kotter and Schlesinger propose six different strategies, each suited to dealing with different types of resistance:

1. *Education and communication* is likely to be the best strategy where there is a lack of information or where inaccurate information or analysis is an issue.

2. *Participation and involvement* can be a powerful strategy where others in the organization have significant power to resist or the change initiators do not hold all the information.

3. *Facilitation and support* will be necessary where people are struggling to adjust to change.

4. *Negotiation and agreement* is recommended where people have power to resist the changes, for example where workers are unionized, and will clearly lose out as a result.

5. *Manipulation and co-optation* may be resorted to where other tactics have failed or are unlikely to work.

6. *Explicit or implicit coercion* are the final strategy, to be used where speed is essential and the change initiators possess considerable power.

The choice of which strategy to adopt is said to be determined by the amount and type of resistance expected, the power relations between change initiators and change resistors, who holds the information needed to design effective change, and the stakes involved.

A case in point: Schlumberger—dealing with resistance

Schlumberger Limited is the world's largest oilfield services company. Incorporated in the Netherlands Antilles, it employs over 113,000 people, operates in 85 countries and has revenues in excess of US$39 billion (FY 2011). In 2006, Schlumberger relocated its US corporate headquarters from New York to Houston as part of a wider restructuring package designed to extend its commitment to core energy industry tools and services. Andrew Gould, Schlumberger chairman and chief executive since 2003, said the move would consolidate the company's presence in the community that was instrumental in its development. When he experienced resistance to some of his restructuring ideas by members of the senior management team, Gould brought together a group of younger, more junior managers in a team he called 'Forum 2005'. Their remit was to envision how they believed the company should look in 2005: Gould then adopted their ideas. By collaborating with this group—and building on the talent and commitment thus nurtured—Gould effectively used collaboration as a means of bypassing resistance. Whilst this was a risky strategy—and certainly would not work everywhere—it is a dramatic example of how change leaders may need to be both resolute and creative in addressing individual resistance.

Sources: www.slb.com; Edgecliffe-Johnson, Andrew (17 May 2002) Nurturing talent to oil the wheels of change. *Financial Times*, p. 14; Balogun, J. and Hope-Hailey, V. (2004) *Exploring Strategic Change* (second edition). Prentice Hall/FT.

The Kotter and Schlesinger model focuses narrowly on change strategies as a response to employee resistance. In contrast, Dunphy and Stace (1988) take a wider view and identify two macro dimensions as driving the change process, namely the type of change and the mode of change. Drawing on the contrast between the incremental approach to change advocated by OD (Organization Development) consultants and the more rapid, coercive restructuring which they observed to be prevalent in organizations, they suggested two types of change— incremental and transformative. Alternative typologies for this distinction can be seen, for example, in Greiner's (1972) organizational life cycle model of evolution and revolution, Tushman, Newman, and Romanelli's (1986) convergence and frame-braking change, and Levy's (1986) first order and second order change. Similarly, the mode of change can be divided into collaborative or coercive, depending upon how potential resistance is to be overcome and, more fundamentally perhaps, the degree of harmony that is perceived between stakeholder interests. The work of Kotter and Schlesinger, as discussed here, is acknowledged in this context as one attempt to address this theme. Putting these two dimensions together, Dunphy and Stace suggest a matrix of options resulting in four distinct types of change, as shown in Figure 9.3.

Thus *Participative Evolution* consists of incremental adjustments achieved by collaborative means; *Charismatic Transformation* is the name given to large-scale, discontinuous change, still achieved by collaborative means; *Forced Evolution* is when adjustments are at an incremental scale but are brought about through coercive means; and *Dictatorial Transformation* results when large-scale, discontinuous change is brought about through coercive means.

Dunphy and Stace foresaw situations when each of these types of change might be appropriate and were not making a negative judgement in describing the means as coercive: they give the example of statutory authorities (such as the Hunter River and Sydney Water Boards), and other organizations that are highly regulated by government, who often require legislative changes to force them to respond to environmental issues and other

	Incremental change strategies	Transformative change strategies
Collaborative modes	*Type 1 Participative Evolution*	*Type 2 Charismatic Transformation*
Coercive modes	*Type 3 Forced Evolution*	*Type 4 Dictatorial Transformation*

Figure 9.3 A typology of change strategies

Dunphy, D. C. (1988) Transformational and coercive strategies for planned organizational change: Beyond the O.D. model. *Organization Studies* (Walter de Gruyter GmbH & Co. KG.), 9 (3) 317–34. Reproduced with permission.

discontinuities in their operating environment. In the case of the Sydney Water Board, they recount an enforced transformational change which, over a period of 24 months, resulted in massive reductions in staffing levels and hierarchical layers within the organization, together with a major shift from a centralized to a regionalized structure. In later work, Stace and Dunphy (1993) expanded their typology to include four types of change (fine tuning, incremental adjustment, modular transformation, and corporate transformation) and four styles of change leadership (collaborative, consultative, directive, and coercive), each on a continuous scale. This revised typology was depicted as a 4×4 matrix, producing sixteen combinations of change type and leadership style. In a survey of twenty-six change situations (from thirteen organizations over an extended period) the majority fell into the 'directive transformation' category, reflecting the turbulent economic environment and hence the need for enforced, radical change. This said, Stace and Dunphy went on to offer detailed case studies of how each of the major type and style combinations has been effectively applied in practice.

 Leadership in the media: Gung Ho

On the surface, the film *Gung Ho* is a comedy centring around the cultural clash between American and Japanese workers in a car factory, but it also shows us an example of transformational organizational change. We see this change through the eyes of Hunt Stevenson, who works for a large American car manufacturer that has just been bought out by a Japanese firm. The scale of the change is apparent as the seemingly impossible Japanese work ethic that the new owners have brought with them brings new working practices—far more regimented and production-oriented than the workers are used to—and the threat of plant closure if production targets are not reached. The change leadership here is directive, with Japanese managers imposing the new regime on reluctant American employees. There is a comic twist in the tail, however, when in a last-ditch attempt to save the situation Hunt contends that the American workers can match the production of the parent company's Japanese factory in its best month, meaning 15,000 completed cars. Amused by this contention, Japanese management agrees that if this output is reached, the factory would remain open and wages would return to the levels in effect prior to the original closing of the factory. In this way, Hunt actually brings about the very changes the new management were trying to force upon him and his colleagues. Which of Kotter and Schlesinger's strategies for dealing with resistance do we see working itself out here?

From a critical perspective

From a critical perspective, there are two main challenges to the n-step models of change and the planned approach they represent. The first of these is the question of whether change can ever be managed in the planned and linear way these models suggest. The contingency models we have already looked at go some way towards suggesting that the n-step models take an oversimplified view of how change happens and the ability of managers to control and direct it. More radical challenges are presented by contextual models of change, most notably Balogun and Hope-Hailey's (2004) change kaleidoscope, discussed below, and explicitly emergent views of change, which suggest that the whole idea of change as a planned process is nullified by the tendency of change to continuously emerge on an unplanned basis. On this latter view, change is always happening but cannot be determined and directed by change leaders. At best, they can influence its direction or capitalize on what is happening anyway! In this vein, Pascale and Sternin (2005) explore the potential of 'positive deviance'—people in the organization who are already doing things differently—and the potential for leaders to create lasting change by finding such people and 'fanning the flames'. The role of the leader here is not as a 'path breaker' who literally leads change by being the first to do something new, but as an 'inquirer' who seeks out pockets of changed activity and explores how they can help to advance it.

The second challenge brings us back to the issue of leading versus managing change, and the association that has been made between change and specific approaches to leadership, in particular transformational and charismatic leadership. The question here—bringing us back to the title of this chapter—is whether these types of leadership are, in fact, an essential underpinning of effective change and, more broadly, whether such leadership is always beneficial in seeking to bring about organizational change. We will explore both these challenges in the sections which follow.

Contextual models of change—recognizing complexity

The type of programmatic change envisaged by n-step models—top-down, led from the centre, linear in nature, and with a pre-determined goal in view—is not without its critics. For example, Beer, Eisenstat, and Spector (1990) suggested that this approach was fundamentally flawed and that bottom-up, ad hoc change, gaining momentum from initiatives at the periphery of the organization, was far more likely to generate fundamental, lasting change. In what they called the 'fallacy of the programmatic change', they suggested that focusing attention on the alignment of key competitive tasks was more likely to produce results than trying to achieve change through an emphasis on abstractions such as participation or culture. Similarly Higgs and Rowland (2011) observe that programmatic change approaches fail because they oversimplify the nature of change, whereas approaches that recognize change as a complex responsive process are more likely to be successful. This is one critique of n-step models: Ladkin, Wood, and Pillay (2010)—as we saw earlier—offer a more fundamental critique in suggesting that all 'synoptic' models of change are founded on an Enlightenment-based fallacy concerning the nature of change. Instead, they suggest an alternative view of change which draws on process thinking. Process thinking prioritizes processes of becoming over the distinct being of things, and hence sees change as the norm and the 'stasis' at the start and end of planned 'change processes' as illusory. If this is the case, then the role of leaders is not to make change happen but to make sense of changes that *are* happening and to serve as an 'event'—a perceived discontinuity in the flow; an artificial 'snapshot', perhaps—such as to influence the future direction of that flow. As such, they should focus on attending to patterns, using 'declarative powers' to institutionalize localized changes, and creating disruption where this is required to dislodge habitual ways of seeing or understanding. In this way, they may act to enable 'organizational change' as being distinct from 'change in organizations'.

The contextual approach offers a third—and perhaps more implementable—critique of n-step models. The basic premise of contextual models of change is that the n-step models to which they are an alternative are too linear to deal with the complexity and uncertainty of attempting to initiate change and that they propose a 'one size fits all' solution to an essentially context specific problem. Thus authors such as Balogun and Hope-Hailey (2004) contend that

> the design and management of any change process should be dependent on the specific situation or context of each organisation. It is dangerous to apply change formulae that worked in one context directly into another (Balogun and Hope-Hailey, 2004: 7).

They see n-step models as taking the lessons learned from a few case studies—whether by researchers, practitioners, or consultants—and turning them into prescriptive 'best practice' models of how to do change, with no real consideration of the generalizability of their prescriptions. In presenting their 'change kaleidoscope', Balogun and Hope-Hailey outline a number of elements of the change context which they claim need to be taken into account in designing a 'one off' change process each and every time change is contemplated. They also suggest a series of stages which need to be undertaken in identifying the right design choices in any particular context. These include answering 'why and what' questions around the changes needed based on an analysis of the organization's competitive position and an identification of its desired future state, followed by 'how' questions relating to an analysis of the critical features of the change context, the choice of change approach, and the levers and mechanisms needed to support the transition process, leadership issues relating to the change and—finally—how the success of the change outcomes will be evaluated. As shown in Figure 9.4, the kaleidoscope itself consists of an outer wheel of contextual factors which need to be taken into account in designing the change process (time available, scope of change contemplated, what needs to be preserved from existing practices, etc.) and an inner wheel of design choices which require to be made based on an assessment of these factors.

The design choices, at the heart of the model, demonstrate the true complexity of organizational change and why the 'one size fits all' approach is deemed so inadequate. These choices fall into six categories, as follows:

1. *Change path*—the type of change to be undertaken in terms of the nature of change and the desired end result.
2. *Change start-point*—the main choice here is whether change is to be top-down or bottom-up, but other variations in between are also possible.
3. *Change style*—the extent to which the change will be brought about collaboratively or directively.
4. *Change target*—the main focus of the change, be it in people's attitudes and values (i.e. culture change), or their behaviours, or specific outcomes.

Figure 9.4 The change kaleidoscope

Balogun, P. J. and Hope Hailey, V., (2008) *Exploring Strategic Change* 3rd edition. Pearson Education Limited. Reproduced with permission.

5. *Change levers*—what mechanisms and interventions will be deployed in actually bringing about change—options here include technical, political, cultural, and interpersonal.

6. *Change roles*—decisions about who will lead the change and what roles different individuals and groups will play in the implementation process.

 Blog box

In a 2004 article recommending a holistic approach to change (see suggestions for further reading at the end of the chapter) Nadler and Chandon (2004) suggested that their big picture approach—which they named Future Ideal Solution Target or FIST—brought about more effective change by expanding the solution space within which change leaders operated. Nadler and Chandon suggest that this is achieved by focusing on what you are trying to accomplish—in the broadest sense—and then working backwards to consider all the different ways that this might be arrived at. Thinking about a current issue faced by your own organization, reflect (in around 300 words) on how a more holistic view of the situation might expand the solution space and thus generate more innovative solutions.

Whilst clearly more complex and context sensitive than previous change models, the change kaleidoscope is not without its limitations. Not least of these is the potential for it to be viewed in much the same way as its authors saw contingency models, namely as appearing 'to offer a "recipe" for making the highly complex business of change simpler and more manageable' (Hope-Hailey and Balogun, 2002: 155). The need to 'continuously reconfigure' the elements within the change kaleidoscope offer some protection from this criticism, however, whilst the approach which surrounds it can be seen as suggesting that change is 'a process in itself rather than a controllable sequence of transition events between present and future states' (Hope-Hailey and Balogun, 2002: 159). The authors also note a number of limitations to the approach, most notably that it requires the application of other models within the design process (such as the transition curve and the cultural web) to generate a comprehensive change design, and that—as with all models—it is only as good as the people applying it and thus raises issues of change agent competencies (interestingly, Balogun and Hope-Hailey refer to change agents rather than change leaders throughout their work). They also acknowledge that the kaleidoscope remains a mechanism for leading planned change, and is thus less applicable to emergent or evolving change situations. This raises the inevitable question as to how 'planned' any change process can be in a constantly changing economic, technical, and competitive environment. The argument could be made that all planned approaches to change are trying to achieve the impossible—moving from A to B when B is inherently a moving target!

Discussion point: Contextual factors for your industry/organization

What are the key contextual factors and sources of change likely to impact on your organization or sector in the next 10 years:

● Will sustainability issues or other regulatory frameworks impact on how you conduct your business in the future?

● What advances in technology can be expected to change the way you design, market, or produce your products or services?

● How will diversity issues, the need to operate globally or changes in the psychological contract, affect how employees in your organization interact with each other or view their relationship with the company?

● What changes will be needed for your organization to sustain its competitive position within the sector?

Leadership and change—transformational and charismatic leadership revisited

Whilst we have already seen definitions of leadership that link it inextricably to change, and transformational and charismatic leadership seem particularly relevant in this context, this association is not without its limitations. Nadler and Tushman (1990) suggest that visionary or charismatic leadership is insufficient on its own to sustain large-scale, systemic change, which is said to also require instrumental or executive leadership (management, we might say) supported by systems, structures, and processes aimed at transferring the individual leader's vision into the actual workings of the organization. They see the role of leadership in any change process as being as a powerful role model and psychological focus point rather than necessarily producing the actual changes required. On this basis, charismatic leadership is about envisioning, energizing, and enabling, whilst instrumental leadership consists of structuring, controlling, and rewarding—where both are seen as equally necessary. Nadler and Tushman emphasize the importance of everyday, mundane behaviours—'walking the talk'—in support- ing or negating change. They also suggest that it is unlikely that one individual will be able to perform both types of leadership required in change situations—making the establishment of a broader leadership base—a guiding coalition, in Kotter's terms—a vital ingredient of success- ful change. At a personal level, they also suggest that a charismatic leader can have a number of shortcomings—the holding of unrealistic expectations, the potential to disenfranchise the next level of management, and the creation of a climate of conformity to name just three.

More generically, Hughes (2006) suggested that change leaders—particularly transforma- tional change leaders—could be dangerous, dysfunctional, and devious; that they may be unethical either in the changes they attempt to introduce or the way they go about it; and that it is potentially problematic that power remains implicit in orthodox accounts of change leadership. In so saying, he drew attention to what has been called the 'dark side' of leader- ship, although arguably failed to make the case that such failings applied to change leaders to a greater extent than any others. Higgs and Rowland (2011) also drew attention to the dark side of leadership, suggesting that pseudo- or inauthentic leadership would have detrimental effects on change initiatives where a leader acting for their own ends or manipulating follow- ers was found out. Stadler and Hinterhuber (2005) saw charismatic or over-ambitious lead- ership as presenting the greatest danger to the performance and survival of an organization. Based on case studies of Daimler Chrysler, Shell, and Siemens, they concluded that collective leadership, drawing on a wide talent pool, was more likely to deliver long-term change in line with company values, and hence secure the organization's future. In a similar vein, Taylor- Bianco and Schermerhorn (2006) noted the necessity for strategic leaders to balance the need for change with the need for stability or continuity, and to focus on both prevention and promotion in their decision making processes. In contrast, Starke et al. (2011) question the conventional wisdom concerning the importance of leadership to transformational change by suggesting that information systems and interpretive schemas act as effective substitutes for strategic leadership in this context.

RESEARCH IN FOCUS: Charismatic leadership as a force for stability?

From the earliest writings of Max Weber, charismatic leadership has been associated with social and other forms of change. In this challenging article, Charlotta Levay (2010) turns this idea on its head by reporting on evidence which demonstrates how charismatic leadership can equally well be a force for stability and resistance to change. Drawing on case studies of two departments within a Scandinavian university hospi- tal, both of which were facing significant change, she catalogues how change which challenged the values and interests of established groups within each department created a crisis which stimulated the formu- lation of charismatic figures in opposition to change. So, for example, she relates the case of Professor A, a prominent figure in his country's medical life, head of a major medical department at a prestigious teaching hospital, and renowned for his spectacular oratory and merciless interrogation of medical stu- dents during ward rounds. He was also known to have strong views on everything from emerging special- ties within the department—which he viewed as 'deplorable'—to the proper attitude towards patients ('the customer is always right'). Levay catalogues how, in the face of plans to introduce specialized wards within a previously undifferentiated department of internal medicine, Professor A put his considerable charisma to good effect in resisting the change and advocating the continuation of the current departmental structure. Whilst the proposed changes were eventually introduced, Professor A held them back for nearly a decade!

Levay offers examples from public life to further support the idea of charismatic leadership in resistance to change: the Northern Ireland Protestant loyalist politician Ian Paisley and the Iranian revolutionary leader Ayatollah Khomeini are both seen as charismatic leaders who staunchly attempted to preserve their customary way of life and that of their followers. In doing so, she contends that the behaviours observed from such leaders are likely to be indistinguishable from those employed by charismatic leaders in support of change. Based on the case studies presented, she offers testable propositions for future research in this area and proposes that her findings should influence how we define charismatic leadership in relation to change, even though the evidence is as yet limited.

Source: Levay, Charlotta (2010) Charismatic leadership in resistance to change. *The Leadership Quarterly*, 21, 127–43.

Chapter summary

In this chapter we have considered:

- The different roles leaders might play in initiating and implementing change, and how these align with earlier definitions of leadership which suggest that leadership and change are synonymous
- The idea that change can be emergent rather than planned, and the implications of this for would-be leaders of change
- The causes of resistance to change and how leaders might go about dealing with resistance from different sources
- Normative, contingency, and contextual models of change and the implications of each for how the change process is understood and the implementation options which are seen to exist
- How transformational and charismatic forms of leadership have been linked to change and the counter-arguments against this seemingly 'natural' association

 ### Integrative case study: Major changes at Yahoo!

Yahoo! Inc is a multinational internet corporation, headquartered in Sunnyvale, California. It is one of the United States' largest websites and best known for its web portal and search engine. Yahoo! was founded in 1994 by Stanford electronics graduates Jerry Yang and David Filo, and has in the region of 700 million visitors to its websites every month. Yahoo! grew rapidly throughout the 1990s, both organically and through a number of acquisitions. In 2000 Yahoo! began using Google for search results, later developing its own search technologies. By 2008, however, the company was struggling and instigated several large redundancy programmes. Also in 2008, it was the subject of an unsolicited bid by Microsoft Corporation which valued the company at US$44.6 billion. The bid was rejected as 'substantially undervaluing' Yahoo! and not being in the best interests of shareholders despite the fact that it represented a 62 per cent premium to where Yahoo!'s shares were trading at the time. After lengthy negotiations the deal fell through and three years later Yahoo! was still sitting on a market capitalization of just US$22.24 billion. Thus began a turbulent period in the company's history, which still continues to the present day. In January 2009, Carol Bartz replaced co-founder Jerry Yang as CEO. Two years later, in September 2011, she was removed from this post by company chairman Roy Bostock and CFO Tim Morse was named as Interim CEO. Scott Thompson was appointed CEO in early 2012, at which time rumours began to circulate of more large-scale redundancies. Several key executives, including Chief Product Officer Blake Irving left Yahoo! during this period, and in April 2012 Yahoo! announced 2,000 job cuts (around 14 per cent) from its staff of 14,100. Together with a complete reorganization of the company, instigated by Scott, these measures were expected to save around US$375 million annually. Before his departure, Irving had largely opposed Thompson's reorganization strategy—not least because it had serious consequences for his own area of responsibility—and disagreed with the proposed redundancies, which he believed would further contribute to the loss of engineering and research talent which the company had been suffering in recent years and add to the demoralization of staff, already weighed down by earlier failed reorganizations and senior management departures. Ongoing turbulence in the Yahoo! boardroom led to the final resignation of Jerry Yang in early 2012, a move that was viewed favourably by shareholders who had long been concerned by his continuing influence over the company after the failed Microsoft bid—by many put down to his reluctance to see control of the company he had co-founded slip away. His departure was also expected to ease negotiations over the sale of the company's Asian assets, which together accounted for a large proportion of the company's stock market value but were not seen as central to its ongoing growth and strategic direction.

Thompson reorganized the company into three core groups—Media, Connections, and Commerce—and announced the intention to sell off or close down a number of peripheral activities, including ad technology. A new leadership structure was brought in—including Sam Shraugher from PayPal, Scott's previous company—to run the new core businesses, Sales were devolved to the regions, and the central product development group (Blake Irving's territory) was decentralized and moved back into the business units. According to Thompson, the moves were part of a strategic plan to make the company 'smaller, nimbler, more profitable and better equipped to innovate as fast as our customers and our industry require'. Thompson planned to bring dedicated product engineering resources into each business unit to bring them closer to their customers. It was also seen as important to leverage the data Yahoo! had collected from this large audience in order to personalize the Yahoo! customer experience and improve the return on investment for its advertisers. With the bulk of Yahoo!'s annual revenues derived from advertising, there was pressure to resolve an increasingly bitter intellectual property battle with Facebook—relating to the licensing of Yahoo!'s patented personalization technology—and to regain the top slot (which they lost to Facebook in 2011) in the display advertising market.

In part, these moves were aimed at heading off dissident shareholder Dan Loeb, manager of New York hedge fund Third Point—whose 5.8 per cent stake in Yahoo! makes it one of the company's largest institutional shareholders—in his attempt to introduce his own nominees onto the Yahoo! board in a bid to overhaul the ailing business. Said Loeb, 'in the absence of independent shareholder oversight, the Yahoo boards of the past five years have given shareholders five CEOs and strategic plans in as many years and seriously damaged the value of the core business.' Loeb believes that the new directors recently brought in by Thompson don't go far enough in broadening its leadership base from the purely technology-focused and that its strategic restructuring will be insufficient to stem its decline against key competitors Google and Facebook. The amount of revenue and net income Yahoo! generates per employee is currently half the average produced by its main rivals, giving shareholders every right to be unhappy.

Thus it is a difficult environment all round for Thompson to be trying to push through changes: pressure from shareholders to raise performance, a challenging competitive environment, and a new structure to bed in with demoralized employees.

Sources: <www.allthingsdigital.com>; Wikipedia; Financial Times (various editions 18 January 2012–18 April 2012); <www.bbc.co.uk> (11 February 2008); <www.guardian.co.uk> (4 April 2012)

Case study questions

- Using Balogun and Hope-Hailey's change kaleidoscope, how would you assess the contextual factors shaping the need for change at Yahoo! currently? Which of these factors are likely to be most significant in determining how Thompson goes about implementing his proposed restructuring?

- Thompson can expect considerable resistance from employees and management alike, given the past history of failed reorganizations and departing senior executives. How might he go about dealing with this resistance?

- What style of leadership does Yahoo! need from Thompson himself if it is to navigate through this difficult period in its history, and how should his approach differ from that of Jerry Yang, the company's co-founder?

N.B. One week after completing this case study, Thompson was sacked as CEO due to the emergence of falsifications on his CV. All the questions raised by the case study will still exist for his successor, however, along with an increased need to be absolutely 'squeaky clean' to combat the high degree of cynicism likely to be showered down upon yet another incoming CEO!

Further reading

Balogun, Julia and Hope-Hailey, Veronica (2004) *Exploring Strategic Change.* (second edition) Harlow: FT Prentice Hall.

Caldwell, R (2003) Change leaders and change managers: different or complimentary? *Leadership and Organization Development Journal*, 24 (5) 285–93.

Kotter, John P. (1996) *Leading Change.* Boston, MA: Harvard Business School Press.

Nadler, Gerald and Chandon, William J. (2004) Making changes: The FIST approach. *Journal of Management Inquiry*, 13, (3) 239–46.

Morrison, D. (1994) Psychological contracts and change. *Human Resource Management*, 33 (3) 353–72.

Critical approaches to leadership

Learning outcomes

On completion of this chapter you will:

- Be familiar with the critical theory school of thought and its application in critical management studies

- Understand the similarities and differences between critical management studies and critical leadership studies

- Have considered seminal examples of critical leadership writing in relation to the three most frequently considered minority standpoints, namely gender, class, and ethnicity

- Be aware of the more general critique of leadership writing in terms of its Western cultural bias, and considered alternative Eastern perspectives on how leadership may be understood and practised

Introduction

In broad terms, a critical perspective on leadership is one which 'challenge[s] the traditional orthodoxies of leadership and following' or the 'hegemonic view that leaders are the people in charge and followers are the people who are influenced' (Jackson and Parry, 2008: 83). Under this definition, we might consider distributed leadership, team leadership, and self-managed teams (all considered elsewhere in this book) as challenging the traditional hegemonic view of leadership. There is a more fundamental genre of critical leadership writing, however, to which we turn in this chapter. It is based on the inherently political and emancipatory goals of critical theory as a research paradigm, and challenges the notion of leadership from the perspectives of a number of 'disadvantaged' minorities with a view to improving their lot. In this chapter we present the reader with an overview of some of the main critiques of leadership which have merged from this paradigm, from the thesis that it is fundamentally problematic because it bolsters the dominant belief in patriarchal social structures that serve to oppress under the guise of empowerment (Sievers, 1993), to the more issue-driven critiques based on feminist or other standpoints. Thus, for example, Alimo-Metcalfe's (1995) examination of leadership as a gendered construct provides a specifically feminist standpoint within the broader, diversity-related critiques, whilst Gemmill and Oakley's (1992) classic description of leadership as an 'alienating social myth' represents a wider, Marxist-led critique. Puwar's (2001) observations on a 'racialized somatic norm' within the British Civil Service exemplify the position of ethnic minorities within a dominant culture, thus completing the triumvirate of frequently explored standpoints.

> ### Discussion point: Personal perceptions of leadership
>
> How are your perceptions of leadership shaped (and perhaps limited) by the culture you have grown up in, the family roles you observed as a child, your experiences as an adult, and the organizations you have worked in?
>
> - What are the cultural traditions around leadership and leadership roles? Who can expect to achieve leadership positions? Who might be excluded from these roles? Is there a 'ruling class' of people more likely to be appointed to top jobs?
>
> - How are women leaders seen? Do they have to be 'masculine' in their style and behaviours to be successful? Or is there a recognition of women as effective leaders in their own right?
>
> - What about people from ethnic minorities—are they able to achieve leadership roles? If so, how are they viewed by their colleagues?
>
> It may be quite challenging to really see past your own assumptions and preconceived ideas in order to answer these questions. This is one of the difficulties of culturally embedded ideas—that they become invisible to us. To help you get a true picture, try talking to friends and colleagues from other classes, ethnic groups, or of different genders about their perceptions of leadership.

Given the subject matter of the chapter—or more specifically, its inherently critical nature—we have moved away from the mainstream versus critical format adopted elsewhere in this text. Instead, the chapter is divided into three broad sections designed to address the following aims. This first section will locate critiques of leadership writing in the wider field of critical management studies, and explore the emergence of a sub-field of critical leadership studies in the academic sense of the phrase. The middle section will offer a series of 'research in focus' pieces, which represent seminal examples of critical leadership writing in relation to the three most frequently considered minority standpoints, namely gender, class, and ethnicity. In the final section of the chapter, we will consider the more general critique of leadership writing in terms of its Western cultural bias—a bias, the observation of which was one of the motivations for offering this (hopefully) more culturally diverse leadership textbook. Specifically, this section will look at how Chinese writing on leadership is beginning to challenge the Western hegemony by presenting a more culturally sensitive view of how leadership is understood and practised.

Critical management studies

In 1992, on the back of a small and, at the time, largely uncelebrated, conference bringing together a number of critical scholars from Europe and North America, the first volume of *Critical Management Studies*, edited by Mats Alvesson and Hugh Willmott was published. The contributions sought to apply the tradition of Critical Theory established in Frankfurt in the 1930s to the field of management studies. In the words of Alvesson and Willmott (2003) Critical Theory:

> proceeds from an assumption of the *possibilities* of more autonomous individuals, who, in the tradition of the Enlightenment, in principle can master their own destiny in joint operation with peers—possibilities that are understood to be narrowed, distorted and impeded by conventional managerial wisdom. (Alvesson and Willmott 2003: 2)

The Frankfurt School and its followers provide a key source (though not the only source) of critical writing designed to stand against the mass of mainstream management writing. In so doing, they seek to 'interrogate and challenge received wisdom about management theory and practice' (Alvesson and Willmott, 2003: 1) and to develop a 'less managerially partisan position' in relation to a range of management disciplines. Whereas mainstream writing has considered the various activities of managing as purely technical functions, the critical perspective sees the issues of who occupies positions of authority within the division of labour and who thus derives most benefit from this division as inherently political in nature. Who does the physical work of producing versus who does the intellectual work of controlling and managing becomes a social distinction. Studies of management which take no account of the disparity produced and perpetuated by this system of management are thus seen as politically naive as well as ethically problematic, and the goal of Critical Theory is to reorganize management into a form that does not systematically privilege one element of the organizational population over another. It seeks to do this by drawing attention to the perspectives of previously underrepresented interest groups and by broadening the means of communication and interrelating between these groups such as to allow for the contestation of previously accepted power relations and ideologies.

Defining the terrain of critical management studies

Critical Management Studies (CMS) have their roots in the Marxist doctrine of the state as a device for the exploitation of the masses by a dominant class. Whilst concerning itself with capitalist institutions rather than the state per se it retains the emancipatory aims of redressing the class imbalances prevalent in society and restructuring management activity to demolish the existing hegemony of the few over the many. As a movement, however, it has moved beyond its origins to a more pluralistic and hence less specifically class-based collection of ideas. Alvesson and Willmott (2003) suggest the following foci as being representative of the current interests of CMS scholars:

- Developing a socially constructed (that is, a non-objective) view of management techniques and organizational processes in contrast with the technicistic, functional (and hence supposedly objective) view of mainstream writing. So, for example, CMS would reframe leadership—previously seen as an unproblematic response to the 'need' to have an authority figure to direct activity and provide meaning—as something which can be seen as creating 'leader-dependent' subjects (Alvesson, 2003).

- Exposing asymmetrical power relations by drawing attention to practices and discourses which, though presented as neutral, are inherently political and serve to reproduce structures in which there is differential access to the rewards of labour. In so doing, the aim is to challenge the centrality of and necessity for a managing elite and posit the potential for a differently defined reality and emancipatory change.

- Counteracting the tendency for 'discursive closure' around taken-for-granted assumptions and ideologies which perpetuate the existing social order. Such closure suggests the impossibility of change which, by suggesting other discourses and 'readings' of the world, CMS would seek to counteract.

- Revealing the partiality of shared interests and consensus previously assumed to exist within organizational settings. In this respect, CMS treads a relatively moderate line between the traditional consensus views and weaker forms of pluralism—which assume that workers and owners have the same interests, or that where this is not the case, the difference arises from misunderstanding or miscommunication—and more radical Marxist views—which see an inescapable conflict between the interests of capital and workers. They thus draw attention to the contradictions in society and the latent social conflicts these might produce at the same time as acknowledging that conflict may exist as a liberating and constructive force.

- Appreciating the centrality of language and 'communicative action' to how structures and actions within an organizational context are understood and oriented to. Language is seen as carrying historically established meanings which support and reproduce certain versions of the world, capable of being revealed and challenged through critical examination. Thus meanings are seen as inherently ambiguous and constitutive, rather than self-evident and unproblematic.

Discussion point: Do we need leaders?

One of the foci of CMS interest identified by Alvesson and Willmott (2003) was the challenge to the perceived 'need' to have a leader as an authority figure to direct activity and provide meaning. Whereas mainstream writing would see the idea of leadership as 'natural' and hence unproblematic, CMS thinking would suggest it is something which can be seen as creating 'leader-dependent' subjects and reproducing existing class divisions.

- Do organizations need 'leaders', or can 'leadership' be exercised in more flexible and socially equal ways?

- Are some types of people naturally more suited to leadership than others and, if so, can this be determined on the basis of gender, class, race or other generic categorizations?

- To what extend does your own experience suggest that leaders and leadership replicate existing class structures and social patterns? Is this a good or a bad thing?

Having answered these questions, consider to what extent your answers are the result of critical thought and reflection, versus the extent to which you have been drawn in to the cultural norms you have grown up with.

In an alternative typology that covers much of the same ground, Grey and Willmott (2005) see the dominant themes within the field as being around the 'de-naturalization' of the taken-for-grantedness of the existing social order, 'anti-performativity' in relation to ends–means relationships, and 'reflexivity' as a challenge to objectivism and scientism.

Critical leadership studies

Whilst critical management studies might be concerned with any discipline within the management field, critical leadership studies are concerned 'to critique the power relations and identity constructions through which leadership dynamics are often reproduced, frequently rationalized, sometimes resisted and occasionally transformed' (Collinson, 2011: 181). Whereas the primary question asked by mainstream paradigms of leadership research is 'what makes an effective leader?', critical leadership studies would suggest that a less leader-centric approach which focuses on followers as well as leaders is likely to produce more informative insights. In this context, Collinson identifies three perceived weaknesses of mainstream leadership study, which it is the aim of critical leadership studies to address, namely:

- *Essentialism.* In rethinking leadership as a socially constructed and discursive construct, CLS scholars reject the search for the essence of leadership that lies at the heart of mainstream, psychological, positivist approaches to leadership study (Lakomski, 2005). This 'syndrome of individuality' (Mintzberg, 2006) and the tendency to romanticize leadership (Meindl, Ehrlich, and Dukerich, 1985) is seen as stemming from the largely Western individualistic cultural tradition from which the bulk of leadership writing has historically sprung.

- *Romanticism.* There has been a tendency within mainstream leadership writing to privilege leaders over followers and/or over relations between the two (as well as privileging leaders over managers), and to ignore the exercise of leadership within the wider social, economic, political, and cultural context in which it necessarily resides. Recognition of the tendency to romanticize leadership of which this is seen as a symptom is said to have prompted a growing interest in 'post-heroic' leadership, and a consequent focus on social, relational, and collective forms of leadership. In this genre, we have seen distributed (Gronn, 2002), shared (Pearce and Conger, 2003), servant (Spears and Lawrence, 2004), quiet, (Badaracco, 2002), and collaborative (Huxham and Vangen, 2004) leadership to name but a few. There has also been a growing emphasis on followership and an interest in exploring the asymmetrical power relations between leader and follower. Similarly Fairhurst (2001) has highlighted what she referred to as the 'primary dualism' of leadership research as being that between the individual and the collective, and argued for a better appreciation of the need to develop a combined understanding of the agency of leadership alongside the dynamics of the collective rather than focusing on either to the exclusion of the other.

- *Dualism.* Mainstream writing has tended to consider leadership in dualist terms of leader versus follower and to see their relative positions and relationships as static. CLS propose a more dialectical approach in which the shifting interdependencies and power asymmetries of these relations are recognized and explored. This requires us to rethink followers as knowledgeable agents rather than passive recipients, and to acknowledge leaders as influenced as well as influencing. In this context, Giddens' (1984) structuration theory represents just one attempt to overcome the individual/society dualism in social theory by reframing the 'dialectics of power relations'.

Collinson goes on to explore three interrelated dialectics, which he sees as being frequently evident in leadership dynamics and hence productive of critical insights. The dialectic of control/resistance problematizes the issue of power, which is frequently neglected in mainstream leadership writing. Within this dialectic we see ideas of disciplinary power from Foucault (1977) but also the notions of 'destructive consent' and 'constructive dissent' (Bratton, Grint, and Nelson, 2004). We see 'identity regulation' (Alvesson and Willmott, 2002) as a prevalent form of organizational control and studies of follower resistance. Taken together, these contributions begin to open up the debate around issues of power and leadership. The second dialectic is that of dissent/consent, which CLS see as inextricably linked rather than as a polarized dichotomy. It is suggested that the boundaries between dissent and consent are likely to be blurred by disguised forms of dissent—absenteeism or withdrawal of discretionary effort, for example—and partial forms of consent, such as inertia or impression management. The motivation behind either dissent or consent has also been problematized, specifically through the recognition that it is an oversimplification to automatically impute subversive or emancipatory motives to dissention. The third dialectic suggested by Collinson—and perhaps the most prevalent one in the literature—is that of men/women. This is also indicative of wider diversity and inequality issues recognized as being present in leadership dynamics. Gender has frequently been stereotyped in leadership writing, with men being said to be more task oriented and women more relationship oriented, or men being more transactional and women being more transformational (Alimo-Metcalfe, 1995). Whilst critical feminist writing has viewed people as being inherently gendered in the way that they are socially constructed, such that the dialectics between masculinity and femininity are thus inescapable, other critical writers have argued that the two are inextricably linked and that leadership research needs to move towards greater fluidity in relation to gender by recognizing that people have multiple, interrelated, and shifting identities in this respect. More broadly, CLS writing in relation to this dialectic explores how 'certain gendered, ethnic and class-based voices are routinely privileged in the workplace, whereas others are marginalized' (Collinson, 2011, citing Ashcraft and Mumby, 2004). Collinson concludes by suggesting that the most pressing challenge for critical leadership studies is to find ways of theorizing these interrelated and often contradictory dialectics, at the same time as locating them in a more nuanced fashion in the diverse economic and cultural contexts in which they actually occur.

Research in focus: class, gender, and ethnicity

Class-based critiques of leadership

Stemming from its Marxist roots, class-based critiques of leadership are, not surprisingly, a significant component of CLS writing. Challenging the need for a powerful leadership elite, operating to maintain the existing social structure, such critiques problematize the division of labour and the 'natural' exertion of power by the few over the many. Thus issues of power are seen as inextricably linked with issues of class and class division. Critical writing seeks to expose the manner in which mainstream writing colludes with practice in seeing the superior power of the leader over his or her followers as a normal and accepted part of the social order: of the way things are and are meant to be. Even newer forms of leadership and their accompanying forms of organization, whilst speaking of the need to empower followers still retain the image of the leader as different and apart from followers. The identity of 'leader' thus retains all of the old historical and socio-cultural trappings of superiority and of a particular place in the structure and systems both of organizations and society in general. Once again, we see the traditional leader/follower dualism being reinforced in terms of a vertical power differential in relation to followers and a privileging of the views and perspectives of the leader.

 Blog box

Who gets to lead in your organization? And how is suitability for promotion to leadership roles assessed? In no more than 300 words, reflect critically on the criteria used to assess leadership potential and the objectivity and consistency with which such criteria are applied. Is there evidence of a 'ruling elite' within the culture of your organization and, if so, what are its characteristics—are most senior managers male or female? From a particular ethnic group or diverse? From a particular class or educational background or a mixture? What do you think this says about the organization?

It is in this context that we now turn to two seminal examples of class-based critiques of leadership. The first denounces the reification of leadership and the alienation which results from its perpetuation in organizational life, whilst the second presents a Marxist-informed critique of how managerial work has been interpreted in academic writing. Whilst the first piece may appear extreme, and overtly political, compared with much that we have seen elsewhere in this text, the second provides a more balanced and accessible take on the limitations of mainstream theorizing. Both nonetheless represent an important challenge to the hegemony of mainstream leadership theory and the construct of leadership itself.

RESEARCH IN FOCUS: Leadership as an 'alienating social myth'?

In 1992 Gary Gemmill and Judith Oakley wrote their radical critique of the leadership construct as an 'alienating social myth', which remains powerful to this day. In it, they proposed that the social construct of leadership is a myth that functions to reinforce existing social beliefs and hierarchical structures. They do not see it as in any way being necessary, in a practical sense, to the achievement of organizational outcomes. In so saying, they are taking a radical humanist perspective incorporating a deconstructionist approach: a central concept within the approach is that of alienation and how this arises due to the intellectual and emotional deskilling which reliance on a leader is said to produce. At its most radical, the critique goes on to suggest that leadership as a social myth symbolically represents a regressive wish to return to the 'symbiotic environment of the womb' and breeds a desire to be rescued by heroic leaders.

Leadership is thus seen as a reification of a social fiction—a fiction which we inhabit as a 'psychic prison': we are trapped by our own constructions of leadership which induce 'learned helplessness' (Seligman, 1977) in individuals at the same time as continuing to prop up the existing social order. Organizational outcomes are explained by attributing them to leadership, thus creating the illusion that leaders are 'in control' and that the whole system will collapse without them. And because this social myth is inculcated outside conscious awareness, reality-testing is blocked and the need for leadership becomes an unrecognized and undiscussable ideology. Within this context, Gemmill and Oakley see the revival of trait-based and charismatic forms of leadership as a 'ghost dance' aimed at restoring a lost but familiar form of civilization: hence their suggestion that the desire for strong, heroic leaders represents a wish to regress to the safety and nurturing of childhood.

This powerful piece of writing offers an extreme perspective on how the leadership construct is socially constructed and the political and psychological purposes this construction serves. In suggesting new paradigms for leadership—around dynamic collaboration and feminist notions of power—the authors conform to the emancipatory stance of the critical school of writing, seeking to eliminate the alienation of followers which they have so vividly brought to our attention.

Source: Gemmill, Gary and Oakley, Judith (1992) Leadership: An alienating social myth? *Human Relations,* 45 (2) 113–30.

RESEARCH IN FOCUS: Managerial work and the technical division of labour

In his review of studies of managerial work, Willmott draws on the Marxist identification of the contradiction between socialized production and private appropriation, but then explores the limitations of this position. In opening the discussion, he notes that academic accounts of managerial work are informed by a liberal-pluralist perspective that fails to situate what managers do within a wider structure of domination and power. Such accounts reinforce a dualist separation of the institutional (i.e. capitalist) versus behavioural (i.e. individual) dimensions of managerial work. Hence such studies are said to fail to appreciate how the technical division of labour is fundamentally a class-based division that operates to secure the process of private appropriation of rewards through a socialized production of value.

In going beyond the traditional Marxist division of capital and labour, Willmott recognizes the ambivalent position of managers. Management is not the neutral technology it is usually portrayed as in the management literature, but nor is it solely serving the interests of the dominant capitalist class. Instead, managers are recognized as having a vested interest in managing their own career outcomes, not necessarily aligned with those sought or endorsed by shareholders, at the same time as needing to sell their labour for wages along with more subordinate workers. He notes that the response of shareholders to this ambiguity is to emphasize the creation of shareholder value at the same time as issuing stock options to senior executives.

In challenging the unproblematic portrayal of managers' position power within the unitarist or pragmatically pluralist frame of reference (drawing on Fox, 1974), Willmott also critiques the radical frame of reference which is often seen as the solution to this uncritical position. The radical frame is seen as ignoring the structural contradictions and forms of resistance which exist within social systems, and the extent to which labour and capital are each dependent on the other. Giddens' (1979) 'structuration' theory is used to bridge the gap between 'action' and 'system' in the interpretation of managerial work, and to illustrate the comparative openness and contingency of capitalist relations of production.

Source: Willmott, Hugh (2005) Studying Managerial Work: A critique and a proposal. In C. Grey and H. Willmott (eds) *Critical Management Studies: A Reader.* Oxford. Oxford University Press, 324–47.

Gender-based critiques of leadership

We have long been familiar with the idea of a 'glass ceiling' preventing women from reaching the top of the corporate ladder, and of legislative and Human Resource Management attempts to combat this deficit. There has also been a wave of leadership writing seeking to identify the differences between male and female leadership and 'fix' the gap either by suggesting women should lead more like men or by promoting the efficacy of female styles of leadership. But in more recent years, we have seen that the complexity of gender issues in the workplace is greater and more subtle than the absence of women in corporate boardrooms.

Hoyt (2010: 305) suggests the metaphor of a 'leadership labyrinth' to convey 'the impression of a journey riddled with challenges all along the way, not just near the top, that can and has been successfully navigated by women' but which still remains a barrier to many more. These challenges take the form of differences in human capital, the impact of physical gender differences, and the continued existence of prejudice, either implicit or explicit. As Hoyt observes, enabling more women to navigate the labyrinth will require changes at the individual, interpersonal, and societal levels.

 Blog box

During my corporate career I was fortunate enough to be on the receiving end of a lot of corporate entertainment from banks wanting to do business with my organization—this was in the heady days of the 1980s when corporate entertainment was lavish, and before we worried much about either its cost or its ethics! As a Corporate Treasurer responsible for a £400 million investment portfolio and a range of other banking needs, I was a client worth wooing. Knowing that I had rowed at university, and was still keen on the sport, one of the banks we did business with invited myself and my husband to Henley Regatta. When we arrived at the riverside hospitality suite, my contact at the bank handed me (as the client) a name badge—as the 'hanger on' there was no name badge for my husband. About half an hour later, the head of the bank in London was doing the rounds, meeting and greeting the bank's guests. As he walked towards my husband and myself, he stuck out his hand, looked towards my husband and said, 'Nice to see you again Mr . . .' before realizing that my husband didn't have a name badge and hence wasn't the client. He had made the assumption that I was the hanger on because I was female, and looked very embarrassed when he realized his mistake! Not good client relations!

   This was not the only time I experienced this kind of reaction. I think my 'favourite' one was when a participant in a meeting suggested I should pour the tea because I was the only women present! The more serious point here is the subtle—or not so subtle—ways in which stereotypical views and insidious prejudices show themselves in the working environment. They didn't stop me achieving a leadership position, but they did impact on how I occupied it. (MIW)

Given this background, the article which follows is a classic example of work which has sought to explore the differences between male and female constructs of leadership, and to consider the impact of these differences on the ability of women to achieve promotion to senior leadership positions. The second article in this section considers the impact of 'second generation' forms of gender bias—those which are more subtle and more insidious than blatant discrimination—and the potential for deliberately gendered pedagogies, applied in women only development programmes, to enable women to undertake the 'identity work' needed to see themselves, and to be seen, as leaders.

RESEARCH IN FOCUS: Leadership as a gendered construct

'An investigation of male and female constructs of leadership and empowerment', a seminal article from 1995 published in *Women in Management Review,* begins by noting the relative paucity of women in senior leadership positions and speculating on the possible reasons—cultural, social, legal, educational, and organizational—for this lack. Focusing on the process of assessment adopted by large organizations the author, Beverly Alimo-Metcalfe, posits the existence of an insidious gender bias in the recruitment and pro-motion of individuals to senior positions. The suggestion here is not that those already at the top deliber-ately discriminate against women but rather that, being largely male and recruiting 'in their own image' they replicate the (masculine) characteristics and skills which they themselves possess. It is in setting the criteria upon which new leaders will be selected that a fundamental source of bias is introduced into the assessment process. As Alimo-Metcalfe goes on to observe, this argument only holds water if men and women perceive the qualities and behaviours of effective leadership differently. In addressing this question, she reviews evidence from three studies which, collectively, demonstrate consistent differences in how men and women perceive leadership and locate these differences in the leadership literature.

Sparrow and Rigg's (1993) study of UK Housing Managers revealed significant differences in the key attributes which participants considered to be important for their jobs, as perceived by men and women performing the role. For example, women saw the priorities of the job as being team management and effective service delivery, whilst men saw them as being vision, entrepreneurship, and an ability to pack-age ideas so as to raise funding. Women saw the appropriate working style as being people-oriented, measured, and participative, whilst men believed they should be political, forceful, high profile, confident, and paternalistic. Similar differences—often to the point of outright contradiction—were seen in how they made decisions, their relations with their own team, and their relations with clients. Alimo-Metcalfe draws attention to the very different 'person specifications' which the two groups would draw up to be used by assessors in a recruitment process.

Her own study of senior managers in the British National Health Service produced similar results. For example, focusing on working style, men saw themselves as needing to show drive and clarity of pur-pose, and to give clear directions, be independent, career driven, and organized. In contrast, women felt they should be busy but accessible, make creative use of others' skills for the benefit of the organization, be strong and supportive, develop teams in which people can grow, and start with the presumption that everyone wants to do a good job. Drawing on a third study, conducted in the USA by Rosener (1990), Alimo-Metcalfe concludes that women are thus more likely to use transformational and interactive styles of leadership, whereas men are more likely to adopt transactional or authority based styles. In this context she also explores gendered perceptions of empowerment, suggesting that men see empowered followers as 'recipients of power'—and empowerment as a gift that is given but can also be taken away—whereas women see them as 'sharers of power'—a much more genuinely connected and collaborative perception of what it is to empower.

Alimo-Metcalfe concludes by noting the irony of the growing demand for leaders to be transforma-tional in order to meet the complex demands of delivering strategic goals in an uncertain world, at the same time as skewing the assessment processes which might—if allowed to be gender-neutral—deliver a higher proportion of leaders fitted to meet this challenge.

Source: Alimo-Metcalfe, Beverly (1995) An investigation of male and female constructs of leadership and empowerment. *Women in Management Review*, 10 (2) 3–8.

RESEARCH IN FOCUS: Second generation types of gender bias

Despite much legislation and 'positive discrimination' aimed at helping women climb the corporate lad-der, Ely, Ibarra, and Kolb observe that subtle forms of 'second generation' gender bias—embedded in cul-tural beliefs and workplace structures and practices—are still preventing many women from making it to the top. Not only are these forms of bias influencing how others view would-be women leaders, they are also said to be having a negative impact on the 'identity work' women need to undertake in order to see themselves as leaders. This identity work is said to consist of the internalizing of a leader identity, together with the development of an elevated sense of purpose.

Ely, Ibarra, and Kolb identify a number of impediments faced by women in performing the identity work of leadership development, as well as noting how both leadership training programmes and organizational reinforcement can work against the successful performance of this transitional task. Foremost amongst the barriers to women's leadership identity work is the prevalence of quintessentially masculine leader prototypes, drawn from culturally available ideologies. Thus leaders are seen as being decisive, assertive, and independent—culturally masculine characteristics, whilst women are seen as being friendly, unselfish, and caretaking—and hence unsuited to leadership roles. Herein lies a double bind in that effective women leaders are likely to be disliked as unfeminine whilst ineffective women leaders are likely to be dismissed as not tough enough! Other challenges which women must overcome are the relative absence of female role models and the lack of social support within the workplace, the gendered nature of traditional career paths (for example, global assignments with a 'trailing spouse' assumed not to have any career aspirations), a lack of access to same-sex networks and sponsors, and the pitfalls of heightened visibility and scrutiny when they do achieve senior positions. Whilst all of these cultural biases are seen as being inadvertent in the extent to which they favour men or impede women in developing an identity for themselves as leaders, their impact is nonetheless significant on women's progress in rising above the 'glass ceiling'.

Ely, Ibarra, and Kolb propose taking a deliberately gendered approach to leadership development as a counter to these challenges. They suggest the value of women only leadership development programmes, and the explicit exploration of such topics as negotiation skills, leading change, and interpreting and using 360 degree feedback from a gendered perspective. This is not the same as the 'add women and stir' or the 'fix the women' attempts at gendered pedagogy which they observe to have been nothing more than existing development programmes delivered in the absence of men. Instead, and based on their collective experience of working in this way, they suggest three principles for the design and delivery of women's leadership programmes, based around the idea of identity work, as follows:

1. Situate topics and tools in an analysis of second generation gender bias
2. Create a holding environment to support women's identity work
3. Anchor participants on their sense of leadership purpose

Taken together, these principles are said to give women a better chance of making a successful transition into leadership roles by seeing themselves, and being seen, as leaders.

Source: Ely, Robin J., Ibarra, Herminia, and Kolb, Deborah M. (2011) Taking gender into account: Theory and design for women's leadership development programs. *Academy of Management Learning and Education*, 10 (3) 474–93.

Ethnicity-based critiques of leadership

As issues relating to diversity have gained a higher profile in organizational studies, so ethnicity and race have emerged as an important strand in leadership writing. As with gender issues, the focus has gone beyond the kind of crude discrimination which has been the subject of government legislation and organizational HR policies to consider the more subtle and insidious ways in which ethnicity can impact on an individual's ability to rise to a position of leadership. The first article in the section is a seminal piece of work by Nirmal Puwar, which explores how preconceived somatic norms of leadership remain white, male, and middle class and the impact these norms have on those from ethnic minorities who do manage to attain leadership positions. We are concerned here with the inward-looking exploration of one ethnic group living and working within the domain of another: later in the chapter, we will look at the broader question of the transferability of leadership models across cultural groupings. In the second article, Ospina and Foldy (2009) review the different types of research which have been conducted in relation to race-ethnicity and why the insights they have produced have remained marginal to the field.

RESEARCH IN FOCUS: The racialized somatic norm of leadership

Written shortly after the MacPherson Report exposed the prevalence of institutionalized racism in the British police force, following the murder of black teenager Stephen Lawrence, Nirwal Puwar's (2001) seminal study explores how institutionalized racism is experienced by those black people who are successful in entering occupational spaces that they are not expected to be in. Specifically, she reports on the experiences of senior black Civil Servants in an institution which—despite its claims to be neutral, impartial, and objective—retains a historically located corporeal image of power as naturalized in the body of the white, middle-class, male. Whilst the gender and class issues inherent in this 'somatic norm' have been explored elsewhere, Puwar's focus is specifically on the experience of race—which she sees as the ongoing legacy of a European Colonial past. In this context, the Civil Service—the professional, impartial bureaucracy which supports the British political system—is seen as the embodiment of the Western Enlightenment ideal, in which notions of white supremacy were so deeply entrenched as to be invisible. In Mills (1997: 76) metaphor, '[t]he fish do not see the water, and whites do not see the racial nature of the white polity because it is natural to them, the element in which they move.'

Puwar coins the phrase 'Space Invaders' to describe those black Civil Servants who do manage to rise to positions of leadership, thus seeking to give a sense of their non-belonging in this senior space and the discomfort experienced by both sides as a result of their presence. She goes on to explore the ways in which they must seek to assimilate themselves into the ways of the white somatic norm, thus denying their black identity in order to be accepted.

Puwar identifies six important features of their presence in the 'white landscape', as follows:

- *Dissonance*—the most obvious sense in which black bodies are seen as 'not fitting'—and therefore being a source of dissonance, a jarring note—in a largely white space

- *Disorientation*—the display of shock—the 'double take'—often in evidence when white Civil Servants come face to face with black Civil Servants where they don't expect them to be—that is, in senior grades or positions

- *Infantalization*—a term coined by Fanon (1986) to express the way in which black people are simply imagined to be capable of much less than white people and are thus assumed to be in more junior positions than their white colleagues

- *The burden of invisibility*—by which Puwar refers to the fact that, once black people do reach senior positions, they are under increased pressure to prove their worth and to work against their invisibility to gain recognition

- *The assimilative pressure of the 'soft things'*—this is a reference to the need to become 'white' in terms of dress, mannerisms, adherence to informal rules, and codes of conduct in order to try to fit in with the norm

- *Language and symbolic power*—foremost amongst the 'soft things' that must be assimilated is the use of 'correct'—by which is meant upper class or Oxbridge as opposed to regionally accented or slang—English, as the hegemonic and 'legitimate' language, and the perceived voice of reason.

Puwar's attempt to problematize the experiences of black bodies in spaces accustomed to the presence of white bodies could easily be extended to other institutions and types of work—for example the legal profession or academia. Its wider significance is in terms of our whole conception of 'difference' and the extent to which it is genuinely accepted in the workplace.

Source: Puwar, Nirwal (2001) The racialised somatic norm and the senior civil service. *Sociology*, 35 (3) 652–69.

RESEARCH IN FOCUS: Shifting views of race-ethnicity in relation to leadership

In a review of the intersection between research on race-ethnicity (where the term race is used to refer to visible, physical traits and ethnicity refers more to customs and traditions learned from ancestors) and the leadership literature, Ospina and Foldy identify three distinct phases in how race-ethnicity has been treated by researchers. They saw this research as addressing the effects of race-ethnicity on perceptions of leadership, the effects of race-ethnicity on the enactment of leadership, and how social actors dealt with the social reality of race-ethnicity. Early research in the field thus viewed it as a constraint and considered race-ethnicity as some kind of disadvantage which would-be leaders needed to overcome. This research was predicated on a US/UK context of white dominance. Research then moved on to seeing race-ethnicity as a personal resource, and as having a positive impact on the leadership styles adopted by black leaders and the sense of purpose they saw for themselves as leaders. Most recently, research has considered race-ethnicity as both a constraint and a resource, seeing it in the context of collective identity. This latest research explores black leaders' responses to systemic inequities based on race-ethnicity. Alongside these shifts in research focus, they observe a shift in treatment of context from simple to complex, the gradual incorporation of more explicit analysis of power dynamics, and increasing efforts to link the micro and macro levels of analysis.

Whilst acknowledging the development of a context sensitive standpoint and intersectional strands of research, as discussed above, Ospina and Foldy also note that the insights gained from such research have, in the main, not been incorporated into mainstream leadership writing, but remain marginal and that people of colour are seldom treated as 'paradigmatic humans' who 'can serve as a source of data . . . to develop theories about the human condition' (Williams, 2001: 1). They suggest two possible reasons why this might be the case. First, the different ontological, epistemological, and methodological assumptions of standpoint research may cause such research to be 'invisible' to mainstream authors as not complying with their assumptions and standards in relation to quality research. Secondly, the assumption by mainstream leadership writing of the generic relevance of Western ideas makes 'whiteness' the default category for measuring leadership and hence one which it becomes impossible to explore: and if whiteness is not recognized as a factor in leadership, then nor is its opposite. As a result of both these reasons, they suggest that the mainstream leadership literature presents a distorted and questionable knowledge about the relationship between race and leadership that can be detrimental both to the field and to the referenced identity groups. They conclude by suggesting an ambitious research agenda aimed at addressing these distortions and hinting at the new mindsets and toolkits researchers will need to take on board if they are to pursue it.

Source: Ospina, Sonia and Foldy, Erica (2009) A critical review of race and ethnicity in the leadership literature: Surfacing context, power and the collective dimensions of leadership. *The Leadership Quarterly*, 20, 876–96.

 Blog box

How do you see your identity as a leader? (Or do you see yourself as a manager?) Do you draw on ethnic or other cultural roots? Do you see your style of leadership as characteristic of or related to your gender or class in some way? In around 300 words, write a 'biography' of yourself as a leader including what has influenced you, what has made you want to be a leader, and how you see your unique contribution as a leader. When you have written it, share it with someone who knows you well and see if they recognize the biography as unmistakably you.

Challenging the hegemony of Western perspectives on leadership

Just as early leadership research looked for the 'one best way' of doing leadership within a national (or rather, Western) context, so early attempts to codify leadership in a global context focused on attempting to identify universal principles of leadership that applied across all cultures. This, in itself, was progress since it involved an implicit acknowledgement of the existing hegemony of Western notions of leadership based on individualism, masculinity, hierarchy, and performativity, and a recognition that these notions might not be universal. The result was an increasing application of dimensions of culture (such as those identified by Hofstede, 1980) to describe variations in leadership styles, practices, and preferences around the world—see, for example, Dickson, Den Hartog, and Mitchelson's (2003) review of cross-cultural leadership research during this transitional phase. More recently still, the limitations of this cross cultural approach—particularly as represented by House et al.'s (2004) GLOBE project (that is, the Global Leadership and Organizational Behaviour Effectiveness research project)—have been highlighted, with specific reference to the reductionist, quantitative methodology adopted (at least for a significant percentage of the findings), its exclusively individual level focus, its simplified conception of national culture, and the difficulties of language/meaning inherent in its mono-linguistic origins (Jepson, 2009). Whilst Jepson goes on to propose a 'more dynamic and interactive approach' aimed at overcoming the shortfalls of projects such as GLOBE, we are still in the realms of Western authors writing from an inherently Western perspective (and we acknowledge ourselves to be part of this Western tradition and to be guilty of replicating many of the same faults we are drawing attention to in the current chapter). In this final section of the chapter, we attempt to offer some small insight into the truly culturally diverse perspectives on leadership which are now beginning to emerge by providing an example of leadership scholarship based on Chinese cultural traditions, and crafted by authors from within that tradition.

RESEARCH IN FOCUS: Getting to grips with guanxi

Based on extensive research with Sino-American joint ventures based on mainland China, this important article notes how the Chinese relational system of guanxi can render Western leadership relations—such as those articulated by Leader-Member Exchange (LMX) theory—compromised. Whilst both are based on the importance of relationships, the former draws on Confucianist notions of exclusive, deterministic feudal/family based ties, with those within this network automatically being granted trust, respect, and performance of obligations, whereas the latter involves choice of a personal network based on competence and liking. Hui and Graen (1997) explore the contribution of an understanding of guanxi to building successful partnerships in China, and suggest the need for the development of 'third cultures'—cultures which synthesize the cultural values and practices that are acceptable to people from both the cultural groups involved in the partnership—as a way of increasing the likelihood of success in cross-cultural joint venture contexts.

Guanxi is said to be an important concept in China, both in terms of its practical impact on people's lives and as a mechanism of social control. The relational network it produces for an individual is governed by *wu lun*, or the five fundamental relationships: individual to government, father to son, husband to wife, elder to younger siblings, and friend to friend. One's position within each of these relationships provides order and stability to the social system and denotes specific roles the individual is required to play in any given situation. Importantly—in the light of confused Western writing on this topic—it is also the basis of cultural collectivism, to the exclusion of people not within the network or clan of which one is a member. Thus Chinese collectivism can be viewed as network first, country second, and culture third—for those trying to instigate teamwork in China, the absence of organizational collectivism within that list is an important omission!

Hui and Graen note six influences of guanxi on Chinese management, as follows:

1. Loyalty and commitment are to the guanxi 'in-group' not to the organization or leader

2. Job satisfaction and involvement will be moderated by the strength of the guanxi network in the workplace—is one in the right network?

3. Role reinforcement and fulfilment of obligations are more important than fairness and equity

4. Chinese management values loyalty more than competence

5. Maintaining guanxi and the obligations it calls forth can be more important than morality

6. Guanxi produces a tendency to be person-oriented rather than solution-oriented in the face of organizational problems

Overall, these influences lead them to summarize guanxi relations as being deterministic, loyal, based on personal networks, amoral, and family-oriented. They contrast this with the notions within LMX theory as being about choice, competence, organizational networks, morality, and employment. They suggest that the success of Sino-American joint ventures will be based on building 'third cultures' which synthesize the important features of each system. To do this, they propose that foreign leaders trying to build partnerships on Chinese soil need to:

7a. Cultivate long-term, holistic relationships with their Chinese partners

7b. Build quality, long-term LMX relationships with competent individuals

8. Develop functional relationships—that is, relationships aimed at organizational and individual growth—with the joint venture partners

This article is one of a growing number showing an understanding of and sensitivity to the unique features of Chinese management and leadership, and assimilating these into Western leadership traditions.

Source: Hui, Chun and Graen, George (1997) Gaunxi and professional leadership in contemporary Sino-American joint ventures in mainland China. *The Leadership Quarterly*, 8 (4) 451–65.

Chapter summary

In this chapter we have considered:

- The origins of critical theory in Marxism and the assumption of 'natural' class-based divisions between leaders and workers

- How critical management studies have challenged the hegemony of mainstream management theory, and how a separate critical leadership studies genre is now developing

- What critical leadership studies have added to our understanding of leadership, and their specific contributions in relation to the minority standpoints of gender, class, and ethnicity

- The prevalence of a Western cultural bias in leadership writing and the emergence of alternative, Eastern perspectives on how leadership can be practised and understood.

Integrative case study: Leadership and connectedness: a remarkable life

In 1992 Carrie Pemberton was the ordained wife of an ordained Anglican priest. They had two children and Carrie was pregnant with their third. It had taken eight years for Carrie to receive ordination, against the grain of the prevailing norms in the Anglican Church and this—together with a sense that there was little truly transformative work being done by her UK counterparts—led her to suggest to her husband that they should make themselves available to serve the church overseas. After a number of meetings with the Anglican Archbishop of the Democratic Republic of Congo—then Zaire—followed by six months of preparatory training in a centre in Selly Oak, Birmingham, she and her family left the UK for the Congo with the remit of re-establishing a failed theological training college for Anglican priests and their wives. Speaking of the decision, Carrie talks about its congruence with what had gone before in her life and about its being the 'next thing' in a series of connected and meaningful transitions. 'It didn't matter that we were packing our lives into six barrels and that we didn't know where we were going—we had made ourselves available for good and God had decided that this was where it should be.'

Not that it was an entirely straightforward decision. As a mother, Carrie had to balance the competing issues—both ethical and practical—of taking young children to an unknown and potentially unstable situation: she describes these as 'keeping them as safe as you can at the same time as making them citizens of the world and giving them a spirit of adventure'. There were also the cross-cultural issues of an international posting to be considered—with a long history of colonization, both on religious and commercial grounds, Britain has not always had the interests of its international neighbours uppermost in its mind when heading for foreign shores. Whilst the current venture was sanctioned by the local church in the Congo, it was still important to Carrie and her husband that they should be the last white Directors of the Institute they set up, and should be replaced by a local Congolese. After the collapse of a previous attempt to establish the Institute under Congolese leadership, it was felt that non-locals were better placed to get key stakeholders on board and establish the core curriculum and stable financial arrangements without hindrance from the ethnic tensions which could constrain insiders. That this should not be a permanent imposition of external leadership was still of fundamental importance to Carrie and an integral part of the remit she saw for herself and her husband. As things turned out, the family returned to England after only 2½ years due to the serious illness of Carrie's husband, but the work they had already done in that limited time was sufficient to establish the Institute on a firm footing and for their local deputy to take over as Institute Director. He is now the Anglican Archbishop of the Congo, whilst his wife—an integral part of this leadership team—is directing the country's response to the profound challenge of rape. According to United Nations estimates, the Congo is said to have the worst figures for the incidence and intensity of rape anywhere in the world, with over 200,000 women having suffered in this way in the wake of the prolonged armed conflict which has dogged the country's history. The Institute itself is now the base for the first University in the Ituri region, where it is located.

Part of Carrie's role during her time in the Congo was to work with the wives of male ordinands to prepare them for their role as pastors' wives. Working though organizations such as the Mother's Union, their role is often critical in delivering social progress within the local community and addressing some of the tribal and gender-based inequalities which persisted in the society of the time (many of which are still problematic). Driven by her strong values, Carrie made a number of decisions about how to play her role in this context which arguably went beyond her stated remit. As an ordained priest—teaching women who at that time had no possibility of being ordained themselves but only of working as helpers to their ordained husbands—Carrie always wore her dog collar in public as a visual symbol of the possibility of change and, specifically, of female ordination within the Institute. More profoundly still, perhaps, she entered into the local issue of tribal differentiation and friction by raising the normally taboo subject as a topic for discussion within her women's group. Speaking of the local situation—and of the over 250 different tribes which populate the Congo—Carrie is adamant about the necessity of 'facing out' the way in which unspoken tribal distinctions are very present in Africa as a whole and exploited by local politicians to leverage power in under-penetrated democracies: 'you need to bring it out into the open if you are going to resolve it. You need to be able to talk about it.' Carrie saw the church as being complicit in the tribal taboo—along with everyone else they refused to address or even discuss the issue despite the fact that everyone, including themselves, operated within this controlling landscape.

Carrie's discussions within her women's group sowed the seeds for some remarkable developments as events in neighbouring Rwanda spilled over into the Congo. In 1996 the civil war between Hutu and Tutsi had led to Hutu militia forces fleeing Rwanda, following the ascension of a Tutsi-led government, and using Hutu refugee camps in eastern Zaire (as the Congo was called at this time) as a base for incursions back into Rwanda. These Hutu militia forces soon allied with the Zairian armed forces to attack Congolese ethnic Tutsis in eastern Zaire. In turn, a coalition of Rwandan and Ugandan armies invaded Zaire with the aim of overthrowing the Mobutu government and gaining control of local mineral resources. Aided by this foreign force, Kabila, a long-time opponent of Mobutu's dictatorship was able to oust the existing government and re-establish Zaire as the Democratic Republic of the Congo—its name from before the Mobutu era. The problem came when Rwandan and Ugandan forces were reluctant to return to their own countries: it took the arrival of the United Nations peacekeeping forces, MONUC, to restore order and broker a peace deal which led to democratic elections. In the Ituri region, however, continuing rebel offensives led to a refugee crisis and to the UN being unable to contain the ongoing conflict between numerous tribal militias. With the UN forces camped in the school grounds which were shared by the Anglican Institute, some of the women whom Carrie had trained became peace negotiators: armed with the courage and mindset to look beyond their own ethnic issues, they went out into the community on behalf of the UN. Self-deprecatingly, Carrie says of her involvement, 'all I was doing was equipping women to be self-authoring, equality-minded, diversity accepting individuals who could be leaders in their own communities.' All, indeed!

Carrie has also worked in one of the UK's 'removal centres'—run by the UK Borders Agency for the temporary detention of asylum seekers and others who have no legal right to be in the UK but have refused to leave voluntarily—seeking to maintain and ensure their human rights during the removal process. She describes both the social psychology (uniformed versus un-uniformed) and the political discourse (the fine line between 'having no right to be here' and 'having no right to be') of the centres as having presented the biggest challenge to her understanding of what it is to 'be human'. Drawing on the Christian message of 'loving thy neighbour as thyself', she sees this in terms of a profound need to share the planet with others—with all that this entails—and a fundamental respect for people whatever and whoever they are. As a leader, she sees herself as 'being a point of disruption' around which others can gather and choose to learn. Her role is to 'put the process of learning in their hands' but not to tell them what to do with it. Carrie (Dr Carrie Pemberton Ford as she now is) is currently Developmental Director for the Cambridge Centre for Applied Research on Human Trafficking, where her most recent research has related to the trafficking risks attaching to the 2012 London Olympics. Speaking of the many remarkable projects she has taken on in her life (only some of which have been recounted here) she says, 'women's lives are joined up—they look for connection'. Whilst struggling with some of the church's current pronouncements in the area of gender and sexuality, she still sees her faith as a strong guiding influence throughout her life and as underpinning this sense of connectedness.

Case study questions

- Carrie's sense of 'connectedness', both as a leader and as a person, was important for her and for the women she worked with. How do you think this might translate into a specific style of leadership or approach to leadership roles? Do you think this is a genuinely gendered aspect of leadership?

- Carrie had a number of different roles to fulfil: priest, wife, mother, teacher, to name but four. As a leader, how would you address the issues of competing loyalties and competing identities which multiple roles produce?

(Continued...)

- Carrie made a deliberate choice to use her status as an ordained woman priest to act as a 'point of disruption' for the women she was teaching. How does the idea of leadership as a 'point of disruption' align with current theories of transformational and change leadership? What role do you think our sense of identity has to play in how we choose to be as a leader and the issues we choose to lead on?

Further reading

Alvesson, Mats and Willmott, Hugh (eds) (2003) *Studying Management Critically*. London: Sage Publications.

Collinson, D. (2005) Critical leadership studies. In A. Bryman, D. Collinson, K. Grint, B. Jackson, and M. Uhl-Bien (eds), *The SAGE Handbook of Leadership*. London: Sage Publications Ltd, 181–94.

Fairhurst, Gail (2001) Dualisms in leadership research. In F. M. Jablin and L. L. Putnam (eds), *The New Handbook of Organizational Communication*. Thousand Oaks, CA: Sage, 379–439.

Grey, Christopher and Willmott, Hugh (2005) *Critical Management Studies: A reader*. Oxford: Oxford University Press.

Hofstede, G. (1980) *Culture's Consequences: International differences in work-related values* (abridged edition) Newbury Park, CA: Sage.

Strategic leadership: The 'perennially unfinished project'

Learning outcomes

On completion of this chapter you will:

- Understand the notion of strategy as a discipline, and its historical origins in the military

- Understand what is meant by 'strategic leadership' and how it relates to other forms of leadership we have considered in this book

- Be aware of the central theories of strategic leadership and how they have been developed both theoretically and empirically

- Be aware of the 'practice turn' in strategy and how this might be applied to issues of the enactment of strategic leadership

- Have considered the extent to which transformational and visionary leadership may be considered as synonymous with strategic leadership

Introduction

In this chapter, we will consider what is meant by strategic leadership, and the various ways in which it has been discussed in the literature. As such, we will start by considering strategy per se and how it has come to prominence as a management discipline. Drawing on leading writers in this field, including Johnson, Balogun, and Jarzabkowski, the chapter will lay out mainstream approaches to strategizing and strategic leadership before developing Knights and Mueller's (2004) view of strategy as a 'perennially unfinished project'. This latter view sits within the 'strategy as practice' perspective, which offers the practising leader a radical challenge to traditional ways of thinking about and doing strategy. Tapping into the authors' own research, the critical section of the chapter will consider how the 'practice turn' relates to strategic leadership—a theme which is developed further in the integrative case study which concludes the chapter. The case study thus sets out some of the leadership practices through which the strategy process is enacted by leaders on an ongoing basis, and asks readers to consider how this compares with more traditional views of 'strategic planning'.

Made up of two Greek words—*stratus*, meaning the manner in which an army or a large body of people may be spread out, and *egy* from the verb 'to lead', the word strategy has its origins in the Greek terms for the senior commander of an army (a *strategos*). Equating to the word 'general' in English, and meaning literally 'applicable to the whole', a military general is thus the person who is accountable for the whole body of the army—how it is deployed, its welfare, and the outcomes it delivers. Interestingly, in its original usage 'strategy' was synonymous with 'strategic leadership', referring as it did to the role of being commander-in-chief—we have since developed separate disciplines of strategy or strategic planning and leadership, which may be at different levels within an organization (thus incorporating what the Greeks would have referred to as tactics). In bringing the terms together again within this chapter, we recognize a specific sub-division or strand within the panoply of leadership writing and theorizing.

So what do we mean, in modern parlance, when we talk about 'strategic leadership'? Yukl (2002) equates the term with executive leadership, and the responsibility of senior executives—and specifically CEOs—for the performance of large organizations. Hitt and Ireland (2002) define the role of strategic leaders in terms of their responsibility for managing the resources and capabilities of the organization such as to create and maintain competitive advantage. Alternatively, strategic leadership can be seen as leadership *of* organizations, and contrasted with supervisory theories of leadership which relate to leadership *in* organizations (Boal and Hooijberg, 2001). As such, it relates to the creation of meaning and purpose for the organization (House and Aditya, 1997) and is 'marked by a concern for the evolution of the organization as a whole, including its changing aims and capabilities' (Selznick, 1984: 5).

A case in point: A traditional growth strategy

In June 2012 Tam and Lan, respectively the biggest airlines in Brazil and Chile, agreed a merger that would make them the second-largest carrier by market value in the world. It was a deal that was expected to spark further consolidation in the airlines industry as carriers seek to survive the impact of the financial crisis in an industry where the high costs of operation mean that many operators see economies of scale as vital to competitive advantage. It represented a traditional growth strategy for a sector where economies of scale and market access are important to long-term success. Founded in 1975 by Rolim Amaro, Tam was the largest Latin American airline prior to the merger and had a history of growing by merger and acquisition. Even though passenger numbers had doubled in Brazil in the previous 10 years, fierce competition, high fuel costs and airport fees, and the effects of currency volatility made the merger a sound cost and resource sharing move for Tam, who retained 80 per cent of the voting shares of the Brazilian company to comply with local ownership regulations. For Lan, Chile's flagship carrier, the merger forms part of a 7-year, $8.9 billion fleet expansion plan intended to provide a firmer financial footing in the face of a heavy debt burden and falling profits. This aim has been partially met as the merger does give Lan access to more profitable long-haul flights, but the Fitch credit rating agency downgraded Lan on the back of the merger, making future debt more costly. The Cueto family, Lan's major shareholders, have retained control of the merged company with Enrique Cueto in the position of CEO. The newly formed Latam Airlines Group, which still operates flights under its component brand names, is now seeking to gain market share on international routes to the east coast of America and to Asia, as well as realizing estimated synergies of $600m–$700m in order to fund further acquisitions. Time will tell whether this strategic merger will deliver the anticipated benefits, and whether big really is best in the airline industry.

Sources: Financial Times (22 June 2012) Brazil and Chile finally land merger; <www.wikipedia>; <www.businessweek.com>

Rohlin, Skärvad, and Nilsson (1998) see strategic leadership as an integration of the multi-faceted perspectives on leadership prevalent during the 1980s, and specifically as a combination of previous personal and administrative perspectives. As such, it is said to unite 'the analytically oriented tradition of the strategy domain with the process and action oriented leadership tradition' (Rohlin, Skärvad, and Nilsson, 1998: 182). They go on to suggest six requirements for a leader to be considered as strategic, namely:

- The ability to build knowledge of the environment
- Personal leadership
- An understanding of business and its processes
- The ability to create shared understanding and build learning teams
- To feel comfortable with change and to enjoy the paradoxes which change entails
- To be rooted in functional skills

Whilst Yukl defined strategic leadership in hierarchical terms, Rohlin, Skärvad, and Nilsson see it as an attitude, specifically as an attitude towards the enterprise within its social context. Figure 11.1 sets out this thesis and its implications for the specific concerns to be addressed by a strategic leader and what 'good' strategic leadership might look like.

Jim Collins (2001b) took a similar approach in framing his notion of 'level 5 leadership': based on a hierarchy of executive capabilities, he saw a truly executive leader as being characterized by humility and fierce resolve. Thus, counter to the more traditional view of transformational leaders as being larger-than-life, charismatic personalities, he suggests that:

> The most powerfully transformative executives possess a paradoxical mixture of personal humility and professional will. They are timid and ferocious, shy and fearless. They are rare—and unstoppable. (Collins, 2001b: 66)

An attitude towards ...	Specifically concerning	Good leadership is characterised by
... society	One's own company's role in society	Broad perspectives; responsibility; environmental consciousness; ethics
... oneself and others	One's own role as strategist, manager and leader	Integrity and genuineness; respect for differences; self-knowledge; empathy and energy; social competence
... the business of one's company	The whole and the parts: coordination and independence	Analysis of business environment; objectives and meaningfulness; overview and insight; results oriented; logic and aesthetics
... stability and change	The uncertain, the complex and the unpredictable	See new patterns; openness and involvement; seek challenges; timing and intuition
... action and reflection	The unknown, the risky, the relative	Asking questions with curiosity; experiment and innovate; business driven; action reflection learner

Figure 11.1 Strategic leadership is ...

Rohlin, Lennart, Skärvad, Per-Hugo and Nilsson, Sven Åke (1998) *Strategic leadership in the Learning Society.* Vasbyholm: MiL Publishers AB. Reproduced with permission.

Based on empirical research—later to form the basis of his book *Good to Great* (2001a)—Collins, explored what makes the difference between a company that achieves merely good performance and those that consistently deliver great performance. His aim was not to focus his attention on the activities of these companies' CEOs, but that was where his findings consistently led him. This resulted in the identification of a cumulative pyramid of leadership characteristics from those required by highly capable individuals, through those exhibited by contributing team members and competent managers, to those found only in effective leaders and 'level 5' executives.

Collins illustrates his findings with a selection of CEOs from his research—for example, Darwin E. Smith, CEO of Kimberly-Clark in the 1970s and 1980s, a period when it was transformed from a stodgy, old-fashioned paper company into a leading paper products company and when its cumulative stock returns were over four times those of the general market, and outperformed those of Hewlett-Packard, 3M, Coca-Cola, and General Electric. What his examples have in common is that most of us will never have heard of them! He contrasts their quietly determined success with the more noisy and self-publicizing approach of such corporate icons as Lee Iacocca and Jack Welch. Interestingly, he notes the ongoing success of Kimberly-Clark—that is after the departure of Smith—and sees this as another difference between level 5 leaders and 'big personality' leaders: the former select good successors because their ambitions are for their companies rather than themselves, whereas the latter need to demonstrate their irreplaceability by leaving behind them a less impressive performance at the hands of a 'lesser' leader. In a final summing up of the attitude of level 5 leaders, Collins suggests that, 'inherently humble, they look out of the window to apportion credit' at the same time as looking 'in the mirror to assign responsibility'—an attribution that is usually the complete opposite of their actual role in their company's transformation.

Discussion point: Humility and fierce resolve as leadership?

Collin's 'level 5 leadership' is at odds with more traditional views of charismatic leadership, and with the larger than life leaders we often hear about in the media. How would you reconcile these two views of strategic leadership?

- How might the characteristics of level 5 leaders act as a substitute for charisma? And how would such leaders communicate their vision to others?
- What kind of senior management teams would each type of leader build, and how would these contribute to the performance they were able to deliver?
- When might each kind of leadership be most effective? Are there specific industry sectors or situations which would favour each of the approaches and how might each type of leader come to power?

Boal and Hooijberg (2001) claim that the interest in strategic leadership since the 1980s represents a rejuvenation and metamorphosis of the entire leadership field. According to them, at the end of the 1970s no new leadership theories were emerging and the wider field of management was losing interest in leadership as a phenomenon. The move away from supervisory leadership to strategic leadership in the 1980s was a reflection of the increasing ambiguity and complexity of the environment within which organizations were called upon to operate and the degree of information overload to which leaders and managers were increasingly subject. In this context, Boal and Hooijberg see the essence of strategic leadership as being the creation and maintenance of 'absorptive capacity' (Cohen and Levinthal, 1990) or the ability to learn, 'adaptive capacity' (Hambrick, 1989) or the ability to change, and managerial wisdom (Malan and Kriger, 1998). This latter combines properties of discernment in relation to variations in the environment and 'Kairos time' (Bartunek and Necochea, 2000), that is the capacity to take the right action at a critical moment. The extent to which strategic leadership is important in determining the performance of organizations thus becomes a function of the degree of discretion enjoyed by top managers—and hence the potential for their decisions to impact on organizational outcomes—and the timing of their decisions to coincide with strategic inflection points in the organization's trajectory, such as changes in fundamental industry dynamics or the development of new technologies.

 Blog box

Within your own experience, either at work or in other areas of your life, who have been the strategic leaders you have admired? Reflect on one such leader, relating their leadership to the various ways in which academic writers have characterized strategic leadership. In no more than 300 words, what was it about them that made them stick in your mind? Was it their attitude? Was it their ability to combine administrative and personal leadership? Or how about their modesty and compelling resolve?

So far, we have taken for granted the idea that focusing on top executives is a valid pastime, and that strategic or executive leadership has an important role to play in determining organizational performance. Yukl (2002) reminds us that there is considerable debate around this issue, and sets out some of the constraining factors which may, in fact, limit the extent to which this is the case. These factors are discussed under the following headings:

- *External determinants*—it can be argued that organizational performance depends largely on external factors which are beyond the control of the CEO. Such factors include fluctuations in the economic environment, current market conditions, the existence of government policies and regulations, and the pace of technological change.

- *Limited discretion*—An incoming CEO inherits an organization with an existing culture, structure, and range of stakeholders. This may result in their ability to act being constrained by powerful internal forces or coalitions, the financial condition of the company, a deeply embedded organizational culture, rigidities within the organization's primary markets, powerful external stakeholders, and perceptions of the organization's performance.

- *Biased attributions*—organizational members may make biased attributions in relation to the actions of their CEO and the impact these actions have. Thus they might exaggerate the influence of individual leaders—either positively or negatively—as a way of making sense of complex and confusing events. Leaders, in their turn, may engage in impression management activities, to deliberately play on this tendency and to thus make themselves appear more powerful and/or effective than they really are. In this context, symbols and rituals—such as elaborate inauguration ceremonies—reinforce the perceived importance of leaders and their responsibility for delivering high level performance. Not surprisingly, successes are announced and celebrated, whilst failures are suppressed or downplayed (Yukl, 2002).

Notwithstanding these constraints, Yukl acknowledges the role of strategic leaders in evolutionary change within an organizational context. He draws on Tushman and Romanelli's (1985) 'punctuated equilibrium model' to explain how the role of top executives in organizational evolution is a function of the organization's evolutionary stage of development. Strategic leadership is seen as a mechanism for mediating between forces for stability and forces for change through alternating periods of reorientation and convergence. Reorientation occurs as relatively short-lived but intensive periods of activity during which top level leaders initiate major changes to the organization's strategy, structure, or culture, usually in response to equally major environmental changes, such as the arrival of a new competitor, major changes in technology, or significant decline in product demand. By contrast, these periods of upheaval and dramatic change are interspersed with much longer periods of only incremental change, during which the major changes are reinforced and internalized into organizational practice. These periods of fine-tuning are referred to as convergence and offer relatively limited scope for the CEO to make an impact on performance. Even in these periods, however, it is important for strategic leaders to continue to perform another of their key functions, namely that of monitoring the external environment in order to identify potential opportunities and threats to the future of the organization. This activity is a major contributor to feeding the process of strategy formulation, for which they are also responsible.

> ## Discussion point: Is it really all down to the CEO?
>
> Thinking about the organizations you have worked in and the performance they have generated, how much of it was down to the CEO?
>
> - What impact have changes in strategic leadership had on organizational performance? What other factors or events were in play at the same time which might have been significant in this regard?
>
> - What was the role of middle and junior managers in translating the strategic leadership from the top into implementable 'tactics' or operations, and how would the performance have been effected by their absence?
>
> - What were the constraints on the exercise of strategic leadership—such as the existence of events beyond their control or the limits placed on their discretion to act—which were also in play and how did these impact on organizational outcomes?

Finally, in introducing the topic of strategic leadership, it is worth noting that we are not limited here to a consideration of CEOs only. Executive teams or 'dominant coalitions' (Cyert and March, 1963) can exercise strategic leadership in a collective or collaborative fashion and can often have advantages over a single, high profile individual. By bringing a broader range of skills and experience to the decision making process, they can often make better decisions than a single individual (although the potential for compromise decisions also exists!). Their collective strength can compensate for individual weaknesses, ensuring that important tasks don't get overlooked; and a team-based structure is more likely to support effective succession planning and leadership transitions. This said, there is no guarantee that these potential advantages will actually bear fruit in practice, with the development of an effective executive team still being largely down to the skill and attitudes of the CEO who remains the 'first among equals'.

 Leadership in the media: A strategy for good against evil

In the first part of the *Lord of the Rings* trilogy—*The Fellowship of the Ring*—we see the character of Gandalf in the role of strategic leader. The film tells the story of the finding of an ancient ring of power, lost for centuries and now in the possession of Frodo, one of an unworldly and peace-loving race of Hobbits. With many races within Middle Earth—elves, dwarves, men, hobbits—disturbed by rumours of the reappearance of the Ring's maker, Sauron, it is Gandalf who guides the coalition that must decide what to do. Some would choose to hide the Ring, and trust that without its power, Sauron will be unable to gain power over them. Others would seek to wield the Ring in battle against Sauron, and so defeat him—ignoring warnings that they would inevitably become evil rulers in his stead. Still others would leave Middle Earth to its fate, departing from its shores forever. It is Gandalf who determines that the Ring must be destroyed if there is to be any chance of peace, and Gandalf who crafts a coalition between the 'free peoples of Middle Earth' who stand against Sauron, and guides their every move in seeking to destroy him and his Ring once and for all.

This epic fantasy can be seen as deeply allegorical (written as the original story was in the dark days of the Second World War) or as just a ripping good yarn—either way, the character of Gandalf offers a fine example of a strategic leader directing the capabilities and managing the resources of his 'organization' so as to create 'competitive advantage'—in this case, literally, by winning a war!

In the mainstream

Strategic leadership theory can be broadly divided into three separate streams of research, some more directly related to the field of strategy than others. Upper echelon theory (Hambrick and Mason, 1984) deals specifically with the notion of those at the top of the organizational hierarchy being responsible for its strategic direction and considers the question of executive accountability. Evolving over time into strategic leadership theory (Finkelstein and Hambrick, 1996) per se this strand of research treats organizational performance as a dependent variable, and measures it in terms of return on investment, return on equity, etc. The second strand, comprised of the so-called 'new' leadership theories—such as charismatic, transformational, and visionary—is less concerned with strategic outcomes and more focused on the practice of leadership by individuals. As we have already seen, the theories in this strand represent a transition from supervisory leadership as the focus of research to leadership as the 'management of meaning' (Smircich and Morgan, 1982). Charismatic and transformational leadership are well covered in their own chapter of this text, and will not be revisited here. Visionary leadership—defined as the articulation of how past, present, and future come together to shape organizational change (Gioia and Thomas, 1996)—is discussed in the critical section of this chapter. The third stream of research—which has been termed by Boal and Hooijberg (2001) as 'emergent'—consists of theories that explore issues of behavioural and cognitive complexity within the practice of leadership, as well as such themes as the role of social intelligence, and competing values theory (Quinn, 1988). These theories are diverse and fragmented—unsurprisingly given their emergent nature—and are not discussed in detail in this chapter. They are of interest, however, as a marker of some of the ways in which research continues to push the boundaries of understanding in relation to leadership practice.

RESEARCH IN FOCUS: The essence of strategic leadership

In their fascinating paper on the 'essence of strategic leadership' Hitt and Ireland (2002) claim that the dynamic and uncertain environment of the twenty-first century requires a new kind of strategic leadership if organizations are to successfully negotiate a path to competitive advantage. The role of strategic leaders in this context, they suggest, is the building of company resources and capabilities with an emphasis on human and social capital. Human capital refers to the knowledge, skills, and capabilities of individuals within the organization, whilst social capital concerns the relations between individuals and organizations that facilitate action and create value. Such relations may be internal to the organization or external. Although physical capital and resources are also strategically important, it is in their emphasis on people that Hitt and Ireland see strategic leaders as adding most value—hence they see this element of the role as its true essence. This approach draws on a resource-based view of the firm, and is referred to by the authors as 'effectuation'. To create value, the resources must be configured to develop capabilities that can be leveraged to create and maintain competitive advantage. The twin components of effectuation—managing firm resources and building teams and communities—are said to be a requirement of top-level leaders but can be exercised at all levels within the organization.

Hitt and Ireland go on to identify four stages in the process of leadership as resource management. The first stage involves the evaluation of existing resources, in the case of human and social capital through the operation of performance appraisal systems and the evaluation of intangible capabilities through personal observation. The second stage requires the active management of these resources through recruitment and selection of new employees, the development of capabilities in existing employees and—where necessary—the 'shedding' of employees who don't fit the required profile and are not viewed as having the capacity to develop. The danger of 'core rigidity' (Leonard-Barton, 1992) within the human capital of the firm is viewed as a real risk to competitive advantage. Stages three and four of the process involve the effective configuring and leveraging of the resources thus assembled. This requires the leader to assign roles, construct teams, and develop communication channels such as to ensure that the whole is greater than the sum of the parts. They must instil challenge and purpose, break through perceived barriers, and encourage potential in order to effectively leverage the resources at their disposal. In delivering on this essential task of strategic leadership, Hitt and Ireland see leaders as requiring astute interpersonal skills and relational competence, in order to operate as 'human modems' in an increasingly networked environment.

Source: Hitt, Michael A. and Ireland, R. Duane (2002) The essence of strategic leadership: Managing human and social capital. *The Journal of Leadership and Organizational Studies,* 9 (1) 3–14.

Upper echelons theory

Writing on strategic leadership can be seen as having its origins in Hambrick and Mason's (1984) upper echelons theory. This theory takes the perspective that organizational outcomes—by which is meant strategic choices and performance levels—can be at least partially predicted by a consideration of the managerial background and characteristics of those at the helm. In putting forward this theory, the authors acknowledge that they make what they describe as 'relatively crude assumptions about the psychological processes of top managers' (Hambrick and Mason, 1984: 193) and that a focus on background characteristics—such as age, tenure, functional background, education, and socio-economic roots—is in any case only a proxy for these processes. Nonetheless, they present their model of strategic choice under conditions of bounded rationality as a counter to the previous argument in favour of 'inertial organizations' (Lieberson and O'Connor, 1972), which suggests that large organizations are swept along by events or that they somehow 'run themselves', leaving no room for a significant contribution by top management. In contrast, upper echelon theory claims that top managers do matter and that their specific impact on organizational outcomes can be identified and accounted for. The underpinning argument here is that, based upon their values and beliefs as well as their past experience, CEOs bring their own 'givens' to any new situation, which limits the CEO's field of vision and how their attention is directed, causes selectivity in perception of events and their significance, and results in a filtering of the ways in which information is evaluated. A condition of bounded rationality is thus produced which constrains the manner in which strategic choices are made. It is suggested that these constraints can be traced to specific organizational outcomes. Whilst this is an intuitively appealing idea, the process of theory building undertaken by Hambrick and Mason was not followed by empirical testing, and their propositions in relation to the model remain largely speculative.

 Blog box

It could be argued that strategy—and the need for strategic leadership—exists at a number of levels within most large organizations. As Director of Lancaster University Management School's Executive MBA, I am responsible for determining and implementing the strategy for the programme. The strategy at this level is about ensuring that the programme remains successful both academically and financially by meeting and exceeding the needs of current students and attracting future ones. But I need to do this within the context of the strategy for the MBA Suite, which includes the full-time and global programmes and is set by the Suite Director. The strategy here is about the brand contribution which the MBA makes to the School as a whole. This in turn, must align with the strategic aims of the Management Faculty, which must be aligned with the strategic goals of the University as a whole. At this level, goals will include financial stability and global reach as well as academic excellence. Translated into a corporate environment, we could be talking about strategy at product, business line or divisional, and national or international levels. Whilst the lower levels of strategy will be constrained by the upper, the potential for goals and their implementation to be shaped by those responsible for them remains considerable. Perhaps 'upper echelon theory' needs to be renamed to reflect this complexity? (MIW)

Positive agency theory

The notion that 'top management matters' was taken in a different direction through the development of strategic leadership theory proper and its alter ego, positive agency theory. Whilst strategic leadership theory argues that organizations are a reflection of their top management and that the specific knowledge, experience, and values of top managers will serve to shape their strategic decisions, positive agency theory views top managers as agents of shareholders, but recognizes that they also have their own interests and agendas separate from those of the shareholders they represent (Jenson and Meckling 1976). Not surprisingly, perhaps, agency theory tends to downplay the positive aspects of executive leadership, focusing on the costs associated with the separation of ownership and control rather than the part played by senior executives in organizational success. This being the case, agency theorists have tended to focus their attention on the devices available to business owners (i.e. shareholders) in shaping and controlling the interests of their agents (i.e. managers). These devices include contracts, reward structures, boards of directors, the operation of the executive labour market, and so on. In their critique of contrasting perspectives on strategic leadership, Cannella and Monroe (1997) suggest that there is only limited empirical evidence to support the successful operation of such devices. Cannella and Monroe also considered strategic leadership theory, seeing it as offsetting some of the limitations inherent in positive agency theory. Its focus on the psychological make-up of executives is said to enable it to take into account individual differences in a way that is not accounted for in agency theory. Seen very much as a decision making theory, it is said to be generally supported by empirical evidence.

 Leadership in the media: Gandhi

In 1893, British-educated attorney Mohandas Gandhi is thrown off a South African train for being an Indian and travelling in a first class compartment. Quietly incensed by the existence of biased laws which allow for such segregation, Gandhi decides to start a non-violent protest campaign for the rights of all Indians in South Africa. After numerous arrests and the unwanted attention of the world, the government finally relents by recognizing rights for Indians, a victory for Gandhi's quiet, non-violent form of protest. When Gandhi is invited back to India, where he is now considered something of a national hero, and urged to take up the fight for India's independence from the British Empire, his strategy is the same—non-violent non-cooperation on an unprecedented scale, coordinated across millions of Indians nationwide. Although the campaign is successful in bringing about independence for India, their troubles are far from over as religious tensions between Hindus and Muslims erupt into nation-wide violence. Still pursuing a strategy of non-violence, Gandhi declares a hunger strike, saying he will not eat until the fighting stops. His 'success' this time is mixed as the fighting ends with the partition of the country into separate nations along religious lines. Religious tensions remain, however, and Gandhi spends his last days trying to bring about peace between the two nations. Angering dissidents on both sides, he is eventually assassinated in 1948, still believing in the power of peaceful protest.

This film is a powerful portrayal of how one man's strategy becomes his life and changes a nation. Few organizational leaders can expect to have the kind of impact achieved by Gandhi, but we may perhaps see his resolve and persistence on a lesser scale in what Collins has called 'level 5 leaders'.

One of the perceived difficulties with strategic leadership theory is the fact that what is really of interest here are the psychological characteristics of top managers, but that much of the research in this area has used demographic characteristics as a proxy for psychological profiles due to the difficulty of measuring the former. One attempt to bring these two measures closer together is Hambrick and Fukutomi's (1991) five seasons model, in which they divide a CEO's tenure into five sequential 'seasons' and trace the executive's psychological orientation during the different periods. The 'seasons' are suggested to be response to mandate, experimentation, selection of enduring theme, convergence, and dysfunction. Underpinning the move from one season to another are changes in the breadth of information sources the executive is tapping into and the degree of filtering that is occurring in relation to information received. Thus the executive begins their tenure open to a wide range of sources of information and receives that information relatively unfiltered. As their skill and experience in post develop, they move from merely seeking to fulfil their stated remit to beginning to experiment with how that remit can be shaped in line with their own values and beliefs. As they become increasingly committed to their own view of what the organization is about and where it should be heading, they filter out more sources of potential information such as to only hear what supports their own view. By this time, they are said to have reached a point of convergence in their thinking, and dysfunctionality—the inability to operate effectively by drawing objectively on a wide range of information—is not far behind. There is empirical evidence to support this idea, suggesting that as tenure increases executives become an inhibitor of strategic change rather than an initiator (Gabarro, 1987) and that this tendency has a negative impact on organizational performance. (Norburn and Birley, 1988).

From a critical perspective

Leadership, strategy, and practice

As we have seen, there is a strong theme within both the leadership and strategy literatures concerned with producing normative frameworks, such as the long-established situational (Hersey and Blanchard, 1982) and contingent (Fiedler, 1967; Vroom and Jago, 1988, 2007) models of leadership, or Porter's (1980) near-ubiquitous '5 forces' framework for developing competitive strategy. In the name of parsimony and clarity, the descriptors of these respective typologies become bland and generic, bearing little resemblance to the day-to-day lived experience of *doing leadership work* or *developing and enacting strategy*. These are also, in many ways, static rather than dynamic models. By contrast, the 'strategy as practice' perspective and more particularly its leadership counterpart see leadership as an ongoing, practical accomplishment: leadership is 'brought off' *as* leadership on a minute-by-minute basis as members of the setting orient to particular leadership practices in a manner which recognizes them as such. In a similar way, strategy is 'brought off' through the mundane practices of strategic leaders rather than by the mere act of having written a strategic plan.

The need to understand the ongoing practical accomplishment of such theoretical notions as strategic leadership through mundane practices has now been recognized and considerable work done to redress the theory-versus-practice balance, with the main thrust of this work emanating from the field of strategy. Hence the 'practice turn' (Jarzabkowski, 2003; Johnson, Melin, and Whittington, 2003) is concerned with 'the myriad micro-actions through which human actors shape activity in ways which are consequential for strategic outcomes' (Jarzabkowski, Balogun, and Seidl, 2007: 6) and recognizes that strategy is 'not something that an organization *has* but something its members *do*' (Jarzabkowski, Balogun, and Seidl, 2007: 6, original emphasis). This is in contrast to the more traditional view of strategy as a more complete, pre-formed entity: a series of 'logically coherent actions emanating from deliberate intentions and purposes: the acting out of prescribed roles, the performing of routines and the implementation of plans' (Chia, 2004: 30). The departure from traditional approaches to strategy represented by the practice turn is not just in the acknowledgement that strategy can be emergent (Mintzberg and Waters, 1985) or can produce unintended outcomes (Balogun and Johnson, 2005) in the face of environmental factors 'for which one cannot plan' (Hamel and Prahalad, 1989): it is not—as is emergent strategy—about 'coming to understand through the taking of actions what [strategic] intentions should be' (Mintzberg, Ahlstrand, and Lampel, 1998: 189) but a micro-level examination of the processual activities which collectively contribute to the accomplishment of strategy, either 'planned' or emergent. Thus from a strategy-as-practice perspective, 'strategy is conceptualized as a situated, socially accomplished activity, while strategizing comprises those actions, interactions and negotiations of multiple actors and the situated practices they draw upon in accomplishing that activity' (Jarzabkowski, Balogun, and Seidl, 2007: 7–8).

A case in point: 'Bringing off' a change in strategy

The difficulties experienced by BP—formally British Petroleum—in trying to respond to increasing concerns about the environment and the need for sustainable supplies of energy provide a very public example of how the accomplishment of strategy on an ongoing basis can be hugely problematic. Their environmental strategy—called 'beyond petroleum'—was launched in 2000 with a $200 million high profile public relations campaign aimed at positioning the company as environmentally friendly. The strategy was largely dismissed as 'greenwashing', however, by those in the media who saw little substance to it. The campaign, which saw the company change its 70 year-old shield-style logo to a green and yellow sunburst, was dismissed by PR watchers as 'ludicrous', emphasizing as it does BP's renewable energy sector at the same time as ignoring what continues to be its major field of operation, that is, fossil fuels. The fact that BP spent $45 million in 1999 to buy a solar energy company called Solarex was largely ignored in favour of reports of the $26.5 billion it invested to buy ARCO by way of expanding its oil drilling portfolio. The 2010 massive oil spill in the Gulf of Mexico further damaged the credibility of BP's claims, with commentators within the sector seemingly expecting BP to instantly change the profile of its energy portfolio in order to grant credibility to its intentions.

Part of the problem with the BP strategy was said to be the misalignment between the company's business processes and its corporate culture. The fact that the claims made for the brand were often ahead of the corporate culture left the company tremendously exposed to risk, particularly—as with the Gulf of Mexico—when things went wrong. This is when anything less than 100 per cent commitment to dealing with potential environmental catastrophes will almost inevitably undermine the success of the strategy: in BP's case, the absence of shut-off valves as standard operating procedure on their numerous rigs pumping oil in the Gulf was treated by the media as a blatant piece of hypocrisy—as was the fact that none of their tankers are double hulled.

Whilst the media were sceptical, the strategy seemed to be working with consumers. Sales from 2004 to 2005 rose from $192 billion to $240 billion then to $266 billion in 2006. Moreover, a survey of consumers found that 21 per cent of them thought BP was the greenest of oil companies, whilst BP saw its brand awareness go from 4 per cent to 67 per cent between 2000 and 2007. It was also rated the world's most accountable company in 2007. The differing fortunes of the strategy between sector commentators and consumers illustrate the constant effort required to 'bring off' a strategic change of direction and the near impossibility of achieving universal success in doing so.

Source: <www.environmentalleader.com> (15 January 2008); <www.prwatch.org> (3 May 2010); <www.talentzoo.com> (2 June 2010).

Samra-Fredericks (2003) produced a fine-grained analytic study of the talk-based interactive routines through which strategic leaders were able to shape the attention and opinion of others in order to produce desired strategic outcomes. In this fascinating study, she explores the skills concerning the choice of which discourse to deploy, what and how much emotion to show, when to bring elements of company history into play, and how to use mitigating language to turn the flow of debate used to shape how strategic direction comes to be determined. Also interesting is Suchman's (1987) work in outlining the relevance of plans to human action in which she says that 'plans are resources for situated action but do not in any strong sense determine its course' (Suchman, 1987: 52). Suchman's central argument is that plans do not thoroughly *determine in advance* and *causally direct* in every detail courses of action. Instead, plans are abstract constructions that need to be applied in specific circumstances rather than somehow 'executing themselves'. Nor is the relationship between the plan and the action it directs a mechanical one. Plans are *accomplished* activities and the successful accomplishment of a plan is consequently dependent on the practical understandings about

---

RESEARCH IN FOCUS: Organizations as 'complex adaptive systems'

Boal and Schultz (2007) draw on a view of organizations as 'complex adaptive systems' to explore the consequences for strategic leadership. In this view, the behaviour and structure of an organization emerges out of the interaction of a collection of organizational agents—a view which would suggest that there is no role to be played by strategic leaders because the system self-organizes. By delving deeper into the characteristics of complex adaptive systems—and in particular by picking up on the notions of 'tagging' and 'edge of chaos' which this theory includes—the authors reinstate leaders in a crucial role and suggest how they use dialogue and storytelling to shape the evolution of the organizations they lead. Through these mechanisms they see strategic leaders as playing a central role in the organization's capacity to learn from its past, adapt to its present, and create its future.

The concept of complex adaptive systems shows how novel and innovative behaviours and courses of action can arise from the interaction of groups of agents acting without the necessity of centralized control. At first sight, viewing organizations in this way would suggest that the role of leadership disappears since it fails to add value to a system that is self-organizing. Boal and Schultz dispute this viewpoint and suggest that there is still a role to be played in shaping the context and structure within which organizational agents operate. They suggest that strategic leadership is needed to push organizations out of the stasis that would otherwise occur—in the language of complex systems, to move them to the 'edge of chaos'—in order to prevent stagnation and allow for change. This 'edge of chaos' is the transition zone between stable equilibrium points and complete randomness and is thus perceived as a place for innovation and creativity. Strategic leadership operates to promote 'strange attraction'—regularly visited patterns or zones of activity within the system that are neither stable nor chaotic, but act as constraints upon overall behaviour. In this way, the general direction of the system can be guided whilst the organizational agents can still be free to organize their own day-to-day activities.

Boal and Schultz draw on the idea of 'tagging' to explain how leaders go about this shaping process. Tagging is a process that facilitates the creation of aggregates within the system—for example brands, teams, and functions —and coordinates activities around the identities thus formed. It is claimed that strategic leaders use the tagging process to influence the context and structure which underpins agent activity. Thus creating new tags around products, divisions, or regions shapes the focus of activities and the pattern of interactions between agents. Tags are an important feature of information handling and learning processes within the system, acting as 'memes'—genetic units of cultural transmission—through which ideas are passed on and evolve. Dialogue and storytelling are suggested as the primary transition mechanisms through which these memes are passed from leader to agent and then spread more widely throughout the organization.

Source: Boal, Kimberly B. and Schultz, Patrick L. (2007) Storytelling, time, and evolution: the role of strategic leadership in complex adaptive systems. *The Leadership Quarterly*, 18, 411–28.

what the plan specifies in *these* circumstances, using *these* resources, *these* people, and so on. As such, the specific activities taken to realize them are a practical matter of making the plan work through all the various and inevitable contingencies that can arise.

The tension between what is planned and what must be responded to in order to implement the plan is articulated by Knights and Mueller in terms of 'a continuous process of self-formation and reconstruction' in which 'numerous stakeholders make demands and serve to condition its development' (Knights and Mueller, 2004: 55–6) as those involved respond to the contingencies of its pursuance. It is thus iteratively developed and elaborated from within in the light of unforeseen developments in the situation and the reactions of a range of stakeholders. It is not the external contingencies that shape the strategy, but the strategy itself which 'keeps itself whole' at the same time as establishing how unforeseen needs and claims can be incorporated into its existing goals. As suggested by its inclusion in the title of this chapter, this notion of the 'perennially unfinished project' seems to us to get more truly to the heart of the minute-by-minute, processual character of action involved in the doing of strategy than many of the more established theories of strategic leadership and strategic planning.

 Blog box

Do the strategic leaders in your organization share their strategy with you? Are you invited to participate in strategy formation, and if so how? In no more than 300 words, reflect on the processes of strategy development and communication within your organization and how they influence the level of understanding and commitment generated. How do you go about translating the strategic goals of the organization into implementable plans and activities for your own level of operation?

Visionary leadership

As noted earlier in the chapter, the transition from supervisory leadership to leadership as the 'management of meaning' (Smircich and Morgan, 1982) as the focus for research resulted in the development of so-called 'new' theories of charismatic, transformational, and visionary leadership within the field of strategic leadership. Visionary leadership—defined as the articulation of how past, present, and future come together to shape organizational change (Gioia and Thomas, 1996)—can alternatively be viewed as being in opposition to strategic leadership, on the basis that it is less concerned with strategic outcomes and more focused on the practice of leadership by individuals. It is on this basis that visionary leadership is now discussed in the critical section of the chapter. Rowe (2001) suggested that strategic leadership was a synergistic combination of managerial and visionary leadership, where managerial leadership is concerned with stability and the preservation of the existing order, and visionary leadership is future oriented and involves risk-taking. He sums up this view in relation to the long- and short-term respective focuses which need to be combined in strategic leadership by saying:

> They [strategic leaders] dream and do something about their dreams. They are a synergistic combination of managerial leaders who never stop to dream, and visionary leaders, who only dream. (Rowe, 2001: 86)

It is Rowe's thesis that managerial and visionary leaders have a tendency to destroy wealth and deliver below average organizational performance, whilst strategic leadership enhances wealth creation and delivers above average returns. There is some resonance here with Cannella and Monroe's (1997) critique of both strategic leadership theory and positive agency theory, both of which are viewed as providing incomplete explanations of the role of top management in organizational performance. Cannella and Monroe suggest that visionary leadership is a necessary element in understanding executive leadership, although they would include personality theory as the final ingredient in the mix rather than Rowe's more prosaic managerial leadership.

Turning to visionary leadership in its own right, Westley and Mintzberg (1989) use a dramaturgical metaphor to develop a dynamic model of how visionary leadership is enacted, which they see as entailing three stages, namely envisioning, articulating, and empowering. They proceed from three assumptions in relation to how visionary leadership is said to differ from more traditional leadership approaches, namely: (1) visionary leadership is a dynamic, interactive phenomenon rather than a merely top-down one; (2) both the content and the context must be taken into consideration when considering vision; and (3) visionary leadership can occur in a number of different styles or types.

Whilst none of these assumptions appears particularly radical in marking out visionary leadership as differing from other forms of leadership, the inclusion of the first seems particularly problematic in relation to their adoption of a dramaturgical metaphor. They are, perhaps, more reflective of the contrast with the discipline of strategic planning, with which at least one of the authors is historically better associated. Nonetheless, they go on to draw on the work of Peter Brook—the legendary director of the Royal Shakespeare Company in the early 1960s—in suggesting that visionary leadership is enacted through the following processes. First, the idea of the vision is crafted through endless *repetition* and rehearsal until it feels right: this is akin to an actor rehearsing his lines and crafting his interpretation of the intentions of the playwright. Next the vision is symbolically communicated in a process which parallels *representation* or performance. At this point, the leader employs a range of linguistic and dramaturgical devises to maximize the impact of the vision on his audience. Finally, the 'attendance' of his audience produces a range of emotions and actions which collectively bring forth a feeling of empowerment in both the leader and the followers. The word '*assistance*' is used here to refer to the 'two-way current' which results in a dynamic interaction rather than a unidirectional flow of ideas.

Westley and Mintzberg go on to suggest that visionary leadership can take on a number of styles or forms dependent upon the salient capacities employed by the leader and the process through which they arrive at and share their vision. So, for example, Steve Jobs is described as a Proselytizer, who demonstrates evangelical enthusiasm in promoting the future potential of new ideas at a market level, thus shaping whole industries. By contrast, Lee Iacocca is designated a Bricoleur—someone who relies on sagacity and insight to pull different things together to make a new whole, based on reading the situation and the people and seeing the potential for an emergent strategy. Other types of visionary leaders are labelled as Creators, Idealists, and Diviners. Whilst the dramaturgical metaphor offers a plausible framework for considering the enactment of visionary leadership, the typology appears to be less convincing, with insufficient distinction being apparent in the capacities employed by visionary leaders or the targets to which these capacities are applied for it to offer clear insights into the phenomenon.

Chapter summary

In this chapter we have considered:

- How notions of strategy and strategic leadership have evolved from military origins into being central concepts within corporate organizations, and how strategy has developed as a separate discipline in its own right

- Where 'strategic leadership' sits in relation to other forms of leadership, and in particular the difference between supervisory leadership and leadership at an organizational level

- The debate surrounding the role of strategic leadership in determining the performance of large organizations

- Theories of strategic leadership, including upper echelon theory and positive agency theory, and the empirical support that each has received

- How the practice turn in both strategy and leadership has focused attention on the accomplishment of leadership through routine, daily practices, and how this stands in opposition to more traditional theories of transformational and charismatic leadership.

 Integrative case study: The doing of strategic leadership

Since incorporation—the process through which UK further education (FE) colleges became 'independent' of local education authorities—the learning and skills sector has increasingly taken on the characteristics of a service culture, with students and parents as the 'customers' and educational packages as the 'product'. This service orientation brought with it with an increased emphasis on commercial and educational accountability with a practical consequence being the need for college principals to manage business issues—finance, strategy, personnel, marketing, etc.—which had previously not been part of their remit. The discourses of commercialism, quality, value for money, and the like are clearly reflected in the practice of strategic leadership within the sector.

Downton (a pseudonym for a real town in the South of England) has a sixth form college (an academic institution for post compulsory education) and a more vocational college of arts and technology, the Principals of which are developing plans to 'co-locate'. The two colleges already have combined curriculum planning and entry procedures, and make joint presentations to local schools to emphasize the complementary (rather than competitive) nature of their respective offerings. A Memorandum of Understanding has now been drawn up setting out the aims and extent of a proposed wider collaboration and a framework for how these aims will be pursued, and making clear that it is a co-location and not a merger. The Memorandum covers in principle the areas of collaboration (e.g. curriculum delivery, quality assurance, and property strategy), key objectives for each area, and process guidelines in terms of planning, monitoring, and evaluation. The need to conduct these activities across two organizations, with two strategic leaders, will require a strong degree of improvisation and adaptation as the plan evolves and contingencies arise. With the bones of the collaboration strategy thus agreed and documented, the two colleges now move into the 'pre-implementation' phase, where aspects of the strategy are being developed and made public through interaction with a range of stakeholders.

The need to *clarify* the strategy will arise from sharing its original formulation with key stakeholders, and responding to their perceptions of it. In the course of drafting various announcement documents to staff, the press, and other important stakeholders, the Principals of the two colleges constantly amend and update them as the subtle, unperceived nuances of the original plan are exposed to stakeholders' reactions. So, for example, as Bob (Principal of the sixth form college) is working on a staff presentation for his college, he revises the wording of key elements of the presentation, based on input from his senior team in relation to staff sensitivities, in order to retain the sense of distinctness between the two colleges—changing the phrase 'common timetable' to 'contiguous timetabling' and inserting a reference to 'separate identities' alongside one to 'integrated marketing' and branding. At the same time, the first draft of a press release is amended so that a reference to collaboration on 'recruitment'—intended to refer to the recruitment of students onto educational courses—is clarified (by the addition of the word 'student') when sixth form staff raise concerns about the potential loss of beneficial contract arrangements compared with their colleagues at the other college.

Once outlined, the strategy requires refining and internalizing through the practice of being *rehearsed*. Through repetition of the key elements of the strategy, sketching out its implications, considering possible objections, etc. the strategic leaders prepare themselves, and the strategy, for wider disclosure. In so doing, they build confidence for later 'skirmishes' in which the fundamentals of the strategy are likely to be challenged, and generate 'ammunition' to meet these anticipated challenges. This practice of rehearsal can occur in both private preparatory meetings, where 'scripts' are prepared and anticipated questions addressed, and in meetings with stakeholders, when key points of the strategy evolve through repetition and reinforcement. So, for example, prior to meetings aimed at canvassing the support of key external stakeholders—in particular those who could provide land for a co-located site—they draft out answers to likely questions and consider what their own responses will be to possible options which may be suggested. In running through these scripted Q&As with senior colleagues and with each other, Bob and Gary (Principal of the FE college) use each other as sounding boards while they practise the pre-prepared scripts and identify gaps, inconsistencies, and potential problem areas.

If a strategy is to be more than just a well-crafted document, then its spirit—the values and aims which form its core—must be upheld as setbacks and opportunities arise: ways must be found of incorporating unanticipated events which may change the detail of what has been planned, but which keep intact its core principles. This practice of *upholding* is evident in Bob and Gary's meetings with stakeholders where retention of the core aims of the co-location strategy—to provide a better combined vocational and academic learning experience for students, at the same time as meeting local employer and community needs—enables them to be flexible in responding to issues raised whilst still sticking to the spirit of what they have previously agreed between themselves. So for example, when a representative of the Borough Council proposes a particular location from its own landholdings as being potentially suitable for the new campus, Bob and Gary can respond to this unexpected but potentially positive offer in terms of agreed priorities for students—for example access and parking issues, catchment areas, nearness to local employers—even though they have not considered the specifics in relation to the site on offer. In such instances, the preparation undertaken is a tacit recognition that they cannot know in advance how individual stakeholders will respond to the plan and thus cannot know in detail how they will need to pursue their case. It is not the (as yet un) written details of the strategy that are at stake here but the core principles it is designed to achieve. It is these that the strategic leaders must maintain, at the same time as incorporating the fluidity required to be responsive to the outturn of specific events.

At the same time the strategy—or more likely the manner in which it is pursued—may need to be *adapted* in order to keep its progress on track. To stick doggedly to a plan in the face of unforeseen events may result in unintended and undesirable outcomes: instead specific activities related to the strategy will need to be adjusted in response to unfolding events without losing sight of the underpinning goals to be achieved. So, for example, when the Principals meet with the editor of the local newspaper to brief him about the co-location strategy, the editor suggests delaying the planned staff briefing until after the official press release to avoid the message leaking out to the nearby regional paper as a merger story. This rescheduling of the announcement to college staff requires Bob to adapt existing plans by finding other items to talk to staff about rather than raise suspicion by cancelling the meeting entirely.

The strategy is, almost inevitably, *elaborated*—furnished with more detail and developed into practically implementable actions—as the process continues. Bob and Gary have started this process in the meetings and activities already described. The process continues with the preparation of a transport plan for the new site, and work on a bid for capital funding. In speaking to the slides prepared for the staff presentation, Bill elaborates on the 'Advantages of collaboration' by talking about 'a better deal for students; new buildings with better facilities; wider choice of and access to vocational training alongside existing academic opportunities; improved progression routes; and the potential for a more sustainable funding structure'—with some of these ideas occurring 'on the hoof'. Thus in the course of these and subsequent meetings and discussions, the plans for co-location evolve and develop: at no point can the strategy be said to be complete or fixed, yet the aims which it embodies are always there as a potential 'finish line'. The route towards this finish line, rather than being linear or causal, is a constant sequence of adjustments and adaptations through which those responsible for its development and implementation tack their way along the course.

Case study questions

- How far do the processes of clarifying, rehearsing, upholding, adapting, and elaborating outlined above resonate with your own experience of how strategic leadership—or strategizing—gets done? How does this practice view of strategy compare with more traditional notions of 'strategic planning'?

- As strategic leaders, what are the key attitudes and characteristics exhibited by Bob and Gary, and how important do you think these are likely to be in the ultimate success of the co-location strategy?

- If you were in Bob's position how would you use visionary leadership—the tying together of past, present, and future—to sell the idea of co-location to resistant colleagues? Do you think the commercial environment in which the college was forced to operate would support this line of argument?

- Given the strong strategic lead provided by the college Principals, what other resources—for example human and social capital—will be important in implementing the proposed strategy?

Further reading

Knights, David and Mueller, Frank (2004) Strategy as a 'Project': overcoming dualisms in the strategy debate. *European Management Review*, 1, 55–61.

Rohlin, Lennart, Skärvad, Per-Hugo, and Nilsson, Sven Åke (1998) *Strategic Leadership in the Learning Society*. Vasbyholm: MiL Publishers AB.

Samra-Fredericks, Dalvir (2003) Strategizing as lived experience and strategists' everyday efforts to shape strategic decision. *Journal of Management Studies*, 40 (1) 141–74.

Suchman, L. (1987) *Plans and Situated Action: The Problem of Human-Machine Communication*. Cambridge: Cambridge University Press.

12 Authentic and ethical leadership: A return to morality?

 Learning outcomes

On completion of this chapter you will:

- Gain an understanding of core concepts associated with authentic leadership
- Examine the moral and ethical component of authentic leadership in more depth
- Understand the ideas and importance of ethical leadership
- Consider servant leadership as a practical development of the ideas contained in authentic and ethical leadership
- Appreciate the role of spirituality in authentic and ethical leadership, and understand the dimensions of spiritual leadership

Introduction

In March 2012, in the USA, Alan Stanford, a wealthy banker from Texas who held a knighthood from the government of Antigua, was convicted of stealing $7 billion of his customer's money. His conviction included counts of fraud, conspiracy and obstructing the US Securities and Exchange Commission (*Financial Times*, 2012a). Stanford joined Bernard Madoff as one of America's biggest financial fraudsters. Madoff was convicted and sentenced to 150 years in prison for a $65 billion fraud (*The Guardian*, 2009).

In India, in January 2009, B.Ramalinga Raju, the chairman of Satyam Computer Services, admitted in a letter to the Board that he had been falsifying the company accounts for the past six years, and had effectively invented a $1 billion cash balance (*Financial Times*, 2009).

In China, in July 2012, Yan Limin, a former executive of China's largest e-commerce group, Alibaba, was arrested by police on suspicion of taking bribes. Limin was sacked by Alibaba in March 2012 for mismanagement and not following regulatory mechanisms (BBC News, 2012).

These are just a few examples in a long line of corporate leadership scandals to have hit the headlines in recent times. One could also cite:

- dubious and illegal accounting practices of Enron and Worldcom
- mis-selling of insurance products by UK banks
- UK politicians making expense claims for properties they did not use, or for items such as maintenance on moats, yachts, and tennis courts.
- Olympus Corporation directors in Japan hiding losses and mis-stating corporate accounts

Ethical scandals such as these have raised questions about the nature and impact of lead-ers and leadership in such situations. They have also highlighted the complex and uncertain globalized corporate world in which leaders have to make 'good' decisions with limited and incomplete information. This complexity has led to a body of work being developed that both challenged leaders to ask questions about their own inner morals, values and purpose, and also offered a possible solution to leading in an uncertain environment.

This chapter will consider some of these approaches to leadership. We will start with an examination of authentic leadership, where it is argued that leaders must know and lead themselves first before leading others. Arguably, one key aspect of authentic leadership is a personal understanding of your own ethical stance, something that has been developed in the second approach we will consider, that of ethical leadership. In understanding aspects of ethical leadership, we are led to two other approaches that have increasingly been the focus of discussion by participants on leadership development programmes—that of servant lead-ership and spiritual leadership.

In the mainstream

Authentic leadership

In defining authentic leadership, scholars often begin with the origins of the word authentic-ity, which is commonly said to come from the words inscribed on the wall of the oracle at Delphi in Greece advising visitors 'To thine own self be true' (Avolio and Gardner, 2005; Caza and Jackson, 2011). Some describe the definitions of authenticity from philosophical per-spectives such as existentialism, where authenticity is a measure of how true you are to your own internal value sets, to your character and your spirit, in spite of pressure from the exter-nal environment on you to act in a different way. It is thought that authenticity derives from your personal awareness of your experiences, needs, thoughts, wants, emotions, preferences, and beliefs. To be an authentic person and leader means actively engaging in a continual process of investigating these elements. Authentic leaders accept that these elements are a fundamental part of themselves, and act in a way consistent with their experiences, thoughts, emotions, and beliefs.

Others talk about the influence of positive psychological ideas from psychologists such as Abraham Maslow and Karl Rogers. In the creation of his famous hierarchy of needs, Maslow determined that it was better to study those people who are mentally healthy rather than those who were not, so he could identify the attributes of motivation that made up his hierarchy (Maslow 1987). In the same way, Rogers's work begins with the assumption that people are fundamentally well and, through a person-centred, relational approach to counselling, can be brought back to this state of wellness (Rogers, 2003). In a similar vein, authentic leadership as de-scribed by Luthans and Avolio (2003) seeks to take a positive perspective, describing and search-ing for those positive attributes that enable a leader to be authentic to their own values and morals, rather than describing and studying the inauthentic in order to describe the authentic.

Authentic leadership has been seen as a reaction to critiques of transformational leader-ship theory discussed in Chapter 5. One specific criticism is related to the idealized influ-ence component of transformational leadership. Idealized influence suggests that a leader is attractive to followers to such an extent that followers desire to emulate the leader. This encouragement of emulation could create dependence on the leader, and could even be used by unethical leaders to manipulate their followers.

Bass and Steidlmeier (1999) answered these critiques by suggesting that there were two types of transformational leader, the authentic transformational leader, for whom ethics and morality were important, and the 'pseudo' transformational leader, who was more likely to use idealized influence in an unethical way to manipulate followers. The notion of being authentic was very firmly linked with a focus on morality, something that has carried through into the various popular and academic definitions of authentic leadership.

The descriptive, and to some extent empirical, work on authentic leadership has gained momentum with academics and practitioners alike since the turn of the century. A prominent popular practitioner of authentic leadership is Kevin Cashman (2008), who starts his book *Leading from the Inside Out* with the story of a priest and a soldier during the 100 years war. The soldier stops the priest and asks him three questions:

- Who are you?
- Where are you going?
- Why are you going there?

The priest, recognizing the importance of these questions, offers to double the soldier's salary if he will ask him these three questions every day. In answering these questions, the priest will gain a degree of self-awareness and self-knowledge that will help him to discern his true purpose in life, and his direction of travel.

Discussion point: Three important questions

Find a quiet space to consider your answers to the following three questions:

- Who are you?
- Where are you going?
- Why are you going there?

Now meet up with a colleague you trust and discuss the answers you both have to these questions.

The three questions above describe components that commonly occur in descriptions of authentic leadership. George (2003) describes authentic leaders as being leaders who possess a keen insight into their own self and are aware of their strengths, weaknesses, values, and principles. They are consistent in the application of these principles, despite any external pressures that may encourage them to act in another way, thus being true to themselves. The consistency of application attracts followers.

George says that an authentic leader will

use their natural abilities, but they also recognise their shortcomings and work hard to overcome them. They lead with purpose, meaning and values. They build enduring relationships with people. Others follow them because they know where they stand. They are consistent and self disciplined. When their principles are tested, they refuse to compromise. Authentic leaders are dedicated to developing themselves because they know that becoming a leader takes a lifetime of personal growth." (George, 2003: 12)

 Leadership in the media: Dead Poets Society

This 1989 film charts the arrival and impact of a new English teacher, Mr Keating (Robin Williams) on a group of young men at a private preparatory school, the Welton Academy. The Academy has four values, 'tradition, honor, discipline, and excellence' and is deeply traditional in its teaching method. Keating uses unusual teaching methods to encourage the boys to think for themselves, to understand their purpose, to see the existential nature of their lives, and to seek to grasp every minute and make their lives extraordinary.

In one scene, Keating has the boys walking around the school quadrangle. The boys start walking at different paces, but soon fall into a marching step with each other. Keating's point is to encourage the boys to walk a different path, not to conform with others' opinions or ideas, to know what they stand for and to stick with this despite the external pressure to conform. In this sense he is encouraging the boys to discover their authentic selves, to explore and find what they truly believe, and to take a stand on this belief. A small group of the boys take up this challenge, understanding and pursuing their core beliefs in spite of strong opposition, and at great personal cost to themselves.

What beliefs are fundamental to you? On what will you take a stand, in spite of external pressure?

Both Cashman and George's work focus on the first two elements, with George suggesting that individual and leader authenticity is made up of five main dimensions:

- Understanding and pursuing your purpose/mission with a passion
- Holding and applying strong values—knowing what is right
- Creating relationships defined by trust that will endure over time
- Demonstrating self-discipline
- Leading from the heart

George related five characteristics that an authentic leader will display in their everyday behaviour that are linked to the five dimensions of authentic leadership mentioned above.

 Blog box

For me, the discovery of purpose has always been a key element of the best education programmes. During my MBA year I discovered a passion for developing people, for always trying to see the potential that they have, and striving to help them achieve that potential. This ties in with some deeply held beliefs, linked to my personal faith, through which I aim to see all people with both realism—as they are now—and through the eyes of God—as they could be if their potential was fulfilled. Gaining clarity on my purpose has helped me focus on dealing with people so they are always developing their potential. This purpose has been a central core through my varied activities, from serving on the leadership teams and running youth groups, to being OD champion on the Board of a company, and especially in my design and development of the MBA and leadership programmes.

Take some time to consider and write about your purpose. What is the thing that most excites you? What are you passionate about? Sometimes you can discover what you really care about by understanding what makes you annoyed, angry, or upset—this could be linked to your purpose. (CS)

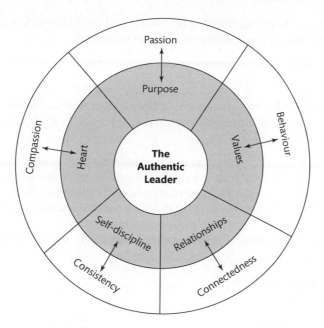

Figure 12.1 George's five characteristics of an authentic leader

Bill George (2003) *Authentic Leadership: Rediscovering the secrets to creating lasting value.* Reproduced with permission of John Wiley & Sons Inc.

Authentic leadership, therefore, is a multidimensional construct. Caza and Jackson (2011) point out that theory covers three broad areas of description for this construct, the authenticity of the individual as a person, the leader's authenticity as a leader, and the phenomenon of authentic leadership itself. According to Avolio, Luthans et al. (2004), the authentic leader knows

> who they are, what they think and behave and are perceived by others as being aware of their own and others' values/moral perspective, knowledge and strengths; aware of the context in which they operate; and who are confident, hopeful, resilient, and of high moral character. Avolio, Luthans et al. (2004: 4)

The academic research and theory of authentic leadership has developed at a pace since Luthans and Avolio's chapter defining this concept appeared in 2003 (Caza & Jackson, 2011). This has largely focused on describing the concept, although there has been some attempt to measure the impact of authentic leadership empirically.

Luthans and Avolio viewed previous work on the subject of authenticity as being focused on possible negative consequences of leaders who exhibited unauthentic, pseudo, or immoral leadership. They drew together several academic ideas including transformational or full-range leadership, positive organizational behaviour, and ethical perspective taking to form a working definition of authentic leadership (Gardner et al., 2011). Avolio and Luthans called for a form of authentic leadership that is positive in its psychological foundations, in which the authentic leadership is both self-aware of thoughts, values, and beliefs, and self-disciplined in a way that is congruent to this self awareness. This authentic leader would be equally interested in the development of themselves and their followers, and would exhibit positive characteristics such as confidence, hope, and optimism.

Authentic leadership dimensions

This original conceptualization of authentic leadership was developed over time by Avolio and his colleagues and collaborators. They produced a model with four dimensions, that Walumbwa et al. (2008) defined as:

> a pattern of leader behaviour that draws upon and promotes both positive psychological capacities and a positive ethical climate, to foster greater self-awareness, an internalised moral perspective, balanced processing of information, and relational transparency on the part of leaders working with followers, fostering positive self-development. (Walumbwa et al., 2008: 94)

The four dimensions of authentic leadership are summarized well by Hannah, Avolio, and Walumbwa (2011):

- Internalized moral perspective
- Self-awareness
- Relational transparency
- Balanced processing

The term 'internalized moral perspective' describes a leader who is guided in decisions and actions by their own moral standards and values. It implies that authentic leaders know what they stand for, what their morals and values are, essentially what they find admirable and acceptable, what they will do and what they will not do. There is an assumption here that an authentic leader has a higher level of moral development than an unauthentic leader, a more acute sense of what is right and what is wrong in any given situation. This internal perspective will dominate, even in situations where there is significant pressure put on a leader to act in a less moral way by peers, by organizational or industry norms, or by those in more senior positions.

This level of moral perception is obviously linked with self-awareness. Self-awareness is made up of two elements. The first is the amount of accurate knowledge a leader has about themselves. The second is how aware a leader is of the impact their behaviour has on others. It is implied that there may be several levels of self-knowledge. Those with the beginnings of self-awareness will have an understanding of their own strengths and weaknesses. Those with a well developed sense of self will have gained an understanding of their purpose, values, morals, and beliefs. Of course, self-awareness in itself only produces interesting information about yourself. The authentic leader uses this information to inform their thoughts on key leadership and organizational issues, and to influence the actions they take on a daily basis.

These daily actions directly influence the next dimension of an authentic leader, relational transparency. Here a leader behaves in a way that develops trusting relationships with colleagues. This may involve the sharing of information about ones-self and about the organization, and behaving in an honest and open way. Gardner et al. (2005) highlight the importance of the authentic leader being authentic in both their self-awareness and their behaviour, and having authentic relationships with their staff. These are defined as being transparent, open, trusting, focused on the development of the follower, and pursuing worthy goals for the organization. The authentic leader will also possess a strong self-regulatory mechanism which will constantly evaluate whether the leader is being true to themselves. Gardner et al. (2005) suggest that self-regulation will result in the leader being a positive role model who will develop high levels of trust, engagement, and well-being in followers.

One of the characteristics of the positive role model is the final element of Hannah's four dimensions, balanced processing. Here a leader takes time to come to decisions, seeking out relevant information and views that may challenge their own. This is a process of investigating issues gives the leader a deeper understanding of the issue, and allows followers to be engaged in the process of decision making. Hannah, Avolio, and Walumbwa (2011) make a link between this process and the opportunity to consider ethical perspectives and standards when weighing up a decision.

To be an authentic leader requires a leader to actively pursue all four dimensions at once and for this to be evident in both their thoughts and their deeds.

Causes and results of authentic leadership

Two elements are thought to have an impact on the creation of an authentic leader, and the development of authentic leadership. These are personal antecedents and environmental conditions. Gardner et al. (2005) first developed this idea in their conceptual model for authentic leader and follower development (Figure 12.2).

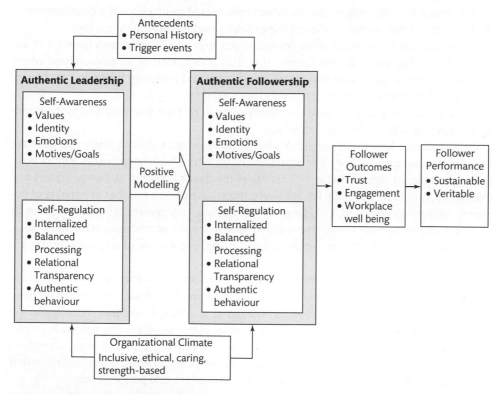

Figure 12.2 Model of authentic leadership

From Gardner, W. L., Avolio, B. J., Luthans, F., May, D. R., and Walumbwa, F. (2005) Can you see the real me? A self-based model of authentic leader and follower development, *Leadership Quarterly*, 16, 3, 343–72. Reproduced with permission.

Table 12.1 The conditions for the development of authentic leadership (Reproduced with permission.)

Environmental conditions	• Supportive • Positive organisational context
Personal elements	• Role models • Training • Personal history • Interpretation of past events • Highly developed personal morality • High psychological capacity • Concern for others • Emotional intelligence • Positive self image/concept • Integrity • Low self-monitoring

Gardner and colleagues suggest that a leader's understanding and interpretation of their experiences will have an impact on their authenticity, especially if they have a significant person in their history who has been a role model for integrity or morals. They link this with critical moments, called trigger events, which have served to influence the development of the individual. Self-knowledge of these things helps develop the authentic leader.

The environmental element is the context which may allow for the development of authentic leadership and authentic followership. This is described as an environment where leaders create an organization that shares information and resources freely, and enables all members of the organization to continually learn and grow.

Caza and Jackson (2011) provide a summary of the conditions that may lead to the development of authentic leadership (Table 12.1).

Various authors have made suggestions for the likely impact authentic leadership can have on followers and organizations. For organizations, authentic leadership creates a more positive organizational climate that in turn facilitates the development of authentic leaders and followers (Gardner et al., 2005). For followers, there have been a number of benefits of authentic leadership proposed, including increased effort, engagement, and performance by followers; improved trust; better attitudes and mindsets; positive emotions in the work place; moral development of followers; improved well-being; and a sense of empowerment (Caza and Jackson, 2011).

Finally, whilst there has been much work done on defining authentic leadership, there has been little empirical work done on proving the claims of improved climate and follower well-being. In one of the few studies, Yammarino et al. (2008) found that most studies on authentic leadership were focused on the individual, either self-reporting against authentic leader questionnaires, or giving opinion on the authentic leadership of their immediate supervisor. These studies did find a link between authentic leadership practice and improved levels of positive emotions, commitment to the organization, and performance.

Authentic leadership has been described as the core of leadership, rather than as a new idea about leadership. As we have seen in this section, the heart of the majority of authentic

---

Case in point: Authentically leading your team

Mary is a senior leader in a UK housing association. Housing associations were created to take on the ownership and management of housing stock that formerly belonged to local Councils across the UK. This type of housing exists for those who cannot afford to buy their own houses, either because they are unemployed, retired, or are in low wage employment. As private companies, some with charitable status, housing associations are in a position to use the stock to raise funds from banks in order to invest in the improvement of housing stock for their tenants.

Mary was recently promoted to head a team of directors who were each responsible for a large amount of stock in different geographic areas of the UK. At the first meeting of this new team Mary wanted to ensure that she clearly communicated her purpose for choosing to work in this sector. She opened the meeting by describing how she passionately believed that everyone, regardless of income or employment status, deserved to have a decent standard of accommodation, and as the market could not provide this at affordable prices, housing associations must seek to provide this for the poorest in society. Mary emphasized her belief that she was there to serve the needs of her team, and that they were all there to serve and enable their employees, so that their customers, the tenants, could have the best possible service.

Mary's openness and honesty about what drives her allowed those who would report directly to her to see her as an authentic leader in the context of the work they were doing. It enabled them to be equally honest about why they chose to be in this line of work. It established a vision or common purpose around the vocational calling of all team members, from which they could pursue a common goal. Whilst there was little discussion about the values that would underpin this, subsequent behaviour by Mary towards the team set the climate as one of honesty, openness, trust, and acceptance.

- How important do you think it is to be authentic with your immediate team? What are the benefits and potential drawbacks of being fully authentic?

---

leadership descriptions is a well developed sense of moral and ethical purpose. An authentic leader has knowledge of their ethical and moral beliefs, and has the courage to act on these. The next section will examine theories and ideas of ethical leadership.

Ethical leadership

We contend that the moral authenticity of the leader explains the authenticity of that person's leadership. (Jackson and Parry, 2008: 99)

Thinking, philosophizing, and discussing ethical leadership is not a new phenomenon. Bass and Steidlmeier (1999) trace the origins of thinking about ethical leadership back to Sophocles and Plato for Western perspectives, and Confucius for Eastern perspectives. In each of these cases, ethics is seen as a core part of what makes a leader effective. In effect, ethical leadership is not seen as a new approach to understanding leadership, but is described as an essential element of all conceptualizations of leadership or descriptions of leader behaviour. Ciulla and Forsyth (2011) point out that when you ask people the question 'what is a leader' you are actually asking 'what is a good leader', and when you dig into the meaning of good it tends to be interpreted as having both a moral and an effective dimension. A leader has to be both morally good and good at what they do in order to be called a leader.

So what is an ethical leader? Ciulla describes an ethical leader as 'someone who not only does the right thing but also does so in the right way and for the right reasons' (Ciulla and Forsyth, 2011: 230). This description brings together two philosophies that dominate the writing on business ethics, that of deontology and teleology. A deontological perspective argues that a leader should act out of a sense of duty, or an adherence to the rules. These rules or duties, should be rationally determined and a leader would follow these rules because they are right, rather than because of the effect they have. If a leader follows their duty then they are deemed to have acted in an ethical way, regardless of the outcomes. Here the focus is very much on the means used to achieve an end, and whether those means are informed by a moral intent. The deontological perspective highlights the morality of the leader as a person, and questions whether a leader has a set of reasoned principles that they adhere to in their actions and decisions.

The teleological, or consequentialist, perspective argues that a leader should be judged ethical if the outcomes of their actions can be judged to have conceived something good, regardless of the actions themselves. Here the focus is on the ends achieved by an action, even if the action itself is morally dubious. The best known consequentialist philosophy is utilitarianism, where an action would be deemed to be good if it results in the greatest good for the greatest number of people. As John Stuart Mill points out, the consequentialist perspective informs us of the morality of the action, rather than the morality of the person undertaking the action (Ciulla, 2001).

These descriptions highlight two key elements in the thinking academics have done on ethical leadership, the character of the leader and the actions of a leader. Ethical leadership focuses on the moral character of the leader, their integrity and ethical awareness, and the leader's ability to communicate and extol this sense of ethics to a team or organization.

This distinction between the character of the individual leader and their attempt to ethically influence followers has been termed moral person and moral manager by Treviño, Brown, and Hartman (2003). The moral person represents the personal characteristics of an ethical individual that Treviño, Brown, and Hartman discovered through a series of interviews with senior executives and ethics officers. This and their subsequent research led to the description of the ethical leader as being caring, honest, trustworthy, and fair, evidenced by the principled manner in which a leader took decisions. The authors suggested that leaders with these characteristics were moral persons. A moral person as an ethical leader considers others and wider society in their decisions, and would make decisions in an open, fair, and principled way (Brown and Treviño, 2006; Jordan et al. 2011).

The research also described an ethical leader as one who communicated their ethical principles in a variety of ways to their followers and to the wider organization. This was termed the moral manager aspect, and is the attempt to influence others in the organization to act in an ethical manner. This could be done through role modelling ethical behaviour, through the allocation of rewards to encourage ethical behaviour, and by consistently giving out an ethical message through all communications (Treviño, Hartman and Brown, 2000; 2003; Brown and Treviño, 2006).

Empirical studies suggest that leaders who are both moral persons and moral managers can expect to see an increase in workplace effort, citizenship like behaviour and verbal contributions, and a decrease of incidents of deviousness from their followers (Jordan et al. 2011).

The works of Treviño, Brown, and Jordan are all influenced by Kohlberg's work on cognitive moral development (Kohlberg, 1969) which focuses on the moral reasoning individuals have when faced with ethical and moral issues. Kohlberg suggested that there are three different stages of moral development that an individual can pass through. The first is the preconventional stage, where ethical and moral norms are as seen as being imposed externally, and the individual will only comply with these if there are rewards or punishments. The second is the conventional stage, where ethical and moral norms come from an individual's close associates (family, friends, role models, etc.), and the individual ensures that they conform with the morals of 'significant others' for the sake of the group.

The third and highest stage is postconventional. Here the individual reasons for themselves what is right and wrong from ideas of rights and justice. The individual here is less likely to be influenced by significant others, and more likely to act in accordance with these morals in the face of pressure to conform to a lower moral standard (Jordan et al. 2011).

Treviño, Brown, and Jordan all suggest that an ethical leader would exist at the highest level of moral development, thus becoming similar to the theories that depict leaders as being exceptional individuals, better than others. Ciulla (2001) disagrees, suggesting that leaders

 Leadership in the media: The Company Men

The Company Men (2011) charts the impact of the recent financial crisis on the employees of a fictional company, GTX. The company is a conglomerate, with interests in such diverse areas as ship building and health care. The global recession puts pressure on company sales and profits, leading to the markets pushing their share price down, and the senior management, fearing that they will be the subject of an aggressive acquisition, begin several rounds of redundancies. The film shows how redundancy and the difficulty of finding new work impacts on several long standing employees of the ship building division, from the bright MBA sales leader, Ben Afleck, to the senior manager who has worked his way up from the factory floor, Chris Cooper.

Gene McClary (Tommy Lee Jones), the CEO of the ship building division, is involved in the discussions regarding redundancies. It becomes clear that he has no knowledge of the first round of redundancies, which happen when he is out of town. His complaints to his boss about the lack of communication and about the process used are met with a requirement for him to publicly demonstrate support for the policy, and not to question the Group CEO's judgement.

In one scene, McClary is in a meeting discussing a second round of 5,000 redundancies. When questioning why some names are on the list he gets a response which suggests that the company would not be legally at risk by laying off these employees. McClary is clearly uncomfortable about the redundancies, thinking more about the people and the impact on them of being out of work, than about the company. He expresses the hope that the company could have been more ethical in their decision making, rather than just considering the legal position.

The film also makes a clear point about the difficulties of ethical leadership and the temptations of senior management. It transpires that McClary, despite demonstrating some core ethical beliefs, is having an affair with the company HR lady. In another scene, after being made redundant himself, McClary confronts the Group CEO, only to have the high value of his own stock options thrown back in his face.

The Company Men raises a number of difficult questions for business leaders:

- When faced with the difficult choices a business leader has to make, what will be important to you?
- Are share price, shareholders and your own stock options more important than your colleagues?
- Where will you stand on legal and ethical issues when taking difficult decisions?

are as human as the rest of us, and we should expect them to be subject to the same temptations as everyone else and not expect them to be of a higher level of moral development. We should, however, expect them to be more successful at the arts of ethical decision making and self control, as the impact a leader can have through their unethical action is greatly magnified compared to that of a follower.

Ciulla suggests that whilst it is important for a leader to understand themselves and their values, not all leaders translate these values into action. She recommends a focus on virtues, which, unlike values, are developed through continual practice. Drawing on the ancient philosophers such as Aristotle, Plato, Aquinas, Confucius, and Buddha, Ciulla creates a list of virtues that ethical leaders would do well to adopt and continually practice. The include altruism, prudence, temperance, justice, fortitude, wisdom, holiness, courage, and righteousness (Ciulla, 2001; Ciulla and Forsyth, 2011).

Discussion point: Are virtues important?

Consider the virtues listed by Ciulla that are mentioned above. What virtues do you see demonstrated by leaders you admire? What virtues are you attracted to? In doing this exercise consider:

- Are these virtues or values? for example do you think they are admirable or do you practise them on a daily basis?

RESEARCH IN FOCUS: Ethical leadership across societies

A recent piece of research by Resick et al. (2011) sought to discover what managers from six different parts of the world understood to be the meaning of ethical and unethical leadership. The authors undertook qualitative studies with managers in China, Hong Kong, Taiwan, the USA, Ireland, and Germany. They were examining whether there was convergence or divergence in the understanding of these terms across different cultures and societies.

The study found that in the USA, Ireland, Hong Kong, and Taiwan there was a strong belief that the leader's character determined the quality of their ethical leadership. In China and Germany there were traits and behaviours linked to character that were identified as embodying ethical leadership. China, Germany, and Hong Kong also held that consideration and respect for others, and a collective orientation were important elements of ethical leadership.

For unethical leadership there was some consensus across the countries that acting from self-interest and misusing power were key elements of being unethical. China, Hong Kong, Germany, and Ireland also found that incivility was linked to unethical leadership, whereas in the USA and Taiwan this was rated as less important.

This study suggests that there are some broadly similar understandings surrounding ethical leadership across different societies, mainly the importance of character and respect for others. The fine grained understanding of ethical leadership does differ in each country, and a multi-national leader will need to be aware of how his actions are perceived differently in different countries. For example, in Germany or China a leader will need to demonstrate a higher level of respect for others than in the USA or Ireland in order to be considered an ethical leader.

Source: Resick, C. J., Martin, G. S., Keating, M. A., Dickson, M. W., Kwong Kwan, H., and Peng, C. (2011) What ethical leadership means to me: Asian, American, and European perspectives. *Journal of Business Ethics*, 101, (3) 435–57.

These virtues all involve an individual acting in a way that will in some way benefit others, and at the extreme, may involve personal cost to the ethical leader themselves. This idea of serving others leads us to the idea of the leader as a servant of others that we will explore in the next section.

Servant leadership

The idea of the servant leader was first written about by Robert Greenleaf (1977). Greenleaf was writing in response to a loss of trust in business leaders, suggesting a practical method that could help set right the perceived wrongs of the business world.

For Greenleaf a leader is a servant first. The potential leader wants to serve others, then consciously aspires to lead in order to serve. To want to serve first is to put the needs of others first. Evidence for a servant leader can therefore be found in their followers, and specifically in whether their followers are growing and developing under their leadership. Greenleaf describes this growth as followers becoming healthier, gaining wisdom, being freer, having increasing autonomy, and becoming more likely themselves to choose to be servants. He also describes the outcome of servant leadership from a broader perspective. For Greenleaf (1977), the actions and decisions of the servant leader will have a demonstrable impact on the poorest in society, ensuring that at the very least their situation is not made worse, and preferably it is improved. All of these elements describe a leader who is operating not out of self-interest, but very definitely in the interest of others (van Dierendonck, 2011).

Being a servant leader is therefore a choice a potential leader needs to make. Rather like the virtues described by Ciulla and Forsyth (2011), becoming a servant leader is something that develops with practice. As Greenleaf points out, choosing to serve may be something a leader has to choose on a frequent if not daily basis, and practise continuously. This is why the servant leader needs to desire to be a servant first, as those who do are more likely to continue on this path when times are hard.

Greenleaf (1977:16–30) defined the attributes he sees a servant leader as having:

- Listening, understanding, and broad communication skills
- *Withdrawal*—the ability to withdraw and reorient oneself
- *Acceptance and empathy*—the ability to accept what is offered, even if it is imperfect, and to understand and be interested in the thoughts, feelings and positions of others
- *Intuition*—'a sense for the unknowable' and the ability to 'foresee the future' (Greenleaf, 1977: 21–2).
- *Awareness and as wide a perception as possible*—through which the leader sees past, present, and future as one entity (Spears, cited in van Dierendonck, 2011: 1232, calls this conceptualization); which enables a leader to have foresight and develops discernment
- *Persuasion*—rather than relying on the resource of power discussed in Chapter 4, a servant leader will persuade people to their vision
- *Healing*—both to provide healing for others, and to gain healing for oneself through service to others

To this list have been added stewardship, being a leader who sees their position, their staff, and their organization as being given to them in trust; commitment to the growth of people; and building community (Spears, cited in van Dierendonck, 2011; Reinke, 2004).

Dirk van Dierendonck (2011) reviewed the available research on servant leadership and produced a list of the characteristics of a servant leader that have emerged from the empirical research in this area (Table 12.2).

From this research van Dierendonck distils servant leadership characteristics down to six main categories, described in the following way:

> [Servant leaders] empower and develop people; they show humility, are authentic, accept people for who they are, provide direction, and are stewards who work for the good of the whole. (van Dierendonck 2011: 1232)

There are some obvious similarities between servant leadership, ethical leadership, and authentic leadership, and all could be said to contain elements of the others. Scholars working in each of these areas have claimed that their theory is the root from which other theories are derived. The key difference between authentic leadership and servant leadership is that authentic is focused primarily on one-self, the search for self knowledge and self restraint, whereas servant leadership is focused on others, their development and growth. Similarly ethical leadership has a focus on normative behaviours for an individual, on understanding values and acting out virtues in a way that will influence others. Servant leaders seek to influence through their service and their focus on the growth of others.

What is clear from the writings on servant leadership, particularly the work of Greenleaf, is that servant leadership is heavily influenced by a spiritual understanding of the world. Greenleaf uses a number of Biblical examples to illustrate his points, demonstrating the spiritual roots of this theory. It is to the ideas of spiritual leadership that we now turn.

Spiritual leadership

Spiritual leadership encompasses two main areas, an individual's purpose, calling, or vocation, and generating a sense of meaning, social engagement and membership in the workplace. Authors in this area have drawn on some of the core theories of leadership, and aligned them with academic work on workplace spirituality (Fry, 2003; Dent, Higgins, and Wharff, 2005).

Discussion point: Do you have a vocation?

With a colleague, discuss the following questions:

- Have you ever been, or are you now in a job that you could describe as a vocation?
- What is your core purpose in life? How are you moving towards this purpose?

Several authors credit Fairholm (2011) with developing the spirituality element of Greenleaf's servant leadership work, and bringing together the ideas of spirituality and leadership to form an initial working model for spiritual leadership. Fairholm saw the very idea of leadership as the manifestation of a leader's spiritual core. The case for leaders to engage with their

Table 12.2 Key characteristics of servant leadership related to measurement dimensions

Key characteristics	Laub (1999)	Wong and Davey (2007)	Barbutu and Wheeler (2006)	Dennis and Bocarnea (2005)	Liden, Wayne, Zhao, and Henderson (2008)	Sendjaya, Sarros & Santora (2008)	Van Dierendonck and Nuijten (in press)
Empowering & developing people	• Develops people	• Serving and developing others	• Altruistic calling	• Empowerment	• Empowering	• Transforming influence	• Empowerment
Humility	• Shares leadership	• Consulting and involving others	• Emotional healing	• Trust	• Helping subordinates grow and succeed	• Voluntary subordination	• Humility
Authenticity	• Displays authenticity	• Humility and selflessness	• Persuasive mapping	• Humility	• Putting subordinates first	• Authentic self	• Standing back
Interpersonal acceptance	• Values people	• Modelling integrity and authenticity	• Organizational stewardship	• Agapao love	• Emotional healing	• Transcendental spirituality	• Authenticity
Providing direction	• Providing leadership	• Inspiring and influencing others	• Wisdom	• Vision	• Conceptual skills	• Covenantal relationship	• Forgiveness
Stewardship	• Builds community				• Creating value for the community	• Responsible morality	• Courage
					• Behaving ethically		• Accountability
							• Stewardship

Source: van Dierendonck, D (2011) Servant Leadership: A review and synthesis. *Journal of Management*, 37, 4, 1228–61. Reproduced with permission.

spirituality was made by both Fry and Fairholm, who describe how in the late twentieth and early twenty-first centuries the workplace changed radically from one where the environment was reasonably predictable, and management of firms was described as controlling, enforced through cultures of fear and coercion, to one where the environment was unpredictable, creating a need for firms to be much more innovative, flexible, and adaptive in order to remain competitive in a globalized market (Fry, 2003; Dent, Higgins and Wharff, 2005). Leaders, it is argued, need to create organizations that generate intrinsic motivation from their employees by helping them consider their work as a vocation or calling, and the organization as a membership group they want to contribute selflessly to, rather than managing through the methods of extrinsic motivation—punishment and reward.

Fry (2003) draws on several academic fields in his description of spiritual leadership. He puts forward the argument for intrinsic motivation and couples this with ideas of workplace spirituality. Here a holistic view is taken of an organization, arguing that an organization should have a culture that allows employees to generate a sense of transcendence through their work, fulfilling their fundamental desire to serve others and work at something that has meaning and purpose. This should be done in an environment where employees feel a sense of social engagement, of membership of their workplace and with their colleagues. Fry (2003) suggests that these two core elements, calling and membership, are essential for spiritual survival, which he later renames as spiritual well-being (Fry et al., 2011).

Spiritual leadership taps into a wider movement which recognizes and examines the employees' need for fulfilment at work. The amount of time people spend in the workplace has led to an increased desire to ensure that their work is meaningful and will make a difference in the world. Employees also wish to feel they are part of something greater than themselves, of a group that is striving together to form a better world. Fry et al. (2011) see spiritual leadership as a method of facilitating a culture in the workplace that allows employees to find this greater purpose and feel socially connected in a membership sense.

> The emergence of spiritual leadership then taps into the fundamental needs of both leader and followers for their spiritual well-being through enhancing their sense of calling toward the unit and its goals and vision and a sense of membership of the group. (Fry et al. 2011: 261)

As can be seen from the model of spiritual leadership shown in Figure 12.3, the suggestion is that this form of leadership is very much in the interests of the organization, fostering increased levels of commitment to the organization and higher levels of performance from the leaders and employees.

The model highlights the central dimensions of spiritual leadership. A spiritual leader will provide a vision of where the organization is headed in the future. This should be compelling and perhaps most importantly for this perspective, it should provide people with a clear sense of meaning for their work that they can commit to and strive towards. Fry (2003) points out that the vision of a spiritual leader should encompass high ideals or moral standards, and encourage in the followers a sense of hope and faith.

The second dimension is termed altruistic love. This is similar to the concept of altruism from the servant leadership literature in that it is more in the service of others than in the service of self. Altruistic love produces feelings of wholeness, harmony, and well-being in the workplace through a focus on recognizing others, appreciating them, and being caring and having concern for all. The use of the word love is deliberate as an antidote to

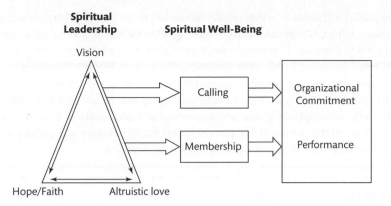

Figure 12.3 Model of spiritual leadership

From Fry, L. W., Hannah, S. T., Noel, M., and Walumbwa, F. O. (2011) Impact of spiritual leadership on unit performance. *The Leadership Quarterly,* 22, 259–70. Reproduced with permission.

the former management regimes which resorted to control through fear. Underpinning this concept of altruistic love are a set of values, virtues, and behaviours including acceptance, kindness, patience, forgiveness, compassion, humility, selflessness, truthfulness, self-control, trust, and loyalty.

The final core dimension is hope and faith. Here the writers on spiritual leadership are at pains to separate the spiritual from the religious, suggesting that religion is comprised of a set of theological beliefs, rites, and rituals, while spirituality is more to do with the qualities that make up the human spirit such as love, compassion, and forgiveness. In keeping with the other ideas in this chapter, spirituality is conceived as a desire to give self-sacrificing (altruistic or charitable) service to others.

 Blog box

Reflecting on your own understanding of the word spirituality, write a short blog on how your acceptance or rejection of ideas of spirituality have impacted on how you perceive the world of work, and how you interact with others. Do you believe that having a sense of spirituality makes it easier or harder to deal with difficult business issues?

Hope in this case is aligned with the vision of the organization and as such is a destination or desire which is expected to be reached. The faith element suggests that all employees will have a firm belief that the organization can reach its goal, even in the face of great difficulties.

Spiritual leadership, therefore, requires a leader to build a culture of altruistic love, where employees can derive a sense of membership while they are pursuing a common vision. It is proposed that the development of an altruistic culture will enable levels of trust to be built up such that all will have hope and faith in the achievement of the vision. In turn, the vision gives rise to a calling for the employees to find meaning and purpose in their work.

Harvey (2001) highlights a further reason for leaders to be interested in spiritual leadership. In discussions with CEOs about decision making, Harvey found that many senior business executives made their most important decisions following a period of reflection and prayer. Although this was found to be quite common, there were few opportunities to share this process of decision making—leaders just do not discuss this aspect of their decision making very often. He also found that in discussing spirituality and leadership these leaders would frequently refer to religious figures, and use religious words such as church, worship, and prayer. Contrary to the writing of Fry, Harvey found that spirituality was uniquely connected with faith, and was more than just a willingness to self-sacrifice.

A case in point: Steve Jobs

Steve Jobs, the founder and CEO of Apple Inc, was famous not just for the simple, Zen-like design of his products, but for his own personal beliefs and actions. One of the stories of Jobs' early life tell of how he dropped out of college to go to India with a friend in search of enlightenment. He spent time with Neem Karoli Baba on his Kainchi Ashram, before returning to the USA and studying with Kobun Chino Otagawa. Whilst it is uncertain whether Jobs was a practising Buddhist, the spiritual beliefs and Buddhist principles he found on this trip can be seen throughout his life, his work at Apple, and his speeches.

Descriptions of Jobs' house tell of a sparsely furnished home, almost empty of furniture, in line with Buddhist teachings on achieving an unattached state from objects. In business the founding principles of Apple were focus and simplicity, demonstrated in an interview he gave to *Businessweek* in 1998: 'Simple can be harder than complex: you have to work hard to make your thinking clean to make it simple. But it's worth it in the end, because once you get there you can move mountains.'

It is also clear that Jobs valued contemplation, knowing your own self, and not letting others unduly influence you. In a speech to graduating Stanford students, Jobs famously advised them not to 'let the noise of other's opinions drown out your own inner voice'. Jobs advised that it takes practice to calm ones thoughts, but by calming your thoughts you allow intuition to grow, allowing you to see more clearly and be more focused, more present.

It cannot be denied that Jobs was one of the greatest business leaders of his generation. His ability to foresee the future, innovate, and change markets is strongly linked to his spirituality, giving a very clear demonstration of how spiritual leadership has the capability of creating competitive advantage for a business.

Sources: <http://abcnews.go.com/Health/steve-jobs-buddhism-guided-life-mantra-focus-simplicity/ story?id=14682458&page=2> accessed 29 August 2012; <http://www.ft.com/cms/s/2/d9cb7940-ebea-11e1- 985a-00144feab49a.html#axzz24vXGwzZY> accessed 29 August 2012; <http://www.usatoday.com/news/ religion/story/2011-11-02/steve-jobs-faith-buddhism/51049772/1> accessed 29 August 2012.

From a critical perspective

Authentic, ethical, servant, and spiritual leadership have all faced similar criticism. One of the main criticisms is on the very definitions attached to these ideas. As discussed earlier in this book, the very concept of leadership is a contested one, with many different definitions of what leadership actually is and how this differs from leading. When an equally ill-defined term such as authenticity or spirituality is added to leadership, then the clarity of what is meant by these terms becomes blurred, and consensus around a definition becomes almost impossible (Fernando, 2011; Caza and Jackson, 2011; van Dierendonck, 2011; Dent, Higgins, and Wharff, 2005).

A second critique that has been levelled particularly against authentic leadership is that there is an assumption that authenticity is a good thing and that the adoption of authenticity in your leadership style will produce good results. This is similar to critiques of leadership itself, which predominantly is assumed to be a positive concept, attached to desirable outcomes. Caza and Jackson (2011) suggest that being inauthentic may actually be beneficial in certain circumstances, and that being too authentic may in fact produce negative outcomes.

As we have seen in this chapter, each of these four ideas are linked to beneficial outcomes for the leaders, for followers and for the organizations themselves. However, in each case the empirical studies that back up these claims are under-developed. Most empirical research has happened in the last ten years, and there is now some data which can be seen to support some of the claims made, as we saw in the section on authentic leadership. For ethical, servant, and spiritual leadership the majority of research seems to have been individually based, and mainly focused on self-assessment tools used to measure your own spirituality, for example. There is little evidence of observational studies or studies of the impact of these approaches to leadership on followers. Hence the theories presented here, like many suggested in the area of leadership, are instinctively attractive, but empirically unproven (Caza and Jackson, 2011; Fernando, 2011; Dent, Higgins, and Wharff, 2005; Avolio and Gardner, 2005).

It should also be noted that the writings on authentic, ethical, servant, and spiritual leadership are dominated by a US focus, with a small number of authors contributing to the development of each area as a concept. For example, authentic leadership is dominated by the writing of Avolio and his colleagues; from this group Walumbwa crosses over into the areas of ethical and spiritual leadership; servant leadership theory is heavily influenced by Greenleaf and the school founded in his name; and Fry dominates the spiritual landscape. It should also be noted that an inordinate number of peer reviewed articles on these subjects come from a US based journal, the *Leadership Quarterly*. There is an obvious need for other parts of the world to explore authenticity, ethics, servanthood, and spirituality as regards leadership from their own cultural and social norms.

Finally, questions have been raised about the underpinning assumption of a positive psychological demeanour, especially in the work on authentic leadership. It is argued that the case for the inclusion of a positive psychological mindset in authentic leadership theory has not been fully made (Northouse, 2010).

Chapter summary

In this chapter we have considered:

- the core dimensions of authentic leadership
- the moral and ethical components contained in the authentic leadership concept
- how a core dimension of authenticity is a sense of morality, and how this links to ideas of ethical leadership
- servant leadership as a practical development of the ideas contained in authentic and ethical leadership
- the role of spirituality in some of the leadership ideas discussed, and the dimensions of spiritual leadership

Integrative case study: Bob Diamond and Barclays Bank

In a lecture given for the BBC *Today* programme in 2011, Bob Diamond, CEO of Barclays Bank stated that he passionately believed banks should be better corporate citizens than they had been, and that this was necessary if they were to rebuild the trust of the public. To rebuild this trust they had to accept responsibility for what had gone wrong and act as better, more effective citizens. Citizenship was defined in how they behave towards clients and customers; how they contribute to economic growth; and how they contribute to the communities they serve.

Mr Diamond went on to discuss the importance of culture in an organization, which he defined as 'how people behave when no-one is watching'. He described how the interests of others—clients, customers, and society—should be at the heart of decisions, and that these decisions should be based on trust and integrity.

On 30 June 2012 news broke of another corporate scandal. Barclays Bank Plc had been fined $360 million for actively interfering with the setting of the London interbank offer rate (LIBOR) rate, the interest rate used when banks borrow and lend to other banks. The Libor rate is used in the daily transaction of $10 trillion of mortgages, credit cards, and corporate loans, plus an additional $350 trillion in interest rate swaps and other derivatives. Any attempt to influence this rate in favour of a bank was considered to be a very serious matter.

In 2008, at the height of the financial crisis, when the liquidity of banks was looking particularly worrying, traders at Barclays had asked submitters, employees at Barclays, and other banks responsible for telling the British Banking Association what interest rates they agreed on a daily basis, to lie about the rate the bank was actually paying. The traders wanted the submitters to claim that their interest rate was lower than it actually was, thus making the bank look healthier to the market. At the time of this manipulation of the LIBOR rate, banks were finding it difficult or impossible to borrow the funds needed to continue trading. Several banks were being bailed out by Governments across the world, and the LIBOR rate was seen as evidence of the financial strength of a bank. Barclays were also involved in negotiations with the Qatar, China, and Singapore based investment funds for loans that would re-capitalize their balance sheet, so had a major incentive to make themselves look like a safe investment option, and to avoid being closely scrutinized by regulators who would look closely at any bank out of step with the average LIBOR rate.

Barclays also admitted that their traders had been manipulating the LIBOR rate even before the financial crisis that began in 2007. This was to improve the profitability of their trades. Several emails between traders and submitters were published showing their appreciation at getting the rate rigged. One such email said 'Dude I owe you big time! Come over one day after work and I'm opening a bottle of Bollinger!' The submitters were obviously happy to oblige.

The traders were working for the investment banking arm of Barclays, Barclays Capital, under the leadership of Bob Diamond. In 2010 Mr Diamond was made CEO of the whole bank. Naturally questions were asked about his leadership of Barclays Capital and the culture this created, of his knowledge about what was going on, and about the responsibility he bore as a consequence of holding the leaders position.

Following the breaking of the LIBOR scandal story on 27 June 2012, Barclays put out the following statements:

> Barclays Chief Executive, Bob Diamond, said: 'The events which gave rise to today's resolutions relate to past actions which fell well short of the standards to which Barclays aspires in the conduct of its business. When we identified those issues, we took prompt action to fix them and co-operated extensively and proactively with the Authorities. Nothing is more important to me than having a strong culture at Barclays; I am sorry that some people acted in a manner not consistent with our culture and values. To reflect our collective responsibility as leaders, Chris Lucas, Jerry del Missier, Rich Ricci and I have voluntarily agreed with the Board to forgo any consideration for an annual bonus this year.'
> Barclays Chairman, Marcus Agius, said: 'The Board takes the issues underlying today's announcement

extremely seriously and views them with the utmost regret. Since these issues were identified, the Authorities acknowledge that Barclays management has co-operated fully with their investigations and taken, and continues to take, prompt and decisive action to correct them. In addition, the Board welcomes the example set by Bob Diamond, Chris Lucas, Jerry del Missier and Rich Ricci in recognising their collective responsibility as leaders of Barclays.' (<http://www.newsroom.barclays.com/Press-releases/Barclays-Bank-PLC-Settlement-with-Authorities-901.aspx> accessed 10 August 2012)

On 28 June Mr Diamond sent a letter to the UK Government Treasury select committee in which he made it clear that the bank viewed the behaviour as being solely belonging to individual traders, and that they were engaged in a process to examine the roles of these individuals in the scandal.

Five days after the story broke, on 2 July, following increased pressure from the media, the Chairman of Barclays, Marcus Agius, resigned. In his resignation, Mr Agius stated that the behaviour of the bank was unacceptable, and that the responsibility for this rested with him. He also announced a review in which a mandatory code of conduct would be created for all Barclays employees that would ensure their actions would not affect the reputation of the bank.

Mr Diamond's response to the scandal was to not resign immediately. Instead, he laid the responsibility and the blame at the feet of the individual traders whose emails showed they were complicit in attempting to manipulate the rate. He sent a message around the company saying that he refused to accept the behaviours were influenced by the culture at Barclays and Barclays Capital, which as a leader he could be seen as having created. There followed a period of press speculation surrounding a telephone conversation that Mr Diamond had with Paul Tucker, deputy governor of the Bank of England. Mr Diamond seemed to suggest that Mr Tucker had advised him to manipulate the LIBOR rate to make Barclay's borrowing costs look lower, a suggestion that Mr Tucker robustly denied.

The outcome of this telephone conversation was for Barclays employees, specifically their Chief Operating Officer, Jerry del Missier, to assume they had support from the Bank of England to manipulate LIBOR. In his evidence given to the Treasury select committee, Mr del Missier admitted passing on the advice he received from Mr Diamond to submit artificially low rates to LIBOR. He assumed this advice had come from the Bank of England. Mr Diamond had previously denied giving such advice. When his involvement in the scandal became apparent, Mr del Missier resigned from his post at Barclays.

On 3 July, Bob Diamond resigned as CEO of Barclays. His resignation followed pressure from the UK regulator, the Financial Services Authority, and the Bank of England for his resignation. Rather than accepting any responsibility for the actions of Barclays, he stated that external pressure on the bank was becoming damaging to the company and as such he would stand down to relieve this pressure. Mr Diamond also decided to forgo a possible £20m bonus as part of his resignation.

Case study questions:

- Do you think the leaders of Barclays acted in a responsible manner?

- Consider what you have learned about authentic leadership and the creation of an ethical climate. Do you think Mr Diamond has acted as an authentic leader in this situation?

- Did Mr Diamond do the right things, in the right way, for the right reasons? Consider what values or virtues you were valuing when answering this question.

- Think about your own values and virtues. How would you have reacted as CEO in this situation?

Sources: <http://efinancialnews.com/story/2012-07-02/wsj-archives-libor-2008> accessed 3 July 2012; <http://www.bbc.co.uk/news/business-18625227> accessed 10 August 2012; <http://finance.fortune.cnn.com/2012/07/30/barclays-libor-diamond/> accessed 10 August 2012; <http://www.newsroom.barclays.com/Press-releases/Letter-from-Bob-Diamond-Barclays-Chief-Executive-902.aspx> accessed 10 August 2012; <http://www.independent.co.uk/news/business/news/memo-documents-bob-diamonds-phone-call-to-paul-tucker-7906625.html> accessed 10 August 2012; <http://www.businessweek.com/news/2012-07-16/del-missier-says-diamond-told-him-to-submit-lower-libor-rates> accessed 10 August 2012.

Further reading

George, W. (2003) *Authentic Leadership: Rediscovering the secrets to creating lasting value.* San Francisco: Jossey-Bass.

Ciulla, J. B. and Forsyth, D. R. (2011) Leadership ethics, in Bryman, A. Collinson, D. Grint, K. Jackson, B., and Uhl-Bien, M. (eds), *The Sage Handbook of Leadership.* SAGE, 229–41.

van Dierendonck, D. (2011) Servant leadership: A review and synthesis. *Journal of Management,* 37, 4, 1228–61.

Dent, E. B., Higgins, M. E., and Wharff, D. M. (2005) Spirituality and leadership: an empirical review of definitions, distinctions, and embedded assumptions. *The Leadership Quarterly* 16, 625–53.

13 Responsible leadership for a sustainable world

 Learning outcomes

On completion of this chapter you will:

- Gain an understanding of the global context within which leaders must operate
- Appreciate the responsibilities that this context confers on business leaders
- Have a basic understanding of corporate social responsibility
- Understand the key issues of sustainability and sustainable development
- Discover ideas about the leadership capabilities needed to be a responsible leader now and in the future
- Appreciate the mindset that leads to a sustainable leadership approach, and understand what this looks like within a business

Introduction

Over the past ten years, the requirement for businesses and business leaders to act in a overtly responsible way has increased at a great pace. Social pressure from customers, activists and governments has demanded that business improve its ethical and environmental record. Legal pressures from changes in both national and international law have required business to pay attention to its impact on the world's natural resources. Scientific and media pressure around the issue of climate change has forced many companies to look hard at the impact they have on the environment, and develop programmes that address the key issue of sustainability.

At the time of writing the world is in the midst of a financial crisis that has seen banks and their employees accused of immense greed and incompetence, and which led to the virtual collapse of the global financial system in 2007/08. Globalization has created a world of high economic growth rates in the East, and recession or possible stagnation in the economies of the West. Inequalities of wealth are becoming apparent not only between countries, but within countries. Capitalism, which promised to lift everyone on a tide of continual economic growth, appears to have created an ever widening gap of inequality of income in both developing and developed economies. The world economy is trying to find ways of dealing with increasingly scarce resources, particularly in energy, food and water, leading to an increase in commodities prices. Developing countries are understandably increasing their energy consumption as they grow, but the burning of fossil fuels and resulting CO_2 emissions has been linked to global warming and climate change, which may threaten our very survival on the planet.

In addition, the developments in technology, particularly internet and mobile technology, mean that very little can be kept secret anymore. Companies employing child labour, whether directly or through third parties in factories around the world, can be sure they will be found out and made front page news within hours.

Leaders must increasingly engage with these crucial areas of responsibility. Maak and Pless (2006) highlight that there has always been an implicit expectation that our leaders will possess a greater sense of the responsibility then the population at large, and that they will be seen to act responsibly once they achieve a position of great influence. Leaders of global companies are therefore under more public scrutiny than ever before for their policies towards their stakeholders, and for their own personal conduct. For example, when BP were desperately trying to cap the Deep Water Horizon well in the Gulf of Mexico, which was causing oil to be washed ashore on the beaches of the US Gulf coast, the CEO, Tony Haywood, was spotted taking some time off to sail a yacht with his son near the Isle of Wight in the UK. This became instant front page news, interpreted by the US media as a dereliction of his duty to fix the oil leak. The media pressure surrounding his personal conduct was seen as a key factor in his decision to resign shortly afterwards.

In this chapter we will examine some of the responsibilities expected of leaders today and in the future. We will explore the areas of corporate social responsibility, sustainability and sustainable development, and discuss the capabilities required by leaders to be able to address these complex and critical issues.

Discussion point: How much responsibility does business have?

Increasingly society is expecting business to be able to play a part in solving big global issues, such as water scarcity, climate change, inequality, and poverty.

- What do you think is the purpose of business?
- Is it the responsibility of private sector companies to reduce climate change or alleviate poverty?
- How would you make the case to shareholders that your business should be taking responsibility in these areas?

In the mainstream

Responsible leadership

Responsible leadership has been defined as a mindset change, from a focus on the purely financial and economic view of business, to one that views business from a much broader perspective, that seeks to understand and engage with all stakeholders, and that strives to use business for the common good (Maak and Pless, 2006). Maak and Pless define responsible leadership as 'the art of building and sustaining morally sound relationships with all relevant stakeholders of an organization'. They suggest that responsible leadership is not just the preserve of certain principled individuals and it is not something that a leader is born with, but, rather like Ciulla's description of virtues in Chapter 12, responsible leadership is something that has to be continuously worked at. It is a balance between the character of the leader and their relations with others; of the tasks a leader has and how they carry these out; and it is something that the culture of the organization can either encourage, or act against.

Schraa-Liu and Trompenaars (2006) expand on this idea of responsible leadership being a balancing act. They discuss how globalization has made peoples and economies interconnected, transforming the leader's role into one that seeks to continually understand and align the interests and demands of multiple stakeholder groupings, from employees and shareholders to communities, the environment, and society at large. They suggest that the ability to reconcile differences amongst stakeholders is a key competency of modern successful responsible leaders.

The definitions above go beyond the legal or governance understanding of responsibility in business. From a governance perspective, a CEO of a listed company is responsible to the board of the business, and through them to the shareholders. This is defined as a fiduciary responsibility, commonly understood to be a financial responsibility to ensure a return on investment for shareholders. Freeman (2007) broadens this fiduciary responsibility to include all stakeholders, requiring leaders to act in a way that holds the business in trust for the good of all.

This requirement to go beyond traditional understandings of governance has led to companies developing and implementing ideas of corporate social responsibility, a concept that we will examine in the next section.

Corporate social responsibility (CSR)

Historically, the term corporate social responsibility (CSR) has risen to prominence during economic periods where events have highlighted corporate ethical inadequacies, environmental pollution and destruction, or the overuse, impact, and potential exhaustion of natural resources. Mostovicz, Kakabadse, and Kakabadse (2009) point out that CSR developed as a reaction against economic ideas that gave a very narrow view of the firm, one that only paid attention to the financial impact and contribution made by a company, and thus did not fully consider a firm's wider impact on society and the environment. CSR questions the role of business in society, whether it is a force purely for economic gain, or could be harnessed as a force for the good of all (Griseri and Seppala, 2011).

Like leadership, CSR is a contested concept. Businesses and academics have many varied interpretations to the meaning and practice of CSR, with different terms such as corporate social performance, corporate citizenship, and corporate responsibility being used almost interchangeably. Some see CSR as being the responsibility to make a profit legally; others see it as having an ethical component that influences the organization's attitude to wider societal issues. CSR has been viewed as a call for companies to be held accountable for all their impacts on all their stakeholders in both legal and ethical terms; and for others it is purely the philanthropic element of corporate donations to good causes, whether this is the straight giving of cash, or clever marketing schemes linked to charitable fundraising initiatives.

Even Governments have tried to contribute to the definition debate. In 2003 the UK Government defined CSR as 'the management of an organization's total impact upon both its immediate stakeholders, and upon the society within which it operates' (DTI, 2003). The following list sets out the core principles within definitions of CSR:

- that CSR is about considering the impact an organization can have not just for and on its shareholders, but for and on its wider stakeholder group
- that CSR is about a process of engagement with stakeholders to consider what role an organization should play in a wider societal context

- that the responsibility an organization has stretches more widely than the confines of the company premises, and includes a responsibility towards wider society, including the environment

Throughout the history of CSR arguments have centred on the role and purpose of business and what this says for the responsibilities that businesses should hold. Milton Friedman (1970) was quite clear in his view that the sole responsibility of business was to only undertake activities that generated profits to be returned to shareholders. He strongly argued that it was unethical to do anything else with profits. Archie Carroll (1979, 1991) developed a CSR model which attempted to bring together Friedman's view with other positions on the responsibilities a business holds within one model, whilst at the same time highlighting the tensions that exist when leaders in organizations have to make decisions that could be seen as a choice between two competing goods, for example, between making an ethical decision and making more profits.

Carroll suggested that the responsibility of business could be defined through understanding the expectations that wider society placed on organizations. This was condensed into four broad areas:

- *Economic responsibilities*—the primary responsibility of business. To offer the things people want and need in a profitable manner, and thus to be able to offer employment that allows the earning of wages, and so the development of an economy.
- *Legal responsibilities*—to comply with the ethical norms of society that have been codified into law in every region and country where a company operates. This applies at the corporate and individual level.
- *Ethical responsibilities*—to understand and comply with those ambiguous and emerging norms of society that have yet to become law for example the belief in equality and diversity in the workplace has taken many years to emerge as an ethical stance that society values, and companies who can forsee these issues are better placed to meet the expectations of their customers than those who only operate against the existing laws of the land.
- *Philanthropic responsibilities*—beyond the expectations of society. Usually characterized by a corporate volunteering scheme, donations to and support for charitable projects, and responses to global environmental disasters, all of which go beyond the economic interests of the firm.

Whilst these responsibilities have been presented in a pyramid (Figure 13.1), they are not meant to be hierarchical. Carroll's four stages are not stepping stones that an organization progresses through to reach the pinnacle. Carroll points out that the stages are not mutually exclusive, but interdependent areas of responsibility. Organizations are typically strong in some areas and weak in others, for example meeting economic responsibilities whilst breaching the legal or ethical ones.

Chandler and Werther (2006) gave three main reasons why businesses should accept the wider view of responsibility implied by CSR. They argued that there is a moral argument, a rational argument, and an economic argument for companies not only engaging with CSR, but making it a strategic decision. The moral argument suggested that business only obtain profits because of the wider society and so cannot be envisaged as a separate entity to society. Society provides the essential elements that business needs to be successful in terms of an

The Pyramid of CSR

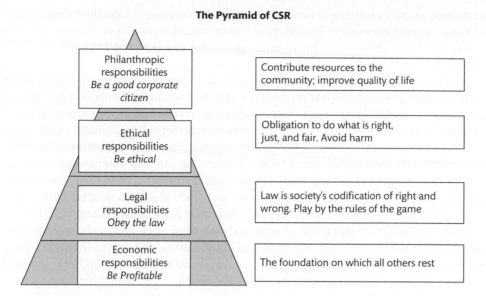

Figure 13.1 The pyramid of corporate social responsibility

Carroll, A. B. (1991) The Pyramid of Corporate Social Responsibility: Toward the Moral Management of Organizational Stakeholders. *Business Horizons* (July–August) 42. Reproduced with permission.

educated workforce, health, safety (protection of property), stability, a legal infrastructure, and a consumer market. As the relationship between business and society is interdependent, business has a moral obligation to understand and act in line with the expectations of society.

The rational argument suggests that organizations need to understand and act in accordance with societal expectations or they will face the resultant backlash. This may come in the form of Government sanctions, consumer boycotts, national and international laws, unwelcome regulation, and even direct fines. All of these actions serve to reduce the profit a company can make. Thus it is rational to adopt CSR policies as a means to avoid sanctions resulting in action that is against societal expectations.

Finally, the economic argument suggests that adopting a CSR strategy gives a company differentiation in the marketplace, leading to competitive advantage. By showing customers that you understand and reflect their expectations, companies can grow their customer base, and improve their relationships with key stakeholders such as suppliers and government. This activity improves the brand of the business, thus attracting customers and reducing the perceived risk for investors.

For some, CSR is not just a rational or economic choice, but is about a company adopting certain ethical principles. Business should do good just because this is the right thing to do, even if this means addressing issues that are seen as beyond the direct legal and financial obligations of the company (Davis, 1973). For others, individuals and businesses should not engage in CSR at all activities as business is only responsible for generating profits for investors, as long as they stay within the rules of the law (Friedman, 1970).

Garriga and Melé (2004) attempted to collate all the theoretical ideas about CSR in one framework. Their framework conceived CSR in four ways. The first was an instrumental approach, where the purpose of business was purely economic and CSR is thus seen as a tool to enhance profitable growth. Theories here include an exclusive focus on shareholder value (Friedman, 1970), CSR as competitive advantage (Porter and Cramer, 2002; Prahalad, 2004), and cause-related marketing (Kotler and Lee, 2005).

The second views CSR as a political perspective on organizations. Here organizations are seen as having power, perhaps as much power and reach as Governments, and thus there is an onus on the organization to act in responsible ways and be held accountable much as an individual citizen is held to account. Theories here include corporate constitutionalism (Davis, 1960; Donaldson and Dunfee, 1994, 1999), and corporate citizenship (McIntosh et al., 1998).

The third conceptualization sees CSR as a process that can help companies to integrate their decisions, systems, and practices with societal expectations. Theories include issues of management or social responsiveness (Wartick and Cochran, 1985), stakeholder management (Freeman, 1984), and corporate social performance (Carroll and Buchholtz, 2011).

Finally the fourth concept is CSR as an ethical idea, drawing on ethical philosophy to determine what ethical duties and responsibilities a business has, and what the right thing to do is. Theories include normative stakeholder theory (Donaldson and Preston, 1995), universal human rights, the common good (Melé, 2002), and sustainable development, which we will discuss later in this chapter.

For business leaders, perhaps the key idea arising from CSR is that of stakeholder management. Core to this idea is the understanding that business is an interconnected set of relationships between a wide variety of stakeholders (Freeman, 2007). Freeman (1984: 46) defines stakeholders as 'any group or individual who can affect, or is affected by, the achievement of the organization's objectives', including employees, customers, suppliers, shareholders, community groups, governments, the wider society, and the environment. This places the onus on the business leadership to engage with, seek to understand the positions, views, and aspirations of all their stakeholders, and be able to manage the conflicts and contradictions that will arise when taking decisions and formulating strategy (Andrews, 1987; Mintzberg, 1983).

The issues of responsibility highlighted by CSR have become increasingly important to business leaders in the twenty-first century, particularly the issue of the impact on the environment. A number of large companies now view sustainability as their key responsibility to society.

RESEARCH IN FOCUS: CSR leaders' skills and capabilities

In their paper, 'CSR leaders road-map', Kakabadse, Kakabadse, and Lee-Davies developed case studies of CSR implementation from 65 organizations from the USA, the UK, Europe, Africa, and Australia. They interviewed 300 managers, seeking to understand how organizations implement CSR and what skills and capabilities are needed by leaders who wish to integrate CSR into everyday business activity.

The study found that there were three stages of CSR implementation, and that each stage required different leadership capabilities for it to be successful. The first stage in making a decision to pursue a CSR agenda required the development of awareness of CSR issues and ideas; the ability to reflect on and make sense of these issues in light of the context of the organization; and the ability to discern appropriate CSR goals for the organization to follow.

The second stage in adopting a CSR policy requires leaders to be able to describe the business case for CSR to organizational stakeholders; to have the persuasive skills necessary to gain support for CSR from stakeholders; to have the wisdom to handle the complexity and conflicting priorities that can arise from the apparently conflicting demands of economic and sustainable growth; to be able to communicate the CSR message consistently across all media; to have the skill to develop appropriate measurement that will hold the organization accountable to its CSR promises; and to have the discipline to persevere with CSR activity.

The final stage is the ability of a leader to create long-term dedication from within the organization for the CSR goals that have been defined. This is a commitment to act on CSR issues throughout the organization, including looking in detail at all policies, practices, and procedures and ensuring that they are all aligned to the CSR vision. The authors' research suggests that this is the most difficult capability to develop, but without it an organization wide CSR strategy may be compromised by previously normal organizational practice.

The authors point out that while these leadership skills are particularly needed at certain stages, they are all needed at other times in order to effectively progress the CSR mission of the organization. Some of the skills and capabilities will be embodied in the person as leader, whilst others are required for the more complex process of leadership through relationships within organizations.

Source: Kakabadse, N. K., Kakabadse, A. P., and Lee-Davies L. (2009) CSR leaders road-map. *Corporate Governance, 9* (1) 50–7.

Sustainability and sustainable development

A study of CEOs carried out by consulting company Accenture for the United Nations Global Compact (2010: 10) found that 93 per cent of CEOs from around the world saw sustainability as important to the future success of their business, with 72 per cent saying that a focus on this issue would help them to rebuild brands, trust, and reputation that was damaged during the financial crisis. Importantly the study showed that CEOs recognize that future leaders of corporations must have the ability to integrate issues of sustainability into their strategy and everyday decisions and actions.

Sustainability is the ability for a business to continue in business over the long term, possibly indefinitely. This ability is tied up with the impact that a business has on the environmental resources of the world that it uses in the process of doing business. Sustainability suggests that business leaders need to critically consider how their companies can reduce and minimize

 Leadership in the media: An Inconvenient Truth

In 2006 former US Vice President and Presidential candidate, Al Gore, made a documentary film which raised international awareness of the issue of climate change. For a number of years prior to the making of the documentary, Al Gore had been touring the USA with a presentation that gave the factual, scientific data that showed the earth was warming. The presentation, which Al Gore estimates he has given over 1,000 times, showed that, according to our records and research data, the rate at which the earth is warming is faster than has ever happened before. Al Gore used research evidence and scientific theories to link this warming data to human activity, suggesting that our use of the earth's resources was having a detrimental effect on our environment.

The presentation became the core of the film, *An Inconvenient Truth*, and detailed the scientific evidence for an increase in carbon dioxide emissions over time. Explanations of how global warming is thought to occur were given, alongside projections of how the earth may change if the temperature continues to climb.

The film has been used in business schools to raise awareness of the issue of sustainability, and as a process to enable students to reflect on their own positions on this important issue.

Watch the film and then ask yourself:

- What are my views on sustainability? Have these been changed by viewing the film?
- What is the impact of my view on sustainability for my company and career?

their impact on natural resources that are utilized in their business. By doing this well, business leaders can help to ensure their businesses will be around in the future, and that future generations will continue to have the ability to support themselves and to flourish.

The first definition of sustainability or sustainable development came from the Bruntland Commission, also known as the United Nations World Commission on Economic Development (1987). The commission was formed to debate environmental strategies that could help the world achieve sustainable development by the year 2000. The instigation of the commission came with a historical background of a growing concern for the environmental impact humanity was having on the world. The realization that natural resources could be finite; the obvious impact of industrial pollution on land, rivers, and species; environmental events such as acid rain, and the discovery of a hole in the earth's ozone layer all contributed to the thought processes and discussions at the commission (Blowfield and Murray, 2011). Following two and a half years of debate between the hundreds of countries, companies, NGOs and intergovernmental agencies present, the commission finally proposed a future where the environment would be firmly in the minds of leaders from both business and governments globally when they were considering their strategic decisions. They defined sustainable development as 'meeting the needs of the present generation without compromising the ability of future generations to meet their own needs' (UNWCED, 1987: 8).

This quote from the UNWCED highlights three timezones that companies were encouraged to consider in their decisions and actions. The first was the past, acknowledging that in the past it had been acceptable for companies to externalize some costs onto the environment, especially in terms of industrial pollution, but that now companies had to deal with this past externalization, and ensure it did not continue.

The second was the present, focusing on meeting the needs and expectations of society today. This included considering issues of intragenerational equity, the responsibility to meet the needs of all peoples no matter where they were based. This was a call for action on issues of inequality between people in their own society, and between countries.

The third was the future, focusing on intergenerational equity, which encouraged decisions to be taken, and resources to be consumed, with an eye on the impact of this for future generations. As former CEO of Novo Nordisk, Mads Øvlisen has been quoted as saying, 'A way of dealing with the planet as if it is on loan from our children rather than inherited from our parents.'

A more recent report specifically focused on business and leadership used the Bruntland report as a foundation for recommendations to future business leaders. The report was created by the Tomorrow's Leaders group, a working group set up by the World Business Council for Sustainable Development, a coalition of 180+ companies committed to sustainable development through equally balancing economic growth, ecological impact, and social progress. The World Business Council is focused on business leadership as the driver for change. The Tomorrow's Leaders group was made up of eight business leaders from global companies including BP Plc, Proctor & Gamble, adidas-Salomon, GrupoNueva, Storebrand, SwissRe, CLP, and TNT. Underpinning the report was a commitment to consult widely with a broad stakeholder group as normal business practice. By consulting widely, the Tomorrow's Leaders resolved to carry out the actions listed in Table 13.1.

Underlying the report is an assumption that economic growth and the goals of sustainability can be achieved together. This is a contentious assumption, and requires that business leaders focus on developing future products and services that have a zero impact in terms

Table 13.1 Tomorrow's leaders report

- We will develop an understanding of how global issues such as poverty, the environment, demographic change, and globalization affect our individual companies and sectors.
- We will use our understanding of the significance of these signals to search for business opportunities that help to address them.
- We will develop our core business strategies to align them to the opportunities that we have identified.
- We will incorporate long-term measures into our definition of success, targeting profitability that is sustainable, supported by a positive record in social, environmental, and employment areas.
- We will develop technologies and products that enable the world to address its environmental and social challenges.
- We will help to create new businesses, new markets, new livelihoods, and new customers among the three billion people who live in poverty today, and the three billion who will be added to the world's population in the next 50 years.
- We will help to set global benchmarks and global frameworks that create universal standards and raise the bar for all companies.
- We will operate and compete successfully in a range of countries, markets, and cultures, maintaining consistent global standards while acting as part of the local community.
- We will responsibly manage the issues raised by ageing populations in the developed world and growing populations in the developing world.
- We will attract new generations of employees, creating an inclusive culture, advancing more women, and enabling people from any nationality, race, or background to fulfil their potential.
- We will set high standards of corporate governance, demonstrating openness about our business activities and building trust.

Source: World Business Council for Sustainable Development and Tomorrow's Leaders (2006) *From Challenge to Opportunity: The role of business in tomorrow's society.* WBCSD Earthprint Ltd. Reproduced with permission.

of resource use and negative impact on eco-systems. It is assuming that through innovative ideas and new technologies, we can continue to grow economically even within an eco-system that is resource stressed.

Dunphy, Griffiths, and Benn (2003) suggest that organizations will respond to the challenges of responsibility and sustainability either by taking a position on, or by moving through six levels or phases of commitment:

- *Rejection*—a focus on exploiting all resources, human and ecological, for the sake of maximizing profit. Leaders here would not accept responsibility or sustainability arguments, and would actively work against possible regulation or activism.
- *Non-responsiveness*—characterised by a lack of awareness or ignorance of sustainable or social issues, rather than active opposition to these issues.
- *Compliance*—either compliance with laws and regulations to avoid risk, or compliance with self-regulatory measures in order to avoid legislation which may limit the activities of the firm.
- *Efficiency*—sustainability seen as a cost reduction and efficiency strategy. Principles of sustainability are incorporated into everyday business practice.
- *Strategic pro-activity*—sustainability viewed as potentially giving competitive advantage as well as cost efficiencies. Leaders here see sustainability as a strategic route to taking a position of leadership in an industry, and thus maximizing returns.

- *The sustaining corporation*—one that is committed to the principles of social and ecological sustainability, that is maintaining returns, but is focused on meeting the needs of the present without compromising the opportunities of future generations.

The level that an organization achieves depicts the manner in which they treat the human and ecological resources they utilize in the process of doing business.

Dunphy, Griffiths, and Benn (2003) point out that an organization does not necessarily progress through this continuum in a regular way, but may jump from one phase to another, and regress depending on internal and external pressures. For example, a change in leadership or governmental regulations may lead to a regression or acceleration on social and sustainable issues.

 Blog box:

During my MBA year in 1998/9 I took an elective on sustainable business. It was this elective, delivered by Gill Coleman of Bath University, that sparked an epiphany moment for me. It has influenced both my view of business and my teaching focus over the past 14 years. For me in my role as MBA Director, and Board member, the biggest issue that current and future leaders have to get to grips with is being able to balance the needs of all stakeholders, including the environment, with the need to make profit and prosper as a business. I completely agree with the Tomorrow's Leaders report which suggests that whilst profit is hugely important, business has to have a purpose greater than just profit to be successful now and into the future. As I write, reports are coming in from the USA where Hurricane Sandy has caused huge damage to the east coast of the USA, flooding New York City and cutting power to millions of people. Scientists have linked the increasing size and power of such storms to rising sea temperatures, potentially caused by emissions from burning fossil fuels and human activity in general. If business wants to stay in business over the long term, then sustainability is not an issue that anyone who aspires to business leadership can ignore.

Consider whether you have had an epiphany moment where you have come to a sudden realization of the fragile nature of our environment and the impact business can have on this. (CS)

Case in point: Patagonia

Under the leadership of Yvon Chouinard and his team, Patagonia have become known for their focus on a sustainable approach to business. They have reached a position where they wish to advocate for an approach to business that improves social justice and environmental responsibility. However, they chose to use the word 'sustainability' as little as possible when talking about their business, preferring 'responsibility' as it implies an acceptance of the impact business can have on human and ecological resources.

Yvon describes how the company gradually developed its understanding of responsibility. It began with a realization that their hard steel pitons, a market leader, were causing the degradation of climbing routes as climbers left the equipment stuck in the rock. The company innovated, produced chocks and wedges, and changed the climbing industry to favour climbing 'clean'. They then realized they were motivated and inspired by nature, and so had a responsibility to act if they could. They became involved in a local campaign to improve the town's polluted river. This led to regular donations to specific environmental causes, acknowledging their responsibility for the environmental impact of their business. Patagonia views this giving as an earth tax, to better price in the full costs of its activities. They were instrumental in creating the 1 per cent for the planet alliance: companies who give 1 per cent of sales to environmental causes. And they began to reduce their own impact, as well as reusing and recycling.

On the employee side, after pressure from employees, including Yvon's wife, Patagonia devoted a part of their site to a nursery for the children of their workers. Having children on site has helped the company to keep its responsibilities to humanity in mind, to be more human and less corporate, and to attract, retain, and motivate good employees.

They see their responsibility to employees as going beyond the immediate and local ones. Over the years they came to understand the pollutant and sometimes toxic chemicals that contribute to the production of cotton, and have worked to reduce this, making it a safer process for employees of their suppliers as well as their own. They have also focused on their overseas manufacturers, trying to ensure the highest standards of health and safety, and to eliminate child labour. As they see it: 'we are responsible for all workers who make our goods and for all that goes into a piece of clothing that bears a Patagonia label' (Chouinard and Stanley, 2012: section 57).

Patagonia also seek to influence their customers, encouraging them not to purchase what they don't need, to repair first, and look to reuse their products, and, as a last resort, to discard and recycle them.

Chouinard and Stanley give a clear message to present and future business leaders:

the time has come for those of us in business to understand ourselves as a part of nature and to walk our fields; we need to make our practices less exhaustive and more intensive and productively alive, so that the world will be habitable for those who come after us. (Chouinard and Stanley, 2012: section 64)

Sustainable leadership

The vision presented by the Tomorrow's Leaders report is one of a sustainable approach to leadership in organizations. It highlights a more sophisticated approach to leadership than one that views leadership as being the possession of an exceptional individual. The Patagonia case demonstrates that leaders who choose the sustainable path for their organizations are the radicals of their generation, those willing to question the conventional wisdom which holds that maximization of profit and shareholder value are the only business of business. Being a responsible leader means accepting that you have obligations to the health of the business, to your workers, to your customers, to the community, and to nature (Chouinard and Stanley, 2012).

This calls for a much more complex and nuanced form of leadership. Marshall, Coleman, and Reason (2011) suggest that the challenges posed by sustainability are systemic, meaning that the dominant economic system we have, capitalism, to some extent drives the unsustainable behaviours of business leaders as they respond to what they believe or have been taught are the 'market' values. A sustainable leader needs to be able to recognize the assumptions that underpin the models of business, capital, and economy that dominate at present, and be able to conceive a different model, where the full price of resource use can be paid, and where an equal focus on profit, people, and planet is good for business rather than something that will make a business less competitive.

This idea of a different conceptualization of good business is fleshed out by Avery and Bergsteiner (2011a). In their book on sustainable leadership they describe two alternative extreme approaches to business, the locust approach and the honeybee approach. Locust leadership is aligned with the idea that the only purpose of business is to do business, to maximize profit and to return these profits to shareholders. In this approach the world is perceived as a primarily competitive place, where the survival of the fittest is the main rule. The authors describe the extreme view of this approach, where leadership is particularly ruthless and asocial, where employees are treated as a means to an end, and not ends in themselves, and where society and the environment are legitimate areas on which to externalize business costs. Typical behaviour of locust companies includes taking short-term decisions aimed at improving share price in the next quarter, paying the lowest wages possible, avoiding or evading tax, and giving or accepting bribes. The mantra of the locust leader is shareholder value, which is sold as the most important value to which the organization has no choice but to adhere.

The term locust is a deliberately provocative one. Individual locusts present little threat. However, when they multiply and act in concert they can strip the environment of all healthy crops. For business, this idea conveys an impression of a type of leadership that is addictive, that grows when economic conditions are favourable, and which may swarm at any time to strip the economy of much needed resources. The global financial crisis can be seen as one example of this: adopting poor financial practices especially in relation to risk becoming vastly popular in the name of profit, and eventually serving to strip nations and economies of their economic wealth.

By contrast, the honeybee approach to leadership presents a more positive idea. This is an approach one characterized by the community-focused behaviour of bees, working together for the good of all, and in the process improving their surroundings by pollinating the various plants in their neighbourhood. Honeybee leadership is therefore more complex, focusing on the business, but also on society and a wide range of stakeholders. Rather than short-term decisions, this type of leadership views business from a long-term perspective, aiming to take all stakeholders of the business on a journey together. Characteristics of a honeybee business include investment in innovation and training and development, high levels of trust between management and workers as employees are seen to be valued in themselves, internal succession plans, ethical and sustainable decision making, and a long-term view taken by investors.

Avery and Bergsteiner (2011a) suggest that anyone seeking to be a responsible leader for a sustainable world would adopt a leadership approach closer to the honeybee model than the locust model, developing successful, productive businesses that work in collaboration and partnership with others and balance the needs of all stakeholders including the shareholders. One example of a possible honeybee leader and company can be found in the integrated case study at the end of this chapter.

 Blog box

Reflect on the ideas of honeybee and locust leadership presented above. Research two companies, one which appears to be closer to the locust model, and the other closer to the honeybee approach. Write a 300 word blog reflecting on these two approaches, how the companies benefit from these approaches, and what you feel is the best way to do business.

By adopting this mindset of long-term decision making, Avery and Bergsteiner claim that a self-reinforcing system can be developed within a company that supports and enhances the honeybee approach. They base their claims on research originally with fourteen European organizations which concluded that there were nineteen leadership practices that noticeably differentiated honeybee companies from locust ones. This theory was then tested on another fourteen companies from across the world, resulting in an additional four leadership practices being added (Avery and Bergsteiner, 2011b). The twenty-three leadership practices are shown in Table 13.2.

Table 13.2 Sustainable leadership: a comparison of different leadership practices. Reproduced with permission.

Leadership elements	Honeybee approach	Locust approach
Foundation practices		
1. Developing people	develops everyone continuously	develops people selectively
2. Labour relations	seeks cooperation	acts antagonistically
3. Retaining staff	values long tenure at all levels	accepts high staff turnover
4. Succession planning	promotes from within wherever possible	appoints from outside wherever possible
5. Valuing staff	is concerned about employees' welfare	treats people as interchangeable and a cost
6. CEO and top team	CEO works as top team member or speaker	CEO is decision-maker hero
7. Ethical behaviour	'doing the right thing' as an explicit core value	ambivalent, negotiable, an assessable risk
8. Long- or short-term perspective	prefers long-term over the short-term	short-term profits and growth prevail
9. Organizational change	change is an evolving and considered process	change is a fast adjustment; volatile, can be ad hoc
10. Financial markets orientation	seeks maximum independence from others	follows its masters' will, often slavishly
11. Responsibility for environment	protects the environment	is prepared to exploit the environment
12. Social responsibility (CSR)	values people and the community	exploits people and the community
13. Stakeholder consideration	everyone matters	only shareholders matter
14. Vision's role in business	shared view of future is essential strategic tool	the future does not necessarily drive the business
Higher-level practices		
15. Decision making	is consensual and devolved	is primarily manager-centred
16. Self-management	staff are mostly self-managed	managers manage
17. Team orientation	teams are extensive and empowered	teams are limited and manager-centred
18. Culture	fosters and enabling, widely shared culture	culture is weak except for a focus on short-term results that may or may not be shared
19. Knowledge-sharing and retention	spreads throughout the organization	limits knowledge to a few 'gatekeepers'
20. Trust	high trust through relationships and goodwill	control and monitoring compensate for low trust

(Continued...)

Leadership elements	Honeybee approach	Locust approach
Key performance drivers		
21. Innovation	strong, systemic, strategic innovation evident at all levels	innovation is limited and selective; buys in expertise
22. Staff engagement	values emotionally committed staff and the resulting commitment	financial rewards suffice as motivators, no emotional commitment expected
23. Quality	is embedded in the culture	is a matter of control

An interesting note in this research demonstrates that it is easier for non-listed companies, SMEs, and family owned businesses to adopt the long-term decision making required to be a honeybee company. Listed companies are under pressure from the stock market to deliver short-term returns every quarter, something that encourages the locust approach. To move from one to the other can take years as it requires the senior management, the wider business, and its stakeholders to form new assumptions on how business actually works.

RESEARCH IN FOCUS: Leading for sustainability

A study by Quinn and Dalton (2009) used a qualitative research method to investigate what leaders who are looking to create a sustainable approach in their businesses actually do. The authors drew on a framework depicting the tasks of leadership that was developed by McCauley and Van Velsor (2004). This framework give three tasks that leaders need to accomplish: setting direction; creating alignment, and maintaining commitment. Quinn and Dalton interviewed seventeen people from twelve US based organizations and the results were coded against the three tasks of leadership outlined above.

The research found that when setting a direction towards sustainability, leaders need to frame the delivery of the message in a positive and compelling way which links traditional business language to the language of sustainable practices, and which gives the message that working towards sustainability is a meaningful business objective. The timing and speed of introduction needs to be considered to fit the context and culture of the organization, with some happy to jump in and see what happens, and others wanting a slow, step by step approach. An important factor was ensuring a focus for the work on sustainability, such as the triple bottom line measurement, as this focus helps to drive a sustainability mindset into the organization.

When creating alignment, the study suggested that leaders focus on integrating sustainability into general business practices, getting structures aligned, ensuring goals and measurement systems are focused on sustainability, and frequently communicating the importance of this issue. Frequent engagement with stakeholders at all levels was advocated, which could lead to a focus on the products and services the business offered being developed along sustainable lines.

When looking at maintaining commitment, the study echoed the work of Avery and Bergsteiner (2011a, 2011b). Building good relationships with all stakeholders, treating employees as assets, caring about the reputation of the business, and favouring collaborating over competing.

Whilst this study was limited by its US focus, it does give indications of how a leader interested in developing a responsible and ultimately sustainable company can set about the process of change.

Source: Quinn, L. and Dalton, M. (2009) Leading for sustainability: implementing the tasks of leadership. *Corporate Governance*, 9 (1) 21–38.

When considering the academic work on concepts of responsible and sustainable leadership, what becomes clear is a common view that there needs to be a change in the mindset and behaviour of a leader in order to develop a view of business that favours the sustainable and long-term view. The DTI (2003) report on changing manager mindsets suggested that there were six characteristics needed for managers to be able to integrate responsibility into their every day decisions:

- questioning business as usual—open to new ideas; challenge others to change working practice
- understanding stakeholders and how they interact with one another
- partnership working internally and externally
- identifying, dialoguing with, and balancing stakeholder needs
- respecting diversity, seeking to understand and accept difference
- having a strategic view of the wider business environment

Hind, Wilson, and Lenssen (2009) developed this further by seeking the competencies leaders would need to really integrate responsible and sustainable practice into their businesses. They found that the most important attributes a responsible leader should have were acting with integrity and caring for people. Once again their research produced evidence that supported the honeybee approach to leadership, with attributes such as respecting all employees, honesty and trust, commitment to the development of employees, and respecting diversity and equal opportunities being rated as important. An important finding for leaders was that managers can assume that sustainability is an organizational responsibility, rather than an individual one, that it resides somewhere else in the organization, rather than being the responsibility of everyone in the organization. This highlights the need for responsible leaders to set the tone and show they are leading on these areas, whilst at the same time ensuring all employees are clear that the same level of responsibility is expected of all.

The study produced a list of competencies of leaders who enhanced the development of responsible organizational behaviour, which the authors termed reflexive abilities. These included the ability to think systemically; to embrace diversity; to balance global and local perspectives; to be able to hold meaningful dialogue with all stakeholders; and to have good emotional awareness, including the ability to include empathy, perception, and curiosity in decision making processes. As the authors state, responsible leaders for a sustainable world need to be able to deal with the uncertainty and complexity of divergent stakeholder needs by adopting unorthodox approaches to balancing these demands.

Discussion point: Sustainable leadership

Consider the capabilities and qualities of a responsible and sustainable leader that have been discussed in this chapter.

- Do you believe that these are key qualities of leadership?
- How comfortable are you with the uncertainty, complexity, and increased demands of sustainable leadership?

From a critical perspective

The move towards leaders adopting the issues of CSR and sustainability has been generally welcomed by authors and practitioners alike. Those who oppose the consideration of sustainability issues by companies point to the responsibilities of business being purely for the interests of shareholders and, from this perspective, leaders should be focused on the maximization of profit and the return of these to shareholders (Friedman, 1970; Hendersen, 2001). This argument calls for the continuation of business as usual, and fundamentally holds a belief that issues of sustainability will be solved by existing markets through price changes in response to supply and demand issues.

A more critical approach to sustainability issues suggests that the very idea of CSR gives an impression that companies somehow possess the ability to solve the complex and uncertain issues of sustainability and community development. Company responses to CSR and sustainability focus largely on measurement in order to improve, for example through adoption of the triple bottom line (Elkington, 1999). This enables companies to report on their performance using social accounting methods against three main criteria: economic impact, environmental impact, and social impact. The triple bottom line approach attempts to demonstrate the interconnected nature of these three bottom lines on each other. Unfortunately, companies tend to use this in a limited way, focusing on those impacts that are straightforward to measure. As Marshall (2011) suggests, this measurement and application of monetary value is an attempt to fix an existing system, and perhaps it is the system itself that needs to change. Marshall quotes Gray and Milne (2004), leaders in the social accounting field, who conclude that the current system of capitalism itself may be the systemic factor that is not sustainable, being based on growth, competition, the maximization of consumption, and maximum returns to shareholders. If the system itself is not sustainable, then this raises the question of whether anyone working within this system can actually take action that is sustainable.

The systemic nature of sustainability is something that responsible leaders need to appreciate if they are to take leadership on sustainable issues. Marshall, Coleman, and Reason (2011) describe systemic thinking as an appreciation of the interconnected nature of everything. It is a mindset that seeks to go beyond the reductionism and fragmentation that characterize the current approaches to business taught by most business schools, and is particularly characterized in the traditional financial accounting of companies, reducing performance to elements that are straightforward to measure, and effectively using only one unit of measurement, money. The triple bottom line, properly implemented, with close attention paid to the interaction of, and conflict between the three areas, is an attempt to develop systemic thinking in the measurement systems of companies. A leader attempting to think about responsibility and sustainability issues in a systemic way needs to develop sense-making skills (Weick 1995), seeking to understand whilst at the same time acting to improve.

Leaders adopting this systemic view of business responsibility have to be comfortable questioning the conventional wisdom of the business world. If sustainability and sustainable development are systemic problems, they will require systemic solutions, which go beyond corporate CSR or sustainability activity to questioning the very systems within which business is done. As Avery and Bergsteiner (2011b: 11) put it, 'sustainable leadership requires a major shift in mindsets, values, and assumptions about how business works'. This shift requires leaders to take a long view, rather than a short-term view on business decisions. It requires leaders to gain an understanding of the systemic patterns and the power bases into which they are intervening, to understand their place in this pattern, and to choose carefully the timing of their interventions. They must aim to see the wider consequences of specific actions or projects. This in turn requires a commitment to stakeholder dialogue, to a practice of business that is relational rather than competitive, one that looks to foster and build networks that will enable systemic change to occur (Marshall, Coleman, and Reason, 2011; Avery and Bergsteiner, 2011; Freeman, 2007).

> Only change that permeates practices, assumptions, and organizational priorities has the potential to be systemic. (Marshall Coleman, and Reason, 2011: 228)

The leaders who adopt this mindset, and question the system whilst at the same time acting in responsible ways within the system, have been described as tempered radicals (Marshall Coleman, and Reason, 2011). Meyerson and Scully (1995) define tempered radicals as individuals who have a commitment both to their organization and its aims, and to a cause that possibly appears to be against the aims of their organization. This belief in a cause leads these individuals to be radical within their organizational culture, as they continually question the conventional wisdom that dictates how things are done. However, they are tempered because they are caught between two apparently conflicting worlds, in a position where they want to influence what is with what they believe to be right. They are not trying to completely destroy one world, but rather are seeking ways to influence, cajole, and dialogue in order to bring about sustainable change.

Leaders who are tempered radicals can be described as hypocritical. Colleagues and observers who believe exclusively that business responsibility is only to shareholders or who argue passionately for social justice and sustainable practice can perceive tempered radicals as holding beliefs that are not compatible. However, for the leader that is a tempered radical, it is the very act of holding the tension between these positions that drives them to take action in a myriad of small ways that will incrementally lead to a systemic change.

Whilst the main stream texts of CSR and sustainability imply that the leaders should focus on the business case for responsible action, the critical texts suggest the action should question the very system that advocates the need for a business case. The main stream has moved to solutions that are acceptable to continue the status quo, solutions including energy and waste reduction which saves money, and community engagement that improves a business context. The critical approach encourages leaders to have an edge, to work within the system, but look to see how the system needs to change, to continue to be radical as the majority move slowly to accepting CSR as business as usual.

A case in point: Paul Polman, Unilever

In 2010 Unilever, one of the world's leading suppliers of fast moving consumer goods, launched their Sustainable Living Plan. The plan was an ambitious ten-year plan that integrated the company business plan with its responsibilities as a sustainable business. The company set out to double their sales whilst at the same time halving their impact on the environment. The plan included targets to increase the nutrition in products, to reduce the use of palm oil, and to bring together small scale suppliers and distributors in ways that would improve their supply chains in developing countries.

At the launch of the plan and during subsequent interviews given by CEO Paul Polman, Unilever have taken a radical position with investors. Polman has made it clear that he believes the company

(Continued...)

has a fiduciary duty to a wide group of stakeholders, and not a single focus on shareholders. He decided to ban quarterly reporting to the City, and has actively courted long-term investment funds as shareholders. His aim is to mediate the system that encourages short-term decision making, aiming instead to attract shareholders who share the vision of a long-term sustainable future. He was quoted in the *Guardian* as asking, 'Why would you invest in a company which is out of synch with the needs of society, that does not take its social compliance in its supply chain seriously, that does not think about the costs of externalities, or of its negative impacts on society?'

Polman takes a holistic view of the future of his and others' businesses. He believes that leaders now and in the future need to be at ease with numerous stakeholders, acting openly and in collaboration, rather than in a traditional, closed, private manner. To this end Unilever are working with their business, with suppliers, and with customers to make themselves a more sustainable company. The most difficult area is the work with customers, where they are trying to educate the public to use products in a more sustainable way, for example washing at lower temperatures or having shorter showers.

By taking small steps with all stakeholders, Polman is taking action to lead on issues of sustainability. He is ensuring that the business takes lots of small steps that may lead to the systemic change needed to deal with the issue of sustainability. 'Success' he says, 'cannot be measured by the end state but by progress and what keeps us going is we have a holistic plan and are moving forward.'

Sources: <http://www.guardian.co.uk/sustainable-business/paul-polman-unilever-sustainable-living-plan> accessed 21 November 2012; <http://www.unilever.co.uk/aboutus/introductiontounilever/> accessed 21 November 2012; <http://www.unilever.co.uk/sustainable-living/> accessed 21 November 2012; <http://www.ethicalcorp.com/business-strategy/ceo-interview-paul-polman-unilever-%E2%80%93-sustainable-living-gets-top-billing> accessed 21 November 2012

Discussion point: Can growth be achieved responsibly?

Consider the critical approaches to issues of responsibility and sustainability:

- Would you describe Paul Polman as a 'tempered radical'?
- Do you think Polman and Unilever are taking a systemic view of this issue?
- Can the joint aims of sales growth and sustainability ever be compatible, or do you think this is a dream that cannot be realized?
- If you were an investor, would you invest in Unilever?

Chapter summary

In this chapter we have considered:

- the global context within which leaders must operate
- the responsibilities that this context confers on business leaders
- what is corporate social responsibility
- the key issues of sustainability and sustainable development
- the leadership capabilities needed to be a responsible leader now and in the future
- the mindset that leads to a sustainable leadership approach, and what sustainable leadership looks like within a business
- the critique of responsible and sustainable leadership approaches

Integrative case study: Aditya Birla Group

Aditya Birla Group is one of India's biggest companies. It is a US$40 billion company with 136,000 employees. The Top Companies for Leaders survey 2011 ranks the Group as number 1 in Asia and number 4 in the world. It was also named as the Winner of the 'Excellence in Developing the Leaders of Tomorrow Award 2012', at SHRM India's First People Awards.

The Group is a conglomerate which operates in thirty-six countries worldwide. The Group's Companies are involved in various activities, including the manufacture of metals such as aluminium and copper, viscose staple fibre, carbon black, chemicals, insulators, acrylic fibre, cement, and fertilizer and IT/ITES. In India it has additional business interests in the branded fashion, clothing, telecom, insurance, financial services, and retail industries.

Originally founded in the nineteenth century by Seth Shiv Narayan Birla as a cotton trading business in Rajasthan, the business grew quickly under his son Ghanshyamdas Birla in the early twentieth century. The business really took off under the leadership of Ghanshyamdas Birla's grandson, Aditya Vikram Birla, who embraced globalization by setting up nineteen companies outside of India. Mr Birla built the fundamentals of the business, giving it a structure, making it a world class producer and manufacturer, and ensuring the Group had a strong financial base. He, along with Mrs Birla, was also responsible for the company founding a children's home in Mumbai. Mr Aditya Birla unfortunately died in 1995, and was succeeded by his son, Mr Kumar Mangalam Birla, who has grown the business from US$2 billion in 1995 to US$40 billion in 2012. He is the Chairman of the Aditya Birla Group.

The Group has a strong values system which is best described as a trusteeship view on business. Here the wealth generated by the business is seen as being held in trust for, and used to the benefit of, the wide range of the stakeholders of the business. For the Aditya Birla Group, this is not about charitable giving in a purely philanthropic manner, but is more focused on helping individuals and communities to develop the skills and generate the finance that will enable them to economically improve themselves in a sustainable, long-term way. Mr Kumar Mangalam Birla has integrated this approach into the core management of the business by adopting the triple bottom line approach to measuring the outputs of the business.

On the death of Mr Aditya Birla, his wife, Mrs Rajashree Birla, became involved in the trustee side of the business. In 1998 the process was institutionalized with the setting up of the Aditya Birla Centre for Community Initiatives and Rural Development. It is the apex body responsible for development projects and is chaired by Mrs Birla. The Centre has oversight of the social initiatives of the Group's forty companies and is anchored to the Group's Corporate Communications and CSR Cell, headed by Dr Pragnya Ram.

Mrs Birla has a seat on the board of the Group's major companies. Each Group company has a Rural Development Cell, responsible for the implementation of the social programmes in their community. A dedicated 250 strong team of professionals work exclusively on the Group's CSR projects, supported by 3,000 field workers. The CSR heads report to Dr Ram and she in turn reports to Mrs Birla.

The Centre focuses on providing assistance and development for the communities surrounding the various plants owned by the Group, many of which are located in rural or tribal areas. The leadership and inspiration provided by Mrs Birla and the support of her son Mr Birla has been widely recognized as being largely responsible for the development of this side of the Group's business. Furthermore, Mr Birla has been instrumental in the Group viewing their social vision as being integral to their wider business vision.

The Group's vision for the Centre is 'To actively contribute to the social and economic development of the communities in which we operate. In so doing, build a better, sustainable way of life for the weaker sections of society and raise the county's human development index.'

(Continued...)

This is done by working inclusively with the local communities on projects related to community and social welfare, education, health care, and infrastructure development. Any project can be started with the help of the Aditya Birla Group, but there must be a plan for the project to be self-sustaining at some point, increasing the likelihood of long-term sustainability of these initiatives. Accountability, performance management, and audits are inbuilt.

The Group works in over 3,000 villages and has an impact on over 7 million people. It has aided with the creation and running of eighteen hospitals in India, Thailand, and Egypt, as well as forty-two schools, enabling the education of some 45,000 students, 18,000 of these at no cost to themselves. Examples of the projects that the Group are involved in include:

- Helping communities in water stressed regions gain access to fresh water through the provision of hand pumps. This initiative included training up and equipping the women of the community as water pump mechanics, who could service and repair the pumps.

- Creating 4,000 self-help groups backed by cooperative banks and microfinance that enables local economic development.

- Providing vocational training for over 100,000 people in agricultural, industrial areas as well as arts, craft, and tailoring.

- Salt reduction schemes to make drinking water more accessible. Also replacing traditional wells with bore wells, recharging underground water sources, installation of hand pumps at intervals of 10–15 houses, constructing check-dams, rainwater harvesting, and harvesting the excess run away water. This has helped provide water to over a million people.

- Soil testing and animal husbandry. Aiding over a million farmers in the choice of which plants to sow, and direct help in increasing crop yields, thus making higher profits.

- Community immunization programmes reaching 16 million children.

Mrs Birla and the Aditya Birla Group have demonstrated how a successful business can be both profit making and socially responsible. The integration of solid business fundamentals with a desire to invest profits for the good of society has led to the Indian Government conferring the third highest civilian award on Mrs Birla, the Padma Bhushan. In 2012 two other accolades were conferred on the Aditya Birla Group, the 'Economic Times Corporate Citizen of the Year' and the Asian Centre for Corporate Governance & Sustainability—'Company with Best CSR & Sustainability Award'.

Case study questions:

After reading the case, reflect on the achievements of the Aditya Birla Group. What strikes you about the social activities of the Group?

- Do you think the approach of Aditya Birla Group is one that could be easily copied?

- What part does leadership have to play in the development of such an integrated approach to business and society?

- From what you have learned about Mrs Rajashree Birla, write a short definition of responsible leadership for a sustainable world.

Sources: Written with support from the Aditya Birla Group. Special thanks to Dr Pragnya Ram for her help with this case. <http://www.adityabirla.com/media/press_reports/2012_30_08_mrs_birla_interview.html> accessed 16 November 2012; <http://www.adityabirla.com/the_group/index.htm> accessed 16 November 2012; <http://www.adityabirla.com/social_projects/overview.htm> accessed 16 November 2012; <http://www.forbes.com/global/2012/0604/heroes-philanthropy-rajashree-birla-hospital-school-fund-grand-dame-indian-charity.html> accessed 16 November 2012; Aditya Birla Group DVD (2006) 'The Noble Commitment' Bedi Films Production; Aditya Birla Group DVD 'Mrs Rajashreeji Birla'.

Further reading

Kakabadse, N. K., Kakabadse, A. P., and Lee-Davies L. (2009) CSR leaders road-map. *Corporate Governance*, 9 (1) 50–7.

Garriga, E. and Melé, D. (2004) Corporate Social Responsibility Theories: Mapping the territory. *Journal of Business Ethics*, 53, 51–71.

Marshall, J., Coleman, G., and Reason, P. (2011) *Leadership for Sustainability: An action research approach*. Greenleaf Publishing Ltd.

Avery, G. C. and Bergsteiner, H. (2011) Sustainable leadership practices for enhancing business resilience and performance. *Strategy and Leadership*, 39 (3) 5–15.

14   Leadership development

Learning outcomes

On completion of this chapter you will:

- Understand the ideas and theories of leadership development
- Have knowledge of the use of coaching and mentoring in leader development
- Appreciate the foundations and application of action learning in leadership development
- Have knowledge of the use of experiential learning and reflection in leadership development
- Be aware of the limitations and critiques of current leadership development practice

Introduction

The quest for better leaders and quality leadership in organizations has led to a meteoric rise in the amount spent on leadership development programmes. It is estimated that companies spend billions of dollars on developing the leadership and management skills of their people (Riggio, 2008; Raelin, 2004). Some authors question how effective these programmes are (Gosling and Mintzberg, 2004; Mintzberg, 2004), and point out that there is very little evidence of what actually gets developed on a leadership development programme (Day, Zaccaro, and Halpin, 2004). In fact, some authors suggest that leadership may be too complex and intuitive to teach (Doh, 2003). Others suggest that individuals and companies believe investment in developing leaders is important because leaders are important to business effectiveness, and because the skills of leading are difficult and complex to master (Riggio, 2008).

The rise in leadership development programmes has been linked to changes in the nature of the work organization. The move away from the modern, bureaucratic organization towards the postmodern organization has removed some old certainties from the workplace, and introduced a belief that companies are in a state of constant flux. Whilst management is still vitally important, leadership is seen as the essential ingredient when dealing with complex and uncertain situations. Leaders in the modern, globalized world have to develop the skills and capacity to continually conceive and execute strategies for any given situation (Day, Zaccaro, and Halpin, 2004).

In previous chapters we have explored the arguments around whether leaders are born or made (Chapter 4). Leader or leadership development does not take a position on this argument, but suggests individuals can always improve their skills as a leader or their ability to provide leadership for an organization.

You will notice that there is a subtle distinction being made here between leader development and leadership development. Leader development is said to work at an individual level. It seeks to improve an individual's mastery of cognitive, socio-emotional, and behavioural skills associated with leadership (Day, 2011), to aid the development of self-awareness, and to increase the individual's capacity to undertake the role of leader. By contrast leadership development focuses on developing the quality and collective capacity for leadership in an organization, and as such is more focused on social processes and structures, group or team activity, and more tightly tied with ideas of organizational development (Day, 2011; Amagoh, 2009; Riggio, 2008).

This chapter will explore the ideas and theories attached to both leader development and leadership development. We will examine some of the techniques favoured by companies and consultants, including action learning, coaching and mentoring, experiential learning, and reflection.

In the mainstream

Leader development

The distinction between leader development and leadership development is widely attributed to Day (2000). Day noticed that the majority of development programmes, either run by companies or offered by consultants, were focused at an individual level. These concentrated on developing the capacity of an individual to lead by developing their skills, their self-awareness and, in some instances, their motivation to take the lead (Riggio, 2008).

Leader development is focused on three main areas of skills development: cognitive; socio-emotional; and behavioural (Amagoh, 2008; Day, Zaccaro, and Halpin, 2004). It is proposed that by developing these skills, a leader will have the capacity and the capability to learn their way through situations and problems that are complex, problems that they have not encountered before, and for which there is no obvious answer.

Within the category of cognitive skills, leader development seeks to enhance a leader's ability to recognize, understand, and solve problems, and to develop their capacity for critical thinking. Cognitive skill development focuses on the ability to solve problems and think critically, possibly because these are thought to be the ones that can be enhanced by intensive leader development initiatives.

Socio-emotional skills are perhaps more widely known as interpersonal skills. Development here focuses on a leader's ability to communicate, to understand individuals and situations, and to mentor others in order to develop capability in the wider team.

Behavioural development is focused on how a leader's behaviour impacts on groups and teams. Behavioural skill development has been used to develop the transformational leader attributes of idealized influence, individualized consideration, inspirational motivation, and intellectual stimulation. These attributes are fully described in Chapter 5.

It is usually argued that the development of cognitive, socio-emotional, and behavioural skills should go hand-in-hand with the development of key leader attributes. These attributes are very similar to the characteristics of the authentic leader, described in Chapter 12. They are self-awareness, openness, trust, creativity, and practical, social, and general intelligence. Day, Zaccaro, and Halpin (2004) argue that the acquisition of both the skills and attributes

Table 14.1 Capabilities thought to be developed during leader development programmes

Self-management capabilities	Social capabilities	Work-facilitation capabilities
Self-awareness	Ability to build relationships	Management skills
Balancing conflicting demands	Ability to maintain relationships	Strategic thinking and execution
Ability to learn	Building effective teams	Creative thinking and implementation
Leadership values	Communication skills Developing others	Initiating and delivering change

Source: Adapted from Day (2011). Reproduced with permission.

allows a leader to develop the ability to be adaptable when dealing with the difficult problems that confront senior managers in today's businesses.

For a leader, training in these skills can be useful for reflecting on previous experiences, as well as preparing for future experiences. The point here is that a leader develops their leadership through gaining experiences, having the ability to learn their way through these experiences, and being able to reflect on and learn from the experiences. These experiences have to be varied in their nature, have a certain amount of challenge to them, and be supported by constructive feedback to be most effective (Jackson and Parry, 2008).

Day (2011) quotes the work of Van Velsor and McCauley (2004), who propose a list of the capabilities that it is hoped are developed during a leader development programme (Table 14.1).

There are some obvious links here back to the work of the behavioural theories of leadership described in Chapter 2. Of particular note is the break down into those skills and attributes that will enhance the leaders ability to form and maintain relationships, and those that will enable the efficient delivery of task. It would appear that these core ideas, arising from the University of Michigan and Ohio State studies, have survived the test of time and been translated into best practice for leader development.

Riggio (2008) highlights that leader development often utilizes a tried and trusted training method called needs analysis. Here there is a definition of the capabilities, competencies, or attributes that typically the organization has decided are key to good leadership. The leader is tested against these at the start of the leader development programme, and a gap analysis is performed that seeks to highlight the areas where the individual leader is in some way deficient, and can therefore focus on to improve their leadership. For this method to work, there has to be an accepted definition of what leadership actually is, what the tasks of the leader are, and what skills and behaviours a leader needs to master to be a leader. In this sense, a leader development programme can become very specific to the organizational context in which it is being developed and delivered.

Indeed, Day (2011) points out that for a leader development experience to be at its most effective, it should be embedded in the organizational context. For a leader development experience to have impact, the participants have to be willing to be developed, be willing to learn from experience, and they have to be interested in becoming better leaders. They also have to be willing to work on their development over time, to accept constructive feedback, and to undertake activities and training that will be challenging. Day (2011) points out that any leader development intervention is more likely to have a longer-term effect rather than an immediate effect, and the impact will unfold over time.

Jackson and Parry (2008) add that leader development will be ineffective if the organizational culture is such that it stifles the kind of leadership being developed. They quote Gordon (2002) who suggests that the embedded power structures of an organization can reinforce existing leadership patterns if they are not developed alongside the leaders. This suggests that the development of leaders is a more systemic practice, engaging with power and structures in organizations as well as the capabilities of individuals.

Day's work has been an attempt to bridge the gap between the differences in leader development programmes, and create a general theory of leader development that is applicable to all contexts and climates. In this he reports to have had only limited success, but is encouraged that the work of theorizing leader development seems to have moved beyond merely reporting best practice and has to some extent become slightly more scientific. Day reports that, in particular, there have been advances in the understanding of leader development that develops expertise in leaders; that investigates the changing nature of a leader's identity as they progress through a programme; and a focus on the leader in the team and the ability to adapt in working groups (Day, 2011: 40).

RESEARCH IN FOCUS: Leader development and the dark side of personality

In this study, Harms, Spain and Hannah investigate the impact of subclinical personality traits on the development of a leader over time. Subclinical traits are positioned as being between the 'normal' big five personality traits (extraversion, agreeableness, conscientiousness, emotional stability, and openness—see Chapter 4 for more detail), and those traits that are used in diagnosing psychological pathologies. They do not hamper a leader in everyday activity, but may have an impact in particular situations, especially when relating to others.

The study examined the following subclinical traits drawn from the Hogan Development Survey; excitable, sceptical, cautious, reserved, leisurely, bold, mischievous, colourful, imaginative, diligent, and dutiful. The authors hypothesized that leader development initiatives generally would have a positive impact on participants over time, but the subclinical traits would have a negative impact, thus reducing the responsiveness of participants to the leader development activities.

Hypotheses were tested on a large scale sample of military cadets over a number of years, and the authors found positive evidence that participants do respond positively to leader development activities. They found some evidence that subclinical traits would slow the rate of leader development, but found little evidence that these traits acted negatively in leader development initiatives. Two traits did seem to have a negative effect (sceptical and imaginative), whilst four had a positive effect (cautious, bold, colourful, and dutiful). The authors concluded that the impact of traits may have a greater or lesser effect depending on the context of the leader development programme. They also speculated that regular feedback on subclinical traits during a programme may increase participant self-awareness, and thus reduce the possible impact of these traits on their future leadership effectiveness.

Source: Harms, P. D., Spain, S. M., and Hannah, S. T. (2011) Leader development and the dark side of personality. *The Leadership Quarterly*, 22, 495–509.

Leadership development

Leadership development is seen as a systematic attempt to improve the wider leadership capability across an organization. This is done at a collective or group level, and requires social interaction in order to achieve an improvement in the quality of leadership. The intention of a leadership development programme may be to give everyone a common understanding, or a shared vision on what leadership is for that organization and how it will be enacted.

Day, Zaccaro, and Halpin (2004) suggest that leadership is both dependent on, and is the product of, a social context. Hence leadership development can only occur within this social context, within the context in which you are a leader, be this in an organization or at an accelerated level on an organizational leadership development programme. In keeping with many other authors, Day, Zacarro, and Halpin (2004) recognize the importance of leadership development, but focus only on the level of leader development. The contention here is that by developing the individual skills and attributes of a leader, the ability of that leader to engage in leadership within an organization will be increased. Day, Zaccaro, and Halpin (2004) recognize that more thinking needs to be done on bridging the leader/leadership development gap, and that the ideal development programme will align leader and leadership development, but notes that very little work has been done on this.

McCauley and van Velsor (2004), drawing on work from the Center for Creative Leadership, suggests that a systemic approach needs to be taken for the development of organizational leadership. Leaders' cognitive and interpersonal skills should be developed alongside other organizational factors such as reward and appraisal systems. In line with this approach, London (2002) outlines a structure for a leadership development programme that would seek to integrate leader and leadership development with the needs of the organization. London suggests that this process would involve an organizational needs analysis linked with some form of assessment of the leadership talent within the organization, leading to a gap analysis. There would then follow some individual development planning, and this would be implemented with support from the organization, involving line management, and coaching or mentoring interventions. Of crucial importance here is the inclusion of problem solving activity in any development course that would link improving the leaders' capability to deal with complex problems with work on key organizational issues. Finally, development would not be a one-off, but would involve an on-going process of assessment and development.

As can be seen above, London's proposal broadens the development of a leader from individual skills development, to development linked with the needs of an organization. John Adair, goes further, suggesting that the development of leadership involves interaction that is wider than just the business organization. Adair suggests that the development of leaders happens throughout their lives, with particular development coming during the years in education. He makes the case that developing leadership is not just about skills training, but about education as well. As such he advocates that business organizations should be interested in schools and Universities, as this is where the growth of leaders begins (Adair, 2005).

London's approach is very traditional, assuming that learning about leadership occurs either in the heads of individuals, or is captured in the systems and processes of an organization. Concepts from the organizational learning literature challenge this, and offer a different approach to development. For example, the social construction approach to learning proposes that learning occurs mainly during interaction between people, in conversations and other interactions. Here, an understanding of leadership is developed between people in an organization. Through their interactions and conversations within the context of the organization, they are constructing an understanding of what leadership is for that context (Easterby-Smith, Crossan, and Nicolini, 2000).

This approach talks directly to Adair's idea of broader influences. Leadership develops through a broader engagement with the organization and wider society, and the interactions involved in this engagement allow for learning to occur and knowledge about leadership to develop. The key here is for leadership development programmes to allow the time and space for groups to discuss, contextualize, and develop their own understandings of issues to do with leadership. The role of a leadership development programme is to create a safe space for these discussions, and to facilitate individual and organizational learning about leadership. The next section outlines processes and interventions that seek to create these safe spaces for dialogue and learning, all of which are widely used by practitioners of leadership development.

Leader/leadership development tools and techniques

Action learning

> There can be no learning without action and no (sober and deliberate) action without learning. (Pedler, 2011: xxi)

Action learning, as suggested by its title, is a learning approach (rather than a training approach) to individual and organizational development. At its essence, action learning is collaborative problem solving, in which individuals come together in a learning set to discuss the difficult issues they face. As such, it is a method of learning through experience, using workplace issues as the main vehicle for learning, asking questions to further understanding about the issue, and generating action to be taken to address the issue (Rimanoczy, 2007).

Recently action learning has gained momentum as a leadership development tool. The rapidly changing nature of the global economy, and the continuous change faced by companies has led to a need for leaders to be able to understand and learn their way through complex problems, being at ease with this complexity and purposeful in action at the same time. Marquardt (2000) argues that traditional forms of leadership development focus on the attributes of the leader, or on developing personal capabilities and competencies. The result is leaders who are technically competent to deliver the task, but who may struggle with the emotional and human aspects of changing organizations.

Action learning, on the other hand, allows leaders to develop critical skills in listening, questioning, and learning through complex problems, whilst ensuring the complexity of the whole system is being considered. As such, action learning is not a reductionist approach to developing leaders or considering complex problems. Rather it is a process which focuses leaders' attention on the whole system (Marquardt, 2000), in which leaders appreciate that they are part of the system and any change necessary to address a complex problem will involve change for everyone, including the leader (Revans, 2011).

The idea of action learning was developed by Professor Reg Revans. Revans was originally a research student in physics at the University of Cambridge. Here he noted how faculty members in the Cavendish Laboratory developed their knowledge through sharing their issues and uncertainties with each other in group discussions, and allowing others to question them.

Revans' career took him to the National Coal Board, where he initiated this form of learning, with managers coming together in groups called action learning sets to discuss their issues. He found that this approach helped the individuals solve their own problems without resorting to 'expert' help, and this in turn raised productivity (Revans, 2011).

At the core of Revans work is a belief in the power of learning by doing (Revans, 2011), and the value of the 'non-expert' in solving problems. He believed that managers were the best people to solve their own problems, and that this could be best facilitated in an action learning set.

Revans suggests that individuals and organizations operate from programmed knowledge, information, and techniques that have been appropriate to the growth of the person or company up to this point. Whilst programmed knowledge is important, Revans suggests that this will not allow the organization to be adaptable to a continuously changing world. He therefore suggests that in addition to programmed knowledge (P), an individual must employ critical reflection, or exploratory insight (Q), so they can learn their way through difficult problems. Thus for Revans, learning (L) can be expressed in the form of an equation: $L = P + Q$. Rimanoczy (2007) suggests that the equation should actually be written $L = Q + P$, as in practice action learning sets use the questions first to access the programmed knowledge in the set, and use this to help address the problem being discussed. Revans goes on to suggest that an individual or organization cannot flourish unless the rate of learning (L) is equal to, or greater than, the rate of change (C) being experienced: $L > C$ (Revans, 2011).

Marquardt (2004) suggest that there are six main components of action learning. The first is that the issue or problem is important to the set. The second is the composition of the set, being four to eight members drawn from different functional and professional backgrounds. Third is the process, which is focused on reflecting on the problem and the use of questioning to draw out new insights. Fourth is that the member of the set bringing the problem has the ability and power to act on the action plan that will be developed. Fifth is the approach of the set, that each member must be committed to learning not just for themselves, but for the set and for their organization. Finally Marquardt suggests that sets should be facilitated in some way by an action learning coach, whose focus is to help the group grasp their learning, and improve their action learning skills.

A critical element of a successful learning set is the creation of a safe space in which participants can explore their difficult issues. This space should enable set members to support and challenge each other, provide difficult feedback if necessary, allow for mistakes to be shared and accepted, and enable the participant with the issue to be the expert on that issue. In other words, set members have to restrain their programmed knowledge at times in order to allow the process of questioning and reflection to occur (Marquardt, 2000; Pedler, 2011).

Pedler (2011) describes how action learning as a moral philosophy is underpinned by humanistic values which describe how to be and how to act in a learning set. These begin with participants accepting that they start from a position of ignorance about the problem being discussed. Effective learning sets require a high level of personal honesty, and a commitment to action. Interaction in the set should be done in a spirit of friendship, and the ultimate purpose of an action learning set should be to make the world a better place.

Action learning has continued to develop since Revans' original ideas, and is now used in the majority of leadership development programmes in both developed and developing countries (Waddill and Marquardt, 2011). An on-going debate is around the necessity of a trained facilitator. Revans argued that the set members should be given a brief introduction to action learning, and then be allowed to develop their own processes without an expert guide. He saw the inclusion of a trained facilitator as an attempt to re-insert an 'expert' into the process, a process that was originally conceived to allow participants to develop their own problem solving skills without a dependence on an expert other. As seen above, Marquardt favours facilitation by an action learning coach, and Rimanoczy (2007), when describing action reflective learning, describes the coach as someone who not only manages the process, but also inputs with theory and ideas at relevant moments.

With the world of business growing ever more global, action learning as a leadership development tool appears to be one possible solution to an increasingly complex world.

Discussion point: Action learning

Form a group of between 4-8 participants. Choose a difficult problem that one of you is facing on your course or at work and then follow the process described below:

- The participant with the problem presents (and is the expert on her issue). All other members must listen without interruption.

- Once the presenter has finished, the others respond in three stages:

  1. Immediate feelings about the problem

  2. Questions to fill *factual* gaps—what don't you know?

  3. Open questions to make the presenter think in a different way about the problem

- The presenter is then put behind an 'invisible screen' and the group explores the options for action. The presenter listens and takes notes, but does not respond at this stage.

- Once the discussion is concluded, the presenter offers her reactions and feedback.

- The presenter crafts an action plan with help from the group.

Once the session is finished, reflect on what you have learned in this process individually, as a group, and for your wider organization.

Coaching and mentoring

The terms coaching and mentoring are used interchangeably in the leadership development literature. In this section we will consider the difference between these concepts, and will define coaching and mentoring as leader development activities.

At the simplest level, coaching is a process and a relationship within which the person being coached decides what their course of action will be and devises their own solution. In this sense, coaching is seen as a non-directive form of cognitive development, where the coach facilitates the coachee to discover their own solutions.

For mentoring, the mentor is usually a more experienced person from the same company or a similar sector or industry to the person being mentored. The mentor's job is to provide advice and specific knowledge about the area of issue. One possible danger of mentoring

Table 14.2 Differences between coaching, mentoring and counselling

Coaching	Counselling	Mentoring
• Non-directive	• Looks backwards and at the present	• Mentor has expert knowledge/experience
• Advice is not given	• Non-directive	• Specific advice is given
• Solutions focused	• Advice is not given	• May be solutions focused or explorative
• Belief that individuals hold the answers	• Not usually solutions focused	• Mentor has 'real' answers
• Based in present and future	• Belief that individuals hold the answers	• Usually directive at some level
• Strengths focused	• Operates at emotional level often	• May/may not result in specific actions
• Commitment to specific actions	• May promote degree of dependence	• Can promote dependence upon mentor
• Promotes high degree of independence	• Dependent on style of counselling, may use skills of questioning, reflecting, clarifying, and regressing	• Uses skills of questioning, reflecting, clarifying and telling
• Uses skills of questioning, reflecting and clarifying		

advice is the status difference between the mentor and the mentee, which could lead the mentee to feel pressured to act on advice that they are not convinced about. In contrast to this, coaching seeks to enable people to take their own decisions and seek their own advice and guidance as necessary (Table 14.2).

 Leadership in the media: Star Wars

The development of an individual through skills enhancement and individual mentoring is depicted in some detail throughout the six Star Wars films. The apprentice system of developing a Jedi Knight is shown in most detail in *The Empire Strikes Back*, where Luke Skywalker goes to learn from the only remaining Jedi Master, Yoda. Yoda acts as a cross between a military training instructor, improving the fitness of Luke's body and mind, and a mentor, advising him with words of wisdom. Luke is encouraged to look internally, to learn to relax and focus his mind, to self-reflect, become self-aware, and to develop self-resilience.

The apprentice system can be seen clearly in Episodes I (*The Phantom Menace*) and II (*Attack of the Clones*) of the series. Here the system of masters mentoring young apprentices is clearly depicted, demonstrating that becoming a Jedi, rather like becoming a leader, is a continuous process of learning and development. The mentoring relationship is very much one of a more experienced leader using their experience and expertise to tell a more junior colleague how to best act. There are some rules in this world that may be useful for companies to adopt. For example, a master only has one apprentice at a time, and they give that apprentice close individualized consideration. The apprentice is involved in every aspect of the master's work, learning from consistent close contact with a role model, rather than one meeting every two months or so, and being exposed to stretch assignments that would seem beyond the capabilities of the apprentice at any given time.

Interestingly, the development depicted in the Star Wars films focuses on the physical, mental, and spiritual fitness of the apprentice. Here the beliefs and the mental state of a leader are as important as the ability to solve complex problems.

Coaching

Ely et al. (2010) describe leadership coaching as a dynamic relationship, usually one-to-one between the leader and the coach, which is geared towards the development of the leader. They suggest that leadership coaching as a form of leadership development focuses on four main areas:

- The needs of the client within the organizational context
- The unique skill set required by the coach
- The importance of the relationship between the coach and the coachee
- Flexibility in the process used during coaching in order to achieve pre-agreed objectives

Wise and Jacobo (2010) describe the purpose of leadership coaching as to enhance skills and performance, and possibly to enable the development of vision, direction, or objectives for an organization. As Miles Downey (2003) puts it, 'Coaching is the art of facilitating the performance, learning and development of another.'

Typically leadership coaches work on improving self-awareness in their clients, to help leaders think through immediate or future work situations which usually involve people issues, or to facilitate the development of certain skills or behaviours in leaders. Organizations can sometimes favour the use of leadership coaching to help leaders cope with new areas and levels of responsibility or to facilitate their thinking about difficult organizational change situations (Ely et al., 2010).

Ely et al. (2010) suggest that leaders engaging in self-directed development activities such as coaching will have different degrees of readiness for this development, and that this degree of readiness will define how successful the activity can be. Readiness could be related to cognitive skills such as reading and thinking, to an appropriate level of conscientiousness, or a desire to seek and receive feedback. The level of commitment of a coachee is also seen as critical in creating a successful coaching relationship. Commitment may include being open to coaching as a development experience, being willing to create the necessary time, and viewing the coaching experience as a useful activity to aid self improvement.

On the other side of the relationship, the coach should also be properly prepared. Whilst there are no universally accepted coaching qualifications, there have been a number of attempts to list the knowledge and skills a coach should have to be effective. These include communication, analysis, and feedback skills, as well as personal qualities such as integrity, empathy and flexibility (Ely et al. 2010). In the context of business leadership, it is also an advantage to have a good general awareness and knowledge of business activities.

Coaching has borrowed heavily from work on therapeutic approaches to counselling. Kets De Vries, Korotov, and Florent-Tracey (2007) draw on a clinically orientated psychodynamic perspective for their work in developing leaders at the Insead business school. This approach seeks to understand the hidden or subconscious dynamics behind a range of leaders thoughts and behaviours, at both an individual and systemic level.

Other leadership coaches draw on the work of Carl Rogers (1980) in defining how a coach should approach arguably the most important element of coaching, the relationship with the client. Rogers thought there were three core conditions that were essential to generate a good counselling relationship: congruence, unconditional positive regard, and empathy.

Congruence means the coach is totally themselves during the coaching session, and does not create a professional front or other barrier that can get in the way of the development of the relationship. The congruence aspect is the coach being aware of how they are reacting internally to the coachee, and allowing this to be matched by their behaviours and words in the coaching session.

Unconditional positive regard requires the coach to have a positive, accepting attitude towards the coachee, accepting where the coachee is emotionally at that moment. It is defined by acceptance, respect, and warmth for the coachee.

Empathy refers to the coach sensing how the coachee is feeling, understands the context in which these feelings arose, and communicates to the coachee the understanding of these feelings.

Rogers argues that the presence of these three core conditions will enable a counsellor and client to create a relationship that will allow for positive change. The same can be said for a coaching relationship between a leader and an executive coach.

Ely et al. (2010) suggest that the individual nature of the coaching relationship, and the flexibility in approach during coaching different leaders, makes it difficult to create a general evaluation technique for leadership coaching interventions. The authors suggest an evaluation model that examines the process and the outcomes of leadership coaching. The outcomes focus on evaluating the client's reactions to the coach, the relationship and the process used; the learning gained, in terms of self-awareness, cognitive development, efficacy, and attitude to work; behaviour, examining whether the coachee's behaviour has changed; and results from an organizational perspective. Process evaluation focuses on the readiness, expectations, and organizational support of the coachee; the competencies and expertise of the coach; the relationship between coach and coachee; and the level of assessment, challenge, and support in the coaching process itself.

In general, the literature on coaching as a leader development activity is very positive. It differs from traditional forms of leader development in that it is individually focused and is flexible to deal with issues that will improve the effectiveness of that individual.

Mentoring

As stated earlier, mentoring is a relationship between a more experienced leader and a less experienced leader. As with coaching, the relationship is focused on the development of the mentee, sometimes referred to as the protégé (Baranik, Roling, and Eby, 2010). The mentor can help the mentee to feel more comfortable in their new role as a leader, and it is argued that gaining an effective mentor can increase the effectiveness of leader development in individuals (Solansky, 2010). Allen et al. (2004) claim that effective mentoring can lead to improved morale and commitment to the organization, plus promotion and better pay for the mentee.

Baranik, Roling, and Eby (2010) suggest that employees enter into mentoring relationships largely due to the benefits they perceive they can gain from such a relationship. They list two main benefits, careers related support and psychosocial support. The careers related support involves the mentor championing the mentee to gain challenging work assignments, coaching them for success in these assignments, and in the process giving them increased visibility in the organization. Psychosocial support involves giving the mentee a sense of personal worth, or value to the organization. This can involve providing support, counselling, and acceptance to the mentee, which in turn can increase the mentee's sense of themselves being a more effective, competent leader.

Case in point: Unilever Global Mentoring Programme

Unilever developed a mentoring programme for future leaders in 2009. The intention of the programme was to meet a diversity target which sought to increase the number of women in senior leadership positions. The assumption was that an effective mentoring relationship would help to accelerate individuals moving up the company hierarchy.

The programme pairs senior leaders from Unilever's business with high potential candidates who have been identified as future leaders in the organization. Over the course of a year the mentor and mentee typically meet every couple of months for two hours, and the discussion can include business and personal issues faced by the mentee at work.

To make the relationship effective, participants talk about the importance of the mentor sharing issues they are struggling with as well, and about the importance of being fully committed to the relationship. From a mentee perspective this means preparing properly for each session. For the mentors this means making the space in a very busy diary, and using questions that will make the mentee think wider and deeper about the issue they are discussing.

The mentoring programme is clearly seen as important and valuable by both mentor and mentee in successful mentoring relationships. Mentees also describe the relationship as motivating, giving them a perception that they are valued by the organization.

Source: Friends in High Places. *Management Today* October 2012, 48–51.

Experiential learning

Experiential learning in leader development programmes can be thought of in two ways. The first is the development of a leader's ability to reflect on their own practice, essentially to be able to learn from everyday opportunities and experiences, and thus be able to continuously self-develop. The second is the training that occurs to develop this capability, usually problem solving activities linked to reflection and feedback sessions. These activities can include role plays, simulations, structured activities, sensitivity training, and outdoor adventure training (Boot and Reynolds, 1983).

The argument that leaders learn mainly from experience was formulated in the management learning literature. Kempster (2006) draws on the work of Burgoyne and Stewart (1977), and Burgoyne and Hodgeson (1983) to make the case that learning to lead occurs though naturalistic processes and accidental events, in other words, through experience. Davies and Easterby-Smith (1984) suggest that experience is the main method that managers learn from, but that some experiences have a greater effect than others. McCall, Lombardo, and Morrison (1988) would agree, and suggest that the key experiences for the development of leaders through experience are line assignments, notable people, and hardships. In an in-depth study of company directors, Kempster (2006) found that interventions through training and development were considered less important than experience in the development of leaders. The directors suggested that their development as leaders was gained mainly through interacting with notable people and undertaking difficult work assignments, and through a journey of identity transformation in their own minds from follower to leader. There was also evidence of development through everyday interaction with people in the organization, and through collective decisions on how a leader should act that were almost unconscious decisions. A key finding of Kempster's work was that leaders rarely appreciate how they have developed as a leader until they are asked to reflect on their development through experience, either through an interview process, or through an activity on a development programme.

 Blog box: Learning to Lead

Write a 300 word blog describing a notable person who has shaped your development as a leader. What made this person notable? Why is this person more notable than others you could have chosen? What activities did this person do as a leader that you admire? How has this impacted on your own leadership?

Reynolds (2009) argues that experiential learning in executive development programmes is intuitively attractive to managers and educators as it suggests a close link to practice, making the development programme appear to have greater relevance. As a learning method, experiential learning puts the emphasis on the participant of a leader development programme to be aware of their own learning experiences and to generate as much learning as they can from these.

An important aspect in experiential learning can be seen in the methods used to help leaders to learn from their experiences. One of the most well known of these methods was developed by David Kolb. Kolb and Kolb (2005) describe experiential learning as a process that transforms experience into knowledge. Understanding the process that individuals follow to develop their principles and values from their experience is essential to gaining an insight into how people will behave in new situations (Kolb, Osland, and Irwin, 1995). Kolb proposed that people follow a four-stage cycle (Figure 14.1) which incorporates having a concrete experience, observing and reflecting on this experience, forming abstract concepts and generalizations from the observation and reflection, and finally creating a hypothesis which will be tested in future experiences.

Concrete experience has two elements, the objective description of the facts as they happened, and the subjective description of feelings, thoughts, and perceptions that the

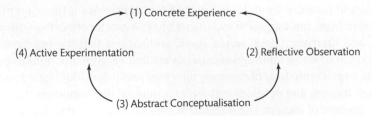

Figure 14.1 Kolb's model of experiential learning. Reproduced with permission.

individual had in the moment of having the experience. Reflective observation considers what meanings or significance the experience may have, and asks the individual to explore different perspectives on the experience. Abstract conceptualization requires the individual to theorize about the experience, either drawing on existing theories or creating their own hypothesis. Finally, active experimentation asks the question 'so what?', how will the individual change in the future to try out a new method in the light of learning from this experience.

Kolb points out that this is a recurring cycle, and that managers can regularly miss out elements of the cycle, thus reducing the effectiveness of their learning. Individuals may have a preference for focusing on one or two areas of this process in more detail than the others. For example, concrete experience and abstract conceptualization are methods that can be used to identify and consider the actual experiences leaders have, whereas practising reflective observation and active experimentation enables leaders to transform this experience into new and useful knowledge (Kolb and Kolb, 2005). Developing self-awareness of their preferences and working on the areas they frequently ignore can increase the effectiveness of their learning from experience.

A case in point: Kevin Roberts, CEO Saatchi & Saatchi Worldwide

Below is a reflection on his most formative leadership learning experience from a highly experienced leader of a global business. Observe how Kevin describes, reflects, theorizes, and applies his learning in this quote.

> When I was 9 years old I was asked by my games teacher to captain 10 and 11 year olds in my primary school football and cricket teams. Since then I've captained every sports team—and business unit—I've been involved with. I learned to relish the accountability early, and loved inspiring others—older and better than me—to join together as one unit and perform together at peak.
>
> Since then I've given responsibility and accountability to loads of people 'before they were ready' and have rarely been disappointed. At the heart of Saatchi & Saatchi's talent agenda today are the 4 things I learned back then that players in my primary soccer team thrived on. The timeless keys to inspiring leaders... Responsibility, Learning, Recognition and Joy.

A second popular model for analysing the experience of a leader or manager is Action Centred Learning (ACL), developed by John Adair (2005). This model focuses on how a leader leads a group to solve a problem or task. Adair proposes that there are three areas of need associated with the completion of the task, and that these three are all equally important. The first is the focus on the task, which includes the need to define the task and plan to achieve the required outcome. The second is the need to maintain the coherence and motivation of the team, which includes agreeing team standards, developing the team spirit, and clarifying team hierarchies. The final element is the needs of the individual, including the leader. Here the focus is on individual attention, relationship forming, encouragement and individualized motivation. The ACL model has been widely used in the development of military leaders, particularly in the UK.

Both of these models have been suggested for managers and leaders to utilize when learning from their own experience, as well as learning from experiences gained on leadership development courses. Experiential learning generally involves some form of problem solving activity, which may be in the outdoors. Gold, Thorpe, and Mumford (2010) suggest that outdoor management development can provide physical and mental challenges through solving problems in sometimes difficult conditions. Traditionally, outdoor development programmes have involved testing activities and difficult situations, designed to push the participant to the limit. Kanengeiter and Rajagopal-Durbin (2012) suggest that this type of physically challenging wilderness experience can give participants the opportunity to practise leadership, to learn how to lead from any organizational position, to develop the necessary skills to work well in and lead multi-cultural groups, to learn how to keep calm in stressful situations, and to discover the value of disconnecting from the world in order to realign oneself with your values.

Physical outdoor development can increase self-confidence and create a desire for future challenges, although there is some doubt as to how much of the impact of an outdoor event actually gets translated back into the work place (Watson and Vasilieva, 2007). Recently the outdoors has been used in a more thoughtful manner to aid the development of a key leadership skill, reflection.

 Blog box:

I am not naturally a reflective person. However, a powerful experiential exercise from a leader development programme has proved to me the value of taking time out to reflect on my purpose, values, and beliefs and how these are enacted in my leadership activities.

The exercise was called a solo. Following some reflective exercises designed to slow down and begin the process of reflection, I was placed alone on a hillside in the Borrowdale valley, with equipment to keep me warm and dry, and a very small amount of food and drink. There I sat for between 6 and 7 hours on a beautiful clear, cold December day, with only my thoughts and memories to consider.

The solo allowed me to bring to the surface things in work that I felt conflicted about, and areas where I wanted to improve. It has proved to be particularly powerful when used in conjunction with executive coaching, through which I have found some very useful ways to address some very difficult relationships at work. (CS)

Reflection

The ability to reflect has been identified as one of the main processes in using experiential learning successfully (Abe, 2011). We saw in Chapter 12 that a key element in authentic leadership was the ability to develop a good level of self-awareness. The process of reflection on leadership experience, and on values and beliefs, is seen as critical in developing high levels of self-awareness.

Reflection in the context of development is defined as serious thought or consideration. Through this serious thought a leader can examine experience and decide on the meaning to be gained from that experience. The process of reflection enables leaders to surface what may be a hidden understanding or belief about reality. Once this is surfaced, the leader can decide what is to be learned from this process (Amble, 2012).

Schon (1987) is credited with first highlighting the importance of reflection for leadership development. He describes in detail the way people hold tacit knowledge and are thus able to do things without necessarily being able to describe what they do or how they do it. It is this type of knowledge that allows them to act quickly in certain situations. Schon argues that reflection on our actions allows us to investigate and understand the tacit knowledge we have. This is particularly important when our learned activities lead to unforeseen results, and we have to re-examine what we do and how we do it to learn from the experience. Schon's work focused on this area as he was interested in why leaders do not typically learn from their mistakes. He proposed that reflecting on action, and reflecting in action may be helpful methods to allow leaders to improve their leadership.

Reflecting on action involves looking back at a later date on what has happened and examining how our previous knowledge may have contributed to the unforeseen outcome. Reflecting in action involves examining what is happening in the moment, during the action itself, which allows for immediate experimentation in order to come up with new ways of solving an issue. Schon suggests that similar to tacit knowledge, reflection in action is an intuitive process that can only be brought to light by later employing the technique of reflection on action (Schon, 1987).

De Rue et al. (2012) underline the importance of structured reflection to enhance leadership development. They point out that the experience of leadership is often a complex, highly visible, and confused one, involving ambiguous situations, numerous stakeholders, and multiple inputs. As such it is not a straightforward thing to reflect on. The authors propose that a structured After Event Review (AER) can help leaders who struggle to learn from their reflection on experience. They suggest that unstructured and self-directed reflection, along the lines of the Kolb cycle described above, are not as efficient and effective as the more structured approach of the AER. An AER is a facilitated process made up of three core elements; self-explanation, data verification, and feedback. During self-explanation an individual examines their behaviour and hypothesizes on the impact of their behaviour on a situation. Data verification asks the individual to challenge this initial view, asking for data on other possible influences on that situation which may also explain the outcome. The feedback element asks the individual to develop specific changes they will make to their own behaviour.

One common traditional method of encouraging reflection has been for leaders to keep a learning journal in which they record the facts and feelings of their leadership experiences. This leadership log can then be used as a set of data to use when reflecting on action, or carrying out an AER. Absalom and De Saint Léger (2011) suggest this is a method of encouraging a learner to be more engaged with their own learning, having to first chart and then reflect on what they have put in their log. The authors go on to suggest that modern web 2.0 technology can also act as an encouragement for reflection, especially the use of blogs to record experiences and reflections. The main differences between the journal and the blog is the public availability of a blog. Whereas a journal is primarily for oneself, a blog is primarily shared, even if this is just with a blog tutor, and this difference in relationship may influence the detail, depth, and effectiveness of the act of journaling. Reflection as a process for personal development, and the use of blogs to aid reflection will be explored further in Chapter 15.

Discussion point: Journaling

Write down an experience of leading that you have personally had. Describe the facts? Describe the feelings you had at the time. Why was this an important experience for you?
   Now discuss the following questions.

● What does the description of your experience tell you about yourself?

● What other possible perspectives can be taken on this experience?

● What have you learned here?

● In light of your learning, what will you do differently in the future?

From a critical perspective

This chapter began by defining a difference between leader development and leadership development. It is commonly acknowledged that most leadership development programmes actually focus on the leader rather than leadership (Day, Zaccaro, and Halpin, 2004; Day, 2011). These programmes also tend to be available for those individuals who either already hold a position of leadership, or are about to be promoted to such a position, raising the question of whether leadership development is focused on the wrong people (Mintzberg, 2004). If leaders can develop from across an organization, as shared or dispersed leadership theory suggests, then why are leader development programmes restricted to this 'elite'?

There is a need for programmes that focus on exploring the fundamental relationships between the leader and follower within the context of where they are leading. Raelin (2011) questions the approach to leadership development that removed individuals from their work context in order to give them knowledge in a classroom or outdoor environment. He advocates leadership development happening in the home environment, with all the constituents of the leadership relationship working together to develop the social practices that make up leadership for an organization. To this end, Raelin places learning and the ability to learn within the social context of work as the key to leadership development, and he advocates the use of techniques such as action learning to allow leaders to stop and learn on the job. Kempster and Iszatt-White (2012) agree with this position, and chart the journey of leadership development from a traditional classroom based activity to one that is more situated in the work experience, and accessed through interventions such as mentoring, coaching and action learning.

Cooper et al. (2005) also identify the context within which leadership development occurs as an important issue that leadership development should address, especially if the development is focused on aspects of authentic leadership. They suggest that development programmes must be genuine, avoiding the desire to be normative, but rather taking into account the context within which the leaders work, their individual differences, their national cultural differences, and being designed as a longer-term, in-work intervention.

Cooper at al. (2005) also raise an interesting issue about trigger events. As discussed in the previous section, scholars speculate that the identity of a leader can develop through difficult assignments and hardship. They cite the example of Mother Teresa who can trace her desire to help the poor of Calcutta to an encounter with a dying lady who could not get help at the Calcutta hospital. Bennis and Thomas (2002) discuss trigger events, suggesting that these can be transformative in nature, creating a desire in the individual to better their world in some way. They point out that these events do not have to be difficult, and can include a film or book that strikes a chord with the individual and inspires their life work. The question Cooper et al. (2005) raise is whether development programmes are able to deliberately create these trigger events and develop the personal insight that is necessary to transform the trigger event into something larger. Research would suggest that very few trigger events or, in the words of Janson, leadership formative experiences, occur on leadership development programmes (Janson, 2008). This raises the question of the value of off-site leadership development, and whether practitioners would be better focusing on developing a leader's ability to learn from experience, facilitated through processes of action learning and coaching.

Reynolds (2009) points out that many forms of management and leadership development, especially forms of experiential learning, fail to address the social and political realities of organizations in which people work. Whilst the design of activities on development programmes has become more sophisticated, the methods and tools used to draw the learning from these activities has had less attention paid to it. He highlights some good practice in this area, where educators have drawn on different perspectives to help leaders deepen their learning from experience, including aesthetics, feminism, discourse, and ecology.

Grint (2007) questions the premise of many organizations' leadership development activities. He suggests that the focus on measurement and selection through competency frameworks implies that the leader is more important than the situation, the context, and even the relationship with followers. This method also suggests that leaders are chosen by competencies they already possess, rather than on their ability to learn new approaches, or learn their way through the complex problems that face leaders. Grint proposes that learning to lead may be a social process rather than an individual one, and that we need to 'understand how *leadership* works *in* organizations rather than how formal *leaders* work on organizations' (Grint, 2007: 233).

This challenge against traditional measurement processes has led to traditional forms of evaluating leadership development programmes to be questioned. A traditional evaluation process, as exemplified by Kirkpatrick and Kirkpatrick (2006), seeks to assess the programme against preconceived learning outcomes focused on the knowledge, skills, and behaviours that have been learned and which are measurable or observable in some way. Watkins, Lysø, and deMarrais (2011) suggest that these fixed outcomes do not allow enough flexibility to completely measure the full range of outcomes of a programme, many of which may not be predictable in advance. Edwards and Turnbull (2013a, 2013b) build on this, suggesting that traditional evaluation focuses on the individual level, thus not considering the impact on learning of the cultural context in which a leader is called to lead. This culture may hinder the transfer of new leadership approaches or ideas back into the organization, and so can have a major effect on the outcomes of a development programme. They call for evaluation models that can evaluate innovative ideas of leadership, such as a distributed or complexity perspective on leadership.

These challenges to competency based leadership development programmes and calls for new forms of evaluation are all part of a desire to find new ways to help leaders develop their leadership. Some new ideas in this field will be explored in our final chapter.

Chapter summary

In this chapter we have considered:

- the ideas and theories of leader development
- the ideas and theories of leadership development
- the use of coaching and mentoring in leader development
- the foundations and application of action learning in leadership development
- the use of experiential learning and reflection in leadership development
- the limitations and critiques of current leadership development practice

 Integrative case study: General Mills Leadership Development

General Mills is one of the world's largest food companies, with brands such as Cheerios, Yoplait, Wanchai Ferry dumplings, and Häagen-Dazs. In October 2012 the Leadership Excellence magazine ranked General Mills and the General Mills Institute as the best large company leadership development programme. The ranking was based on measuring the quality of their leadership development against seven principles (Leadership Excellence, 2012):

- Is the vision of the program in line with the business strategy and outcomes, and meaningful to participants?
- How well designed is the programme? How credible is the content? How relevant is the curriculum? How customized is the programme?
- How broad is the involvement across the company and how deep the participation?
- What ROI measures are made and reported and to what degree is accountability for performance and results part of the programme?
- What are the qualifications of the presenters, how effective are their presentations, and how is the programme delivered?
- What do participants take away and apply to improve themselves, their families, teams, and volunteer work?
- What is the impact of the programme on all stakeholders? Does the programme and its participants benefit a broader community?

General Mills put their success down to continuously developing programmes that are at the cutting edge of leadership development. Across their business they offer an individual development plan focused on career advancement, mentoring, taught courses at the General Mills Institute, access to leadership experts, and funding for external courses.

In 2006 Janice Marturano, deputy counsel of General Mills, developed a partnership with University of Massachusetts Medical School to develop the Mindful Leadership Program series. The aim of this series is to develop the leader's ability to be present and pay close attention to themselves, to others, and to their work.

The Mindful Leadership Series uses a combination of meditation, yoga, and dialogue to develop the skills of presence and intense listening. With the series are programmes such as 'Cultivating Leadership Presence through Mindfulness', 'Catching lightning: Innovation and Mindfulness', and 'Mindful Leadership at Work'.

Participants on these courses report an increased ability to step back and examine their work priorities, making them more effective. They suggest that the course has enabled them to make decisions with greater clarity, and to listen more attentively to both themselves and others.

One commonly reported outcome of the course is the realization that it is a leader's responsibility to be fully present at each and every interaction with people. Course participants describe multitasking as merely switching attention between competing things very quickly. Through developing themselves on the leadership course, they are able to focus their attention on one element for a longer period, thus making them more effective, and more present.

General Mills has acted to integrate this approach into the business through the built environment of their office campus in Massachusetts. Every building now has a meditation room where employees can retreat in order to refocus themselves on the important matters of the day.

Whilst this leadership development initiative started out as a small, niche programme, it is now central to General Mills leadership courses, and is credited with driving a cultural change in the business. In 2011 *Fortune* magazine listed General Mills as the second best global company for leaders, suggesting that their leadership development programmes really are at the cutting edge of modern leader development.

Sources:

The Mind Business. *Financial Times*, 24 August 2012.

<http://www.ft.com/cms/s/2/d9cb7940-ebea-11e1-985a-0144feab49a.html#axzz2BR8VlLd3>. accessed 6 November 2012; Inside General Mills: Leadership program helps train the mind.

<http://www.generalmills.com/en/Media/Inside_General_Mills_archive/leadership_6_8_2010.aspx> accessed 6 November 2012; News Release: General Mills No.1 in Leadership development ranking.

<http://www.generalmills.com/en/Media/NewsReleases/Library/2012/October/LeadershipExcellence.aspx> accessed 6 November 2012; *Leadership Excellence* (2012) 2012 Leadership 500: Leadership Development Program Supplement 29 (10).

<http://www.leaderexcel2.com/edownloads/2012/10october/10le5215478/2012-leadership500.pdf.> accessed 6 November 2012;

<http://management.fortune.cnn.com/2011/11/03/top-companies-for-leaders/> accessed 6 November 2012.

Case study questions:

- The General Mills leadership programs have clearly been successful in developing leaders in the organization. Are meditation, taking time out, and being focused attributes you would ascribe to leaders you admire?

- Consider the literature that has been discussed in this chapter. What elements are General Mills drawing on in their programme to develop their leaders?

- From your knowledge of how leaders develop, what, if anything, would you say is missing from the General Mills approach?

Further reading

Doh, J. P. (2003) Can leadership be taught? Perspectives from management educators. *Academy of Management Learning and Education*, 2 (1) 54–68.

Gold, J., Thorpe, R., and Mumford, A. (2010) *Leadership and Management Development*. 5th edition. CIPD.

Grint, K. (2007) Learning to lead: can Aristotle help us find the road to wisdom? *Leadership*, 3 (2) 231–46.

Kempster, S. and Iszatt-White, M. (2012) Towards co-constructed coaching: exploring the integration of coaching and co-constructed autoethnography in leadership development. *Management Learning*, published online 25 June 2012 at <http://mlq.sagepub.com/content/early/2012/06/24/1350507612449959>.

15 The mindful leader

 Learning outcomes

On completion of this chapter you will:

- Be aware of the relative importance of a leader developing knowledge (episteme), and skills (techné)
- Understand the concept of phronesis (practical wisdom) and appreciate the crucial part this has to play in leadership judgement and decision making
- Gain a working knowledge of mindfulness and understand how the development of mindful practice can benefit leaders
- Appreciate the importance of reflexivity, reflection, and critical thinking in the development of managers and leaders
- Understand the importance of developing sound wisdom in judgement and decision making

---

 Blog box: Oluwafunke Amobi, Nigeria

Given the changing dynamics of the market place, and the ever increasing competitive pressures organizations face today, effective leadership and people management have fast become key differentiating competencies that most companies are seeking to remain ahead of the competition. After my course, I got promoted to General Manager level, with responsibilities which directly impact business strategy and organizational performance. Success in this role requires that I demonstrate a high level of leadership capability as well as design and deploy tools to support other line managers across the business to be effective leaders. I can reliably submit that the learning and deliberate practice of the mindfulness skills developed from the course has been a critical part of my success as a manager in the past five years.

I find that day to day I am constantly drawing from the 'mindful' suite of managerial skills, especially reflectivity and the ability to learn from experience, as well as active collaboration. To succeed in the global marketplace as a General Manager a strong sense of self-awareness and good managerial judgement are indispensable. My ability to self-reflect and review my actions and inactions as a manager has strongly aided my performance on the job. I am able to proactively ask the question 'what have I learnt from this? What am I missing?' I have also deliberately worked with my team leaders to develop these skills which have improved my ability to build high performing teams with a focus on continuous improvement. Today, I use the mindfulness skills to successfully lead cross functional project teams that deliver high impact business objectives.

Introduction

Henry Mintzberg suggests that 'Effective managing ... happens where art, science, and craft meet' (Mintzberg, 2005). This idea of managing and leading businesses being a blend of knowledge, skills, and artistry encapsulates the starting point for innovative approaches to leadership development that have been introduced onto MBA and corporate leadership programmes. A colleague of ours at Lancaster University Management School, Dr Peter Lenney, is well known for suggesting that teaching people how to manage or how to lead in a classroom is like trying to teach swimming by waving your arms around in a damp room. The fundamental knowledge of core business areas can be taught in classrooms, and traditional business and management programnes do this very well. But learning to manage and lead people is like learning a foreign language. In class you can learn the basics of the vocabulary, grammar, and punctuation, but you only really learn when you are immersed in practising the language in everyday situations. A focus on becoming a mindful leader seeks to integrate these perspectives, the teaching of core knowledge and skills, alongside the practice of managing and leading.

In 2009, the influential US leadership journal, *Leader to Leader*, published an article by Deepak Sethi which extolled the virtues of leaders making a practice of mindfulness. This article defined mindfulness as a technique of mental exercise and a rigorous mental practice that was practical, action orientated, and allowed leaders to develop focus, awareness of self and others, and an ability to lead in the moment (Sethi, 2009). More recently, the *Financial Times* (2012b) published an article about the mindful leadership course run by General Mills, described in the previous chapter. This was quickly followed by a blog by Bill George (2012) on the *Harvard Business Review* website, which advocated mindfulness as a means to develop employees to become better leaders. George describes mindfulness as being present and aware in any and every given moment, having awareness of your own thoughts and emotions as well as awareness of the impact of your behaviour on others. It is maintaining control in stressful situations, and having the ability to be acting, observing, and reflecting in a given moment. These articles demonstrate a growing interest in mindfulness as a method of developing leaders and leadership.

 Leadership in the media: Living in the moment

There are several films which can be used as examples of being mindful of staying in the present moment. The obvious series of films that has been used as an example before in this book are the Star Wars films. Here we see Jedi Knights frequently being advised to remain in the present. For example, the beginning of Episode I, *The Phantom Menace* (1999), has Jedi QuiGon Ginn advising a young Obi Wan Kenobi to keep his thoughts in the here and now, and not to lose sight of the present moment.

A less obvious example is the film, *Ferris Bueller's Day Off* (1986). Here Ferris Bueller, played by Matthew Broderick, takes a day off school to give himself and his friends experiences that will open up their thinking and allow them to challenge their categories. The desire to be in the present is summed up by the main quote of the film:

Life moves pretty fast. If you don't stop and look around once in a while, you could miss it.

A final example, and one that is popular with students, is *Kung Fu Panda* (2008). This sees the Kung Fu master, Oogway, mysteriously teaching the hero of the film, Po, that 'Yesterday is history. Tomorrow is a mystery. But today is a gift, and that is why it is called the present.' The film follows Po on his journey to become the Dragon Warrior, a journey that highlights the need for self-awareness, self-acceptance, and focus.

Where is your focus? Do you spend more time reviewing the past, worrying about the future, or being in the present?

Using the concept of mindfulness as a leadership development tool is something that is being introduced and refined on corporate leadership and business school programmes across the world. Mindful Leadership goes beyond the meditation techniques used by General Mills, and the descriptions given by Sethi and George. It is linked with Aristotle's concepts of episteme, techné, and phronesis, particularly focusing on developing phronesis, or practical wisdom, that helps leaders gain the judgement and decision making skills needed at senior levels of business.

This chapter will explore the concept of mindfulness. It will highlight the other influences that have shaped thinking on developing mindful leaders, and it will describe how leadership development programmes can aid the creation of mindful practitioners.

The concept of mindfulness, and its use as a leadership development method, is certainly not a mainstream leadership idea, and so this whole chapter will represent a critical perspective on leadership development. The ideas presented in this chapter will be interspersed with blogs from MBA alumni, and from senior managers who have been participants on mindful leadership courses. These business leaders describe how they have changed and developed through the adoption of mindful practices.

 Blog box: Maik Leonardt, Germany

The mindfulness course was one of my personal highlights during my MBA. The module encouraged us to deal with past experiences, and to reflect on what happened and what we would do differently if a similar situation would arise in the future.

What I found whilst doing these reflective exercises was that the technique we used (Gibbs reflective cycle) came quite naturally to me as I habitually asked myself 'what could I have done better'. However, I think the module helped me to apply reflection consciously and moreover structured my approach to learning from experience. During the reflective exercises we did I even learned from situations that happened 6 to 7 years ago. That was very powerful!

Previously, I felt that always thinking about past situations was a way of doubting my capabilities. Being aware of the power of this practice I came to realise that, contrary to my original beliefs, it helped me improve constantly. Amongst other benefits mindfulness has made me more self-confident about the way my brain works.

Making conscious reflection a habit significantly contributes to a manager's performance as he climbs up the ladder in an organization. I am convinced that it has substantially supported my career. Today I am responsible for 20 plus people including mid level managers. The power of reflection is one of the key managerial tools I implement myself and foster in my team of managers.

From a critical perspective

The traditional business school is focused on developing an individual's knowledge of a broad range of business areas. Through a variety of learning technologies, business school students have gained the analytical skills that enable them to understand and explore a variety of situations, and through this process, gain an ability to apply the same tools and models to analyse the real business situations they will face when returning to work.

This form of learning was developed in the United States in the early part of the twentieth century. In most traditional business schools, the core design of business tuition has remained largely unchanged since its inception. Scholars have begun criticizing this paradigm and the lack of obvious innovation, commenting that the traditional business school teaches the wrong people the wrong things in the wrong way (Mintzberg, 2005; Chia and Holt, 2008).

Knowledge taught in business schools focuses around ideas, concepts, theories, and models that have been refined through a scientific process to create normative descriptions of the world of managing and leading (Chia and Holt, 2008). Chia and Holt propose that this dominance of 'knowledge by representation' in business schools actually curtails the ability of students to gain the necessary practical skills required by managers and leaders in today's world.

The 'knowledge by representation' taught at many business schools has been very good at developing two things which are crucial for the leadership of an organization: knowledge and skills. This type of training prepares people to analyse and make leadership decisions about an organization as if it were a case study rather than a live complex, uncertain, paradoxic environment. Grint (2007) argues that leadership and learning to lead is not just an individual event, focused on the acquisition of knowledge and skills, but is actually a social process, something that is learned whilst in the very processes of working rather than something learned by studying the organization in a detached way. This makes the argument for more leadership development being done in the workplace, rather than in detached ways on business school programmes.

A case in point: Learning on the job

I was promoted to the position of Deputy Chief Executive of a Non Departmental Public Body (NDPB) in my early 40s. My career progression had not been easy. Female line managers had been anxious that no-one should overtake them; male colleagues were openly and publically scathing of their female peers.

Fortunately the Chief Executive of the NDPB was open-minded and keen to progress women. Unfortunately his open-minded approach meant that he also had a habit of upsetting ministers. He managed to do this in a spectacular fashion, about 6 months after my appointment. A decision he made before going on leave, scandalised ministers and hit the tabloids. By the time he returned from leave his desk had been cleared, the Chair I had been working with had resigned, and I found myself running a multi-million pound organization with a newly appointed Executive Chair. We both had to learn a lot very quickly, and we did.

Fortunately we established trust from the start. He was forthright but fair and objective. I knew the organization inside out and was keen to learn more from his commercial experience. We were forced into a position of zero based budgeting but within a year had secured contracts worth £40 million plus. No business school could have taught me so much so fast—although a business school did help.

- In your experience, has your knowledge of leadership and your identity as a leader developed more in a classroom or in live experience?

However, Grint is not suggesting the total abandonment of the traditional learning methods of a business school, as these give leaders two essential elements: episteme and techné.

Drawing on the philosophy of Aristotle, Grint suggests that whilst traditional programmes can develop skills (techné), and knowledge (episteme), they cannot necessarily develop practical wisdom (phronesis). For Grint, a leadership development programme should aim to develop all three elements, techné, episteme, and phronesis so that a leader can decide what to do, and have the understanding and skills in order to carry out this decision.

Grint's ideas are drawn from the *Nichomachean Ethics*, where Aristotle is offering advice to his son Nicomachus on how to deal with problems. The advice is to gain relevant knowledge (episteme) that helps you to understand the problem, to acquire the skills or tools (techné) that will help with how you deal with the problem, and to develop the practical wisdom (phronesis) that enables you to decide what to do.

Episteme can be thought of as scientific knowledge, ideas, and theories that are derived essentially through some form of experimentation, and are thought of as universal and context independent. A traditional general business and management programme can be thought of as an episteme giving machine. Models and theories, derived through research and experimentation, are taught to students so that their knowledge of the areas of business is enhanced. A general management student from any business school will leave with academic or theoretical knowledge of a number of core subjects, from marketing, finance, and operations, to organizational behaviour and strategy. Episteme gives a very good academic understanding of organizations, and can give an insight into why things are as they are, but it does not necessarily help the individual leader to decide what to do in a given situation. As Grint points out (2007: 235), episteme is analytic but not necessarily prescriptive.

Understanding something and having knowledge of why is useful, but a leader also needs the ability to act on this understanding. The knowledge of how to act is what Aristotle meant by techné. Techné has been described as know how, skills, or techniques that can be used to intervene in situations in order to produce something else. For example, a business course may train participants in good negotiation skills, but these skills have no purpose in themselves, they are to be used to achieve an end, in this case a successful negotiation. Grint (2007) argues that development programmes which focus on improving leaders' skills in certain areas start from the perspective that the leader is in some way deficient. They need to go on a course to learn to be more competitive, charismatic, or transformational. They could be better at communication, presentation, negotiation, consultancy, or networking. Some business courses even offer skills courses on dress, what to wear in certain circumstances, how to eat properly, and how to choose fine wine.

The techné elements of a business or management programme are extremely important, allowing students to learn some useful skills that are expected of leaders. These courses allow the students to add a practical, 'how to' element to the vast episteme that a business school teaches. However, the academic understanding of a subject area and the practical understanding of how to do something does not help a leader make the judgements and decisions that are required at senior levels of business. For this an individual needs practical wisdom, or phronesis, an ability to decide on what could and should be done.

Phronesis is 'essentially rooted in action rather than simply reflection' (Grint 2007: 236). Leaders can only develop this through the insights gained by experience, rather than academic learned knowledge, or practical skills development. Aristotle argues that this practical wisdom is an appreciation of what is good for both the individual and the wider society, and this includes some form of moral reasoning. According to Grint (2007), wisdom is:

- Moral knowledge
- Ethically practical action
- Context dependent
- Focused on the collective good rather than the personal good

This is the kind of reasoning that is required in situations of complexity and uncertainty, where there are no clear solutions, indeed where the outcome of any specific action is uncertain. In this environment a leader has to be comfortable making decisions in full knowledge that she does not have the full facts, and can therefore make a wrong decision. This calls for a certain amount of humility, something that is implied by the concept of phronesis. One might say that the uncertain environment has always been the realm of the leader, hence the need for the development of phronesis.

From the perspectives of episteme and techné, most leadership development courses are no different from each other. It is essential that leaders develop the knowledge and skills that will enable them to work at senior levels in organizations. However, few leadership development courses have considered methods of helping individuals develop phronesis that would allow leaders to better discern what the right thing to do would be.

Grint (2007), suggests that phronesis cannot be taught, but is rather a process that must be lived through. The application of phronesis is specific and different for every situation, and thus it is a concept that cannot be reduced to a theory or model that can be taught in a classroom. Rather, phronesis is something that is learned through experience as an apprenticeship, perhaps with the aid of a guide or mentor. The concept of mindfulness, and the adoption of mindful practices is one possible way to aid leaders in the development of their phronesis as a leadership ability.

 Blog box: Shankar Muthamperumal, India

'What did you learn from your education' is the question I have faced most frequently during job interviews. In answering this I discuss all the strategy frameworks, marketing concepts and accounting principles that I have learned, but there was never a moment where I had to recollect and say 'I learned a lot about myself'. I completely agree that these frameworks, concepts and principles are very crucial for any professional during their career, but they will be a mere structure if the person does not have practical wisdom, knowing when to use them, where to use them and how to use them. In order to achieve that capability a leader should have an excellent level of self-knowledge and awareness driven by exceptional emotional intelligence.

At this moment, I sincerely thank my business school for providing me the dual platform to learn business concepts through core modules, and to understand more about myself through the practice of mindfulness. Mindful practices, including writing reflective blogs, leadership essays and the gaining knowledge as an apprentice to a global CEO were excellent tools to accomplish self-reflection and the feedback sessions provided a valuable alternative perception on my strengths and weakness.

Such a mindful and action learning course has already guided me to frame my own 7 leadership and management principles to practise in my future career. In addition, the course has given me the comfort to practise and verify my principles through real time consulting projects and helped me to refine my principles before I take them to the battlefield. Now I can confidently say that these principles are excellent tools for a mindful leader to handle the exponentially growing problems of this VUCA (Volatile, Uncertain, Complex, Ambiguous) world.

Mindfulness

Professor Ellen Langer (1989, 1997), a Professor of Psychology at Harvard, gave one of the first key descriptions of the concept of mindfulness. Langer argued that as individuals we perceive reality as a series of concepts, and in order to organize these concepts our brains automatically place what we experience into categories, making it quick and easy for us to understand life as it occurs. If we did not have categories we would have to constantly understand things anew, and in the process continually challenge our beliefs. This ability to challenge our own thinking, to challenge old categories and to create new categories, is Langer's first characteristic of mindfulness. By contrast, a mindless individual will always accept what they believe as true, without attempting to understand their categories or assumptions.

Langer's second characteristic is an openness to new information. If one is constrained by categories, it will be hard to conceive of a different or better world. Being open allows an individual to challenge their categories, understanding that their previous beliefs and assumptions could be changed. This openness is perfectly captured in the quotation famously carved into the front step of the London office of Saatchi & Saatchi—'Nothing is impossible'!

The third characteristic seeks to broaden the thinking of an individual. Langer argues that a mindless approach is one where an individual may view things from a single perspective without the understanding that this perspective will be based on biases and assumptions, and on the situation or context. A mindful approach includes an awareness that there are multiple perspectives, based on multiple assumptions, given different meanings dependent on the context in which they are interpreted.

Langer also talks about a mindful person being more aware and involved in the process, in the doing of something, rather than being focused on the achievement or outcome. In this sense a mindful characteristic is to be interested in the means, or the how, more than the end, something that links mindfulness to ethical approaches which value people as a means in themselves, rather than a means to an end. Langer also advocates that a mindful thinker will allow their intuition to develop, as intuition allows us to break

---

 Blog box: Andrew Ponnambalam, Sri Lanka

Mindfulness has helped me to look at life in a completely different way. It helped me filter out all the superficial things in life and learn to appreciate what I had around me. Nothing is permanent, and you are only good so long as the bottom and top lines are growing. Therefore rather than getting carried away by momentary glamour and glitz associated with the corporate life the course has made me take a step back and re-evaluate my life and the road I was travelling.

It showed me the importance of not focusing on what I did not have, but instead making the most of what I had in life. My lack of capital for a prime example did not impede my ability to bring two Foreign Direct Investments valued at USD$200 million to Sri Lanka since 2011. I was able to finesse and use my skill of networking to bring in such investments to the country successfully.

Learning through reflection has influenced the way I work and has impacted both my personal life and business. Learning to control my emotions while having a kaleidoscopic, open mind has made me more objective when tackling issues. This has significantly improved my decision making skills. I also learnt why God gave me one mouth and two ears, to ensure I listen well before I speak.

The course has empowered me with skills to be a good leader, to see things for what they are, and to envision how I want it to be. Academic theory and actual results can be poles apart, and mindfulness made me value the practical experience and soft skills which are essential to make or break a deal.

free from the traditional categories that can restrain mindful thought (Langer 1989, 1997; Gartner, 2011).

These ideas of mindfulness are applied to the organizational area by Weick and his co-authors, who describe mindfulness as the 'capacity to induce rich awareness of discriminatory detail. By that we mean that when people act, they are aware of context, of ways in which details differ...and of deviations from their expectations' (Weick and Sutcliffe, 2006: 32). Langer's categories become Weick and Sutcliffe's expectations. The ability to be aware how you expect any given context to be, and to be able to question and refine these expectations are core concept of mindfulness. In this sense, mindfulness is about being present in the moment, with your full focus and attention on the act you are engaged in.

Weick and Sutcliffe are writing in the context of the management of high reliability organizations, where close attention to small details and changes can have a major impact on the reliability and safety of the organization. Their list of the characteristics of mindfulness reflect this context: a preoccupation with failure, a reluctance to simplify (or rely on categories), an awareness or sensitivity to on-going operations, a commitment to developing resilience, and a deference to expertise (Weick and Sutcliffe, 2006). The mindful leader here resists the natural tendency to reduce experiences into 'normal' events, and strives to focus intently on what is being observed, being aware of and managing distractions in order to gain a detailed understanding.

Case in point: Phil Jackson and the Chicago Bulls

Under coach Phil Jackson, the Chicago Bulls were one of the most successful basketball teams in US history. Jackson's book, *Sacred Hoops*, describes the approach to developing a team he used to such success with first the Bulls and later the LA Lakers. This included a core belief in the players being fully aware and present at all times through the practice of mindfulness.

To facilitate this, Jackson led the players in meditation sessions. The aim was to quiet the mind, so that they would all be fully aware and engaged during a game, and so they would be free to react to what was happening in the game without being distracted by negative thoughts and unhelpful judgements. This training included holding some practice sessions in complete silence. Jackson also developed a method of play that ensured all members of the team had to be present and involved in all aspects of the game in every single minute.

Jackson's approach combined a deep knowledge of the sport of basketball, with wisdom gained from ancient spiritual sources, including Christianity, Buddhism, and Native American principles. The core idea of developing mindfulness to be continuously present can be seen in the leadership development approaches being adopted by companies today.

Source: Jackson, P. and Delehanty H. (1995) *Sacred Hoops: Spiritual lessons of a hardwood warrior.* Hyperion, New York.

By contrast, a mindless leader would be content with operating from the categories that have been created by previous experience. They would not question these categories, nor so closely scrutinize an operation in a way that would enable them to question their own assumptions. Unknowingly, a mindless person is subject to self-fulfilling prophecies, as their actions are based on pre-existing categories which lead to repetitions of previous outcomes. These categories allows their minds to simplify the complexity of life in order to facilitate a quick route to decisions, and these decisions are then justified retrospectively, which serves to reduce any disappointment or anxiety at making what may be a wrong decision.

From an organizational perspective, the mindful leader must create the conditions and cognitive processes which will enable collective mindfulness (Weick, Sutcliffe, and Obstfeld, 1999). These include methods that help create shared understandings of situations across an organization. This concept of collective mindfulness has developed into the idea of Mindful Organizing (Gebauer, 2012).

The purpose of Mindful Organizing is to enable leaders and managers to be able to deal with uncertainty and unexpected events, over which they have little control and imperfect information. Mindful Organizing assumes that uncertainty exists everywhere in an organization and, because of this, control systems, processes, and procedures are limited in preventing incidents from happening. The most critical element is the ability to respond quickly, to change and adapt in light of new scenarios. This calls for a constant reassessment of what is actually happening now, asking leaders to be mindful of the current external and internal environments, to be preoccupied with failure (Weick and Sutcliffe, 2006), and to have productive paranoia (Collins and Hanson, 2011). Central to this is a belief that learning is crucial to everything. By seeing every mistake, complaint, problem, and issue as a learning possibility, and by adopting processes of mindful reflection that help bring out this learning, leaders can develop mindful organizations that are characterized by their adaptability and resilience.

Similar to Chia and Holt's views on the knowledge taught at business schools, Mindful Organizing questions the belief that decisions can be made rationally. Instead, there is an acceptance that any decision will create conditions of risk in other areas, requiring the leader to be constantly vigilant about the impact of their decision making. This approach requires leaders to apply multiple perspectives to the rational data they receive, constantly questioning, debating, doubting, and contradicting the knowledge they hold. A mindful approach resists the desire to simplify in order to allow decision making to be easier. Rather it requires the leader to engage with the complexity of any situation, encouraging multiple perspectives in order to ensure they are getting a full picture of the present situation (Gebauer, 2012).

Becoming mindful, therefore, is a process of developing the ability to pay close attention to things that previously may have been taken for granted or assumed. It is the process of identifying one's own mental models and challenging these in order to be open to new perspectives and ways of operating. It is a continuous process of remaining present in any and every moment, ensuring that the leader remains fully aware of themselves, their thinking and actions, and of the experiences they are having. As such it is something that allows the leader to be aware of their learning in each situation, and thus develop their phronesis.

Developing these mindful abilities is not a quick process. It requires leaders to fully reject the traditional premise of the leader being the hero, having all the answers, and solving all the problems. Instead the leader must be willing to admit what they do not know, and to show a desire to continually learn their way through problems. In this sense it places an importance on leadership, on the ability to work through relationships with numerous others in order to gain multiple understandings of situations, and to make decisions with the awareness that these are only temporary solutions.

Mindfulness and the development of phronesis also suggest that leaders learn mainly from their lived experience (Kempster, 2006), and that there are key practices they can develop that will help them to draw out their learning from every experience. Ashford and DeRue (2012) call these practices Mindful Engagement, a combination of having a learning mindset, practising learning behaviours, and engaging in a process of reflection to help question categories or assumptions.

The learning mindset means that leaders view every experience as an opportunity to gain new knowledge and a different understanding of the task at hand.

Learning behaviours include a willingness to try new situations, to find new experiences in order to learn by doing. This is coupled with seeking feedback on collaborative conduct, or how others see the behaviour of the leader, and regulating emotions. Ashford and DeRue suggest that experiences which lead someone to have an excessive positive or negative emotional reaction can obstruct the learning process, and a conscious regulation of emotions can aid the individual in being able to reflect on and thus learn from experiences.

The final element of Mindful Engagement, reflection, is described by Ashford and DeRue (2012: 151) as 'an active process of probing cause-and-effect, questioning assumptions, and analyzing the meaning of experiences'. The purpose of reflection is to gain a deeper understanding of what actually happened, of why the group were successful or not, of how each individual member and the complexity of their interaction contributed to this success or failure. Reflection encourages leaders to question the categories that have influenced their thinking and action, their cognitive and collaborative conduct, in that experience.

Chapter 14 contains a more detailed discussion on reflection as a leadership development process. One approach that seeks to use the beauty of nature to enhance the practice of reflection, and thus the ability to understand experiences and categories, is wilderness thinking. Wilderness thinking blends the ancient spiritual tradition of a retreat with the use of a beautiful natural environment as a means to aid reflection. A retreat has traditionally been used as a time to reconnect with that which is most important, a time of solitude in which to consider one's life, and to ask fundamental questions of meaning and purpose. This concept of retreat has been brought into leadership programmes to focus the individual on the self-awareness aspect of leadership development, using the outdoors as a classroom that will aid the development of self-reflection capabilities. The idea of retreat has been blended with the idea of a 'solo', that was developed by the Outward Bound movement in the UK as a means for teaching individual survival skills whilst at the same time creating a space on a personal development programme for a participant to consider who they are, where they are going, and what is their purpose in life. The original solo consisted of being isolated in a remote place for a period of days. Wilderness thinking has developed this into a one-day experience, where the main focus is now to create the time and space for a leader to reflect without distraction. It has been argued that using the remote outdoors for a short, intensive period of quieting the mind and focusing attention on reflection enables the participants to develop reflective skills and have time to examine their leadership capabilities, leading to more sustainable outcomes of the leader development process (Watson and Vasilieva, 2007).

RESEARCH IN FOCUS: The impact of being mindful

Ashford and DeRue (2012) describe a piece of research they have conducted on the effects of mindful practice amongst MBA students. They split their MBA students into two sets, both of which would go through the same experiential activities over an 8-month period. One group were asked to reflect on experience in an unstructured way, and the other using a method called an after event review (AER). The after event review allows the group to systematically analyse their behaviour and judge how this behaviour contributed to the outcomes of the group's work. This is done from three perspectives. One is self-evaluation of behaviour and outcomes. The second is data verification, where the self-evaluations in the group are discussed and different views on the experience gained. Finally there is a process of giving and gaining feedback. The AER allows the students to consciously process information they have automatically gathered during the experience (Ellis and Davidi, 2005).

In Ashford and DeRue's research the groups who used the AER method of structured reflection saw an 8 per cent increase in the ratings they received of the effectiveness of their leadership, a 9 per cent increase in the number of job offers they received, and a 10 per cent increase in their salary offers when compared to the other group.

Whilst these results are from a small scale study, they prove extremely interesting for MBA students, who generally have decided to do an MBA in order to gain a better job and a higher salary!

Source: Ashford, S. J. and DeRue, D. S. (2012) Developing as a leader: the power of mindful engagement. *Organizational Dynamics*, 41, 146–54.

Discussion point: The after event review

Leaders are constantly working in groups or teams to deliver important outcomes for the organization. After your next piece of group work has finished, gather your group and conduct an after event review:

- Ask each member to individually evaluate their own behaviour and allow each group member to explain to the group how this behaviour contributed to the success of failure of the activity. Do not contradict or interrupt each group member during their explanation.

- Once all members have had their say, discuss as a group the different perspectives being presented. Be aware of and open to those perspectives that challenge your own.

- As a group, agree on the main learning points from this review and record this as feedback. Consider how you individually and as a group could change your behaviour in order to improve performance in the future.

Chapter summary

In this chapter we have considered:

- the relative importance of a leader developing knowledge (episteme), and skills (techné)
- the importance of phronesis (practical wisdom) in leadership judgement and decision making
- definitions of mindfulness and how the development of mindful engagement can benefit leaders
- the importance of reflexivity, reflection and critical thinking in the development of managers and leaders
- how to develop sound wisdom in judgement and decision making

Integrative Case Study: Developing mindful leaders

The following case is derived from a combination of leadership development programmes which use the core principle of mindfulness to aid the development of leaders and leadership.

The concept and practice of mindfulness, the gaining of episteme, techné, and especially phronesis, and an active process of openness, experimentation, and reflection are the core ideas that underpin mindful leadership programmes run by companies and business schools. This approach requires participants to be open, honest, and self-critical of their own actions, continually reflecting on and learning from their experience. It requires them to actively seek out new opportunities to lead in their work or private lives, in order to enrich the experiences they can then reflect on. It requires them to pro-actively seek out group working that will stretch their abilities, allow them to try out the new knowledge and skills they have learned, and give them opportunities for reflection and the questioning of their own mental categories.

When considering how best to develop phronesis, mindful programmes tend to utilize some knowledge (episteme) and skills (techné) training to begin the process of developing mindful leaders. The knowledge and skills that have proven most useful for drawing practical wisdom from experience include:

- Reflexivity—focused on a deep self-awareness of collaborative conduct
- Critical thinking skills
- Collaborative-deliberative competence
- Reflectivity and an increased ability to learn from experience
- Understanding of the nature of knowledge
- Criticality—particularly with respect to the ideas, theories, and concepts taught at business schools
- Managerial/business judgement and decision making practices

By developing these areas a mindful leader can become someone who is reflective and reflexive, proactively learning from experience through reflection, and constantly being 'mindful' of her personal cognitive, deliberative, and collaborative conduct and her continuous personal development.

 Blog box: Jeff MacKenzie, Canada

In the academic world, textbook teaching has to be generalised to a certain extent to appeal to a wide audience. This is also the case in most businesses, which have generalised training programs and feedback mechanisms. The difficulty in taking a generalised approach is that it is extremely difficult to cater to different people with unique personalities and various sets of skills.

Mindfulness has helped me to better understand and interpret generalised information so I can more effectively apply what I learn and use it according to my own specific strengths and weaknesses. Many people do not take the time to reflect on the deeper meaning of what they are being taught. Mindfulness has taught me to open my mind and get rid of the filters that prevent information from being clearly and impartially received. I have learned the value in taking time to understand more than just the language that is being communicated but to understand the deeper meaning of a person's actions and intentions.

Most people understand very little of what they are actually being told. Moving into leadership positions in the future, mindfulness has, above all, helped me learn how to effectively learn. I have experienced first-hand the value in taking time to step back and reflect on the past so that I can make better decisions in the future.

(Continued...)

Reflexivity, Critical Thinking and Reflection

As discussed earlier, the reflection process is essential for leaders to gain the most learning from experience. However, reflection in many development programmes tends to be focused on individual leader development. By combining reflection with reflexivity, the focus can be put on both leader and leadership development. Reflexivity is a sociological concept which highlights the involvement and influence of the person or self in any given situation. The practice of being constantly reflexive is one that asks leaders to constantly be aware of and question the assumptions and beliefs on which arguments are built (Holland, 1999). This requires them to both understand and be aware of their own prejudices, assumptions, and beliefs, and to critically question the prejudices, assumptions, and beliefs of the episteme that they have been taught by both business schools and their own functional experience. Drawing on the work of Thomas Nagel (1986), leaders can be challenged to question the very idea of objectivity and thus develop self-awareness of their assumptions and biases (categories).

The reflexive process begins with training in critical thinking skills (techné). This allows leaders to begin to question their episteme, the very ideas that they 'mindlessly' assumed to be true. The development of high level critical thinking and discourse skills allows leaders to gain a deeper critical understanding of the contribution of leadership theory to actual leadership practice. Leaders are generally aware that the output of business schools do not always speak to practice, and critical thinking development will allow practising leaders to become mindful of the limitations of the traditional ideas around leadership that have made up the majority of company and business school training on leadership.

Underpinning the development of reflexivity is the formation of reflective skills, and a strong habit of reflective practice. Delegates on leadership programmes need space to practise how to be reflective practitioners by having to systematically, thoughtfully, and frequently reflect on their experiences. The involvement of a tutor to facilitate and deepen these reflections can aid this process, but this should always be done with the purpose of enabling the leader to be self-sustaining in their reflective practice.

Structured reflection allows students to develop the quality of their self-awareness, critical thinking, and collaborative skills that are vital to effective leadership. To aid this process of reflection, leaders need to ensure they are engaging in different and varied experiences so that they are gaining appropriate experiences that can be used as reflective learning opportunities. These experiences could include challenges or projects with different organizations, company exchanges, team working on different projects, interaction with senior business people, international trips to gain knowledge of business in different countries, and the use of wilderness thinking activities (Watson and Vasilieva, 2007). The aim here is to allow leaders to develop an ability to be continuously self-critical, to apply critical thinking to their own thinking and behaviour, to their cognitive and collaborative conduct.

Some mindful leadership programmes will supplement experiences with psychometric tests to aid leaders with the development of their self-awareness. Blending psychometrics with online critical thinking courses and tests can help leaders to develop the awareness and criticality necessary for them to question their assumptions and categories.

This approach to psychometric tools reflects an understanding that psychometric assessment is not merely a process that discovers some unchangeable personal chemistry. Rather it is an active process of discovery. Active reflection on one's psychometric profile can lead to substantial personal development, and it is used on leadership programmes as one part of a leader's journey to a greater understanding of themselves and others.

The writing of reflective blogs can further develop the ability to reflect on and learn from experience. This is especially important during and after each experiential event on a programme. Reflective blogs are a useful method for leaders to use the principles of mindfulness and criticality when reflecting on experiences as they are happening and once they have finished. The intent here is to aid the development of self-awareness and phronesis (practical wisdom). These are particularly useful in programmes that aim to develop leaders in their own context, using real workplace experiences as the focus of reflections. Here the blogs would look to explore some of the systemic issues within an organization that enable or constrain the practice of effective leadership.

The blogging process requires leaders to adopt a continuous learning mindset for all the experiences they have. The blog is a learning focused one, that focuses on the individual's collaborative conduct and that of the people they interact with during their experience. Through regular reflective blogging, leaders can:

- Confront and understand the difference between their desired conduct and their actual conduct
- Gain insights into themselves and in doing so to become more reflexive
- Become aware of the creative tension in seeing the disjunctions between their thinking, intensions, and observed behaviours

The reflection has to be deliberate and focused, with a consideration of their own thinking and action, as well as the action of others. Ideally leaders work with blog tutors, who give feedback on the mindfulness of their thinking as evidenced in the blogs, and who can help to develop the depth of their criticality and the practical usefulness of their insights.

A further aid to reflection that is specific to leadership is a hand written journal which records experiences and reflections on all the moments during the year when participants have encountered leaders or observed what they consider to be good or bad leadership. This could include their own and other CEOs, leaders who have given talks they have attended, examples they have read about in the media or academic research, characters they have observed in the film and entertainment media or on the sports field, leaders they have encountered during their work, and individuals demonstrating leadership on courses they have been involved in. This type of journal gives developing leaders a source of evidence from which they can challenge their previous assumptions about what a leader looks like and what the act of leadership actually entails.

Businesses that are serious about developing mindfulness and phronesis in their leaders would also offer opportunities for them to test out their practical wisdom in action. This would involve opportunities to engage in live judgement and decision making with the senior management of the business. By asking aspiring leaders to understand the main aspects of their business, and suggest the areas that the CEO should focus on in the coming year, businesses give future leaders the opportunity

---

 Blog box: Pulaq Pathak, UK

The phrase 'the art is in hammering, and not in the hammer' resonates in my mind whenever I think of the mindfulness module.

This module helped me gain management insights, but I was not sure if all this was just philosophical and wondered if I would be able to execute these once I was back in the corporate world. More than a year into work after the MBA now, I see my answers in many circumstances.

There are many people who have inspired and guided me through my life and career. However, it is now that I am able to spot characteristics that differentiate them as successful managers and leaders. I realise that there are different coloured lenses to look at things as opposed to just black or white, just right or wrong. This makes me more observant in my workplace and gives me a choice of the characteristics I would like to practise more.

If I need to understand a financial balance sheet, I can revise a few chapters from my MBA finance book (the hammer) and get up to speed quickly. Mindfulness put me into the habit of present awareness and reflective thinking which cannot be found in books. It is a continuous process. Sometimes when I am on the train from work, I unconsciously blog in my mind and reflect on that days events and decisions. It seems that the mindful blogs I wrote during the course have become a habit. A habit that I will cherish for life.

(Continued...)

to develop their thinking on what is the right thing to do from a senior leadership context. To fully answer this question, participants would need to gain a deeper knowledge (episteme) about their business and its clients and markets, use their skills (techné) in the analysis, and utilize their phronesis to decide what could and should be done.

These judgement and decision making sessions offer direct engagement with the hard, real-time realities of a competitive global business. Through openly engaging with this experience, coupled with a high degree of personal reflection and reflexivity, practical wisdom and judgement can be developed.

In conclusion, mindful leadership courses develop the practices of mindfulness described in this chapter. The intention of these courses is for leaders to be more open to, and able to learn from, new experiences. They aim to create a greater degree of awareness of self and others, to develop the ability to understand and question one's own beliefs, assumptions, and categories, and to teach a set of practices that allows leaders to practise leadership through the continual pursuit of practical wisdom.

Case study questions:

- In light of the understanding you have gained from this chapter, write down your own definition of mindfulness. This is the episteme you have gained.

- Which practice will you adopt to develop your own mindful ability? This is the techné you have gained.

- Consider how you can gain as much learning from your past and future experiences as possible, both for yourself and for the groups you will work in. In this way you can begin to consciously develop your phronesis.

Further reading

Ashford, S. J. and DeRue, D. S. (2012) Developing as a leader: the power of mindful engagement. *Organizational Dynamics*, 41, 146–54.

Grint, K. (2007) Learning to lead: can Aristotle help us find the road to wisdom? *Leadership*, 3 (2), 231–46.

Gartner, C. (2011) Putting new wine into old bottles: Mindfulness as a micro-foundation of dynamic capabilities. *Management Decisions*, 49 (2), 253–69.

Weick, K. E., Sutcliffe, K. M., and Obstfeld, D. (1999) Organizing for high reliability: processes of collective mindfulness. *Research in Organizational Behavior*, 21 (1), 81–123.

References

Abe, J. A. (2011) Positive emotions, emotional intelligence, and successful experiential learning. *Personality and Individual Differences*, 51, 817–22.

Absalom, M. and De Saint Léger, D. (2011) Reflecting on reflection: Learner perceptions of diaries and blogs in tertiary language study. *Arts and Humanities in Higher Education*, 10, 2, 189–211.

Adair, J. E. (2005) *How to Grow Leaders: The Seven Key Principles of Effective Leadership Development*. London: Kogan Page.

Adams, J., Hayes, J., and Hopson, B. (1976) *Transition: Understanding and managing personal change*. London: Martin Robertson and Company.

Alimo-Metcalfe, B. (1995) An investigation of male and female constructs of leadership and empowerment. *Women in Management Review*, 10, (2, 3–8.

Alimo-Metcalfe, B. and Alban-Metcalfe, R. J. (2001) The development of a new transformational leadership questionnaire. *Journal of Occupational and Organisational Psychology*, 74, 1–28.

Allen, T. D., Eby, L. T., Poteet, M. L., Lentz, E. and Lima, L. (2004) Career benefits associated with mentoring for protégés: A meta-analysis *Journal of Applied Psychology*, 89, 27–136.

Alvesson, M. (2003) Critical organization studies. In B. Czarniawska and G. Sevon (eds), *Nordic Lights*. Malms: Liber/Oslo:Abstrackt.

Alvesson, M. and Sveningsson, S. (2003) Managers doing leadership: The extra-ordinarization of the mundane. *Human Relations*, 56, 12, 1435–59.

Alvesson, M. and Willmott, H. (2002) Producing the appropriate individual: identity regulation as organizational control. *Journal of Management Studies*, 39, 5, 619–44.

Alvesson, M. and Willmott, H. (eds) (2003) *Studying Management Critically*. London. Sage Publications.

Amagoh, F. (2009) Leadership development and leadership effectiveness. *Management Decision*, 47, 6, 989–99.

Amble, N. (2012) Reflection in action with care workers in emotional work. *Action Research*, 10, 3, 260–75.

Ancona, D., Bresman, H., and Caldwell, D. (2009) The X-Factor: Six steps to leading high-performing X-teams. *Organizational Dynamics*, 38, 3, 217–24.

Andersen, J. A. (2005) Leadership, personality and effectiveness. *The Journal of Socio-Economics*, 35, 6, 1078–91.

Andrews, K. R. (1987) *The Concept of Corporate Strategy* 3rd edition. Scarborough, ON: Irwin.

Antonakis, J. (2010) Predictors of Leadership: The Usual Suspects and the Suspect Traits in A. Bryman, D. Collinson, K. Grint, B. Jackson, and M. Uhl-Bien (eds), *The SAGE Handbook of Leadership*. London: Sage Publications.

Appelbaum, S. H., Berke, J., Taylor, J., and Vazquez, J. A. (2008) The role of leadership during large scale organizational transitions: lessons from six empirical studies. *Journal of American Academy of Business*, 13, 1, 16–24.

Ashcraft, K. L. and Mumby, D. K. (2004) *Reworking Gender: A Feminist Communicology of Organization*. London: Sage.

Ashford, S. J. and DeRue, D. S. (2012) Developing as a leader: the power of mindful engagement. *Organizational Dynamics*, 41, 146–54.

Avery, G. C. and Bergsteiner, H. (2011a) *Sustainable Leadership: Honeybee and locust approaches*. Abingdon: Routledge.

Avery, G. C. and Bergsteiner, H. (2011b) Sustainable leadership practices for enhancing business resilience and performance. *Strategy and Leadership*, 39, 3, 5–15.

Avolio, B., Luthans, F. & Walumbwa, F.O., (2004). Authentic leadership: Theory-building for veritable sustained performance. *Working paper*. Gallup Leadership Institute, University of Nebraska, Lincoln.

Avolio, B. J. and Gardner, W. L. (2005) Authentic leadership development: getting to the root of positive forms of leadership. *Leadership Quarterly*, 16, 315–38.

Avolio, B. J., Walumbwa, F. O., and Weber, T. J. (2009) Leadership: Current theories, research, and future directions. *Annual Review of Psychology*, 60, 421–49.

Awamleh, R. A. (2003) A test of the transformational leadership model: The case of Jordanian bankers. Paper presented at the Academy of International Business (UK Chapter), Leicester, 11–12 April.

Babiak, P., Neumann, C. S., and Hare, R. D. (2010) Corporate Psychopathy: Talking the Walk. *Behavioral Sciences and the Law*, 28, 174–93.

Badaracco, J. (2002) *Leading Quietly: An unorthodox guide to doing the right thing*. Boston, MA: Harvard Business Press.

Ball, K. and Carter, C. (2002) The charismatic gaze: everyday leadership practices of the 'new' manager. *Management Decision*, 40, 6, 552–65.

Balogun, J. (2006) Managing change: Steering a course between intended strategies and unintended outcomes. *Long Range Planning*, 39, 29–49.

Balogun, J. and Hope-Hailey, V. (2004) *Exploring Strategic Change*. 2nd edition. Harlow: FT Prentice Hall.

Balogun, J. and Johnson, G. (2005) From intended strategies to unintended outcomes: The impact of change recipient sensemaking. *Organization Studies*, 26, 11, 1573–601.

Balthazard, P. A., Waldman, D. A., and Warren, J. E. (2009) Predictors of the emergence of transformational leadership in virtual decision teams. *The Leadership Quarterly*, 20, 651–63.

Baranik, L. E., Roling, E. A. and Eby, L. T. (2010) Why does mentoring work? The role of perceived organizational support. *Journal of Vocational Behavior* 76, 3, 366–73.

Barge, J. K. (1996) Leadership skills and the dialectics of leadership in group decision making. In R. Y. Hirokawa and M. S. Poole (eds), *Communication and Group Decision Making* 2nd edition. Thousand Oaks, CA: Sage, 301–42.

Bartunek, J. M. and Necochea, R. (2000) Old insights and new times: Kairos, Inca cosmology and their contribution to contemporary management inquiry. *Journal of Management Inquiry*, 9, 2, 103–13.

Bass, B. M. (1960) *Leadership, psychology, and organizational behaviour*. New York: Harper

Bass, B. M., (1985) *Leadership and Performance*, New York: Free Press.

Bass, B. M. (1990) 'Concepts of leadership', in B.M. Bass and R. M. Stodgill, *Handbook of Leadership: Theory, Research and Managerial Applications*. New York: Free Press.

Bass, B. M. (1996) *A New Paradigm of Leadership: An inquiry into transformational leadership*. Alexandria, VA: U.S. Army Research Institute for the Behavioural and Social Sciences.

Bass, B. M. (1998) The ethics of transformational leadership. In J. Ciulla (ed.), *Ethics: The heart of leadership*. Westport, CT: Preager, 169–92).

Bass, B. M. and Avolio, B. J. (1990) The implications of transactional and transformational leadership for individual, team and organisational development. *Research in Organisational Change and Development*, 4, 231–72.

Bass, B. M. and Avolio, B. J. (1994) *Improving Organisational Effectiveness through Transformational Leadership*. Thousand Oaks, CA: Sage.

Bass, B. M. and Avolio, B. J. (1997) *Full Range Leadership Development: manual for the Multifactor Leadership Questionnaire*. Palo Alto, CA: Mindgarden.

Bass, B. M. and Riggio, R. E. (2006) *Transformational Leadership* 2nd edition. Mahwah, NJ: Lawrence Erlbaum.

Bass, B. M. and Steidlmeyer, P. (1999) Ethics, character, and authentic transformational leadership behaviour. *The Leadership Quarterly*, 10, 2, 181–217.

BBC News (2012) *Alibaba: Former executive detained amid bribe probe*. <http://www.bbc.co.uk/news/business-18732720> accessed 6 July 2012

Beer, M., Eisenstat, R. A., and Spector, B. (1990) Why change programs don't produce change. *Harvard Business Review*, November–December, 158–166.

Bennis, W. G. and Nanus, B. (1985) *Leaders: The strategies for taking charge*. New York, Harper & Row.

Bennis, W. G. and Thomas, R. J. (2002) Crucibles of leadership. *Harvard Business Review*, 5–11 September.

Biggart, N. W. and Hamilton, G. G. (1987) An institutional theory of leadership. *Journal of Applied Behavioral Science*, 23, 4, 429–41.

Blake, R. R. and McCanse, A. A. (1991) *Leadership Dilemmas—Grid Solutions*, Houston, TX: Gulf, 29.

Blake, R. R. and Mouton, J. S. (1981) Management by Grid Principles or Situationalism: Which? *Group and Organizational Studies*, 6, 4, 439–63.

Blanchard, K., Zigarmi, P., and Zigarmi, D. (2000) *Leadership and the One Minute Manager: Increase Effectiveness by being a good leader*. London: Harper Collins.

Bligh, M. C. and Robinson, J. L. (2010) Was Gandhi 'charismatic'? Exploring the rhetorical leadership of Mahatma Gandhi. *The Leadership Quarterly*, 21, 844–55.

Bligh, M. C. and Schyns, B. (2007) The romance lives on: Contemporary issues surrounding the romance of leadership. *Leadership*, 3, 3, 343–60.

Blowfield, M. and Murray, A. (2011) *Corporate Responsibility*. 2nd edition. Oxford: Oxford University Press.

Boal, K. B. and Hooijberg, R. (2001) Strategic leadership research: Moving on. *The Leadership Quarterly*, 11, 4, 515–49.

Boal, K. B. and Schultz, P. L. (2007) Storytelling, time, and evolution: the role of strategic leadership in complex adaptive systems. *The Leadership Quarterly*, 18, 411–28.

Bolden, R. (2011) Distributed leadership in organizations: a review of theory and research. *International Journal of Management Reviews*, 13, 251–69.

Boot, R. L. and Reynolds, M. (eds) (1983) *Learning and Experience in Formal Education*. Manchester: Manchester Monographs.

Bowers, D. G., and Seashore, S. E. (1966) Predicting organizational effectiveness with a four-factor theory of leadership. *Administrative Science Quarterly*, 11, 2, 238–63.

Boyatzis, R. E. (1982), *The Competent Manager: A Model of Effective Performance*. New York: John Wiley & Sons.

Bratton, J., Grint, K., and Nelson, D. (2004) *Organizational Leadership*. Mason, OH: SouthWestern/Thomson.

Bresnen, M. J (1995) All things to all people? Perceptions, attributions, and constructions of leadership. *The Leadership Quarterly*, 6, 4, 495–513.

Brown, M. E. and Treviño, L. K. (2006) Ethical Leadership: a review and future directions. *The Leadership Quarterly*, 17, 6, 595–616.

Bryk, A. (1999) *Trust in Schools*. New York: Russell Sage Foundation.

Bryman, A. (1986) *Leadership and Organisations*. London: Routledge & Kegan Paul.

Bryman, A. (1992) *Charisma and Leadership in Organisations*. London: Sage.

Burgoyne, J. G. and Reynolds, M. (eds) (1997) *Management Learning*. London: Sage, 249.

Burgoyne, J. G., and Hodgson, V. E. (1983) Natural learning and managerial action: a phenomenological study in the field setting, *Journal of Management Studies*, 20, 3, 387–99.

Burgoyne, J. G. and Stewart, R. (1977) Implicit learning theories as determinants of the effect of management development programmes, *Personnel Review*, 6, 2, 5–14.

Burke, C. S., Stagl, K. C., Klein, C., Goodwin, G. F., Salas, E., and Halpin, S. M. (2006) What type of leadership behaviours are functional in teams? A meta-analysis. *The Leadership Quarterly*, 17, 288–307.

Burns, J. McG. (1978) *Leadership*. New York: Harper and Row.

Bushe, G. R. and Chu, A. (2011) Fluid teams: Solutions to the problems of unstable team membership. *Organizational Dynamics*, 40, 181–8.

Calder, Bobby J. (1977) An attribution theory of leadership. In B. M. Staw and G. R. Salancik (eds), *New Directions in Organisational Behaviour*. Chicago, IL: St Clair Press.

Caldwell, R. (2003) Change leaders and change managers: different or complimentary? *Leadership and Organization Development Journal*, 24, 5, 285–93.

Cannella Jr, A. A. and Monroe, M. J. (1997) Contrasting perspectives on strategic leaders: Towards a more realistic view of top managers. *Journal of Management*, 23, 3, 213–37.

Carlin, J. (2008) *Playing the Enemy: Nelson Mandela and the game that made a nation* London: Atlantic Books.

Carlyle, T. (1846) *On heroes, hero-worship and the heroic in history*. New York: Wiley and Putnam.

Carroll, A. B. (1979) A three dimensional conceptual model of corporate performance. *Academy of Management Review*, 4, 4, 497–505.

Carroll, A. B. (1991) The pyramid of corporate social responsibility: toward the moral management of organizational stakeholders. *Business Horizons*, July-August, 39–48.

Carroll, A. B. (1999) Corporate social responsibility: evolution of a definitional construct. *Business & Society*, 38, 3, 268–95.

Carroll, A. B. and Buchholtz, A. (2011) *Business and Society: Ethics and stakeholder management*. 8th edition. Andover: South-Western/Cengage Learning.

Carroll, B. and Levy, L. (2008) Defaulting to management: Leadership defined by what it is not. *Organization*, 15, 1, 75–96.

Carroll, B., Levy, L., and Richmond, D. (2008) Leadership as practice: Challenging the competency paradigm. *Leadership*, 4, 4, 363–79.

Cascio, W. F. and Shurygailo, S. (2003) E-leadership and virtual teams. *Organizational Dynamics*, 31, 4, 362–76.

Cashman, K. (2008) *Leadership from the Inside Out: Becoming a Leader for life*, 2nd edition. San Francsco, CA: Berrett-Koehler.

Caza, A. and Jackson, B. (2011) Authentic leadership, in A. Bryman, D. Collinson, K. Grint, B. Jackson, and M. Uhl-Bien (eds), *The Sage Handbook of Leadership*, London: Sage, 352–64.

Chandler, D. & Werther, W.B. (2006) *Strategic corporate social responsibility: stakeholders in a global environment*. SAGE.

Chen, C. and Meindl, J. (1991) The construction of leadership images in the popular press: the case of Donald Burr and People Express. *Administrative Science Quarterly*, 36, 4, 521–51.

Chia, R. (2004) Strategy-as-practice: Reflections on the research agenda. *European Management Review*, 1, 29–34.

Chia, R. and Holt, R. (2007) Wisdom as learned ignorance: integrating east-west perspectives in E. H. Kessler and J. Bailey, (eds), *Handbook of Organizational and Managerial Wisdom*. London: Sage, 505–26.

Chia, R. and Holt, R. (2008) The nature of knowledge in business schools. *Academy of Management Learning and Education*, 7, 4, 471–86.

Chouinard, Y. and Stanley, V. (2012) *The Responsible Company: What we learned from Patagonia's first 40 years*. Ventura, CA: Patagonia Books.

Ciulla, J. B. (2001) Carving leaders from the warped wood of humanity. *Canadian Journal of Administrative Sciences* 18, 4, 313–19.

Ciulla, J. B. (2005) The state of leadership ethics and the work that lies before us. *Business Ethics: A European Review*, 14, 4, 323–35.

Ciulla, J. B. and Forsyth, D. R. (2011) Leadership ethics, in A. Bryman, D. Collinson, K. Grint, B. Jackson, and M. Uhl-Bien (eds), *The Sage Handbook of Leadership*, London: Sage, 229–41.

Clampitt, P. G., DeKoch, R. J., and Cushman, T. (2000) A strategy for communicating about uncertainty. *Academy of Management Executive*, 14, 4, 41–57.

Cohen, A. R. (2008) Putting a charge in leadership? A response to Clawson's 'Leadership as managing energy' *International Journal of Organizational Analysis*, 16, 3, 182–6.

Cohen, S. and Bailey, D. (1997) What makes teams work: Group effectiveness research from shop floor to the executive suite. *Journal of Management*, 23, 239–90.

Cohen, A. R. and Bradford, D. L. (1989) Influence without authority: the use of alliances, reciprocity, and exchange to accomplish work. *Organizational Dynamics*, 17, 3, 5–17.

Cohen, W. M. and Levinthal, D. A. (1990) Absorptive capacity: a new perspective on learning and innovation. *Administrative Science Quarterly*, 35, 128–52.

Collins, D. (1998) *Organizational Change: Sociological Perspectives*. London: Routledge.

Collins, J. (2001a) *Good to Great: Why Some Companies Make the Leap—and Others Don't*. London: Random House Business Books.

Collins, J. (2001b) Level 5 leadership: the triumph of humility and fierce resolve. *Harvard Business Review*, 79, 1, 66–76.

Collins, J. and Hansen, M. T. (2011) *Great by Choice*. London: Random House Business Books.

Collinson, D. (2005) Critical leadership studies. In A. Bryman, D. Collinson, K. Grint, B. Jackson, and M. Uhl-Bien (eds), *The SAGE Handbook of Leadership*. London: Sage, 181–94.

Collinson, D. (2011) Critical leadership studies. In A. Bryman, D. Collinson, K. Grint, B. Jackson, and M. Uhl-Bien (eds), *The SAGE Handbook of Leadership*. London: Sage, 181–94.

Conger, J. A. (1989) *The Charismatic Leader: Behind the mystique of exceptional leadership*. San Francisco, CA: Jossey-Bass.

Conger, J. A. (1999) Charismatic and transformational leadership in organisations: An insider's perspective on these developing streams of research. *The Leadership Quarterly*, 10, 2, 145–70.

Conger, J. A. and Kanungo, R. (1987) Toward a behavioural theory of charismatic leadership in organizational settings. *Academy of Management Review*, 12, 637–47.

Conger, J. A. and Kanungo, R. (1998) *Charismatic Leadership in Organisations*. Thousand Oaks, CA: Sage.

Cooper, C.D., Scandura, T.A. & Schriesheim, C.A. (2005) Looking forward but learning from our past: Potential challenges to developing authentic leadership theory and authentic leaders. *The Leadership Quarterly* 16, 475–93

Cope, M. (2003) *The Seven C's of Consulting* 2nd edition. London: Financial Times/Prentice Hall.

Cronshaw, S. F. and Lord, R. G. (1987) Effects of categorization, attribution, and encoding processes on leadership perceptions. *Journal of Applied Psychology*, 72, 97–106.

Currie, G. and Lockett, A. (2011) Distributed leadership in health and social care: concertive, conjoint or collective? *International Journal of Management Reviews*, 13, 286–300.

Cyert, R. M. and March, J. G. (1963) *A Behavioural Theory of the Firm*. Englewood Cliffs, NJ: Prentice-Hall.

Daft, R. L. (2003), *Organization Theory and Design*, 8th Student International Division. London: Thomson Learning.

Daft, R. L. (2010) *Leadership*. 5th edition. Andover: South-Western/Cengage Learning.

Dansereau, F. and Yammarino, F. J. (2006) Is more discussion about levels of analysis really necessary? When is such discussion sufficient? *The Leadership Quarterly*, 17, 5, 537–52.

Davies, J. and Easterby-Smith, M. (1984) Learning and developing from managerial work experience, *Journal of Management Studies*, 21, 2, 169–83.

Davis, K. (1960), Can Business Afford to Ignore Corporate Social Responsibilities? *California Management Review* 2, 70–6

Davis, K. (1973) The case for an against business assumption of social responsibilities. *Academy of Management Journal*, 16, 2, 312–22.

Day, D. V. (2000) Leadership Development: a review in context. *The Leadership Quarterly*, 11, 581–613.

Day, D. V. (2011) Leadership development, in A. Bryman, D. Collinson, K. Grint, B. Jackson, and M. Uhl-Bien (eds), *The Sage Handbook of Leadership*, London: Sage, 37–50.

Day, D. V., Gronn, P. and Salas, E. (2004) Leadership capacity in teams. *The Leadership Quarterly*, 15, 857–80.

Day, D., Gronn, P. and Salas, E. (2006) Leadership in team-based organizations: on the threshold of a new era. *The Leadership Quarterly*, 17, 211–16.

Day, D. V., Zaccaro, S. J., and Halpin, S. M. (2004) *Leader Development for Transforming Organizations: Growing leaders for tomorrow*. Mahwah, NJ: Lawrence Erlbaum Associates, Inc.

Den hartog, D. N. and Dickson, M. W. (2004) Leadership and culture. In J. Antonakis, A. T. Cianciolo, and R. J. Sternberg (eds), *The Nature of Leadership*. London: Sage.

Dent, E. B., Higgins, M. E., Wharff, D. M. (2005) Spirituality and leadership: an empirical review of definitions, distinctions, and embedded assumptions. *The Leadership Quarterly*, 16, 625–53.

DeRue, D. S., Hollenbeck, J. R., Nahrgang, J. D. and Workman, K. (2012) A quasi-experimental study of After-event reviews and leadership development. *Journal of Applied Psychology*, 97, 5, 997–1015.

Dickson, M. W., Den Hartog, D. N., and Mitchelson, J. K. (2003) Research on leadership in a cross-cultural context: making progress, and raising new questions. *The Leadership Quarterly*, 14, 729–68.

Doh, J. P. (2003) Can leadership be taught? Perspectives from management educators. *Academy of Management Learning and Education*, 2, 1, 54–68.

Donaldson, T. and Dunfee, T. W. (1994) Towards a unified conception of business ethics: integrative social contracts theory, *Academy of Management Review* 19, 252–84.

Donaldson, T. and Dunfee, T. W. (1999) *Ties That Bind: A Social Contracts Approach to Business Ethics*. Boston, MA: Harvard Business School Press.

Donaldson, T. and Preston, L. E. (1995) The stakeholder theory of the corporation: concepts, evidence, and implications, *Academy of Management Review* 20, 1, 65–91.

Downey, M. (2003) *Effective Coaching: Lessons from the Coaches Coach*. Oakland, CA: Texere.

Downton, J. V. (1973) *Rebel Leadership: Commitment and charisma in a revolutionary process*. New York: Free Press.

Drath, W. H., McCauley C. D., Paulus, C. J. et al. (2008) Direction, alignment, commitment: Toward a more integrative ontology of leadership. *The Leadership Quarterly*, 19, 635–53.

DTI (2003) Changing Manager Mindsets. Report of the Working Group on the Development of Professional Skills for the Practice of Corporate Social Responsibility. PDF available at: <https://www.ashridge.org.uk/>

Dunphy, D. C. and Stace, D. A. (1988) Transformational and coercive strategies for planned organizational change: Beyond the OD model. *Organization Studies*, 9, 3, 317–34.

Dunphy, D., Griffiths, A. and Benn, S. (2003) *Organizational Change for Corporate Sustainability*. Abingdon: Routledge.

Easterby-Smith, M., Crossan, M., and Nicolini, D. (2000) Organizational Learning: Debates, past, present, and future. *Journal of Management Studies*, 37, 6, 783–96.

Edmondson, A. C. (2012) Teamwork on the fly. *Harvard Business Review*, April, 72–80.

Edwards, E. (2011) Concepts of community: a framework for contextualizing distributed leadership. *International Journal of Management Reviews*, 13, 301–12.

Edwards, G. and Turnbull, S. (2013a) A cultural approach to evaluating leadership development. *Advances in Developing Human Resources*, 15, 1, 46–60.

Edwards, G. and Turnbull, S. (2013b) Special issue on new paradigms in evaluating leadership development. *Advances in Developing Human Resources*, 15, 1, 3–9.

Elkington, J. (1999) *Cannibals with Forks: the triple bottom line of 21st century business*, North Mankato, MN: Capstone.

Ellis, S. and Davidi, I. (2005) After event reviews: drawing lessons from successful and failed experience. *Journal of Applied Psychology*, 90, 5, 857–71.

Ely, K., Boyce, L. A., Nelson, J. K., Zaccaro, S. J., Hernez-Broome, G., and Whyman, W. (2010) Evaluating leadership coaching: a review and integrated framework. *The Leadership Quarterly*, 21, 4, 585–99.

Ely, R. J, Ibarra, H., and Kolb, D. M. (2011) Taking gender into account: Theory and design for women's leadership development programs. *Academy of Management Learning and Education*, 10, 3, 474–93.

Emery, C. and Fredendall, L. (2002) The effect of teams on firm profitability and customer satisfaction. *Journal of Service Research*, 4, 217–29.

Ensari, N., Riggio, R. E., Christian, J., and Carslaw, G. (2011) Who emerges as leader? Meta-analyses of individual differences as predictors of leadership emergence. *Personality and Individual Differences*, 51, 532–36.

Etzioni, A. (1961) *A comparative analysis of complex organizations: On power, involvement and their correlates*. New York: Free Press.

Fairholm, G. W. (2011) Real Leadership. How spiritual values give leadership meaning. [online]. ABC-CLIO. Available from: <http://lib.myilibrary.com?ID=305337> accessed 3 July 2012.

Fairhurst, G. (2001) Dualisms in leadership research. In F. M. Jablin and L. L. Putnam (eds), *The New Handbook of Organizational Communication*. Thousand Oaks, CA:. Sage, 379–439.

Fanon, F. (1986) *Black Skin, White Masks*. London: Pluto.

Fayol, H. (1917) (in French), *Administration industrielle et générale; prévoyance, organisation, commandement, coordination, controle*. Paris: H. Dunod et E. Pinat.

Fernando, M. (2011) Spirituality and leadership, in A. Bryman, D. Collinson, K. Grint, B. Jackson, and M. Uhl-Bien (eds), *The Sage Handbook of Leadership*, London: Sage, 483–94.

Fiedler, F. (1967) *A Theory of Leadership Effectiveness*. New York: Mc Graw Hill.

Fiedler, F. (1974) The contingency model—new directions for leadership utilization. *Journal of Contemporary Business*, 3, 65–79.

Fiedler, F. E. and Mahar, L. (1979) The effectiveness of contingency model training: A review of the validation of Leader Match. *Personnel Psychology*, 32, 45–62.

Financial Times (2009) Trail of deceit that did not go unnoticed. <http://www.ft.com.ezproxy.lancs.ac.uk/cms/s/2/7768205a-de7e-11dd-9464-000077b07658.html#axzz1zq2Mklp3> accessed 6 July 2012.

Financial Times (2012a) Stanford faces decade in jail for stealing $7bn <http://www.ft.com.ezproxy.lancs.ac.uk/cms/s/0/437fdb56-6333-11e1-9245-00144feabdc0.html#axzz1zq2Mklp3> accessed 6 July 2012.

Financial Times (2012b) The Mind Business 24 August 2012. <http://www.ft.com/cms/s/2/d9cb7940-ebea-11e1-985a-00144feab49a.html#axzz2BR8VlLd3. accessed 6 November 2012.

Finkelstein, S. and Hambrick, D. C. (1996) *Strategic Leadership: Top executives and their effects on organizations*. St Paul, MN: West Publishing.

Fleishman, E. A. (1953) The description of supervisory behavior. *Journal of Applied Psychology*, 37, 1, 1–6.

Fleishman, E. A., Mumford, M. D., Zaccaro, S. J., Levin, K. Y., Korotkin, A. L. and Hein, M. B. (1991) Taxonomic effects on the description of leader behaviour: A synthesis and functional interpretation. *The Leadership Quarterly*, 2, 4, 245–87.

Foucault, M. (1972) *The Archaeology of Knowledge*, A. M. Sheridan, trans. London: Tavistock Publications (original in French).

Foucault, M. (1977) *Discipline and Punish*. London:. Allen and Unwin.

Fox, A. (1974) *Beyond Contract*. London: Faber.

Freeman, R. E. (1984) *Strategic Management: A Stakeholder Approach*. Boston, MA: Pitman.

Freeman, R. E. (2007) *Managing for Stakeholders: Survival, reputation and success*. New Haven, CT: Yale University Press.

French, J. R. P., Jr., and Raven, B. H. (1959). The bases of social power in D. Cartwright (ed.), *Studies in Social Power*. Ann Arbur, MI: Institute for Social Research, 150–67.

Friedman, M. (1970) The social responsibility of business is to increase its profits. *New York Times Magazine*, 13 September 1970.

Friedrich, T. L., Vessey, W. B., Schuelke, M. J., Ruark, G. A., and Mumford, M. D. (2009) A framework for understanding collective leadership: the selective utilization of leader and team expertise within networks. *The Leadership Quarterly*, 20, 6, 933–58.

Fry, L. W. (2003) Toward a theory of spiritual leadership, *Leadership Quarterly*, 14, 6, 619–22.

Fry, L. W. (2006) Toward a paradigm of spiritual leadership, *Leadership Quarterly*, 16, 5, 619–22.

Fry, L. W., Hannah, S. T., Noel, M., and Walumbwa, F. O. (2011) Impact of spiritual leadership on unit performance. *The Leadership Quarterly*, 22, 259–70.

Fukushige, A. and Spicer, D. P. (2011) Leadership and followers' work goals: a comparison between Japan and the UK. *The International Journal of Human Resource Management*, 22, 10, 2110–34.

Fullan, M. (2001) *The New Meaning of Educational Change* 3rd edition. New York: Teachers College Press.

Fullan, M. and Murphy, A. (2004) *Leading Continuity*. Exeter: Centre for Leadership Studies, University of Exeter.

Gabarro, J. J. (1987) *The Dynamics of Taking Charge*. Boston, MA: Harvard Business School Press.

Gallie, W. B. (1955-56) Essentially Contested Concepts, *Proceedings of the Aristotelian Society*, 56, 167–8.

Galpin, T. J. (1996) *The Human Side of Change: A practical guide to organization redesign*. San Francisco, CA: Jossey Bass.

Gardner, W. L., Avolio, B. J., Luthans, F., May, D. R. and Walumbwa, F. (2005) Can you see the real me? A self-based model of authentic leader and follower development. *Leadership Quarterly*, 16, 3, 343–72.

Gardner, W. L., Cogliser, C. C., Davis, K. M., and Dickens, M. P. (2011) Authentic leadership: a review of the literature and research agenda. *The Leadership Quarterly*, 22, 6, 1120–45.

Garriga, E. and Melé, D. (2004) Corporate Social Responsibility Theories: Mapping the territory. *Journal of Business Ethics*, 53, 51–71.

Gartner, C. (2011) Putting new wine into old bottles: Mindfulness as a micro-foundation of dynamic capabilities. *Management Decisions*, 49, 2, 253–69.

Gastil, J. (1997) *A Definition and Illustration of Democratic Leadership,*. Oxford: Oxford University Press, 155–78.

Gebauer, A. (2012) Mindful organizing as a paradigm to develop managers. *Journal of Management Education*, 37, 2, 203–28.

Gemmill, G. and Oakley, J. (1992) Leadership: an alienating social myth? *Human Relations*, 45, 2, 113–30.

George, W. (2003) *Authentic Leadership: Rediscovering the secrets to creating lasting value*. San Francisco, CA: Jossey-Bass

George, W. (2012) Mindfulness helps you become a better leader. HBR blog 26 October 2012. <http://blogs.hbr.org/hbsfaculty/2012/10/mindfulness-helps-you-become-a.html> accessed 4 Decmebr 2012.

Gibb, C. A. (1954) Leadership. In G. Lindzey (ed.), *Handbook of Social Psychology*, Vol 2 Reading, MA: Addison-Wesley, 877–917.

Giddens, A. (1979) *Central Problems in Social Theory*. London: Macmillan.

Giddens, A. (1984) *The Constitution of Society*. Cambridge: Polity.

Gilley, A., Dixon, P., and Gilley, J. W. (2008) Characteristics of leadership effectiveness: Implementing change and driving innovation in organizations. *Human Resources Development Quarterly*, 19, 2, 153–69.

Gioia, D. A. and Thomas, J. G. (1996) Identity, image, and issue interpretation: Sensemaking during strategic change in academia. *Administrative Science Quarterly*, 41, 370–403.

Gold, J., Thorpe, R., and Mumford, A. (2010) *Leadership and Management Development*. 5th edition. London: CIPD.

Goldberg, L. R. (1990) An alternative 'description of personality': The Big-Five factor structure. *Journal of Personality and Social Psychology*, 59, 6, 1216–29.

Gordon, R. (2002) Viewing the dispersion of leadership through a power lens: Exposing unobtrusive tensions and problematic processes. In K. W. Parry and J. Meindl (eds), *Grounding Leadership Theory and Research: Issues, Perspectives and Methods*. Greenwich CT: Information Age Publishing, 39–56.

Gordon, R. (2011) *Leadership and Power*. In A. Bryman, D. Collinson, K. Grint, B. Jackson, and M. Uhl-Bien (eds), *The SAGE Handbook of Leadership* London: Sage, 195–202.

Gosling, J. and Mintzberg, H. (2004) The education of practicing managers. *Sloan Management Review*, 45, 4, 19–22.

Gosling, J. and Murphy, A. (2004) Leading Continuity. Working Paper. Exeter: Centre for Leadership Studies, University of Exeter.

Gosling, J., Bolden, R. and Petrov, G. (2009) Distributed leadership in higher education: what does it accomplish? *Leadership*, 5, 299–310.

Graef, C. L. (1997) Evolution of situational leadership theory: a critical review *The Leadership Quarterly*, 8, 2, 153–70.

Graen, G. B. (1976) Role making processes within complex organisations. In Marvin D. Dunnette (ed.), *Handbook of Industrial and Organisational Psychology*. Chicago: Rand McNally College Publishing Co.

Graen, G. and Uhl-Bien, M. (1991) The transformation of professionals into self-managing and partially self-designing contributors: Toward a theory of leadership-making. *Journal of Management Systems*, 3, 3, 49–54.

Graen, G. B. and Uhl-Bien, M. (1995) Relationship based approaches to Leadership Development. *Leadership Quarterly*, 6, 2, 219–47.

Gray, R. and Milne, M. (2004) Toward reporting on the triple bottom line: mirages, methods and myths. In A. Henriques and J. Richardson (eds), *The Triple Bottom Line: Does it all add up?* Abingdon: Routledge, 295–337.

Green, S. G. and Mitchell, T. R. (1979) Attributional processes of leaders-leader-member interactions. *Organizational Behavior and Human Performance*, 23, 429–58.

Greenleaf, R. K. (1977) *Servant Leadership: A journey into the nature of legitimate power and greatness*. Mahwah, NJ: Paulist Press.

Greiner, L. E. (1972) Evolution and revolution as organisations grow. *Harvard Business Review*, July-August, 37–46.

Grey, C. and Willmott, H. (2005) *Critical Management Studies: A reader*. Oxford: Oxford University Press.

Grint, K. (2005a) *Leadership: Limits and Possibilities* Basingstoke: Palgrave/Macmillan.

Grint, K. (2005b) Problems, problems, problems—the social construction of leadership. *Human Relations*, 58, 11, 1467–94.

Grint, K. (2007) Learning to lead: can Aristotle help us find the road to wisdom? *Leadership*, 3, 2, 231–46.

Grint, K. (2010a) *Leadership: A Very Short Introduction*, Oxford: Oxford University Press

Grint, K (2010b) A History of Leadership. In A. Bryman, D. Collinson, K. Grint, B. Jackson, and M. Uhl-Bien (eds), *The SAGE Handbook of Leadership*. London: SAGE Publications, 3–14.

Griseri, P. and Seppala, N. (2011) *Business Ethics and Corporate Social Responsibility*. Andover: South-Western, Cengage Learning

Gronn, P. (2000) Distributed properties: a new architecture for leadership. *Educational Management Administration and Leadership*, 28, 317–38.

Gronn, P. (2002) Distributed leadership as a unit of analysis. *The Leadership Quarterly*, 13, 4, 423–51.

Gronn, P. (2003) Leadership: who needs it? *School Leadership and Management* 23, 3, 267–90.

Gronn, P. (2008) The future of distributed leadership. *Journal of Educational Administration*, 46, 2, 141–58.

The Guardian (2009) Bernard Madoff receives maximum 150 year sentence. <http://www.guardian.co.uk/business/2009/jun/29/bernard-madoff-sentence> accessed 6 July 2012.

Guarnieri, R. and Kao, T. (2008) Leadership and CSR—a perfect match: how top companies for leaders utilize CSR as a competitive advantage. *People and Strategy*, 31, 3, 34–41.

Hackman, J. R. (2002) *Leading Teams: Setting the stage for great performances.* Boston, MA: Harvard Business Press.

Hackman, J. R. (2009) Why teams don't work. *Harvard Business Review*, May, 99–105.

Hackman, J. R. and Walton, R. E. (1986) Leading groups in organisations. In P. S. Goodman (ed.), *Designing Effective Work Groups.* San Francisco, CA: Jossey-Bass, 72–119.

Halpin, S. M. (2006) What type of leadership behaviours are functional in teams? A meta-analysis. *The Leadership Quarterly*, 17, 288–307.

Hambrick, D, C. (1989) Guest editor's introduction: Putting top managers back in the strategy picture. *Strategic Management Journal*, 10, 5–15.

Hambrick, D. C. and Fukutomi, G. D. (1991) The seasons of a CEO's tenure. *Academy of Management Review*, 16, 719–42.

Hambrick, D. C. and Mason, P. A. (1984) Upper echelons: The organisation as a reflection of its top management. *Academy of Management Review*, 9, 2, 193–206.

Hamel, G. and Prahalad, C. K. (1989) Strategic intent. *Harvard Business Review*, May-June, 63–76.

Handy, C. (1993) *Understanding Organizations* Harmondsworth: Penguin.

Hannah, S. T., Avolio, B. J. and Walumbwa, F. O. (2011) Relationships between authentic leadership, moral courage and ethical and pro-social behaviours. *Business Ethics Quarterly*, 21, 4, 555–78.

Hardy, C. and Leiba-O'Sullivan, S. (1998) The power behind empowerment: implications for research and practice. *Human Relations*, 15, 4, 451–83.

Harms, P. D., Spain, S. M., and Hannah, S. T. (2011) Leader development and the dark side of personality. *The Leadership Quarterly*, 22, 495–509.

Harris, A. (2008) Distributed leadership: according to the evidence. *Journal of Educational Administration*, 46, 2, 172–88.

Harvey, J. B. (2001) Reflections on books by authors who apparently are terrified about really exploring spirituality and leadership. *The Leadership Quarterly*, 12, 3, 377–8.

Hatcher, R. (2005) The distribution of leadership and power in schools. *British Journal of Sociology of Education*, 26, 253–67.

Hazen, W. A. (2006). *Everyday Life.* Culver City, CA: Good Year Books, 61.

Heenan, D. A. and Bennis, W. (2000) *Co-leaders: The power of great partnerships.* London: Wiley.

Heider, F. (1958) *The Psychology of Interpersonal Relations.* New York: Wiley.

Heifetz, R. (1994) *Leadership Without Easy Answers.* Harvard, MA: Belknap.

Hendersen, D. (2001) *Misguided Virtue: False notions of corporate social responsibility.* London: Institute of Economic Affairs.

Hernandez, M., Eberly, M. B., Avolio, B. J., and Johnson, M. D. (2011) The loci and mechanisms of leadership: exploring a more comprehensive view of leadership theory. *The Leadership Quarterly*, 22, 6, 1165–85.

Hersey, P. and Blanchard, K. H. (1982) Grid principles and situationalism: Both! A response to Blake and Mouton. *Group and Organizational Studies*, 7, 2, 207–10.

Hersey, P. and Blanchard, K. (1982) *Management of Organizational Behaviour: Utilizing human resources.* Englewood Cliffs, NJ: Prentice Hall.

Hersey, P., Blanchard, K. H., and Dewey, E. J. (1996) *The Management of Organizational Behaviour: Utilizing human resources*, 7th edition. Englewood Cliffs, NJ: Prentice Hall.

Hickman, G. R. (2010) Organizational change practices. In G. R. Hickman (ed.), *Leading Organizations: perspectives for a new era*, 2nd edition. Los Angeles, CA: Sage, 510–24.

Higgs, M. and Rowland, D. (2011) What does it take to implement change successfully? A study of the behaviours of successful change leaders. *The Journal of Applied Behavioural Science*, 47, 3, 309–35.

Hill, S. K. (2002) Team leadership. In P. G. Northouse, *Leadership Theory and Practice*. Thousand Oaks, CA: Sage.

Hind, P., Wilson, A., and Lenssen, G. (2009) Developing leaders for sustainable business. *Corporate Governance*, 9, 1, 7–20.

Hitt, M. A. and Ireland, R. D. (2002) The essence of strategic leadership: Managing human and social capital. *The Journal of Leadership and Organizational Studies*, 9, 1, 3–14.

Hofstede, G. (1980) *Culture's Consequences: International differences in work-related values.* abridged edition. Newbury Park, CA: Sage.

Hofstede, G. and Bond, M. H. (1988) The Confucius connection: From cultural roots to economic growth. *Organisational Dynamics*, 16, 4, 4–21.

Hogg, M. A. (2001) A social identity theory of leadership. *Personality and Social Psychology Review*, 5, 3, 184–200.

Hogg, M. A. (2005) Social identity and leadership. In D. M. Messick and R. M. Kramer (eds), *The Psychology of Leadership: New perspectives and research*. Mahwah, NJ: Lawrence Erlbaum Associates, 53–80.

Holland, R. (1999) *Reflexivity. Human Relations*, 52, 463–84.

Hollander, E. P. (1958) Conformity, status, and idiosyncrasy credit. *Psychological Review*, 65, 117–27.

Hope-Hailey, V. and Balogun, J. (2002) Devising context sensitive approaches to change: The example of Glaxo Welcome. *Long Range Planning*, 35, 153–78.

House, R. J. (1976) A 1976 theory of charismatic leadership. In J. G. Hunt and L. L. Larson (eds), *Leadership: The cutting edge*. Carbondale: Southern Illinois University Press, 189–207.

House, R. J. and Aditya, R. (1997) The social scientific study of leadership: Quo vadis? *Journal of Management*, 23, 409–74.

House, R. J., Hanges, P. J., Ruiz-Quintanilla, S. A., Dorfman, P. W., Javidan, M., Dickson, M., and Associates (1999) *Cultural Influences on Leadership and Organisations: Project GLOBE*. In W. H. Mobley, M. J. Gessner, and V. Arnold (eds), *Advances in Global Leadership*. Stamford, CT: JAI Press, 171–233.

House, R. J., Hanges, P., Javidan, M., Dorfman, P., and Gupta, V. (eds) (2004) *Culture, Leadership and Organisations: The GLOBE Study of 62 Societies*. Thousand Oaks, CA: Sage.

Howell, J. M. and Avolio, B. J. (1993) The ethics of charismatic leadership: Submission or liberation? *Academy of Management Executive*, 6, 2, 43–54.

Hoyt, C. (2010) Women and leadership. In P. G. Northouse, *Leadership: Theory and practice*, 5th edition. Thousand Oaks, CA: Sage, 301–33.

Huang, X., Shi, K., Zhang, Z., and Lee Cheung, Y. (2006) The impact of participative leadership behaviour on psychological empowerment and organizational commitment in Chinese state-owned enterprises: the moderating role of organizational tenure. *Asia Pacific Journal of Management*, 23, 345–67.

Hülsheger, U. R., Alberts, H. J. E. M., Feinholdt, A. and Lang, J. W. B. (2013) Benefits of mindfulness at work: the role of mindfulness in emotion regulation, emotional exhaustion, and job satisfaction. *Journal of Applied Psychology*, 98, 2, 310–25.

Hughes, M. (2006) *Change Management: A critical perspective*. London: Chartered Institute of Personnel and Development.

Hui, C. and Graen, G. (1997) Gaunxi and professional leadership in contemporary Sino-American joint ventures in mainland China. *The Leadership Quarterly*, 8, 4 451–65.

Huxham, C. and Vangen, S. (2004) Doing things collaboratively: Realizing the advantage or succumbing to inertia? *Organizational Dynamics*, 33, 2, 190–201.

Ilgen, D. R., Hollenbeck, J. R., Johnson, M. and Jundt, D. (2005) Teams in organisations: from input-process-output models to IMOI models. *Annual Review of Psychology*, 56, 553–43.

Jackson, B. and Parry, K. (2008) *A Very Short, Fairly Interesting and Reasonably Cheap Book about Studying Leadership*. London: Sage.

Jackson, P. and Delehanty H. (1995) *Sacred Hoops: Spiritual lessons of a hardwood warrior*. New York: Hyperion.

Jacobs, T. O. and Jacques, E. (1990) *Military Executive Leadership*. In K. E. Clark, and M. B. Clark (eds), *Measures of Leadership*. West Orange, NJ: Leadership Library of America, 281–95.

Janson, A. (2008) Extracting leadership knowledge from formative experiences. *Leadership*, 41, 1, 73–94.

Jarzabkowski, P. (2003) Strategic practices: An activity theory perspective on continuity and change. *Journal of Management Studies*, 40, 4, 529–60.

Jarzabkowski, P., Balogun, J., and Seidl, D. (2007) Strategizing: The challenges of a practice perspective. *Human Relations*, 60, 1, 5–27.

Jenson, M. C. and Meckling, W. H. (1976) Theory of the firm: Managerial behaviour, agency costs, and ownership structure. *Journal of Financial Economics*, 3, 305–60.

Jepson, D. (2009) Studying leadership at cross-country level: A critical analysis. *Leadership*, 5, 1, 61–80.

Johnson, G., Melin, L., and Whittington, R. (2003) Micro strategy and strategizing: Towards an activity-based view? *Journal of Management Studies*, 40, 1, 3–22.

Jordan, J., Brown, M. E., Treviño, L. K. and Finkelstein, S. (2011) Someone to look up to: executive-follower ethical reasoning and perceptions of ethical leadership. *Journal of Management* published online 15 March 2011.

Judge, T. A. and Bono, J. E. (2000) Five-factor model of personality and transformational leadership. *Journal of Applied Psychology*, 85, 5, 751–65.

Judge, T. A., Bono, J. E., Ilies, R. and Gerhardt, M. W. (2002) Personality and leadership: A qualitative and quantitative review *Journal of Applied Psychology*, 87, 4, 765–80.

Judge, T. A., Piccolo, R. F., and Kosalka, T. (2009) The bright and dark sides of leader traits: A review and theoretical extension of the leader trait paradigm, *The Leadership Quarterly*, 20, 855–75.

Jung, D., Yammarino, F. J., and Lee, J. K. (2009) Moderating roles of subordinates' attitudes on transformational leadership effectiveness: A multi-cultural and multi-level perspective. *The Leadership Quarterly*, 20, 586–603.

Kakabadse, A. and Kakabadse, N. (1999) *The Essence of Leadership*. London: International Thomson Business Press.

Kakabadse, N. K., Kakabadse, A. P., and Lee-Davies, L. (2009) CSR leaders road-map. *Corporate Governance*, 9, 1, 50–7.

Kanengeiter, J. and Rajagopal-Durbin, A. (2012) Wilderness leadership—on the job. *Harvard Business Review*, 90, 4, 127–31.

Kanter, R. M., Stein, B. A., and Jick, T. D. (1992) *The Challenge of Organizational Change: How Companies Experience it and Leaders Guide it*. New York: Free Press.

Kanungo, R. N. (2001) Ethical values of transactional and transformational leaders. *Canadian Journal of Administrative Sciences*, 18, 4, 257–65.

Kanungo, R. N. and Mendonca, M. (2001) Ethical leadership and governance in organizations: A preamble. *Canadian Journal of Administrative Sciences*, 18, 4, 241–3.

Katzenbach, J. R. and Smith, D. K. (1993) *The Wisdom of Teams: Creating the high performance organization*. Boston, MA: Harvard Business School.

Katzenbach, J. R and Smith, D. K. (2005) The discipline of teams. *Harvard Business Review*, (July-August) 162–171 (reprinted from 1993 in the 'Best of HBR' series).

Kelley, H. H. (1971) *Attributions in Social Interaction*. New York: General Learning Press.

Kelley, H. H. (1973) The process of causal attributions. *American Psychologist*, 28, 107–28.

Kempster, S. (2006) Leadership learning through lived experience: a process of apprenticeship, *Journal of Management & Organization*, 12, 1, 4–22.

Kempster, S. and Iszatt-White, M. (2012) Towards co-constructed coaching: exploring the integration of coaching and co-constructed autoethnography in leadership development. *Management Learning*, published online 25 June 2012 at <http://mlq.sagepub.com/content/early/2012/06/24/1350507612449959>.

Kerr, S. and Jermier, J. (1978) Substitutes for leadership: Their meaning and measurement. *Organizational Behaviour and Human Performance*, 22, 374–403.

Ketola, T. (2010) Responsible leadership: Building blocks of individual, organizational and societal behaviour. *Corporate Social Responsibility and Environmental Management*, 17, 173–84.

Kets de Vries, M.F.R. (1994) The Leadership Mystique. *Academy of Management Executive*, 8 (3),73–92

Kets De Vries, M. F. R. (1999) High-performance teams: lessons from the pygmies. *Organizational Dynamics*, 27, 3, 66–77.

Kets De Vries, M. F. R., Korotov, K. and Florent-Tracey, E. (2007) *The Coach and the Couch: The psychology of making better leaders*. Basingstoke: Palgrave Macmillan.

Kirkpatrick, D. L. and Kirkpatrick, J. D. (2006) *Evaluating Training Programmes: The Four Levels*, 3rd edition. San Francisco, CA: Berrett-Koehler.

Kirkpatrick, S. A. and Locke, E. A. (1991) Leadership: do traits matter? , *Academy of Management Executive*, 5, 2, 48–60.

Knights, D. and Mueller, F. (2004) Strategy as a 'Project': overcoming dualisms in the strategy debate. *European Management Review*, 1, 55–61.

Kohlberg, L. (1969) Stages and Sequences: The Cognitive Development Approach to Socialization in Goslin, D.A. Handbook of Socialization Theory of Research Rand McNally pp. 347–480

Kolb, A. Y. and Kolb, D. A. (2005) Learning styles and learning spaces: enhancing experiential learning in higher education *Academy of Management Learning and Education*, 4, 2, 193–212.

Kolb, D., Osland, J., and Irwin, R. (1995) *Organizational Behavior: An Experiential Approach*, 6th edition. Englewood Cliffs, NJ: Prentice Hall.

Korac-Kakabadse, A. and Korac-Kakabadse, N. (1997) Best practice in the Australian Public Service: An examination of discretionary leadership. *Journal of Managerial Psychology*, 12, 7, 433–91.

Korman, A. K. (1966) 'Consideration', 'initiating structure', and organizational criteria—a review. *Personnel Psychology*, 19, 4, 349–61.

Kotler, P. and Lee, N. (2005) *Corporate Social Responsibility: Doing the most good for your company and your cause*. New York: John Wiley & Sons Inc

Kotter, J. P. (1990) *A Force for Change: How Leadership Differs from Management*. New York: Free Press.

Kotter, J. P. (1995) Leading Change: Why Transformation Efforts Fail. *Harvard Business Review* (March-April), 59–67.

Kotter, J. P. (1996) *Leading Change*. Boston, MA: Harvard Business School Press.

Kotter, J. P. (1999) What effective general managers really do. *Harvard Business Review* (March-April), 145–59.

Kotter, J. P. (2001) What leaders really do. *Harvard Business Review* 79, 11, 85–96.

Kotter, J. P. and Schlesinger, L. A. (2008) Choosing strategies for change. *Harvard Business Review* (July-August), 130–9. (reprinted from 1979).

Kouzes, J. M. and Posner, B. Z. (1987) *The Leadership Challenge: How to get extraordinary things done in organisations*. San Francisco, CA: Jossey-Bass.

Kouzes, J. M. and Posner, B. Z. (1998) *Encouraging the Heart*. San Francisco, CA: Jossey-Bass.

Kouzes, J. M. and Posner, B. Z. (2002) *The Leadership Challenge*, 3rd edition. San Francisco, CA: Jossey-Bass.

Kozlowski, S. W. J., Gully, S. M., McHugh, P. P., Salas, E. and Cannon-Bowers, J. A. (1996) A dynamic theory of leadership and team effectiveness: Developmental and task contingent leader roles. *Research in Personnel and Human Resources Management*, 4, 253–305.

Kramer, M. W. and Crespy, D. A. (2011) Communicating collaborative leadership. *The Leadership Quarterly*, 22, 5, 1024–37.

Kübler-Ross, E. (1969). *On Death and Dying*. New York: Macmillan.

Kübler-Ross, E., and Kessler, D. (2005). *On Grief and Grieving: Finding the meaning of grief through the five stages of loss*. New York: Scribner.

Ladkin, D. (2010) *Rethinking Leadership: A new look at old leadership questions*. Cheltenham: Edward Elgar.

Ladkin, D., Wood, M. and Pillay, J. (2010) How do leaders lead change? In D. Ladkin, *Rethinking Leadership: A new look at old leadership questions*. Cheltenham: Edward Elgar.

Lakomski, G. (2005) *Managing Without Leadership*. Amsterdam: Elsevier.

Langer, E. J. (1989) *Mindfulness*. New York: Perseus Publishing.

Langer, E. J. (1997) *The Power of Mindful Learning*. Addison-Wesley.

Leadership Excellence (2012) 2012 Leadership 500: Leadership Development Program Supplement, 29, 10 <http://www.leaderexcel2.com/edownloads/201 2/10october/10le5215478/2012-leadership500.pdf> accessed 6 November 2012.

Leithwood, K., Mascall, B., Strauss, T., Sacks, R., Memon, N., and Yashkina, A. (2007) Distributing leadership to make schools smarter: taking the ego out of the system. *Leadership and Policy in Schools*, 6, 1, 37–67

Lencioni, P. (2002) *The Five Dysfunctions of a Team: A Leadership Fable*. San Francisco, CA: Jossey-Bass.

Leonard-Barton, D. (1992) Core capabilities and core rigidities. *Strategic Management Journal*, 13, 111–25.

Levay, C. (2010) Charismatic leadership in resistance to change. *The Leadership Quarterly*, 21, 127–43.

Levy, A. (1986) Second-order planned change: definition and conceptualization. *Organizational Dynamics*, Summer, 5–20.

Lewin, K. (1958) Group decision and social change. In E. E. Maccoby, T. M. Newcomb, and E. L. Hartley (eds), *Readings in Social Psychology*. New York: Holt, Reinhart and Winston, 197–211.

Lian, H., Brown, D. J., Tanzer, N. K., and Che, H. (2011) Distal charismatic leadership and follower effects: An examination of Conger and Kanungo's conceptualization of charisma in China. *Leadership*, 7, 3, 251–73.

Lieberson, S. and O'Connor, J. F. (1972) Leadership and organisational performance: A study of large corporations. *American Sociological Review*, 37, 117–30.

Likert, R. (1979) From production and employee centeredness to systems 1–4. *Journal of Management*, 5, 2, 147–56.

Ling, W., Chia, R., and Fang, L. (2000) Chinese implicit leadership theory. *Journal of Applied Social Psychology*, 140, 729–39.

Linstead, S., Fulop, L., and Lilley, S (2004) *Management and Organization: a critical text*. Basingstoke: Palgrave Macmillan.

Lipman-Blumen, J. and Leavitt, H. J. (2009) Hot groups and connective leaders. *Organizational Dynamics*, 38, 3, 225–33.

London, M. (2002) *Leadership Development: Paths to Self-insight and Personal Growth*. ebook.

Lord, R. G. and Maher, K. J. (1990) Alternative information-processing models and their implications for theory, research, and practice. *Academy of Management Review*, 15, 9–28.

Lord, R. G. and Smith, J. E. (1983) Theoretical, informational, information processing, and situational factors affecting attributional theories of organisational behaviour. *Academy of Management Review*, 8, 50–60.

Lukes, S. (1974) *Power: A Radical View*, London: Palgrave Macmillan.

Luthans, F. and Avolio, B. J. (2003) Authentic leadership development, in K. S. Cameron, J. E. Dutton, and R. E. Quinn (eds), *Positive Organizational Scholarship: Foundations of a new discipline*. San Francisco, CA: Berrett-Koelher, 241–58.

Maak, T, and Pless, N. M. (eds) (2006) The quest for responsible leadership in business, in T. Maak and N. M. Pless, N.M. (2006) *Responsible Leadership*. Abingdon: Routledge, 1–13.

McCall, M. W., Lombardo, M. M., and Morrison, A. (1988) *The Lessons of Experience*. Lexington, MA: Lexington.

McCauley, C.D. and van Velsor, E. (eds) (2004) *The center for creative leadership handbook of leadership development* San Francisco: Jossey Bass.

McClelland, D. C. (1973), Testing for competence rather than intelligence. *American Psychologist*, 28, 1, 1–14.

McGill, I. and Beatty, L. (1992) *Action Learning: A Practitioner's Guide*. London: Kogan Page

McGrath, J. E., Arrow, H., and Berdahl, J. L. (2000) The study of groups: Past, present and future. *Personality and Social Psychology Review*, 4, 1, 95–105.

Machiavelli, N. (1993) *The Prince*. Louisville, KY: Wordsworth.

McIntosh, M., Leipziger, D., Jones, K., and Coleman, G. (1998) *Corporate Citizenship: Successful strategies for responsible companies*. London: Financial Times/Prentice Hall.

McShane, S. and Von Glinow, M. A. (2009) *Organisational Behaviour*, 5th edition. London: McGraw-Hill Higher Education.

Malan, L. C. and Kriger, M. P. (1998) Making sense of managerial wisdom. *Journal of Management Inquiry*, 7, 242–51.

Malhotra, A., Majchrzak, A. and Rosen, B. (2007) Leading virtual teams. *Academy of Management Perspectives*, 21, 1, 60–70.

Mandela, N. (1995) *The Long Walk to Freedom: The autobiography of Nelson Mandela* London: Abacus.

Marquardt, M. J. (2000) Action learning and leadership. *The Learning Organization*, 7, 5, 233–40.

Marquardt, M. J. (2004) *Optimizing the Power of Action Learning*. Palo Alto, CA: Davies-Black Publishing.

Marshall, J., Coleman, G., and Reason, P. (2011) *Leadership for Sustainability: An action research approach*. Austin, TX: Greenleaf Publishing Ltd.

Martinko, M. J., Harvey, P., and Douglas, S. C. (2007) The role, function, and contribution of attribution theory to leadership: A review. *The Leadership Quarterly*, 18, 561–85.

Maslow, A. (1987) *Motivation and Personality*. 3rd revised edition. Hong Kong: Longman Asia Ltd.

Meindl, J. R. (1995) The romance of leadership as a follower-centric theory: A social constructionist approach. *The Leadership Quarterly*, 6, 3, 329–41.

Meindl, J. R. and Ehrlich, S. B. (1987) The romance of leadership and the evaluation of organisational performance. *Academy of Management Journal*, 30, 91–109.

Meindl, J., Ehrlich, S. B., and Dukerich, J. M. (1985) The romance of leadership. *Administrative Science Quarterly*, 30, 1, 78–102.

Mele, D. (2002) *Not only Stakeholder Interests. The Firm Oriented toward the Common Good* Notre Dame, IN: University of Notre Dame Press.

Melnick, M. J. (1982) Six obstacles to effective team performance: some small group considerations. *Journal of Sport Behaviour*, 5, 3, 114–23.

Messick, D. M. (2005). On the psychological exchange between leader and follower. In D. M. Messick, and R. M. Kramer (eds), *The Psychology of Leadership: New*

perspectives and research. Mahwah, NJ: Lawrence Erlbaum Associates, *53–L 89*.

Meyerson, D. E. (2001) *Tempered Radicals: How people use difference to inspire change at work*. Cambridge, MA: Harvard Business School Press.

Meyerson, D. E. and Scully, M. A. (1995) Tempered radicalism and the political of ambivalence and change, *Organization Science*, 6, 5, 585–600.

Millikin, J. P., Hom, P. W., and Manz, C. C. (2010) Self-management competencies in self-managing teams: Their impact on multi-team system productivity. *The Leadership Quarterly*, 21, 687–702.

Mills, C. (1997) *The Racial Contract*. Ithaca, NY: Cornell University Press.

Mintzberg, H. (1975) The manager's job: Folklore and fact. *Harvard Business Review*, 55, 4, 49–61.

Mintzberg, H. (1983) The case for corporate social responsibility. *Journal of Business Strategy* 4, 2, 3–15.

Mintzberg, H. (2005) *Managers not MBAs: A hard look at the soft practice of managing and management development*. San Francisco, CA: Berrett-Koehler.

Mintzberg, H. (2006) The leadership debate with Henry Mintzberg: community-ship is the answer. *The Financial Times*. FT.Com.

Mintzberg, H. and Waters, J. A. (1985) Of strategies, deliberate and emergent. *Strategic Management Journal*, 6, 257–72.

Mintzberg, H., Ahlstrand, B., and Lampel, J. (1998) *Strategy Safari: A guided tour through the wilds of strategic management*. New York: Free Press.

Morrison, D. (1994) Psychological contracts and change. *Human Resource Management*, 33, 3, 353–72.

Moss Kantor, R. (1979) Power failure in management circuits. *Harvard Business Review*, 57, 4, 65–75.

Mostovicz, I., Kakabadse, N., and Kakabadse, A. (2009) CSR: the role of leadership in driving ethical outcomes. *Corporate Governance*, 9, 4, 448–60.

Mumford, M. D. and Van Doorn, J. (2001) The leadership of pragmatism: reconsidering Franklin in the age of charisma. *Leadership Quarterly*, 12, 279–310.

Nadler, D. A. (1998) *Champions of Change: How CEOs and their Companies are Mastering the Skills of Radical Change*. San Francisco, CA: Jossey-Bass.

Nadler, D. A. and Tushman, M. L. (1990) Beyond the charismatic leader: leadership and organisational change. *California Management Review*, 32, 2, 77–97.

Nadler, G. and Chandon, W. J. (2004) Making changes: The FIST approach. *Journal of Management Inquiry*, 13, 3, 239–46.

Nagel, T. (1986) *The View from Nowhere*. Oxford: Oxford University Press.

Nanus, B. (1992) *Visionary Leadership: Creating compelling sense of direction for your organization*. San Francisco, CA: Jossey-Bass.

Nienaber, H. (2010) Conceptualisation of management and leadership. *Management Decision*, 48, 5, 661–75.

Norburn, D. and Birley, S. (1988) The top management team and corporate performance. *Strategic Management Journal*, 9, 225–37.

Northouse, P. G. (2010) *Leadership Theory and Practice*, 5th edition. Thousand Oaks, CA: Sage.

O'Connor, P. M. G. and Quinn, L. (2004) Organisational capacity for leadership. In C. D. McCauley and E. Van Velsor (eds), *The Centre for Creative Leadership Handbook of Leadership Development*, 2nd edition. San Francisco, CA: Jossey-Bass, 417–37.

Oh, I., Wang, G., and Mount, M. K. (2011) Validity of observer ratings of the five-factor model of personality traits: A meta analysis. *Journal of Applied Psychology*, 96, 4, 762–73

Ospina, S. and Foldy, E. (2009) A critical review of race and ethnicity in the leadership literature: Surfacing context, power and the collective dimensions of leadership. *The Leadership Quarterly*, 20, 876–96.

Palmer, I., Dunford, R., and Akin, G. (2009) *Managing Organizational Change: A multiple perspective approach*. Singapore: McGraw-Hill Education (Asia).

Pascale, R. T. and Sternin, J. (2005) Your company's secret change agents. *Harvard Business Review* (May), 1–10.

Pearce, C. L. (2007) The future of leadership development: the importance of identity, multi-level approaches, self-leadership, physical fitness, shared leadership, networking, creativity, emotions, spiritualityand on-boarding processes. *Human Resources Management Review*, 17, 355–9.

Pearce, C. L. and Conger, J. A. (2003) *Shared Leadership: Reframing the hows and whys of leadership*. Thousand Oaks, CA: Sage.

Pearce, C. L., Conger, J. A. and Locke, E. A. (2008) Shared leadership theory. *The Leadership Quarterly*, 19, 5, 622–8.

Pedler, M. (2011) *Action Learning in Practice*, 4th edition. Farnham, Surrey: Gower Publishing Ltd.

Pendlebury, J., Grouard, B., and Meston, F. (1998) *The Ten Keys to Successful Change Management*. Chichester: John Wiley.

Peterson, M. F. and Castro, S. L. (2006) Measurement metrics at aggregate levels of analysis: Implications of organisation culture research and the GLOBE project. *The Leadership Quarterly*, 17, 5, 506–21.

Pfeffer, J. (1977) The ambiguity of leadership. *Academy of Management Review*, 2, 104–12.

Phillips, J. S. and Lord, R. G. (1986) Notes on the practical and theoretical consequences of implicit leadership theories for the future of leadership measurement. *Journal of Management*, 12, 31–41.

Podsakoff, P. M., MacKenzie, S. B., Moorman, R. H., and Fetter, R. (1990) Transformational leader behaviours and their effects on followers' trust in leader, satisfaction, and organisational citizenship behaviours. *The Leadership Quarterly*, 1, 107–42.

Popper, M. (2011) Toward a theory of followership. *Review of General Psychology*, 15, 1, 29–36.

Popper, M. and Amit, K. (2009) Attachment and leader's development via experiences. *The Leadership Quarterly*, 20, 749–63.

Porter, M. E. (1980) *Competitive Strategy: Techniques for Analyzing Industries and Competitors*. New York: Free Press.

Porter, M. E. and Cramer, M. R. (2002) The competitive advantage of corporate philanthropy. *Harvard Business Review* (December 2002).

Prahalad, C. K. (2004) *The Fortune at the Bottom of the Pyramid: Eradicating poverty with profits*. Philadelphia: Wharton Business Publishing.

Prahalad, C. K. (2012) The bottom of the pyramid as a source of breakthrough innovations. *Journal of Product Innovation Management*, 29, 1, 6–12.

Purvanova, R. K. and Bono, J. E. (2009) Transformational leadership in context: Face-to-face and virtual teams. *The Leadership Quarterly*, 20, 343–57.

Puwar, N. (2001) The Racialised Somatic Norm and the Senior Civil Service. *Sociology*, 35, 3, 652–69.

Pye, A. (2005) Leadership and organising: Sense-making in action. *Leadership*, 1, 1, 31–50.

Quinn, L. and Dalton, M. (2009) Leading for sustainability: implementing the tasks of leadership. *Corporate Governance*, 9, 1, 21–38.

Quinn, R. E. (1988) *Beyond Rational Management*. San Francisco, CA: Jossey-Bass.

Raelin, J. A. (2003) *Creating Leaderful Organizations: How to bring out leadership in everyone*. San Francisco, CA: Berrett-Koehler.

Raelin, J. (2004) Don't bother putting leadership into people. *Academy of Management Executive*, 18, 131–5.

Raelin, J. (2011) From leadership-as-practice to leaderful practice *Leadership*, 7, 2, 195–211.

Rafferty, A. E. and Griffin, M. A. (2004) Dimensions of transformational leadership: Conceptual and empirical extensions. *The Leadership Quarterly*, 15, 329–54.

Raven, B. H. (2008) The bases of power and the power/interaction model of interpersonal influence. *Analyses of Social Issues and Public Policy*, 8, 1, 1–22.

Reinke, S. J. (2004) Service before self: Towards a theory of servant-leadership. *Global Virtue Ethics Review*, 3, 30–57.

Resick, C. J., Martin, G. S., Keating, M. A., Dickson, M. W., Kwong Kwan, H. and Peng, C. (2011) What ethical leadership means to me: Asian, American, and European perspectives. *Journal of Business Ethics*, 101, 3, 435–457

Revans, R. (2011) *The ABC of Action Learning* Farnham, Surrey: Gower Publishing (on-line resource).

Reynolds, M. (2009) Wild Frontiers: Reflections on experiential learning. *Management Learning*, 40, 4, 387–92.

Riggio, R. E. (2008) Leadership development: the current state and future expectations. *Consulting Psychology Journal: Practice and Research*, 60, 4, 383–92.

Rimanoczy, I. (2007) Action learning and action reflection learning: are they different? *Industrial and Commercial Training* 39, 5, 246–56.

Rittel, H. W. J. and Webber, M. M. (1973) Dilemmas in a general theory of planning. *Policy Sciences*, 4, 155–69.

Rogers, C.R. (1980) *A Way of Being*. Houghton Mifflin

Rogers, C. R. (2003) *Client centred therapy*. London: Constable.

Rohlin, L., Skärvad, P.-H. and Nilsson, S. Å. (1998) *Strategic Leadership in the Learning Society*. Vasbyholm: MiL Publishers AB.

Rosener, J. (1990) Ways women lead. *Harvard Business Review* (November--December), 119–25.

Rost, J. C. (1991) *Leadership for the Twenty-first Century*. Westport, CT: Greenwood.

Rost, J. C. (2008) Influence. In A. Marturano and J. Gosling, J. (eds), *Leadership: The Key Concepts*. Abingdon: Routledge, 86–90.

Rowe, W. G. (2001) Creating wealth in organizations: The role of strategic leadership. *Academy of Management Executive*, 15, 1, 81–94.

Sampson, A. (2000) *Mandela: The authorised biography* London: Harper Collins.

Samra-Fredericks, D. (2003) Strategizing as lived experience and strategists' everyday efforts to shape strategic direction. *Journal of Management Studies*, 40, 1, 141–74.

Sandes, F. (1916). *An English Woman-Sergeant in the Serbian Army*. London: Hodder and Stoughton.

Sashkin, M. (1987) A theory of organizational leadership: vision, culture and charisma. *Proceedings of Symposium on Charismatic Leadership in Management*. Montreal: McGill University.

Schein, E. H. (1988) *Organizational Culture*. WP 2088-88. Cambridge, MA: Sloan School of Management

Working Papers, Massachusetts Institute of Technology.

Schon, D. A. (1987) *Educating the Reflective Practitioner*. San Francisco, CA: Jossey-Bass

Schraa-Liu, T. and Trompenaars, F. (2006) Towards responsible leadership through reconciling dilemmas, in T. Maak and N. M. Pless (2006) *Responsible Leadership*. Abingdon: Routledge, 138–54.

Schyns, B. and Blich, M. C. (2007) Introduction to the special issue on the romance of leadership—In memory of James R. Meindl. *Applied Psychology: An International Review*, 56, 4, 501–4.

Schyns, B. and Hansbrough, T. (2008) Why the brewery ran out of beer: The attribution of mistakes in a leadership context. *Social Psychology*, 39, 3, 197–203.

Schyns, B. and Schilling, J. (2010) Implicit leadership theories: Think leader, think effective? *Journal of Management Inquiry*, 20, 2, 141–50.

Seijts, G. and Gandz, J. (2009) One-teaming: Gaining a competitive edge through rapid team formation and deployment. *Organizational Dynamics*, 38, 4, 261–9.

Seligman, M. E. P. (1997) *Helplessness: On depression, development, and death*. San Francisco: WH Freeman and Co.

Selznick, P. (1984) *Leadership in Administration: A sociological interpretation*. Berkeley, CA: University of California Press (originally published in 1957).

Sethi, D. (2009) *Mindful Leadership. Leader to Leader*, Winter 2009.

Shamir, B. (1992) Attribution of influence and charisma to the leader; the romance of leadership revisited. *Journal of Applied Social Psychology*, 22, 386–407.

Shamir, B. and Eilam, G. (2005) 'What's your story?' A life stories approach to authentic leadership development, *Leadership Quarterly*, 16, 395–417

Shamir, B., House, R. J., and Arthur, M. B. (1993) The motivational effects of charismatic leadership: A self-concept based theory. *Organization Science*, 4, 1–17.

Shamir, B., Pillai, R., Bligh, M. C., and Uhl-Bien, M. (2007) *Follower-centred Perspectives on Leadership: A Tribute to the memory of James Meindl*. Charlotte, NC: Information Age Publishing.

Shoa, L. and Webber, S. (2006) A cross-cultural test of the five-factor model of personality and transformational leadership. *Journal of Business Research*, 59, 8, 936–94.

Sievers, B. (1993) Love in the times of AIDS. *Arbeitspapiere des Fachbereichs Wirtschaftswissenschaft der Bergischen Universitat*, Gesamthochschule Wuppertal, No. 163, Wuppertal.

Skuthorpe, T. (2006) Recordings, interviews and field trip notes from Nhunggal country, 2000–6

Slocum, J. W. and McGill, M. E. (1998) A little leadership, Please? *Organizational Dynamics*, 26, 3, 39–49.

Smircich, L. and Morgan, G. (1982) Leadership: the management of meaning. *Journal of Applied Behavioural Science*, 18, 3, 339–58.

Soderquist, K. E., Papalexandris, A., Ioannou, G., and Prastacos, G. (2010) From task-based to competency-based: a typology and process supporting a critical HRM transition *Personnel Review* 39, 3, 325–46.

Solansky, S. T. (2010) The evaluation of two key leadership development program components: Leadership skills assessment and leadership mentoring. *The Leadership Quarterly*, 21, 675–81.

Sparrow, J. and Rigg, C. (1993) Job analysis: Selecting for the masculine approach to management. *Selection and Development Review*, 9, 2, 5–8.

Spears, L. and Lawrence, M. (eds) (2004) *Practicing Servant-Leadership: Succeeding Through Trust, Bravery, and Forgiveness*. San Francisco, CA: Jossey-Bass.

Spillane, J. P., Halverson, R., and Diamond, J. B. (2001) Investigating school leadership practice: a distributed perspective. *Educational Researcher*, 30, 23–8.

Spillane, J. P., Halverson, R. and Diamond, J. B. (2003) Leading instruction: the distribution of leadership for instruction. *Journal of Curriculum Studies*, 35, 5, 533–43.

Spillane, J. P., Halverson, R. and Diamond, J. B. (2004) Towards a theory of leadership practice: a distributed perspective. *Journal of Curriculum Studies*, 36, 1, 3–34.

Stace, D. A. and Dunphy, D. C. (1993) The strategic management of corporate change. *Human Relations*, 46, 8, 905–20.

Stadler, C. and Hinterhuber, H. H. (2005) Shell, Siemens, and Daimler Chrysler: leading change in companies with strong values. *Long Range Planning*, 38, 467–84.

Stagl, K. C., Salas, E., and Burke, C. S. (2007) Best practices in team leadership: What team leaders do to facilitate team effectiveness. In J. A. Conger and R. E. Riggio (eds), *The Practice of Leadership: Developing the next generation of leaders*. San Francisco, CA; Jossey-Bass, 172–97.

Starke, F. A., Sharma, G., Maues, M. K., Dyck, B., and Dass, P. (2011) Exploring archetypal change: the importance of leadership and its substitutes. *Journal of Organizational Change Management*, 24, 1, 29–50.

Stech, E. L (2004) Psychodynamic approach. In P. G. Northouse (ed.), *Leadership Theory and Practice*. Thousand Oaks, CA: Sage Publications, 235–63.

Stewart, G. I. and Manz, C. C. (1995) Leadership for self-managing work teams: A typology and integrative model. *Human Relations*, 48, 7, 747–70.

Stogdill, R. M. (1948) Personal factors associated with leadership: A survey of the literature. *Journal of Psychology*, 25, 64–6.

Stogdill, R. M. (1974). *Handbook of Leadership: A survey of theory and research*. New York: Free Press.

Suchman, L. (1987) *Plans and Situated Action: The Problem of Human-Machine Communication*. Cambridge: Cambridge University Press.

Sveiby, K. (2011) Collective leadership with power symmetry: Lessons from Aboriginal prehistory. *Leadership*, 7, 385–411.

Takala, T. (1998) Plato on Leadership, *Journal of Business Ethics*, 17, 7, 785–98.

Taylor, F. W. (1903) *Shop Management*. New York: Harper & Brothers.

Taylor, F. W. (1911) *The Principles of Scientific Management*. New York: Harper & Row.

Taylor-Bianco, A. and Schermerhorn Jr, J. (2006) Self-regulation, strategic leadership and paradox in organizational change. *Journal of Organizational Change*, 19, 4, 457–70.

Tejeda, M. J., Scandura, T. A., and Pillai, R. (2001) The MLQ revisited: psychometric properties and recommendations. *The Leadership Quarterly*, 12, 31–52.

Thorpe, R., Gold, J., and Lawler, J. (2007) *Systematic Review*. University of Leeds: Northern Leadership Academy.

Thorpe, R., Gold, J., and Lawler, J. (2011) Locating distributed leadership. *International Journal of Management Reviews*, 13, 239–50.

Tichy, N. M. and Devanna, M. A. (1986) *The Transformational Leader*. New York: Wiley.

Tracey, J. B. and Hinkin, T. R. (1998) Transformational leadership or effective managerial practices? *Group and Organization Management*, 23, 220–36.

Treviño, L. K., Brown, M., and Hartman, L. P. (2003) A qualitative investigation of perceived executive ethical leadership: perceptions from inside and outside the executive suite. *Human Relations*, 55, 5–37.

Treviño, L. K., Hartman, L. P., and Brown, M. (2000) Moral person, moral manager: How executives develop a reputation for ethical leadership. *California Management Review*, 42, 128–42.

Trompenaars, F. (1993) *Riding the Waves of Culture*. London: Brealey.

Tsui, A. S, Wang, H., Xin, C., Zhang, L., and Fu, P. P. (2004) 'Let a thousand flowers bloom': Variation of leadership styles among Chinese CEOs. *Organizational Dynamics*, 33, 1, 5–20.

Tuckman, B. W. (1965) Developmental sequence in small groups. *Psychological Bulletin*, 63, 6, 384–99.

Tuckman, B. W. and Jenson, M. A. C. (1977) Stages of small group development revisited. *Group and Organisational Studies*, 2, 419–27.

Tushman, M. L. and Romanelli, E. (1985) Organizational evolution: A metamorphosis model of convergence and reorientation. *Research in Organizational Behavior*, 7, 171–222.

Tushman, M. L., Newman, W. H., and Romanelli, E. (1986) Convergence and upheaval: managing the unsteady pace of organizational evolution. *California Management Review*, 29, 29–44.

Uhl-Bien, M. (2006) Relational leadership theory: Exploring the social processes of leadership and organising. *The Leadership Quarterly*, 17, 654–76.

UN Global Compact and Accenture (2010) *A New Era of Sustainability: UN Global Compact-Accenture CEO Study 2010.* available from <http://www.unglobalcompact.org/docs/news_events/8.1/UNGC_Accenture_CEO_Study_2010.pdf>.

UN World Commission on Environment and Development and Bruntland, G. H. (1987) *Our Common Future.* Oxford: Oxford University Press. *

van Dierendonck, D. (2011) Servant leadership: A review and synthesis. *Journal of Management*, 37, 4, 1228–61. *

Van Knippenberg, D. and Hogg, M. A. (2003) A social identity model of leadership effectiveness in organisations. In R. M. Kramer and B. M. Staw (eds), *Research in Organisational Behaviour, volume 25.* Amsterdam: Elsevier, 245–97.

Van Knippenberg, B., Van Knippenberg, D., De Cramer, D. and Hogg, M. A. (2005) Research in leadership, self, and identity: A sample of the present and a glimpse of the future. *The Leadership Quarterly*, 16, 495–9.

Van Velsor, E. (2009) Introduction: Leadership and corporate social responsibility. *Corporate Governance*, 9,1, 3–6.

Van Velsor, E. and McCauley, C. D. (2004) Our view of leadership development, in McCauley, C. D. and Van Velsor, E. (eds), *The Center for Creative Leadership handbook of leadership development*, 2nd edition. San Francisco, CA: Jossey-Bass.

Vecchio, R. P., Hearn, G., and Southey, G. (1996) *Organizational Behaviour.* Sydney: Harcourt Brace.

Vroom, V. H. and Jago, A. G. (1988) *The New Leadership: Managing participation in organizations.* Englewood Cliffs, NJ: Prentice Hall.

Vroom, V. H. and Jago, A. G. (2007) The role of the situation in leadership. *American Psychologist*, 62, 1, 17–24.

Vroom, V. and Yago, A. I. (1998), *Situation Effects and Levels of Analysis in the Study of Leadership Participation*, Stamford, CT: JAI Press.

Waddill, D. and Marquardt, M. (2011) Adult Learning Theories and the Practice of Action Learning in Pedler(2011)(ed.) *Action Learning in Practice*, (4th edition). Gower Publishing Ltd.

Wageman, R., Fisher, C. M., and Hackman, J. R. (2009) Leading teams when the time is right: Finding the best moments to act. *Organizational Dynamics*, 38, 3, 192–203.

Waldman, D. A., Bass, B. M., and Yammarino, F. J. (1990) Adding to contingent reward behaviour: The augmenting effect of charismatic leadership. *Group and Organization Studies*, 15, 4, 381–94.

Wallace, M. (2002), Modelling distributed leadership and management effectiveness: primary school senior management teams in England and Wales, *School Effectiveness and School Improvement*, 13, 2, 163–86.

Walumbra, F. O. and Lawler, J. J. (2003) Building effective organisations: Transformational leadership, collectivist orientation, work-related attitudes and withdrawal behaviours in three emerging economies. *International Journal of Human Resources Management*, 14, 7, 1083–101.

Walumbwa, F. O., Avolio, B. J., Gardner, W. L., Wernsing, T. S., and Peterson, S. J. (2008) Authentic leadership: Development and validation of a theory-based measure, *Journal of Management*, 34, 1, 89–126.

Wartick, S. L. and Cochran, P. L. (1985) The evolution of the corporate social performance model. *Academy of Management Review*, 10, 4, 758–69.

Watkins, K. E., Lysø, I. H., deMarrais, K. (2011) Evaluating executive leadership programs: a theory of change approach, *Advances in Developing Human Resources*, 13, 1, 208–39.

Watson, S. and Vasilieva, E. (2007) Wilderness thinking: inside-out approach to leadership development, *Industrial and Commercial Training*, 39, 5, 242–5.

Weber, M. (1947) *The Theory of Social and Economic Organisation*, T Parsons, trans. New York: Free Press.

Weber, M. (2002) *The Protestant Ethic and the Rise of Capitalism*, Peter Baehr and Gordon C. Wells, trans. Harmondsworth: Penguin Books.

Weick, K. (1995) *Sensemaking in Organisations.* Thousand Oaks, CA:. Sage.

Weick, K. E. and Sutcliffe, K. M. (2006) *Managing the Unexpected: Resilient performance in an age of uncertainty.* San Francisco, CA: Jossey-Bass.

Weick, K. E., Sutcliffe, K. M., and Obstfeld, D. (1999) Organizing for high reliability: processes of collective mindfulness. *Research in Organizational Behavior*, 21, 1, 81–123.

Weiner, B. (1986) *An Attributional Theory of Motivation and Emotion.* New York: Springer-Verlag.

Wendt, H., Euwema, M. C. and van Emmerik, H. (2009) Leadership and team cohesiveness across cultures. *The Leadership Quarterly*, 20, 358–70.

Westley, F. and Mintzberg, H. (1989) Visionary leadership and strategic management. *Strategic Management Journal*, 10, 17–32.

Wheelwright, J. (2004). *Yudenitch, Flora Sandes (1876-1956). Oxford Dictionary of National Biography*. Oxford: Oxford University Press.

White, R. (1959), Motivation reconsidered: the concept of competence. *Psychological Review*, 66, 5, 279–333.

Wilkinson, J. (2011) *Jonny: My Autobiography*. London: Headline Publishing Group

Williams, R. (2001) Theory from whom? *Conference on the Sociological Perspectives on the Holocaust and Post-Holocaust Jewish Life*. Rutgers University. October.

Williamson, T. (2008) The good society and the good soul: Plato's Republic on leadership, *The Leadership Quarterly*, 19, 397–408.

Willmott, H. (2011) Studying Managerial Work: A critique and a proposal. In A. Bryman, D. Collinson, K. Grint, B. Jackson, and M. Uhl-Bien (eds), *The SAGE Handbook of Leadership*. London: Sage Publications Ltd, 324–47.

Wise, D. and Jacobo, A. (2010) Towards a framework for leadership coaching. *School Leadership and Management*, 30, 2, 159–69.

Woods, P. A. and Gronn, P. (2009) The contribution of distributed leadership to a democratic organizational landscape. *Educational Management Administration & Leadership* 37, 430–51.

World Business Council for Sustainable Development and Tomorrow's Leaders (2006) *From Challenge to Opportunity: The role of business in tomorrow's society*. Stevenage, Herts: WBCSD Earthprint Ltd.

Yammarino, F. J., Dionne, S. D., Schriesheim, C. A., and Dansereau, F. (2008) Authentic leadership and positive organizational behaviour. *The Leadership Quarterly*, 19, 6, 693–707.

Yukl, G. (1999) An evaluation of conceptual weaknesses in transformational and charismatic leadership theories. *Leadership Quarterly*, 10, 2, 285–306.

Yukl, G. (2002) *Leadership in Organizations*, 5th edition. Upper Saddle River, NJ: Prentice-Hall Inc.

Yukl, G. (2010) *Leadership in Organization*, 7th edition. Upper Saddle River, NJ: Prentice Hall.

Zaccaro, S. J (2007) Trait-based perspectives of leadership. *American Psychologist*, 62, 1, 6–16.

Zaccaro, S. J. and Bader, P. (2003) E-leadership and the challenges of leading e-teams: Minimizing the bad and maximizing the good. *Organizational Dynamics*, 31, 4, 377–87.

Zaccaro, S. J. and Banks, D. J. (2001) Leadership, vision, and organizational effectiveness. In S. J. Zaccaro and R. J. Klimoski (eds), *The Nature of Organizational Leadership: Understanding the performance imperatives confronting today's leaders*. San Francisco, CA: Jossey-Bass, 181–218.

Zaccaro, S. J., Rittman, A. L. and Marks, M. A. (2001) Team leadership. *The Leadership Quarterly*, 12, 451–83.

Zaleznik, A. (1977) Managers and leaders: Are the different? *Harvard Business Review*, (May–June), 67–8.

Zimmermann, P., Wit, A., and Gill, R. (2008) The relative importance of leadership behaviours in virtual and face-to-face communication settings. *Leadership*, 4, 3, 321–37.

Index